W9-CKA-314

CROSS CULTURE AND FAITH:
THE LIFE AND WORK OF JAMES MELLON MENZIES

Cross Culture and Faith

The Life and Work of James Mellon Menzies

Linfu Dong

UNIVERSITY OF TORONTO PRESS
Toronto Buffalo London

© University of Toronto Press Incorporated 2005
Toronto Buffalo London
Printed in Canada

ISBN 0-8020-3869-7

Printed on acid-free paper

Library and Archives Canada Cataloguing in Publication

Dong, Linfu, 1961–
    Cross culture and faith : the life and work of James Mellon
    Menzies / Linfu Dong.

    Includes bibliographical references and index.
    ISBN 0-8020-3869-7

    1. Menzies, James M. (James Mellon), 1885–1957.   2. Archaeologists –
China – Biography.   3. Missionaries – China – Biography.   4. Missionaries –
Canada – Biography.   I. Title.

DS734.9.M45D65 2005   931   C2004-907041-X

University of Toronto Press acknowledges the financial assistance to
its publishing program of the Canada Council for the Arts and the
Ontario Arts Council.

University of Toronto Press acknowledges the financial support for
its publishing activities of the Government of Canada through the
Book Publishing Industry Development Program (BPIDP).

Contents

Illustrations follow page 144

Acknowledgments

The story told here about James Menzies is based on my PhD thesis, completed in 2001 at York University. This undertaking could not have happened, however, without the help of many people from institutions in Canada, China, the United States, and the United Kingdom. It is impossible to acknowledge appropriately all the many individuals whose knowledge, insights, and support influenced the development and writing of the thesis and then this book. But there are specific people to whom I am especially indebted. While these individuals share in the quality of the book, any errors or limitations are mine alone.

My thanks go to Song Jiaheng, who taught me how to be a scholar and introduced me to Canadian studies at Shandong University; Peter Mitchell, who has never let me down as a good mentor and who introduced me to the topic and to the Menzies family; William Westfall, Margo Gewurtz, and Bernard Luk, who supervised the writing process of the thesis; Bernard Frolic, who taught me Sino-Canadian relations; Bob Wakabayashi, who introduced me to Japanese culture and history; and Alvyn Austin, who patiently read the second draft of the thesis, correcting my writing almost sentence by sentence, and reformatted the thesis for publication, making it more interesting. Marion, Frances, and Arthur Menzies, James's children, allowed me unconditional access to the family collection of letters and manuscripts. Fang Hui shared his thoughts on Menzies's scholarship. And as every writer acknowledges, no book can be written without archives. I must thank the many librarians and archivists who offered me their dedicated help in retrieving papers and documents.

CROSS CULTURE AND FAITH:
THE LIFE AND WORK OF JAMES MELLON MENZIES

Introduction

Early in the spring of the year Chia Yin the writer was riding his old white horse along the south bank of the Huan River north of Changte City in the province of Honan. The ground had just been harrowed for cotton planting, and the farmers had thrown the freshly ploughed up potsherds and rubble to the edge of the fields. A number of potsherds of a very early date attracted the rider's attention, and led him on from sherd to sherd to a bend in the river ... This was the Waste of Yin.[1]

The young man on the old horse was a Canadian Presbyterian missionary named James Mellon Menzies and the year was 1914, the third spring of the Republic of China. The place was a village named Xiaotun (old spelling Hsiao-t'un), literally 'Little Village,' on the broad North China Plain in North Henan (old spelling Honan). Menzies was an unusual missionary, for he was educated initially as a civil engineer and Dominion land surveyor, and had spent his summers surveying the northern Ontario bush. Although he had been in China for only three and a half years and at Zhangde (which he spelled Changte) for only a couple of months, he had heard of an ancient ruin nearby. As he made his evangelistic tours of the rural districts, he knew what he was looking for, and when he found it, with eyes trained to see signs on the surface of the earth as indicators of what lay below, he understood its significance. He believed he was guided by providence that day, for as he reflected years later: 'God seemed to guide me when he placed in my hands the discovery of the "Oracle Bones," the actual relics of the ancient religious life of the Chinese at 1400–1200 B.C.'[2]

The discovery of the 'Waste of Yin' and its excavation by the Academia Sinica after 1928 was as important to the archaeology of ancient China as Howard Carter's discovery of King Tut's tomb (1923) was to Egyptian archaeology or Leonard Woolley's work at Ur of the Chaldees was to Mesopotamian. The Waste of Yin was as spectacular as the famous, more recent discovery of the pottery army of the First Emperor, Qin Shihuangdi, at Xian – and a thousand years older.

About 1395 BCE (traditional) or 1300 BCE (revised), China's formative Bronze Age civilization known as the Shang dynasty (1766–1122 BCE traditional, 1700–1045 BCE revised) constructed its seventh and last capital city at a bend in the Huan River about seventy miles north of the Yellow River. They called the place Yin and renamed the dynasty itself Yin, the Shang-Yin. Twelve Shang kings ruled at Yin for 273 years, until 1122/1045 BCE, when the Shang was conquered by the Zhou people. The Zhou sacked the city so completely that it was known to history as *Yin-xu*, the Waste (or ruins) of Yin. The ancient records that survived the book burning of China's first emperor, Qin Shihuangdi, are fragmentary and over the millennia the location of Yin was forgotten. Several centuries later, a city was built near the site: named Anyang, it was later renamed Zhangde and relatively recently has reverted to its old name of Anyang. By the beginning of the twentieth century, some historians doubted the existence of the Shang, viewing it as, at best, a 'semi-legendary' state like its supposed predecessor, the Xia (old spelling Hsia) dynasty.

In 1899, an eminent Qing (old spelling Ch'ing) scholar named Wang Yirong made a startling discovery in Beijing. When an illness occurred in his family, the prescribed medicines included something called 'dragon bones.' These had been used in Chinese medicine as far back as the Han dynasty (206 BCE–221 CE) to treat illnesses such as dysentery, gallstones, fevers and convulsions in children, internal swellings, paralysis, women's diseases, and malaria. Similarly, 'dragon teeth' were also used to appease unrest of the heart and calm the soul. In both north and south China, ancient bone fossils served as 'dragon bones.'

To Wang Yirong's great astonishment, he found 'chicken scratches' on the bones that looked like primitive Chinese characters. Although he was a scholar of ancient bronze and stone inscriptions, he could not decipher the characters except for a few simple ideographs. The *Book of Shang* in the *Book of History*, one of the five Confucian Classics, speaks of the Shang custom of divination using animal bones, usually the plastron (lower shell) of turtles or the scapula of sheep or oxen. Wang realized these inscribed 'dragon bones' were actually oracle bones containing the oldest form of Chinese writing. It is difficult to exaggerate the importance of Wang's discovery. It revolutionized Chinese paleography and paved the way for the development of archaeological science in China. Wang immediately ordered his servant to purchase all available inscribed dragon bones from drugstores in Beijing. Since the dealers were loath to reveal their sources, Wang never discovered that they came from the Little Village at a bend in the Huan River.

James Menzies, a shy, almost self-effacing man, never claimed that he had discovered the Waste of Yin: the villagers had known and used those ancient bones for centuries, after all. Rather he was, he claimed, 'the *first foreign or Chinese archaeologist* to *visit* the Waste of Yin with a *purely scientific interest* in these objects' (italics added). Shard by shard, he became the foremost non-Chinese expert on Bronze Age China and helped decipher the oracle bone script. The collecting of potsherds and fragments of bone – so many that his missionary colleagues nicknamed him affectionately 'Old Bones' – started as a hobby, but became his obsession. Working with Western and Chinese colleagues, he helped create the field of scientific archaeology and taught the first related university course (in Chinese), at Cheeloo (pinyin Qilu) University in Jinan, Shandong province. Above all, James Menzies became a collector of oracle bone fragments and an expert on deciphering the ancient script. In the last hundred years, the Waste of Yin has yielded about 150,000 pieces of inscribed oracle bones. Excluding those destroyed by warlord soldiers, the extant inscribed oracle bones collected by Menzies total 35,913 pieces, to which he added another 23,000 ancient artefacts. To put this effort in context, he gathered the largest private collection of oracle bones on the meagre salary of an ordinary missionary. It was mainly through his own economy that he helped collect and preserve these Chinese cultural treasures.

The Royal Ontario Museum (ROM) in Toronto approached him several times to act as its purchasing agent in China, but Menzies declined because he had no interest in sending art and artefacts out of China to be 'preserved' in the West. With his strong religious motivation, he conducted his collecting activities according to a set of principles and ethical standards that set him apart from other collectors. He did not collect clandestinely. He bought from the peasants around him or simply picked up bits of bones from the fields outside his station at Zhangde. He collected in China, for China, and intended to leave his collection in China.

After Menzies refused the ROM's request, his place was taken by Bishop William Charles White, bishop of the adjoining Anglican mission at Kaifeng in southern Henan. Between 1923 and 1934, White sent an astounding number of ancient and medieval Chinese art to Toronto, making the ROM Chinese collections supposedly the largest in the world outside of China.

Then war intervened. In 1936 James Menzies left for a furlough in Canada, without knowing that he would never be able to return. The next year, North China was occupied by Japanese armies, and Cheeloo University was forced to evacuate to Free China in Sichuan. Since he could not return, Menzies utilized his 'detention' in Canada by volunteering his services to the ROM and registering at the University of Toronto as a PhD candidate. He wrote his dissertation on the *Shang Ko* (pinyin *ge*), the typical bronze weapon of the Shang, and received his PhD in 1942. He spent the rest of the war working first for the United States Office of War Information in San Francisco and then the State Department in Washington as a China expert. His working career was ended by two heart attacks in 1946. Until his formal retirement in 1953 he continued to push his mission board to send him back to China to complete his mission there. However, the rapidly changing political situation in China made his plans impossible to realize. To the very end of his life, Menzies kept both his commitment to the missionary enterprise in China and an active interest in Chinese culture and archaeology.

The life and work of James M. Menzies has never been told – perhaps, some might assert, deliberately. Menzies's 'true story' includes a significant intersection with the story of Bishop White. This book raises serious questions regarding Bishop White. The 1920s, when White gathered the astounding collection later housed within the ROM, began a 'now or never' period, a window of ten to twelve years when North China was stripped of many of its ancient treasures. In 1920–1 Henan suffered the worst famine in modern history; in 1922, 1923, 1925, and 1927–8, it was civil war; in 1937, the Japanese invasion. Modernization seemed equally destructive as railways levelled burial mounds and motor roads cut through city walls. Poverty and warlordism combined to create both the means and the justification for large-scale exportation of Chinese art and artefacts. At bargain costs, many public and private collections in Western countries benefited enormously from those conditions. The ROM, through its agent, Bishop White, was one that benefited greatly.

There have always been questions concerning Bishop White's collecting. 'It required ingenuity, imagination, and diplomacy,' his biographer Lewis C. Walmsley wrote diplomatically. 'It required too the mind of a detective to trace accurately the origin of artifacts, and even more to distinguish between genuine objects and forgeries. It demanded patience, insight, and a quick alertness to what was happening in the Chinese archaeological world if one were to be first on the scene of each new discovery and procure its choicest treasures. Beyond that, it called for a man of position who could deal with unscrupulous officials.'[3] The official history of the ROM, *The Museum Makers*, is more candid: concerning White's correspondence with C.T. Currelly, the museum's founder and director, Lovat Dickson wrote: 'Reading through the hundreds of letters that passed between them, one sometimes has the eerie feeling of listening to the whispered conversation of conspirators.'[4]

Indeed, the Menzies/White relationship raises the issue of 'intellectual property.' That is a very modern term, and in this earlier era it was rarely raised in academic circles. Initially, as the museum's purchasing agent, White relied on Menzies's direct experience with the Waste of Yin materials for decisions on the authenticity and provenance of artefacts. Later, when White began lecturing and publishing on the ROM collection, the question of academic originality ('intellectual property') came into play. Menzies complained to C.T. Currelly that White's treatment of him as a doctoral student and research assistant was 'inhuman, for he seemed to take an unholy delight in forcing me to tell him what he would then pass off as his own research. A dozen times a day and often for long stretches of time, he would question me on the objects on which he was lecturing to his classes,' and then hold the lecture within Menzies's earshot. Finally, in desperation, Menzies asked Currelly to stop White from publishing two monographs that contained information and ideas 'borrowed' from Menzies's PhD thesis.[5] These are serious charges worthy of detailed examination.

Although this issue has been well known within the North Henan mission family and whispered in the ROM itself, this book is the first direct examination of the full details of the two men's relationship. One can say that L.C. Walmsley, Bishop White's successor as head of the Department of East Asiatic Studies at the University of Toronto, in his biography of White deliberately obfuscated the bishop's relationship with Menzies. This book is the corrective, attempting to set the record straight. I do not intend to be judgmental but rather to let the facts and documents speak for themselves.

This biography of James Mellon Menzies is not limited to his life. Instead, it examines the complex world of this rural evangelist turned missionary scholar who tried to 'negotiate' with multiple forces: Christian missions and imperialism, Chinese nationalism and intellectual studies. This book tries to shed new light on the modern encounter between China and the West, especially the missionary enterprise. The theoretical framework is neither the 'impact/response' dichotomy nor the post-colonial theories of 'orientalism' and 'cultural imperialism.' Although such general theories do raise important questions about power and coercion, they can also force historical figures into categories that limit multidimensional historical analysis. To highlight the issues that Menzies had to negotiate, I try to put his life and work in the historical context in which he lived. For this purpose, I refrain from applying generic explanations. Instead, historical data from family and archival collections in Canada and China, supplemented by personal recollections, are given the opportunity to play the major role in this reconstructed historical drama. Hence, this study intends to capture the intricate relationship among the forces in modern Chinese history through a detailed study of the complex life of one individual missionary.

In the past two decades, a number of studies of Canadian missions to China have been published.[6] They have explored a wide range of issues such as missions' history, the transfer of medical knowledge, educational reform, famine relief, and rural reconstruction. They focus essentially on the secular aspects of Canadian missions without attempting to evaluate the religious work of the missions in the Chinese context, since few have been able to utilize Chinese archival and oral-history materials. One of the few that does is Karen Minden's history of the medical college at West China Union University, *Bamboo Stone: The Evolution of a Chinese Medical Elite.*[7] As a result, they are told from a Canadian perspective. This study's use of Chinese materials provides another level of understanding.

The missionary encounter in China was dynamic in nature and multiple in interaction, as the growing scholarship on China missions attests. The story of both Protestant and Catholic missions has to be presented from multiple perspectives. It has been recognized that one lasting contribution of the mission enterprise, far eclipsing their evangelical efforts, was their involvement in China's educational modernization and the transfer of Western medical knowledge and skills. Yet, as Jean-Paul Wiest has observed, treating mission history like secular history deprives it of its religious dimension; therefore, study of the missionary enterprise has to be conducted at two levels, the historical as well as the theological.[8] In this study, both *secular* and *theological* aspects of James Menzies's missionary life and work are examined in a balanced approach.

Since most studies of Canada's involvement in China missions are essentially Canadian, they fail to recognize the two-way dialogue in which Canadian missionaries were involved. I have tried to reconstruct, as much as possible, this two-way dialogue as experienced by James M. Menzies. It is based on primary sources from both China and Canada, supported by secondary sources in English and Chinese.

The most important primary source is the extensive Menzies Family Papers, which are used here for the first time. These are currently at the Ottawa home of Arthur Redpath Menzies, James's son.[9] In addition, I have interviewed people who knew Menzies in China and Canada, including his students, Chinese and Canadian scholars, members of his family, and other Canadian 'mish kids.'

To verify and supplement this personal information, I have consulted the major Canadian archives. The United Church of Canada Archives contains the records of the North Henan mission, which was Presbyterian from 1888 to 1925 and United Church after 1925. The University of Toronto Archives has a useful biography file, as well as records of the University YMCA and the Student Volunteer Movement. Bishop White's papers are divided among three archives. The Anglican Church of Canada General Synod Archives contains his mission correspondence. His correspondence as museum collector and curator are in the Royal Ontario Museum and the files of the Registrar's Office and the Far Eastern department in the University of Toronto Archives. His personal and scholarly papers are in the Thomas Fisher Rare Book Library at the University of Toronto. These contain two files of ten letters from Menzies to White between 1928 and 1934, and one letter from White to Menzies, as well as a copy of Menzies's doctoral thesis, annotated in White's hand. These are discussed in later chapters. Other North American archives include those of the Harvard-Yenching Institute at Harvard University and the Yale Divinity School.

Chinese sources include the records of Cheeloo University, Shandong University, the Shandong Provincial Archives, Shandong Provincial Museum, the Nanjing Museum, and the Beijing Palace Museum.

In addition to theoretical considerations, this study tries to make a specific contribution to the study of Canada's role in the China missionary movement. As Peter Mitchell and Margo Gewurtz pointed out when they established the Missionary Studies Program at the University of Toronto – York University Joint Centre for Asia Pacific Studies:

Canada's relations with East Asia demonstrate the need for fuller understanding of the missionary movement, both at home and overseas. While still an underdeveloped colony evolving into conscious nationhood, Canada eagerly joined this international missionary effort ... Until well into the twentieth century, the Canadian presence in East Asia was a missionary presence. While diplomatic and economic ties lagged far behind, East Asia became the dominant focus of Canadian mission enthusiasm, as Canadians became the third or fourth largest national group among mission communities in China, Japan, and Korea.[10]

The first chapters of this book discuss the early life of James Mellon Menzies chronologically. He was born in 1885 at Clinton, Ontario, and lived at several places in rural Ontario before attending high school in Leamington. His grandparents, who had emigrated from Scotland fifty years earlier, bequeathed their piety to the family. Although his family was conventionally religious, he had little opportunity to attend church or Sunday school since Clinton lacked a Presbyterian church. Many missionary biographies stress the influence of a pious mother or an inspiring minister, but Menzies came to his missionary calling when he enrolled in 1904 at the School of Practical Science, the engineering faculty at the University of Toronto. He quickly came under the influence of the fervent missionary enthusiasm then sweeping the college students. He became active in the YMCA and the Student Volunteer Movement, the foremost recruiting agency for college-educated missionaries, whose watchword was the expansive 'Evangelization of the World in This Generation.'

Since the Canadian Presbyterian church did not employ so-called secular missionaries (even male doctors and educationalists had to be ordained), Menzies attended Knox College, the Presbyterian seminary at the University of Toronto, graduating in 1910. A few months later, he was on his way to China as an evangelist of the North Henan Mission, which in 1925 became the North China Mission of the United Church of Canada. He spent more than two decades in North Henan (1910–32), making evangelistic tours of rural towns and villages, building schools, and even finding opportunities to apply his civil-engineering knowledge. The main issues of these early chapters are rural evangelism and Menzies's reflection on missionary policies under the challenge of militant Chinese nationalism. His declining interest in rural evangelism and increasing interest in Chinese culture brought him into direct conflict with his conservative mission.

His tenure in China was broken by a three-and-a-half-year interlude as captain in the Chinese Labour Corps during the First World War, which sheds light on an overlooked aspect of that war. In 1917, before China entered the war, the British government recruited 100,000 labourers mainly from Shandong to act as non-combatant workers in France. This was considered an important part of the British war effort, but its operations in China and France were entrusted mainly to Chinese-speaking missionaries. Like other young men from North Henan, Menzies had to choose between God and King when the British government pressured them to enlist in the Chinese Labour Corps.

The later chapters dealing with Menzies's advancing years are more thematic, as they explore the mind of a scholar. Although Menzies became a recognized archaeologist, he did not feel that scholarship and Christian higher education were ends in themselves, but rather were the means or components of a new evangelism: a living church led by educated Chinese Christians aided by an indigenized gospel. This was far different from the old evangelism imported by foreign missionaries and preached in terms of foreign religious concepts. He gradually came to the view that in order to survive in China, Christianity must be inculturated within Chinese culture as Buddhism had been 'sinicized' fifteen hundred years earlier. This was the path of accommodation or synthesis pioneered by the seventeenth-century Jesuits such as Matteo Ricci (1551–1610) and Protestant missionaries such as W.A.P. Martin (1827–1916) and Timothy Richard (1845–1911).[11] Menzies's ideas started to evolve while he was in North Henan, but their mature evolution was stimulated by the dynamic intellectual atmosphere at Cheeloo University, where he taught archaeology from 1932 to 1936, the happiest and most productive years of his career.

In his studies of Shang religion, Menzies came to the conclusion that the ancient Shang people who lived about the time of Moses in the Bible had worshipped a god they called *Shangdi* (usually translated as 'Lord on High'). This was not a new idea, as it had been promulgated in the seventeenth century by the Jesuits who, with no scientific evidence, speculated that the Zhou people later introduced the idea of *Tian* or 'Heaven,' a supreme impersonal moral force that governs the universe and mankind. This loosely defined idea later became an important concept of Confucianism. *Shangdi*, the Jesuits speculated, was a monotheist creator similar to Jehovah and they used the term to translate 'God the Father.' The term *Shangdi* was rejected by successive popes during 'the Chinese rites controversy' at the beginning of the eighteenth century, and consequently Roman Catholics had to invent a new name for God: *Tianzhu*, the 'Lord of Heaven,' which had no accretions of meaning within Chinese culture. Ironically, after many years of debate over 'the term question,' most Protestants adopted *Shangdi* in their translations of the Bible.

As a missionary, Menzies tended to stand with the Jesuits, although as a scientist, he wanted to *prove with scientific methods* that God, the universal lord of creation, did not exclude the Chinese. In other words, he wanted to find how 'grace' operated in the ancient Shang culture. Once he had identified the ancient ideograph of *di* or god, he believed he had found the scientific evidence. This became his 'mission' in life: the search for God in ancient China.

Menzies's search for God was a tedious and painstaking process. For two decades he collected oracle bones and related archaeological artefacts, and spent his spare time identifying the archaic oracle-bone inscriptions that bore information about the religious concepts and practices of the Shang Chinese. Working in 'the still watches of the night,' he studied all periods of Chinese calligraphy and epigraphy to decipher the original meaning of each character. 'Some of us,' he wrote, have to 'school ourselves in Chinese thought, and ideas, so that we know something of the soul and mind of China as well as the outside form.'[12] After moving to Cheeloo University, he started to theorize his distinctive interpretation that the Shang were worshippers of 'God' or *Shangdi*, a religious belief that continued for millennia thereafter in one form or another.

Out of his experience in North Henan, Menzies concluded that the conversion of China could only be achieved by adapting the Christian gospel to the Chinese reality. As he reflected in the early 1950s: 'While I have counted 1000 persons baptized and many more prepared for the catechumens, yet perhaps my work on the bones permeated deeper into Chinese life than my work among the schools and churches of North Honan ... When one starts from the premise that God is the God of the Chinese and was so recognized by them, Christianity no longer becomes a foreign religion in the eyes of the Chinese and you have a firm foundation for your Christian preaching.'[13]

Chapters 9 to 14 present a picture of Menzies's transition from a rural missionary to an archaeologist and introduce his scholarly studies. The final chapters detail the frustration of the years (1937–51) that he spent in North America, waiting. They examine his doctoral studies at the University of Toronto and the Royal Ontario Museum, his war service with the United States government, and especially his efforts to return to China. During this time, he wrote numerous letters to the Overseas Mission Board of the United Church of Canada, expressing his strong desire to return to China to complete his mission, even at the price of personal safety.

The fate of the Menzies collections of oracle bones and other ancient artefacts is told in detail in the Conclusion and Epilogue; briefly, of the 35,000 oracles he collected, over 30,000 bones remained in China. They were dispersed among the Shandong Provincial Museum, the National Palace Museum in Beijing, and the Nanjing Museum. After his death, his study collection was acquired by the Royal Ontario Museum from his family, who also deposited a smaller collection at the Art Gallery of Greater Victoria (British Columbia).

James Menzies had a unique career and left a distinctive legacy. He was quiet and modest with a strong sense of humility. At the same time, he was a man of commitment, determination, and principle. Physically, he was short, but intellectually, he had a larger presence than most people of his times. He was a rigorous scholar with a mind capable of philosophical thinking. All these personal qualifications made it possible for Menzies to follow a unique career path by crossing gaps that seemed too huge for others to attempt.

Specifically, Menzies crossed three gaps in pursuing his life mission as a missionary expatriate. He was a trained civil engineer who saw the link between engineering and foreign mission, and crossed from mechanical science to foreign evangelism. After more than two decades' evangelical efforts in North Henan, Menzies was ready for the second crossing. This time the gap was between rural evangelism and archaeology. Again, his colleagues could not see the natural link between the two subjects. Once convinced that it was his mission to find God in ancient China, he devoted himself to the study of ancient Chinese cultures and religions.

The last and most important gap was that between Western culture/ faith and Chinese culture/faith. We now live in a world of rapid globalization, with gradually declining barriers between different cultures and faiths. James Menzies's world was very different, with peoples alienated from each other by cultures and faiths. Ethnocentrism was the order of the time, even within the missionary movement. In the process of pursuing his life's mission, Menzies successfully broke the yoke of ethnocentrism and became an advocate of intercultural and inter-religious understanding. Shard by shard, he discovered the concept of *Shangdi* and crossed the gap between two very different cultures.

James Menzies pursued his life mission quietly. In the same fashion, he passed away quietly without leaving a personal monument, even though he could have done so. Now, half a century later, scholars in China have started to recognize his unique achievements in Shang-Yin archaeology and culture, particularly as a collector and scholar of oracle bones. In 1996, his *Oracle Bone Study* was published and reissued by Qilu Press. A dozen papers have appeared in books and academic journals that recognize his important contributions to the study of Shang archaeology and culture. Wang Ruxing, an eminent scholar of oracle-bone studies, wrote: 'Menzies, through his studies, contributed to the development of Oracle Bone Studies, not only in the pioneering stage, but also in pushing its transition from the pioneering stage to the development stage.'[14]

In the 1950s Menzies was condemned in China as a cultural imperialist and thief of Chinese cultural artefacts. For decades, he was among those foreigners that Chinese scholars tried to forget or avoid. Thus, the recent activities constitute a rehabilitation of Menzies. This process culminated in 2000 with the 'James Menzies Conference' held at Shandong University, which had inherited part of Cheeloo University where Menzies taught in the 1930s. Out of this conference came the publication of a biography by Fang Hui, one of the key persons involved in rehabilitating Menzies. Dr Fang is a professional archaeologist well positioned to evaluate Menzies's academic achievements. As it always does, the Canadian government missed no opportunity to celebrate another Canadian hero recognized in a foreign land. As the official Canadian representative to the conference wrote: 'How honoured Canada is to know that the first non-Chinese archaeologist of China was Canadian.'[15]

Chapter 1

Rural Ontario, 1885–1903

'I look back now to my childhood and think of our old home in Clinton,' wrote James Mellon Menzies in 1919, when he congratulated his father on his eighty-second birthday. James was 'somewhere in France,' engaged in the melancholy task of supervising a battalion of Chinese workers mopping up the battlefields of the First World War. 'I can see it in my memory now. I think I see the spring coming. The snow is melting and the green sodden grass is beginning to push its fresh sword like blades toward the warm sun. I can see the steam rising from the ground and I watch a robin hop across the lawn that slopes down to the artistic picket fence with its thick creamy paint. The chestnuts along the fence have sticky leaf buds and later the leaves come out like little umbrellas.'[1] How characteristic of James Menzies, when surrounded by the ravages of man's inhumanity, still to remember the feel and smell of the earth, the grass steaming in the sunshine, the robin pecking for earthworms – scenes of his idyllic rural childhood.

It was a bitterly cold day, 23 February 1885, when James Menzies was born at the comfortable home of David Redpath Menzies and his wife, Jane McGee, in Clinton, Ontario, Canada. He was their second son, born twelve years after Robert. Four years later, in 1889, Margaret was born. Of the three, James would be the brightest and best educated. Like his father, Robert was a worker rather than a scholar, and found farming and managing the family business more interesting than the schoolroom. Margaret was also well educated, a graduate of the University of Toronto who married a fellow student of her brother James, Jack Judge, an engineer who became a prominent civil servant in Alberta in charge of road building for the province. She had a special bond with James and took personal responsibility for keeping the family ties strong.

James Menzies's grandparents, Robert Menzies and Catherine Redpath, emigrated in 1832 from Chapel Hill, Logie Almond, in Perthshire, along the shore of Loch Tay in the Central Highlands of Scotland. Nothing remains of the village today except a stone cairn marking the location of the chapel. The Menzies clan's progenitor, who was of Norman origin, from Mesnièrzies'es, near Rouen, was granted lands in the Lothians in the twelfth century. The Menzies Castle, built in the early 1500s, saw its share of the turbulent history of the Highlands, for it was occupied by Cromwell's forces in the 1650s and sided with the Jacobites in 1715. Bonnie Prince Charlie stayed there for two days during his retreat from Stirling, which ended in the tragedy at Culloden. The official history describes the Menzies as a small, 'relatively peaceful clan, predominantly siding with law and order and the established monarchy ... Differences with their neighbours were mainly resolved [through] diplomacy, litigation or convenient marriage and they became the oldest family in Strathtay.'[2] Perhaps we can see some of these characteristics in James Menzies.

After the Napoleonic Wars, tens of thousands of Highlanders were driven off their ancestral lands by the tragic 'Highland Clearances,' when the lairds fenced in their estates and turned them into sheep farms. The tenant clansfolk were simply 'cleared,' often in brutal, dehumanizing fashion, and their houses and crops were burned to prevent them from returning. Perthshire was effectively cleared without the violence of other estates. The displaced crofters made their way to ports such as Perth, Aberdeen, and Glasgow, and subsequently dispersed to form proud ethnic pockets in all the far corners of the British Empire – in Nova Scotia and Upper and Lower Canada, South Africa, and New Zealand. The clearances were an important episode in Scottish history, for they depopulated the Highlands, giving the glens the empty feeling they have today. Sometimes the refugees left in small numbers, as individuals or families, but more often they left en masse. In 1829, sixty families, over three hundred individuals, left Perthshire for Carleton Place, Upper Canada, where they named the villages of Perth and Glenquaich after their old homes.[3]

The Menzies clan seems to have thoroughly dispersed, if James Menzies's grandparents were any indication. In 1832 young Robert Menzies sailed to Upper Canada with his younger sister Nellie. On the same boat was another Scotsman, Robert Redpath, with his sister Catherine. The two families became friends on the long voyage, and soon after landing the two Roberts married each other's sister. The couples settled near each other in 'the Scottish block' back of Hamilton.

Immediately, they became victims of the heated politics of the colony. Robert and Nellie had come on the invitation of an uncle who had no children and wanted to make them his heirs. However, they were cheated out of his farm by a deceitful lawyer, a member of the notorious 'Family Compact' that ran the government and dispensed patronage. No wonder that five years later, when the red-haired Scottish firebrand William Lyon Mackenzie called for revolution against the oligarchy, Robert Menzies joined the rebels. The family story is that when Mackenzie's band was fleeing to safety on Navy Island in the Niagara River, a messenger brought news that Catherine had given birth to a son, David Redpath, on 21 February 1837.[4]

Born within the sound of rebellion, David Redpath Menzies, James's father, was the second of seven children that Robert and Catherine raised on a 100-acre farm near Milton. He grew up as a farm boy and left home at age fourteen to earn his own living. He apprenticed himself to a woodworker and became proficient in fine cabinetry, specializing in ornate desks and organ cabinets. Working in lumber camps in the winter and farming in the summer, David saved enough to buy a farm at Clinton, where in 1872 he married Jane McGee, whose parents had come from County Antrim in Northern Ireland. David became co-owner of the Doherty Organ Factory in Clinton, which turned out two to three hundred organs a month, sold as far away as England.[5] By the time James was born in 1885, David was successful enough to have built a large house to provide his family with a gracious life.[6]

Located in the rich agricultural area of Huron County, Clinton was a prosperous yellow-brick town on the road from Stratford to Goderich on Lake Huron. Surrounded by forest and farmland, it had sawmills and grain mills that serviced the local farmers. By the 1880s, like most Ontario towns, Clinton's main street had its share of churches. The earliest settlers were Bible Christians, a radical Methodist sect based in Devon, England, who built the first chapel in the 1850s. After the Bible Christians joined the Methodist church union in 1884, there were two Methodist churches, a Baptist chapel, an Anglican church, and even a Salvation Army hall.

David Menzies and his family were Presbyterians, and the family atmosphere was deeply religious. The children were imbued with a spirit of sober devotion. They did not believe in dogmatic principles, but rather in faith exemplified in their daily lives. Theirs was a private faith, nurtured within the family, especially as Clinton did not have a Presbyterian church. Although the children went to Sunday school whenever possible, their parents were not able to attend church regularly. As James Menzies explained in his application to the Foreign Mission Board in 1910, 'our home life was of the very best, but there was no Presbyterian church in the community. A Methodist Church was built by the community but was abandoned after a year or so. Sunday school was kept going. During my boyhood we organized a Boys Club and S[unday].S[chool]. Class. In that I was trained. At high school, no opportunity afforded itself for the course in my life for I was at home part of the time.'[7]

The moral tone of the Menzies home was typically Victorian. Restraint in all things, honesty, thrift, industry, kindness, and charity were fundamental to the development of a 'Christian character.' Of course, they had Bible readings and prayers at meals and bedtime. The parents did not have much formal education, but like most Presbyterians they grounded their religious beliefs on reason and conscience rather than emotion. There was no sense of mysticism or emotional extremes in the family. This devotional, highly personal, non-institutional, and moderate religious experience had a long-lasting influence on James, whose religious life was to remain prominent once he left home.[8]

The family moved from Clinton to Goderich – 'just a sojourn' – where David owned the Goderich Organ Company, and in 1894 (when James was nine) to Staples in Essex County, near Windsor. Like many self-made entrepreneurs, David invested in land. He bought a six-hundred-acre farm at Staples because it contained the best grove of black walnut trees in the area, the finest wood for organ cabinets. Essex County, which includes Point Pelee, the most southerly point of Ontario, contains some of the best agricultural land in the province and was particularly known for its flourishing canning industries as well as tobacco farming. In addition to the farm, David ran a general store and lumber company and travelled as far as Winnipeg selling organs. He invested in land in what became downtown Winnipeg: this he later sold at a good profit, enabling him to retire comfortably and to send money to his poor missionary son. David remained on the Staples farm until 1919, when in his eighties he moved to Edmonton to retire near his daughter Margaret and within visiting distance of his son Robert. He died there in 1929 at the age of ninety-three.

David was a practical man, and as a good Christian he felt that making money honestly and diligently merited God's reward for his 'stewardship' of money and resources. He never tired of telling James the importance of hard work. Writing in 1894 from Staples before the family arrived, he described his daily activities: 'The house here is cold and small and made of rough boards. The wind blows through them and they are very cold when it is windy. Our house is papered with old newspapers. We get up early here. We have breakfast at 6:30 and I am in the office before daylight and make the fire and sweep out by lamplight and do not leave the office until 10 at night.'[9] He was then nearly sixty.

If father instilled a belief in the dignity of work, mother encouraged their offspring not to 'neglect your duty to your maker ... Do not mingle with bad company for their influence is for nothing good ... We are told in His word that we should acknowledge Him in all our ways and He shall direct our paths. You see we have the promise of his guidance providing we do our part. Otherwise we should not expect the promise. They are only a condition.'[10] The symbiotic nature of work and faith was a hallmark of the parental legacy to the Menzies offspring.

The family circle in the Staples farm home was enlarged with the addition of Aunt Lizzie, Mrs Menzies's widowed sister, and her son Harvey. When James and Harvey were ready for high school, David installed Aunt Lizzie as housemother of a rented house in Leamington.[11] Margaret later joined them when she also reached high-school age. Father David did not have much schooling, having moved into the middle class through hard work and business acumen. But he encouraged his children to stay in school and be good students.

In 1901 he wrote to James in Leamington, expressing a common lament of the pioneer generation: 'We did not have as good schools and as good a chance to learn when I was a boy as you have. I always think if I had been a better scholar, I could have done better than I have and made money faster by filling positions that now but men of good education can fill. I hope you will push on at school as you are doing and that I will have the pleasure of seeing you some day filling the place of some of our great men.' James was a good student – 'a good second if not first' – but David projected his own fear of examinations on his son. 'Lots of good scholars have been beaten and plucked as they called it at examinations, even would be members of parliament get beaten at elections and it often happens that the best man gets beaten. So, remember it is no disgrace to get beat if you do not come out first, take a more determined stand next time to come out ahead and no doubt you will accomplish it.'[12] Perseverance thus brought its own rewards.

To his parents' delight, James Menzies passed the university entrance examination in 1903 with flying colours and was accepted by the School of Practical Science at the University of Toronto, majoring in civil engineering. The first stage of James Menzies's life was coming to a close. He had completed his high-school education with good standing and was now ready to move towards a professional career. The idea of becoming a missionary had not yet entered his mind. Nevertheless, his rural Ontario childhood had unconsciously prepared him for the eventual call to China. Moving from Clinton to Staples to Leamington to Toronto developed in him an ability to adjust to new environments, an important prerequisite for a missionary without permanent residence either in the field or in Canada. This spirit of adventure made it easier for James to sail away later as a missionary.

Why would a university-trained civil engineer give up a comfortable life to be a missionary to remote China? Historians of missions frequently probe the question of motivation. Piety was important, the desire to save souls. However, piety was not the only factor in the creation of a missionary. James Menzies followed a unique path to the mission field. He was the first trained engineer to become a Canadian overseas missionary. Unlike most missionaries, he was not inspired primarily by a pious Sunday school teacher or family influences. Rather, the commitment to mission work came to him gradually as a young student through the influence of the missionary movement then sweeping the colleges and universities of North America.

Parental influences were thus important but not totally determinant. Although he welcomed the dedication to hard work and faith, Father David was disappointed that his favourite son did not inherit his business acumen and showed little interest in money. James always considered money as a necessary evil. Later in life, the few dollars he saved from his small mission salary were spent on bits of ancient bones and pots that had inestimable value for the study of ancient Chinese culture but little immediate intrinsic worth. James's life amplified the lessons on the virtue of frugality learned from his mother and the dignity of work stressed by his father. Throughout his life, he tried to spend every minute doing something meaningful. This religious view of work sustained him through the years in China.

Chapter 2

Toronto, 1903–1905

The Skule of Practical Science

When James Menzies arrived in September 1903, 'Toronto the Good' was the metropolis of English Canada. It was almost one hundred years old and yet everything seemed new, built within the last decade or two. It was a big, bustling North American city with electric lights, streetcars, and 'skyscrapers' as befitted its self-proclaimed image as 'the Queen City.' The railways and mass media – national magazines like *Saturday Night* and the *Presbyterian Record* as well as the Eaton's department store catalogue – carried Toronto's ideas and products to every part of the Dominion.

It must have been thrilling for a rural youth to move to the big city, but Menzies had no time for sightseeing. He had registered several weeks late for classes and had to catch up. Only gradually did he become familiar with Toronto, appreciate its physical beauties and rich social life, and develop a strong sentimental attachment to the city.[1] Years later the 'wandering missionary' wrote, 'I am glad to be back in Toronto. Somehow I feel that I belong here. It is 46 years since I came to Toronto first in 1903 and ever since then Toronto has seemed more my home than any place outside of China.'[2]

At that time, Toronto was one of the great evangelical cities of the world, run by and for evangelicals. Ninety per cent of the population were Protestants, with the Methodists counting almost one-third and the Presbyterians not far behind. A decade earlier, the *Toronto Daily Mail* held a contest to determine the most popular preacher of the day. The winner received 160,000 votes, while the runner-up received 140,000: this was in a city of 100,000 people! The idea that preachers were

celebrities may seem astonishing in our secular age, but it was a successful gambit as the newspaper's subscriptions rose dramatically.[3]

Toronto not only had famous preachers and beautiful churches but
also the headquarters of the five national Protestant denominations:
Methodist, Presbyterian, Church of England (Anglican), Baptist, and
Congregational. Toronto also had six seminaries: Catholic St Michael's,
Methodist Victoria College, low-church Anglican Wycliffe, Presbyterian
Knox, high-church Anglican Trinity College, and the Baptist McMaster
University on Bloor Street.

Toronto was also a city of schools. Its post-secondary institutions absorbed a diverse, never-ending stream of young men and women from
the farms and small towns of Ontario, educated and professionalized
them, and then sent them to the far corners of the earth. Established as
a non-denominational provincial college in 1850, University College was
an exception. In 1887, it federated with two denominational colleges
(Methodist Victoria and Roman Catholic St Michael's), three seminaries
(Knox, Trinity, and Wycliffe), and professional faculties such as medicine, engineering, dentistry, and architecture to become the University
of Toronto. In addition to the two universities (Toronto and McMaster),
there were business colleges, normal schools and teachers' colleges,
deaconess training schools, and the Toronto Bible Training School for
missionaries and lay workers. Thus, post-secondary education was strongly
associated with religion in the Arts while the relationship was less secure
in the 'modern' subject areas of business and science.

The School of Practical Science (SPS) was the engineering faculty of
the University of Toronto, located in the southeast sector of the campus.
Founded in 1873 as a diploma school, SPS started granting four-year
Bachelor of Applied Science (BASc.) degrees in 1892 after its incorporation within the new University of Toronto. The term 'practical science'
had two rather different meanings at the time, as the official history
states: 'For some, it meant "serving a useful purpose," and its antonym
was "impractical": thus, practical science would include the thermody-
namics of steam engines, the chemistry of ore refining, or the statistics of
bridge building. But to science educators at the time, it referred instead
to the new style of teaching by involving students in laboratory work –
teaching, in other words, by allowing students to "practice" science.'[4]
Although officially designated as the Faculty of Applied Science in 1900,
the old name SPS – or its irreverent nickname, 'Skule' – continued to be
used for many years.

SPS was known as 'Galbraith's school' after John Galbraith, the first professor of engineering in 1878, then in the middle of his long and illustrious career that spanned thirty-six years until his death in 1914. He 'led the school from an ill-defined concept in the minds of the government and university administrators into a flourishing school of engineering with a place, a mission, and a tradition of its own, a success that should not be taken lightly.'[5] An earlier SPS history was more fulsome: 'The early engineering graduates have not only played a conspicuous part in the building of the Canadian transcontinental railways, and in other public works, but have been almost exclusively the engineers of that epoch-making venture in public ownership, the development of power by the Hydro-Electric Power Commission of Ontario. This is a striking proof of the high quality of the instruction given in the School from the beginning.'[6]

With the increasing demand for trained engineers, the all-male student body of SPS doubled from 223 to 475 in the three years from 1900 to 1903, and would redouble by 1908.[7] The original 'little red schoolhouse' was jammed, despite several additions and the construction of new buildings. Although new courses and specialities were added, the basic thrust of the curriculum had barely changed. In addition to mathematics, physics, mineralogy, the strength of materials, and chemistry of various types, all students had to spend several afternoons a week in surveying.

The centrepiece of the engineering program was 'engineering drawing, a subject that was actually a mix of many things – technical drawing, mapping and topography; the study of projections and perspectives, descriptive geometry; and even such practical matters as drawing out stone-cutting patterns. Students spent fourteen of their forty hours a week on this, and were expected also to spend any free time at their drafting tables. Instilling the skill of visualizing was, obviously, the heart of engineering education.'[8] This intense scrutiny of objects and drawing them in pen and ink was to stand James Menzies in good stead once he became an archaeologist.

Then as now, the engineering students had a reputation as the pranksters of the university. Their lives were filled with hard work and long hours, expanding horizons and plenty of good fun. Fun, the school history notes, 'was something new. Fun was not something that students had much experience of at university before the 1880s. But student life in these turn-of-the-century years was indeed changing, as the old discipline of college life, kept in place for years by small student numbers and traditional respect for authority, was lost once and for all. Students began to organize and take part in extracurricular activities as they never had before, to socialize away from the eyes and rules of the authorities, and, perhaps most striking of all, to demand a say in the affairs of the university.' Sometimes, they got into 'hustles' and 'scraps' that degenerated into 'organized brawls, with hundreds of young men fighting hand to hand outside the university buildings.' When the authorities tried to intervene, the students went on strike. In 1906, several rowdies were suspended after being caught red-handed painting medical students with red ink, prompting the engineering students to boycott classes.[9] It was during James Menzies's student years (1905) that two lines were added to the engineer's identifying yell after a riotous rugby game:

We are, we are, we are the Engineers,
We can, we can, we can demolish forty beers.[10]

James Menzies never got caught up in the 'laddish' side of engineering life. He was quiet and shy by nature, a scholar not an athlete, and sports were not an important part of his life. Below average in height and sturdily built, he was never moved by the cult of games, but kept in good health by regular evening walks. Yet the rowdiness unconsciously prepared him for the turbulent nationalism in China when his middle-school students went on strike in order to attend an anti-imperialist parade.

Although James Menzies registered late for classes, by the end of the first term he was able to catch up and become 'the foremost in a class of about 200 pupils.' He spent his first year almost exclusively on surveying, drawing, and books, with little time for extracurricular activities. 'I have only been to an entertainment once,' he wrote his mother, 'so you see I am not spending much that way.'[11] He worked so hard at exam times that his father advised him not to 'sit up all night, go to bed and get your rest and you will feel fresh in the morning for the ordeals of the day.'[12]

An important part of training in civil engineering was summer internships with land survey teams in the bush. Surveying was becoming an important role of the government as Canada opened vast new territories for mining and agriculture. Before lands could be settled or exploited, they had to be surveyed and registered. To meet the demand, the Canadian government created the Dominion Land Surveyor licence system. In the summer of 1904, Menzies went on his first expedition to New Ontario, the northern land acquired in the 1880s after a long legal battle with the Dominion government. The following summer, he went to the Northwest Territories (now Saskatchewan and Alberta). In 1906 he and his father started a joint venture prospecting for minerals at Cobalt, Ontario, after the discovery of silver sparked a treasure-hunting fever there.[13] After James spent two months in the deep woods and found nothing, he was hired as a topographer by a Geological Survey Team.[14] In 1907 and 1908 he went again to the Prairies. These summer expeditions in the newly opened north and west territories gave James an opportunity to practise the skills he had learned in school. At the same time, they opened his eyes and mind to the wild side of nature. The adventure of living on the frontier tested his capacity for adaptation to unfamiliar living conditions, which later became essential in his life as a missionary in China.

Until 1909 when the four-year degree became compulsory, SPS still operated on an optional basis: a one-year diploma in surveying, a three-year diploma, or an additional fourth year leading to a BASc. Because of the high demand for engineers by expanding Canadian industry, many students chose one of the diploma options. However, James Menzies chose the four-year program and graduated with honours in 1907. He was an outstanding student. Decades later he wrote to Arthur, his son: 'I had always stood near the top of my class. I stood first in civil engineering in my first year and always took honours.'[15] If he had chosen to follow his father's wishes, James could have been 'at the head of some noted engineering staff.'[16] However, to David's disappointment, James chose a much more demanding and rewarding career: that of a foreign missionary.

The Student Volunteer

James Menzies arrived at the School of Practical Science with a deep but private faith, although he seldom attended church or Sunday school and certainly had no plans to become a missionary. Mission apologists stress the formative importance of the family in the creation of missionary heroes: as one historian has noted, 'The seeds that would ripen into a sense of obligation and ultimately bear fruit in a missionary vocation were often planted in the home.'[17] Others have highlighted the early influence of a local minister or Sunday school teacher.[18] Still this does not explain James's conversion to foreign missions. His parents were good Presbyterians, but they opposed their promising son's call to China. Instead, his dedication came from his university experiences.

In one of the most secular sections of the university, Menzies became exposed to 'public religion', the modern piety expressed through public organizations such as the YMCA, bible study groups, and mass student religious conventions. His decision to give up civil engineering for the ministry was not sparked by a sudden and emotional conversion but by gradual, inexorable changes in his spiritual and intellectual life. These changes came naturally, without a traumatic spiritual experience.

Menzies spent his first year at SPS engrossed in his studies. He felt profoundly lonely. When he confided that fact to his high-school friend, Mary MacGregor, she advised him to take up some pastime such as skating, or to join a Christian Endeavour society where he could meet nice young people.[19] Christian Endeavour, an American import that appealed mainly to Presbyterians, brought young men and women together 'for social and cultural activities in a protected setting and a devotional atmosphere ... Its formula for success was the provision of busy-work: each member was expected to participate in every meeting, if only by reciting a Bible verse.'[20]

Interestingly, Menzies chose to join the Young Men's Christian Association instead. The University College YMCA was founded in 1873 and by 1900 was the third largest university association in North America, with a membership of three thousand, and its own building and branch in every college and faculty.[21] The YMCA offered more intellectual content such as scientific lectures and boys' parliaments, although it had the same sense of religious excitement and the involvement of every member.

James Menzies was the ideal candidate for the YMCA: a lonely male student from a respectable, small-town religious background, adrift in the big city. He began to attend the SPS branch of the YMCA in 1904. As he summarized in his application to the Presbyterian Foreign Missionary Committee in 1910, this led him into student and social activism:

I have been a member of the University YMCA Executive as Councillor, Recording Secretary, Bible Study Convenor and Student Volunteer Chairman. I have been closely associated with City Mission work, being an advisory member of the Committee. I am also an advisory member of the Canadian College Mission. Almost all my time has been spent on religious work in the University. I have done some work in the city in young people's work, city missions, street preaching, prison work, and personal work during Revivals. This last summer I spent on the mission field of Lake Joseph, Muskoka ... I have been connected with the Laymen's Missionary Movement and Young People's Missionary Movement at their conferences, also Student Conferences. I have led normal Bible Study groups. In college I have led Bible Study and Missionary Classes.[22]

For James Menzies, Christian activism in a campus setting was the first step to lifetime commitment.

The YMCA had two serious purposes. The first was the training of student leaders, 'the statesmen of the next generation' who would go forth to Christianize Canadian society. The second was to train foreign missionaries to take the gospel to the ends of the earth. Canada had a special place in God's plan of redemption, YMCA leader Newton Rowell stated, which was 'to lead the world in the work of world-wide evangelization.' A young country with limited resources and a vast 'uninhabited' West to be settled, Canada was to be the 'lynch-pin' of a new Anglo-American alliance whose 'high mission' was 'to give light, liberty, peace and good government, civilization and Christianity to all races of men.' Canada's contribution to the world missionary enterprise, noted Alvyn Austin, 'like its contribution to the First World War, was larger than its share: it has been said that in proportion to their size and resources, the churches of Canada sponsored more missionaries overseas than any other nation in Christendom.'[23]

The overseas wing of the YMCA was the Student Volunteer Movement, which became the foremost recruiter of educated foreign missionaries. Founded at Northfield, Massachusetts, in 1886 under the direction of American evangelist Dwight L. Moody, the SVM did not send missionaries on its own but recruited college students for denominational missions by encouraging a signed pledge, 'I will, God willing, volunteer to go as a foreign missionary.' From the beginning, Canadian students sent delegates to Northfield and other SVM conventions and started Canadian conferences at Niagara-on-the-Lake, which became known as the 'Canadian Northfield.'[24] With its slogan 'The Evangelization of the World in This Generation,' it was a powerful recruiting agency. By 1920 it had sent nine thousand North American college graduates to foreign missions.[25]

As enthusiasm for missions coursed through Canadian churches in the 1880s and 1890s, the SVM stimulated the denominations to establish overseas missions. It became '*de rigeur* for each denomination to be represented in at least one "heathen" country.'[26] Because of its decentralized structure, the Presbyterian Church in Canada developed a patchwork of small unrelated missions around the world. The Eastern Division, based in Halifax, was responsible for missions in the New Hebrides (now Vanuatu), Korea, Trinidad, and British Guyana, while the Western Division, centred in Toronto, supported missions in India, Taiwan, and China.

The Ontario Presbyterians sent their first overseas missionary in 1871,

the redoubtable George Leslie Mackay, who established the first independent foreign Canadian mission. He set out 'in Abrahamic ignorance'
of his destination and arrived in Taiwan. Two years later, two profession-
ally trained schoolteachers, Marion Fairweather and Margaret Rodger,
became the pioneers of the Canadian mission at Indore, India.[27] On
mainland China, the Presbyterians had three missions. North Henan was
founded in 1888 by the firebrand from Oxford County, Jonathan Goforth,
his wife, the noted painter Rosalind Bell-Smith, and the scholarly Donald
MacGillivray. MacGillivray was subsequently seconded to Shanghai, the
second Presbyterian mission, where he contributed his literary skills to
the Christian Literature Society. At Guangzhou (Canton) a small medical mission was sponsored by the Presbyterian Women's Foreign Missionary Society of Montreal.

By contrast, the Methodist Church of Canada, highly centralized in
Toronto, concentrated on two large, prestigious missions in Japan and
West China. Every year during Menzies's school career, a large party of
twenty or thirty enthusiastic young people – mostly married couples and
single women – would bid farewell from Toronto. Their widely circulated
letters described how they enthusiastically set the Yangtze gorges ringing
with the Victoria College cheer. By the 1920s, the West China mission
had over two hundred missionaries and was regarded as one of the most
professional anywhere in the world.

The Anglican Church of Canada erected overseas dioceses in Japan,
India (Kangara), and China (Henan). The Canadian Baptists sponsored
missions in India and Bolivia, while the Congregationalists had Angola.

Every four years – one student generation – the SVM held a mammoth
conference. Massey Hall, the largest auditorium in Toronto was the
venue for the 1904 convention, described by Alvyn Austin in *Saving
China*: 'The stage was draped in flags and bunting, representing the
hoped-for alliance of British and American churches.' Among the 2000
registered delegates from all over North America were 494 Canadians
representing 54 institutes of higher learning. Even the *Toronto Daily Star*
reporter put aside objectivity to rhapsodize:

> The platform in Massey Hall these days commands a farther skyline of life
> and service than any meeting in legislature or parliament. The real states-
> men are here. It is they who deal with big affairs, and put their hands on vast
> enterprises. What are our poor parish politics compared with the world-
> wide sweep? What is our trade policy compared to the evangelization of the
> world in this generation? Is it any wonder that such a movement has drawn
> to it the best and the brightest?[28]

These conventions introduced James Menzies to the heroic image of a foreign missionary, but equally important was the inspiration of returned missionaries. In 1904 Menzies 'took a decided stand' and joined Dr McTavish's Central Presbyterian church, a mission-minded congregation. There he heard addresses by Presbyterian missionaries from many parts of the world, especially from North Henan, with which he gradually developed 'a strong attachment.'[29] In 1908, Menzies, as the chair of the university SVM, was the organizer for John Mott's visit to Toronto. Mott's call for men of ability for foreign fields deeply impressed the young student. In a letter to his mother, he wrote, '[H]ow I wish you and father could be here to hear inspiring addresses and meet people who are moulding our country and the world.'[30] It is clear that people such as Mott helped nourish James's spiritual life, shape his life direction, and strengthen his commitment to the foreign-mission cause.

James was a person of commitment. In 1905 and 1906 he kept a diary and seldom did a day pass without some activity related to Bible study or the YMCA. In one typical week, he wrote:

October 8th [1905], Sunday: ... went to church. Rev. [R.P.] MacKay, Foreign Mission Secretary of the Canadian Presbyterian Church preached ... Bible class this afternoon ... Church tonight.

October 9th: sent $10 to International Committee YMCA ... I hope it will help them in turning some man's life as they turned mine while at Lakeside ... Got the invitations to our freshman reception and put them in the envelopes ... Went to Business meeting of YPSCE [Young People's Society of Christian Endeavour].

October 10th: distributed the invitations ... Waited at YMCA after 5 till 6:30 for the fruit to come for our reception. Our reception was all right.

October 11th: made a plan of our Bible Study leaders.

October 12th: get some Lakeside Bible Study notes. Saw Gordon about holding our model group.

October 13th: I saw several of the fellows about having a model group class of Bible Study.

October 14th: I spent considerable time in getting the fellows to promise to come ... to the group tonight ... I had to hurry through dinner to get over to the YMCA to the model group ... It was a success. 16 men out, 10 groups have been started and I have at least 5 more to start right away and expect as many more as soon as we get rightly started.[31]

This week was not the exception but the norm for Menzies's university career.

As chair of the Bible Study Committee, he recruited leaders to set up small groups of four to five members. He organized rallies and receptions, inviting church leaders such as James A. Macdonald, editor of the Toronto *Globe*, to deliver inspiring speeches.[32] In the committee report for 1907–8, Menzies wrote:

> To increase the efficiency, Normal classes were organized for the leaders ... The majority of these Normal classes met on Friday evenings in the YMCA. Each evening the little building was crowded to overflowing and the leaders were well fitted to conduct their groups, which met at a time and place arranged for each group. The campaign was opened by a Rally in Convocation Hall on October 6th, when President Falconer presided and Mr. J.A. Macdonald, of the *Globe*, made a very powerful address. The canvass that followed resulted in the enrolment of 1,050 men. Of these, 748 [members of 106 groups] attended regularly for eight weeks or more.[33]

> The president of the university referred to this remarkable accomplishment in his report: It will not be invidious to make special reference to the work of the Bible Study Committee. The large number of men engaged in daily study of the Scriptures constitutes a force for good that was only excelled in dynamics by the normal classes of young leaders who came together every Friday evening to study under the Professors who gave their services to such good effect.[34]

As a member of the university YMCA executive, Menzies attended conferences at Northfield, Massachusetts, Lakeside, Ohio, and Niagara-on-the-Lake, Ontario. The liberal but devotional atmosphere of these conferences served as a stimulant in directing him to the cause of foreign missions. The conference participants spent regular hours on Bible study, student work, and world problems. 'The whole atmosphere of the conference was such as to encourage the development of a new conception of the Christian leader as a man of intelligence and insight in both theological and social matters, yet interested in games and sports and concerned with the spread and application of the Christian ethic in the world.'[35] In the summer of 1905, Menzies wrote, 'I went to the student conference at Lakeside, Ohio and there decided to become a foreign missionary.'[36]

Chapter 3

From Commitment to Departure, 1905–1910

Search for a Venue

For James Menzies, the year after Lakeside was a period of intense spiritual struggle to confirm and strengthen his new commitment. Many times Menzies felt weak, and prayed for God to guide him and give him strength. At other times he thought he was too sinful to be useful for God's cause on earth. One such day was 4 September 1905, when he started his diary with 'SIN!' in capital letters, followed by: 'I have fallen in sin. Oh God, when I should be striving onward, I have been defeated.'[1] He did not mention the specific sin, but three days later he asked God to 'Create in me a clean heart, Oh God and renew a right spirit within me.'[2]

When Menzies volunteered as a foreign missionary, he planned to become a self-supporting engineer/missionary overseas, where he could teach the gospel in his spare time. By 1900 Western engineers were found at every corner of the world. As imperialism became the dominant force in world politics, engineers were sent to construct railways and ports, to open mines, and to build the physical structures for imperial dominance over the world. Working in colonial countries, they were the representatives of modernization on an exploitive Western model. With their relaxed morals, engineers and businessmen had a bad reputation overseas. As a Christian, Menzies was embarrassed by this tarnished image and, as he explained to the Foreign Mission Committee (FMC), 'I felt I was needed there to offset the bad influence of many engineers.'[3]

This was a bold but impractical idea, prompting Menzies to explore the possibility of going out as a YMCA secretary. By this time, the YMCA was expanding in many parts of the non-Western world such as China, India, and Japan. The first Canadian overseas secretary was Arthur W. Beale, a graduate of Queen's University sent to Japan in 1888 by the International Committee with financial support from the Montreal YMCA.[4] In 1905 David Willard Lyon, an American, arrived in Shanghai as the first YMCA secretary in China.[5]

To prepare himself as a potential YMCA secretary, James planned to take a few courses at Knox College. Yet he was not sure how the YMCA could fit into the mission fields. He wrote, 'I believe YMCA work at home is due to the failure of the various churches to meet the needs of young men. This should not be so in the foreign field where there is but one denomination in each district.'[6] This was, of course, a simplistic view of foreign missions, which in many ways shared the denominational divisions of the homelands. Nonetheless, it was this attitude that led him to broaden his search for a more conventional way to serve overseas.

Although the Presbyterian Church in Canada had sent a few non-ordained educational missionaries overseas, such were the exception. The first trained educationalists in North Henan were women, such as Margaret Brown, who became the mission historian. All male missionaries had to be ordained, including the medical doctors who had degrees in medicine and theology. Ordination would mean another three years of study after graduating from civil engineering, and Knox College had never accepted an engineering student. On the other hand, while the YMCA did not require ordination, there seemed to be no room for engineers in their system. 'I am away at sea as to what to do,' wrote James in his diary. 'Gracious God, in whose hands I have placed my destinies and life. I beg of thee to guide me and place me in the world where I can do the most for thee ... Oh God, throw more light on things now and help me to utilize every moment in such a way that it will prepare me for what shall be of service for Thee in my coming life.'[7]

Since he wanted to live among the Chinese people, Menzies finally chose to pursue the conventional route as an ordained evangelist under the Presbyterian church. As he wrote in his application to the Foreign Mission Committee: 'I want to put my life where I can reach the people directly in evangelistic effort ... So, I desire to become an evangelist and to do what I can for the people over whom I am placed.'[8]

Another factor was that the FMC was willing to bend the rules. Through the YMCA work, Menzies had come to know the foreign secretaries R.P. MacKay and A.E. Armstrong, who between them dominated the Foreign Missions Committee (and its successor, the Board of Overseas Missions) from 1888 to the 1950s. MacKay praised Menzies as a young man of 'good judgment,' and Armstrong said he was 'exceptional' and could 'educate the church at home.' The FMC concluded that if they could do anything to 'recruit James into their missionary force,' they would be glad to assist him in gaining entry into Knox College.[9]

The summer of 1907 was a brief excursion in the life he might have led as a professional engineer. With his BASc. from the Faculty of Applied Science, James left for the Prairies in charge of a reconnaissance party for the Dominion Land Survey, charged with drawing the demarcation line between what would become the provinces of Saskatchewan and Alberta. He had spent several summers in the west serving his apprenticeship for the Dominion Land Surveyor licence. It was hard work and sometimes dangerous. His band kept moving on the featureless grassland, most of the time on foot. Besides mosquitoes, they were attacked by bears. However, James relished this pioneer life, reporting in letters his excitement with hunting, collecting natural specimens, and 'wild thinking' under the star-lit prairie sky.[10]

Knox College

In September 1907 Menzies registered at Knox College, graduating in 1910 with a Bachelor of Divinity degree. Knox College was an all-male world like the School of Practical Science and the YMCA, but if SPS was like a fraternity house, Knox was a combination of seminary and boarding house. It occupied an impressive gothic structure just west of the University of Toronto campus on a spectacular site in a circle in the very middle of Spadina Avenue, facing down the broad boulevard to Lake Ontario. The building, unfortunately, had deteriorated over the years, with poorly ventilated, gas-lit classrooms downstairs and draughty dormitories upstairs. Five years after Menzies graduated, Knox College moved to its present building on the main campus, a designated architectural landmark.

Like SPS, Knox College saw itself as a 'practical' institution dedicated to training a class of professional men rather than a few scholars, professionals who learned by 'practising' theology. As Principal William McLaren stated in 1907: '[The work of the Canadian church] is not to indulge in speculative theology, but to give the gospel and its institutions to a new land. And we venture to think that one of the safeguards which has helped to preserve our theology pure and wholesome has been the concentration of the thought and energy of the Church on its great practical work, the salvation of souls and the upbuilding of the Kingdom of Jesus Christ.' Brian Fraser in the official history, *Church, College, and Clergy*, describes Knox College's mission in this period as the creation of 'a progressive church for a nation transformed.'[11]

Knox was the most important of the five seminaries maintained by the Presbyterian Church in Canada. Founded in 1844 by Free Church Secessionists, Knox was long regarded as a citadel of conservatism, but by 1900 it had moved from confessional orthodoxy, based on the Westminster Confession of Faith and the Shorter Catechism, to progressive orthodoxy, the belief that God speaks in different ways to each generation of human history. Hired mostly from Scottish universities, the professors 'combined a solid grounding in the evolutionary moral and religious worldview of Idealist philosophers, the historical methods of the believing practitioners of higher criticism, and the movements among university students, inspired by Dwight L. Moody and Henry Drummond, to spread the intellectual and social benefits of Protestantism throughout the world.'[12]

The years that Menzies was at Knox, 1907–10, were particularly significant in its history. The respected conservative principal William Caven died in 1904 and his successor, William McLaren, retired in 1908. Alfred Gandier, a noted liberal, was appointed principal and professor of practical theology, a position that he occupied from 1908 until Church Union in 1925. Among the illustrations in Fraser's history is the composite photograph of the 1910 graduating class, twenty students in gowns including James Menzies. Fraser noted that, of the eight faculty, seven were 'progressives' or 'liberals,' the sole exception being Principal Emeritus McLaren. John Edgar McFadyen, who taught Old Testament, was a leading exponent of higher criticism. T.B. Kilpatrick was a prolific and passionate proponent of optimistic nationalism and of progressive and aggressive Protestantism. Robert Law challenged his students to bring out with new fullness and urgency the social significance of Christianity as embodied in the ideal of self-sacrificing service seen in Christ.[13]

Although Knox College did not have the divisive heresy trials that characterized confrontations between liberals and conservatives – or modernists and anti-modernists as they were called – in Scotland and the United States, the transition to progressive orthodoxy was not smooth. As Knox College and the other seminaries were moving away from denominational identity to train a generation of ecumenical ministers who would implement the United Church of Canada, the conservative wing was moving toward fundamentalism.

One sign of the increasingly bitter conflict occurred in Menzies's second year, when Jonathan Goforth returned from China and accused some Knox professors of teaching heresy. A stormy presence in the North Henan mission, Goforth had launched a dramatic revival campaign in Korea and Manchuria in 1907 that he called the 'Holy Ghost revival.' He tried to revive the church at home using the same methods, but was received with shocked silence when he called upon the General Assembly to confess their sins publicly. 'I do not remember another man who came home with such an asset, and who made so little of it,' R.P. MacKay confided. Unsuccessful at rooting heretics out of Knox College, Goforth returned to China and seemed 'to consider it his duty to hunt for heresy' among his missionary colleagues.[14] Paradoxically, James Menzies – an engineer and archaeologist, a theological liberal, and a representative of the new professional – was to live at the same mission station at Zhangde with the Goforths.

James Menzies was the first student to enter Knox with an engineering degree. This caused some problems. The college stressed the importance of liberal arts to 'develop the mental and moral powers needed to communicate the Gospel in meaningful language.'[15] Professor McFadyen supported Menzies's application because 'a mind trained in science was for the purpose of beginning Greek or Hebrew just as good as one trained in philosophy or history.'[16] He proved to be correct, because Menzies always stood near the top of his class.[17]

The practical side of theological studies was reinforced through field work. Some students worked among Eastern European immigrant communities in Toronto, while others took rural charges for practice preaching. Menzies spent two summers in home missions. He returned to the Prairies in 1908 as an itinerant minister at places so remote that his father could not locate them on the map.[18] The following summer he spent among the native people in Muskoka, Ontario. Compared with the Prairies, Muskoka was much more pleasant. The land was covered with dense forest and hundreds of lakes, the 'cottage country' of today. He enjoyed the sojourn, which helped him to get away from 'so much hurry and study.'

Although the YMCA remained high in Menzies's agenda, his focus shifted to the Student Volunteer Movement. He was president of the university SVM and convenor of the Student Volunteer Band. To stir up young people's interest in foreign missions he organized monthly meetings and annual conferences. Leading evangelists were invited to speak: the 1908 speakers included J.A. Macdonald, R.P. MacKay, J. Harvey

Bruce, a missionary on furlough from North Henan, the prominent mission historian Kenneth S. Latourette, and Samuel M. Zwemer of the international SVM.[19]

Between 1886 and 1925, the SVM was the most efficient recruiter for foreign mission fields. It provided a pool of volunteers from which came one-half to three-quarters of the North American Protestant missionaries sent overseas.[20] For Toronto, the number of volunteers was 225 in 1908 and 235 the following year. James, however, seemed disappointed with the lack of interest in missions among the university's young people. 'If Toronto is to do her share of the evangelization of the world in this generation,' wrote James in the SVM annual report, 'she must not only give $500,000, but maintain a contingent of 600 volunteers of whom not 87, but 200 should be members of the University.'[21]

As James expanded his religious activism beyond the campus, he took on more responsibilities. His diary for this period is a record of meetings. In 1908 he served on fifteen committees, which included the Foreign Mission Committee of Knox College, the Student Volunteer Union, the Knox Volunteer Band, the Laymen's Missionary Movement, the Council of Canadian College Missions, the City Mission, and the Missionary Committee of Central Presbyterian Church.[22]

A Lifetime Partner

One happy result of James's involvement in the SVM was his acquaintance with Annie Belle Sedgwick, who would become his wife and partner in mission work. She was a deaconess-in-training at the Anglican Deaconess Training School, while her brother Arthur Sedgwick was Menzies's fellow student at the School of Practical Science. Her sister Maude was also attending the deaconess school. Three years older than James, Annie was born in 1882 at the family farm at Cottam near Windsor, Ontario, not far from the Menzies farm at Staples. (This was to become an important part of the Menzies's family life, since they could alternate visits with an extended family of cousins on both sides.) She was the second oldest of six sisters and a brother and grew up on a mixed farm growing corn, tobacco, and hay, with horses, cows, pigs, and chickens.

'Mother's family background was upper middle class English,' wrote her daughter, Marion F. Menzies Hummel, in her affectionate memoir.[23] Her great-grandfather was a friend of the Duke of Wellington and his sister a Lady-in-Waiting to Queen Adelaide. The Sedgwick pedigree had come down somewhat in the world after Annie's grandfather, a well-to-do director of a London bank, lost most of his money in Irish railways. Annie's father, John Finch Sedgwick, the second youngest of seven, emigrated to the colonies in 1870 and settled at Brantford, Ontario, where he worked as a builder with another English emigrant, John Wright, on the construction of the School for the Blind. He cemented the partnership when he married Wright's daughter Annie Marie, a trained seamstress. They bought the farm at Cottam, where they remained until John Sedgwick's death in 1904.

Annie Belle loved sewing and became a fine seamstress. She was taken out of school to provide clothes and alterations for the other children. 'She learned to make patterns just from looking at an illustration in a ladies' magazine,' Marion wrote. 'This skill came in very handy years later on the mission field where she made all our clothes. She even remade my father's clerical suit when it was becoming greenish. She remade it by turning it inside out ... Mother was a lady. She held herself very upright to emphasize her pride in being descended from landed gentry in England. She had the skills treasured by the gentry, – letter writing, hospitality, dressmaking, making a charming and restful home for her husband and family.'[24]

After John Sedgwick's death, Mrs Sedgwick sold the farm and moved to Windsor, where she invested in rental houses to support the family. At twenty-two, Annie's life changed. Since she now had to support herself, she started training as a nurse in Boston, but her feet gave out after four months. The family life had revolved around the local Anglican church at Cottam, which her father had helped build. He had been a warden and his wife leader of the choir, while Annie had been secretary of the Young People's Association and led a women's Sunday school class. This experience led her and her sister Maude to apply to the deaconess school that had just opened in Toronto in 1906. They both graduated in its first class of 1909. Annie also attended theological classes at Wycliffe, where she was elected to the executive of the Student Volunteer Union, of which James Menzies was president. She too had decided on a China mission career, and after a temporary appointment at All Saints Church in downtown Toronto, she was appointed to join Bishop William C. White, who had just been consecrated as 'Bishop in Honan' and designated to establish a Canadian diocese at Kaifeng.

'Their courtship had many ups and downs,' Marion wrote tactfully. Although James was deeply attracted to the young deaconess, he was a shy, stuttering man who could not speak of his feelings until he finally wrote her a letter just before she left for China. Then he told his mother his 'little secret':

> I love a lassie. I did not know how much I did until I tried to love another. We have known one another for a couple of years or more, very superficially just at volunteer meetings and casually in the city ... She is loved by everyone from the little raga-muffins on the street to the highest church dignitaries ... I liked her and remembered her voice and how bewitching she looked, just imagine a Deaconess bewitching. I could not get away from the visions of the little Deaconess and ended with my spending some pretty anxious days, pondering all the problems concerned and I resolved to let my heart have its way. So, I wrote a letter that took me three days. Well I told her in a clumsy blunt brutal way that I admired her from the crown of her head to the soles of her shoes.[25]

The two sisters, Annie and Maude, were both appointed to Henan. Since they were the pioneers, they were given a grand farewell from the train station, hoisted on the shoulders of Wycliffe students. James could not get near her through the crowd, and so he bought a ticket to the next station and got on the train. There he proposed for the umpteenth time and gave her a diamond engagement ring engraved 'JMM to ABS 1910.' This time she accepted, on condition that she complete her five-year commitment to the Anglican mission before they were married.

A Career Launched

In January 1910, as if making a New Year's resolution, James Menzies applied to the Foreign Missionary Committee of the Presbyterian Church in Canada. This was done pro forma, since the FMC had had their eye on him for many years. He was accepted at the next meeting, along with Dr Frederick M. Auld, a medical doctor from Montreal General Hospital, and both were designated for North Henan. A.E. Armstrong wrote to congratulate him 'upon the wonderful privilege which is yours in investing your life in [what] is without question the greatest opportunity for service in this world.'[26]

David and Jane, James's parents, heard their son's news through the newspaper, the Toronto *Globe*, before they received a letter from him a week later. Although they had expected this outcome for some time, they were still not ready to see their son sailing thousands of miles away to a country about which they knew almost nothing except for its poverty and violence. The Boxer massacre had occurred only ten years earlier. Father lost sleep the night the news came, worrying that, at the age of seventy-three, he would never see his son again. Yet, despite his pain, he wrote James an encouraging and loving letter:

> We received the news with pleasure and pain. We are glad to think you have been called by a higher power and chosen by your fellow men for the work, that of winning souls to Christ and trust you and your mate will succeed in evangelizing your share of the world in this generation. We are sorry when we think of being separated from you by so great a distance and in all possibility never to see you again.[27]

Even at this late moment, practical-minded David did not give up hope that James would become a fully qualified engineer. He pressured his son to complete his exam for the Dominion Land Surveyor licence.

> Are you going to write off your D.L.S. before leaving? I think it would be a mistake if you did not, as it would give you a standing with the official class of the country and strengthen your influence. The men of influence to my mind are the parties to reach and anything that would assist you in that way would be a benefit. Think that matter over seriously and if at all practical, I would like to see you finish your D.L.S. as that is the part of your education I took so much interest in and even looked forward to seeing you at the head of some noted engineering staff. Any financial assistance you require to finish that course I will be glad to furnish you only let me know what is needed.[28]

James Menzies wrote the final test three months before he left for China. His father's advice turned out to be quite useful, for later he often benefited from his Dominion Land Surveyor credentials.

The FMC never let its new missionaries leave the country quietly. It required them to tour Canada to arouse people's interest in foreign missions, which needed not only volunteers but also financial supporters. In February 1910 James undertook a deputation tour of Ontario and Quebec, the central support region for Presbyterian missions. From Quebec, he wrote: 'The church was full last night, full to overflowing with chairs in the aisle. I spoke four times yesterday.'[29] In May, two churches competed for the honour of holding the solemn but joyful ceremonies of ordination and designation. He was ordained at Central Presbyterian church in Toronto by Dr McTavish, who had been an important influence ever since Menzies took his first communion there in 1904. Then at his home church in Staples, Dr Smith held the formal farewell service.

On 21 May 1910 James Mellon Menzies, accompanied by his sister Margaret (engaged to another engineering friend, Jack Judge), boarded a ship at Montreal. As they sailed down the St Lawrence River, the young missionary left behind aging parents and many friends whom he might never see again. The farewell songs seemed particularly poignant. 'Honey Boy, must you really sail away, my Honey boy,' one woman sang:

Must you go – Don't you know
When the ship sails down the bay, my Honey Boy
I'll be true, my Honey Boy, to you
For I love you best of all, my Honey boy
   Don't you sigh – Time will fly
   When you're on the deep blue sea,
   Try and think sometime of me
   I'll be waiting anxiously, Honey Boy[30]

His experiences and education had provided James Menzies with the resilience and adaptability – that indefinable quality called 'character' – that would stand him in good stead overseas. His family had given him a deep private faith, but the missionary fires in his heart came comparatively late, through the campus evangelism of the public religion of the YMCA and SVM. As he worked with these organizations, his horizons widened. 'My training in Hebrew and Greek did not make me either a Hebrew scholar or a Greek expert,' James wrote years later, 'but they did give me the background of all my linguistic research in Chinese language.'[31] His theological training at Knox College was progressive, giving him an open mind when he had to face hostile Chinese nationalism and anti-Christian movements. It made it possible for him to appreciate Chinese culture and search for the hand of God within Chinese religious belief and life. His practical, scientific training would remain dormant but not forgotten. His uncanny ability to read the landscape and visualize objects was little utilized until he discovered the oracle bones at the Waste of Yin. James Menzies had come to his missionary career by a unique path that ensured he would have a unique career.

Chapter 4

North Henan, 1910

Love and Marriage

The experience gained growing up among the rolling hills of Ontario farmland and surveying the unmapped Prairies seemed to breed a love for travel in James Mellon Menzies. Given the chance, he always took the longer route to any destination. His first trip to China set the pattern: instead of the normal trans-Pacific route, James went via England and Scotland and onwards across Russia on the legendary Trans-Siberian railway.

With his sister Margaret, he left Toronto on 21 May 1910 to attend the Edinburgh World Missionary Conference as a delegate of the Presbyterian Church in Canada. This great gathering marked the high point of ecumenical co-operation in the missionary movement. There, Menzies met evangelists and missionaries from all over the world and learned from their passionate discussions on issues commonly faced by overseas missions. One main topic was China, the largest and most important field, then on the eve of revolution. The two weeks at Edinburgh provided an intense spiritual experience wherein Menzies the Student Volunteer was initiated into the real world of missions.

After the conference, James and his sister spent two weeks touring the British Isles, meeting Menzies relatives in Perthshire and McGees in Northern Ireland. Margaret then bade him farewell from Waterloo Station and he was off into the unknown. The journey across the endless Siberian steppes took two weeks. He was fascinated as his trained eyes watched the landscape change from Russian Europe to Chinese Asia. On 8 September 1910 he arrived at Beidaihe (old spelling Pei-tai-ho), a beautiful coastal resort in North China. The opening of the Beijing-

Hankou railway in 1905 meant that his designated field of North Henan could be reached in two or three days, a big change from the pioneer days of that mission's founding 'Henan Seven,' whose similar trek inland took several weeks of bumping across the endless North China plain in springless donkey carts.

However, instead of heading directly to Henan, Menzies diverted further southward to look up his fiancée, the 'pretty deaconess' Annie Belle Sedgwick. She and her sister Maude had arrived in China in April and were studying the language at the Central China missionary resort, Guling in Jiangxi province. At the base of the holy mountain Lushan, Guling was generously watered all year, cool and pleasant in the summer. Covered with pine and bamboo forests, the hills were dotted with pavilions, waterfalls, and other attractions such as the Cave of the Immortals, which later inspired Chairman Mao to write a poem in its honour. After four days on the train, the anxious James arrived at Guling, and in the magical air of Guling won Annie's heart once again.

'I wanted to tell you how happy I am,' he wrote his parents. 'We expected to wait for some years, but the folks out here have decided that it will be best for us to be married at once and then we can settle down to [study] the language together.'[1] Canon George Ernest Simmons, the second-in-command of the Anglican mission, 'persuaded Bishop White to seek permission from his home mission board to let Annie break her contract and marry James.' On a personal level, James understood how difficult it was for her. He was Presbyterian and she was Anglican. Their marriage thus meant not only breaking her promise to serve for at least a five-year term but also leaving her church. 'She was so bound up in it all,' wrote James. 'You know she has been in the actual work at Home for several years and it means almost as much for her to give up her Church as it would for a clergyman.'[2]

Later, he wrote that Annie was 'making her dress now for the occasion,' and that she 'wrote home tendering her resignation ... She is the best woman there ever was. She is my ideal. I have met many many women in Church work but there is none that from mere ability, disposition, and Christian life that ever attracted me one half so much as she. But that is not the reason I asked her to be my wife. I asked her because I loved her and I loved her because I could not help it.'[3] They were married on 23 February 1911 by Bishop White in Kaifeng, Henan, and continued to live this love for fifty years.

James Menzies was to have an intimate but troubled relationship with Bishop White for the next fifty years, but this first encounter was exceptionally auspicious. They had probably met the year before in Toronto, since White was consecrated bishop in November 1909, at the same time as James Menzies was applying to the Presbyterian church and Annie Sedgwick was preparing her outfit. It was a magnanimous gesture from a new bishop building a mission from scratch to give up his first woman missionary evangelist without regard to narrow denominational politics. James Menzies was eternally grateful that White had released Annie, and his gratitude coloured his later regard for the older man: White was not the sort of man to let him forget a favour.

A Canadian Bishop

Born in England and also raised in rural Ontario, William Charles White had associations with the YMCA and Student Volunteer Movement before graduating from Wycliffe College in 1897. His fellow students, supported by the Canadian branch of the Church Missionary Society, appointed him as their personal representative to Fujian province on the southeast coast of China.[4] Twelve years older than Menzies, White had arrived in China before the sweeping changes following the Boxer Uprising. From the beginning he was fascinated by Chinese culture, and in time became a fluent linguist, able to speak several dialects. Like many pioneer missionaries, he tried to adapt to Chinese ways, living in native-style houses and wearing Chinese clothes, including an artificial pigtail (or queue) hanging down his back and thick-soled Chinese boots. There was still a great deal of hostility towards Christian missionaries, and the only converts White made were from the dregs of society, opium addicts and lepers.[5]

In 1907 White was transferred from rural evangelization to Fuzhou (old spelling Foochow) city, the capital of Fujian, and a new world of experience opened up. At Fuzhou he found he had 'more in common with the mandarins than with the lepers and opium smokers. Those unfortunates could not appreciate what he had attempted to do; they could not enter into the world of ideas and inspiration that awaited him ... In short order he managed to meet the intellectual leaders of the city. From those scholars who "took me in as an older brother and treated me handsomely" he acquired a profound interest and appreciation for Chinese culture.' One scholar made a remark that remained fixed in White's mind: 'Every country has its national religion, but one country may adopt and learn the good points of another's religion. Though the religion of China is Confucianism, we should tolerate other religions, assimilating their good points into our own system, and discarding that which is unworthy.'[6]

That same year, 1907, White attended the All-China Centenary Missionary Conference held in Shanghai. After the Boxers, the Qing government tried desperately to modernize. It abolished the old civil-service examination system and the Confucian education system behind it, replacing it with state schools that taught Western subjects. This led to a 'mass movement' towards Christianity, when thousands of young men wanting to learn English filled the mission schools and churches. In response to the euphoria of the 'mass movement,' Protestant missions in China grew dramatically. The Shanghai conference called for the unification of the work of various missions and the extension of work to the untouched parts of the mission fields.

As a result, the British and American Anglicans united to form a national Anglican communion of China and invited the Canadian church to 'join in the extension of Christ's Kingdom in this land, by sending a bishop and clergy to undertake work in one of the provinces, where there is, at present, no missionary work of our communion.'[7] White was asked to write a report outlining where the mission should be located and how much it would cost. The Canadian Presbyterians in North Henan extended 'a most cordial invitation' for him to consider Kaifeng, the capital of Henan.

Kaifeng had a reputation as one of the most bitterly anti-foreign cities of China, and in fact was the last provincial capital not 'occupied' by foreign missionaries. As late as 1902, there were posters on the city wall prohibiting the sale of Bibles. Thereafter the China Inland Mission, the Swedish American Lutheran United Mission, and Southern Baptists had established missions there. Bishop White arrived in March 1910, in the middle of a blinding dust storm.

White's first annual report outlined a five-year plan. In Kaifeng, the mission needed a cathedral seating 1000 people, houses for native and foreign workers, a school for girls and another for women, and a college for men and boys. At Guide (old spelling Kweiteh, now called Shangqiu), he was planning a hospital. By 1913 he could write confidently that, despite initial prejudice, 'the Mission plant had developed considerably' and 'the Mission is in favour with all people from the Governor of the province down.' It had three stations: at Kaifeng, Zhengzhou (old spelling Cheng-chow), and Guide. In addition to Bishop and Mrs White, there were thirteen missionaries in the field: Canon Simmons and his wife, five single men, and six single women.[8]

There may have been another reason why Bishop White was so willing to allow Annie Sedgwick to marry James Menzies. Lewis Walmsley, the biographer, alluded to this when he states that White's personality 'radically changed' when he became bishop.

> At thirty-six he was one of the youngest bishops in the Church of England, a position with power and prestige that cannot be disregarded. A dignity accompanied the bishopric. Deference surrounded it. It carried with it a sense of sovereignty accentuated by the regalia – the robes, mitre and orb – that was reinforced by omnipresent ritual ... Like many men who have felt called of God to a special destiny, and been promoted rapidly to positions of prominence, Bishop White guarded jealously the authority his church had bestowed upon him. He assigned duties and delegated responsibility, but shared none of the prerogatives of his office. This made him seem a dictator to some of the Honan mission.[9]

As a result of his abrasive behaviour, the entire first generation of Canadian missionaries, except for Canon George Simmons and his wife, resigned or left the field within a few years. Maude Sedgwick, Annie's sister, withdrew from the mission because of ill health, but the real reason, according to her nephew Arthur Menzies, was that she was frustrated by Bishop White's interference with her life and work. She became interested in a man in Kaifeng, but Bishop White frowned upon this friendship. She was a trained teacher, sent out to teach in the girls' school, but he insisted on keeping her as his personal assistant, and did not allow her to teach.[10]

The Eve of Revolution

When James Menzies arrived in July 1910, China was a volcano ready to explode. After the Boxer Uprising, as resistance to Western intrusions crumbled, the Qing (or Manchu) court, led by the Empress Dowager Cixi (old spelling Tz'u-hsi) recognize the inevitability of change and attempted to guide reforms in such a way that the Manchus could maintain their dominance over the Han Chinese. The most drastic measure was the abolition of the age-old government examinations, which caused the collapse of the traditional elite system. In 1905 the focus shifted to constitutional reform, following Japan's victory over Russia. To many Chinese, the defeat of a large, modern Western power by a tiny Asian nation was proof of the effectiveness of constitutional reform and revolution. They believed they had found the panacea for the survival of China.[11]

These deathbed reforms were too little and came too late to preserve the Qing dynasty. Mounting anti-Manchu sentiment swung public feeling toward revolution, championed by Sun Yat-sen – a Christian – and his Revolutionary Alliance (Tongmenghui). The revolutionaries, never well organized or efficient, emerged the victors in the revolution in 1911 less because of their strength than through the weakness of the Qing. Nonetheless, the founding of the Republic of China was something new in China's long dynastic cycle, as the country embarked on an uncharted voyage.

The reforms and revolution provided the Christian enterprise with an unprecedented opportunity. When the examinations were abolished, a modern education became the new channel for ambitious young men and women. A lucky few went abroad to study, to Japan, America, and Europe. But for those unable to travel, mission schools provided the best opportunity within China. The missionaries, chased out in 1900 as 'foreign devils,' were now welcomed as 'revered teachers.' The students listened to their preaching, hoping to catch the 'secret' of Western superiority, and sought their advice on national politics. Missionaries, individually and collectively, played an active role in China's national struggle. Some were hired by Chinese governments as advisers, while others became translators, educators, publishers, and institution builders. The influence of missionaries on the Chinese elite reached its summit.[12]

The Boxer Uprising taught the Chinese another lesson: the person and property of foreign missions – Protestant and Catholic – and of their Chinese converts were inviolable. Any violence against missionaries would be visited by swift and disastrous vengeance by Britain or the other Powers. Consequently, the missionary enterprise entered into its golden age of expansion, which lasted for almost two decades. In 1900 there were about 2000 Protestant missionaries and 1000 Roman Catholic priests and nuns in all of China; by 1910 there were 5144 and 1469 respectively. Fifteen years later, a new wave of anti-Christian agitation, epitomized by the May 30th movement of 1925, halted this rapidly expanding momentum. By then, there were 8158 Protestants and 3059 Catholics, a total missionary 'force' of over 11,000 individuals from every country in Christendom.[13]

This expansion was geographical as well as institutional. By 1902 the pioneer stage was over, and every province and most of the large cities had resident missionaries. The unfinished task was to fill the gaps between the major mission stations. Changes in Chinese society created urgent demands for Christian missions to expand their educational and medical institutions. Mission schools were no longer just auxiliary tools to train literate Chinese converts, but a source of Western knowledge in the country. To train the leaders of tomorrow, the missions were forced to adopt new professional standards, better equipment, and professional teachers.

The Chinese need for modern education fitted well with the Social Gospel movement that came to dominate mainline denominational missions after 1900. A progressive theological movement, it moved the churches from concern only for the souls to concern also for the bodies of the people they sought to recruit. Social reform and justice were given a place in the mission of the church. In the mission fields, this movement opened the Church to increased attention to more secular concerns such as education, medicine, and social services, hitherto regarded as purely ancillary to evangelism. Voluntarily, missionaries became partners in China's modernization. With their knowledge of Western science and institutions, many became experts in their professions. James Menzies, a trained civil engineer and surveyor, was part of this new generation of 'professional altruists'[14] who would dominate missions in China right up to 1949. He would soon find uses for his practical skills in building dams and canals.

North Henan

Canada was a relative latecomer to China missions. The Presbyterian church sent George Leslie Mackay to Taiwan in 1871, and he claimed the entire northern half of the island. As for mainland China, it was almost two decades before the Presbyterian Church in Canada (Western Division) sent the 'Henan Seven' to found the North Henan mission (NHM) in 1888. Jonathan Goforth and his wife Rosalind Bell-Smith left Toronto in the spring and arrived at Yantai, a pretty city on the Shandong coast then known as Chefoo, where they were joined by Dr Frazer Smith, his wife, and a nurse, Harriet Sutherland. Dr William McClure, the respected superintendent of the Montreal General Hospital, and Donald MacGillivray, a gold medallist from Knox College and a brilliant student of languages, arrived by the end of the year.[15]

With the help of the American Presbyterians in Shandong, they moved inland towards Henan. They advanced cautiously, according to the mission history, 'on their knees.' It took two years before they could secure a foothold in their chosen field, a temporary mission at Chuwang, a 'wretched village,' just inside the provincial border. They rented a second station the following year at Xinzhen, a market town. Then, in 1894, they acquired the first property in Zhangde (old spelling Changte), the largest of Henan's three prefectural cities north of the Yellow River.

The expected harvest of souls came slowly. Jonathan Goforth baptized his first convert in 1892 after two years' work, a blind *yamen* runner and opium addict called Zhou Laochang, known to generations of Canadian Presbyterians as 'Old Blind Chou, the first convert.' Dr Smith, in a simple operation performed in public, surgically removed his cataracts, and when the bandages were removed, Old Zhou leapt to his feet and proclaimed, 'I was blind but now I see.'[16] By 1900 the NHM had twenty-six male and female missionaries and eighty-two Chinese converts, at three stations with four dispensaries and a primary school for boys.[17]

Henan is located on the broad North China plain, flat with deep loess soil that stretches for hundreds of miles. In winter, the dry icy winds blow in from Mongolia, bringing fine yellow dust storms. In summer, the rains come from the Pacific, though there are many years when they are either short or non-existent. The growing season is seven months long and the soil is soft and fertile, suitable for intensive irrigation agriculture, if indeed water can be brought to it. This was the heartland of Chinese civilization, where the first traces of neolithic humans have been discovered dating back six thousand years or more. Here at Zhangde – which has reverted to its ancient name of Anyang – the Bronze Age began around 1800 BCE. Of the eighteen imperial capitals in Chinese history, fifteen had been within the borders of Henan.[18] The Canadian Presbyterians called Henan the 'old homestead' of Chinese civilization and felt an affinity with its dusty plains.

The name 'Henan' means 'south of the Yellow River,' but a wedge extends north of the river between Shandong and Shanxi provinces. This wedge was the Canadian Presbyterian field, one of the poorest regions of China. Its ancient glories were long past. The people were straitjacketed by poverty and tradition. Cut off from government authorities south of the river and bordered by the black granite cliffs of the Taihang mountains, it was a particularly isolated district until the railway came through. Until then the main connection between North Henan and the rest of China was the Yellow River itself, west to Xian and east to the gulf of Bohai. Although North Henan people were curious about anything new, at the same time they showed a strong sense of animosity against anything too unfamiliar, which explains why it was one of the last provinces opened to Christianity.

North Henan was a rural region. In the late Qing, it had a population of over eight million, most of whom were peasants living in twenty thousand villages or small towns. It was divided into twenty-four counties that were under the jurisdiction of three prefectures: Zhangde in the northern corner, Weihui (old spelling Weihwei) in the southeast, and Huaiqing (old spelling Hwai-king) in the southwest, all of which eventually housed Canadian mission establishments. Although the soil was incredibly fertile, producing two crops a year of millet, wheat, *gaoliang*, and beans, the region was poverty-stricken owing to cyclical floods and drought. As a result, famines were frequent.

In 1900, when the Boxer Uprising swept across the North China plain, North Henan, unlike neighbouring Shandong, Hebei, and Shanxi, did not become a Boxer stronghold. Still, the missionaries were forced to flee. They were beaten by mobs and stripped of their clothes, and although there were no deaths, several missionaries were severely wounded, including Jonathan Goforth and Dr Percy Leslie. When the Canadians returned in 1902, they found ruined missions and terrorized converts. As one missionary noted, however, from active hostility 'the attitude of the Chinese, both officials and common people, had completely changed to one of respect, confidence, and friendliness.'[19] Chinese soldiers escorted the returning missionaries and local officials received them with 'marked tokens of favour.' It seemed a new North Henan was being born out of the fire of the Boxers. Within a few years, railway, telegraph, post office, and newspapers would transform the 'old homestead.'

Between 1902 and 1910, when James Mellon Menzies arrived, the North Henan mission entered the era of the 'mass movement.' If the Canadians advanced on their knees before 1900, now they were carried by local interest among peasants and the elite. In 1902 the NHM had one station at Zhangde; by the end of the decade it had six: large stations at Zhangde, Weihui and Huaiqing, and smaller ones at Daokou (old spelling Tao-k'ou), Wu'an, and Xiuwu (old spelling Hsiu-wu). The missionary staff had doubled to 58 and the number of Christian converts had increased from a few dozen to 2729.[20]

As the mission expanded, two trends emerged to dominate its development for decades. First, as the number of converts increased, the training of Chinese leadership became a contentious issue. At this rural mission in a poor area, most of the converts were semi-literate peasants.

It was therefore a daunting task to secure a capable and intelligent leadership for the native church. As a first step, in 1905 the mission started a two-month summer theological school, in which evangelists were given intensive theological training over six summers. In 1909 the mission organized a Chinese Presbytery separate from the mission council, although all the ordained ministers were still Canadians and the Chinese were deacons and elders. It would take decades for the church in Henan to become a truly 'three-self' church: self-governing, self-propagating, and self-supporting.[21]

Educational and medical work also started to show an increasing professionalism. Compared to the Canadian Methodist or Anglican missions, the NHM retained the traditional conservative approach toward evangelism, viewing educational and medical work as auxiliary tools, not the basic purposes of the mission. However, the drastic social changes after 1900 pushed it to move reluctantly to develop modern educational and medical enterprises. Primary schools for boys and girls were opened in villages with enough Christian families. Except for small grants from the mission, these schools were self-supporting. As the network of village schools (also called district schools) developed, a residential school for boys called the Muye (old spelling Mu-yeh) Junior Middle School was opened at Weihui. This would later be upgraded to a high and normal school, the most ambitious educational undertaking of the NHM. Three years later, the boys' boarding school at Zhangde was transformed into a modern primary school with four teachers and seventy-five students.[22]

This professionalism was also shown in other lines of mission work. In 1910, the same year Menzies arrived in North Henan, Mark Wheeler was appointed specifically for YMCA work, and the first lay member of the staff, Hugh MacKenzie, arrived to be treasurer and business agent of the mission, residing nearby at Tianjin, the closest port with a foreign concession. Medical work was important from the very beginning, as the conversion of Old Blind Zhou testified. Although the board stipulated that medical doctors also be ordained graduates of Knox College or another seminary, medical missionaries, male and female, doctors and later nurses, were professionals. They were not content to remain operating primitive dispensaries or clinics, and pressed for modern hospitals. By 1910 the NHM had four hospitals, including one for women, as the foundation for a medical enterprise in North Henan.[23]

To the conservative older missionaries like Jonathan Goforth and Harvey Grant, the mission secretary, professionalization and bureaucratization did not come easily. They were of the old school, graduates of

Knox College in the 1880s when it was trying to create a national Presbyterian church that needed to emphasize its denominational distinctiveness. Consequently, they considered themselves bound by the Westminster Confession and the democratic form of government through presbytery and synods.

After Goforth launched his revivals in Manchuria and Korea, during his 1908 sabbatical, he embarked on a hunt for heretics at Knox College. Undeterred by lack of success in Canada, he returned to China, convinced that it was 'his duty to hunt for heresy' among the members of his own mission. Eventually, because of his charges, three missionaries were called upon to defend their views before the Presbytery, including Mr Clark, principal of the training school at Weihui.[24]

James Slimmon, one of the older men, summed up the conservative feeling that the decline of evangelism was due to the kind of missionaries the FMC had been sending out since 1900. 'The new ones were not interested in direct preaching and soul-winning. The mission was becoming more and more institutionalized. He granted that there had to be some institutions and missionaries had to be in them, but chapel and village preaching, which was the foundation of any successful mission, seemed to be on the point of vanishing. 'The more Missionaries, the fewer converts,' he concluded.[25]

Despite these rumbles in the background, in January 1910 the North Henan presbytery issued a 'rousing call to the Home Church for more workers. Presbytery asked for twenty-six new appointees, over and above the new pastors and their wives and the three single women who had recently arrived. They described their request as modest. They wanted twelve "pastoral evangelists" – five doctors, two of them women, three male educationalists, five female evangelists, two of whom should have nurse's training, one man for student work and one mechanical engineer.'[26] James Menzies and Dr Frederick Auld were the first representatives of this coming generation, the 'professional missionaries.'

Chapter 5

The Early Years, 1910–1917

Wu'an

After James Menzies left Annie Belle Sedgwick at Guling with a promise of marriage, he spent his first five months from September 1910 to February 1911 at Huaiqing in the southwest corner of North Henan. For a while there was some confusion, for there was another James Menzies already stationed at Huaiqing: Dr James R. Menzies, a pioneer medical missionary who was no relation. In English, they were differentiated by their middle initial: Dr James R. and Rev. James M. In Chinese the confusion was resolved by choosing different surnames. Since Dr James R. had already adopted the name of 'Meng,' the family name of the great Confucian philosopher and teacher Mencius, James M. took the pseudonym 'Ming' of the Ming dynasty as his family designation. Ming means 'bright,' to which was added a personal name of Yishi, which means 'honest.' He noted proudly that Ming was close to the Gaelic pronunciation of Menzies, Mingis.[1]

Perhaps James M.'s happiness influenced his adaptation to China. Instead of suffering culture shock, young Menzies found life to be a great adventure and more comfortable than a survey camp in northern Ontario. Huaiqing station had a 'very fine' compound outside the city wall, protected by its own high brick wall. 'The houses are 8 roomed with a kitchen,' he wrote his parents. 'The ceilings are all 10 feet high, so we have fairly comfortable houses. Just now the compound is very beautiful. In fact it is all the year round. It is one of the most beautiful I have seen. There are all kinds of flowers, more especially roses and chrysanthemum. True it is rather tough out in the country when you are away for a month at a time, sleeping in mud huts with no light, no air and lots of rats and fleas. But, then it is resting to get home again to a place that is at least something like home.'[2]

Menzies's early observations demonstrate an adaptation to the Chinese environment that surpassed the insensitive response of many missionaries. After attending a local fair, he wrote, 'They are much like our fairs, only the people come to sell things and to buy. There is always a religious ceremony held in connection with every fair. They put their gods in litters, deck them up with all kinds of fancy things and cart them around a bit and then put them back in their old temples. There is a big straw dish in front of the idol for people to put money in and an incense burner in which to burn incense to the gods.'[3] Menzies's comments mark his separation from the many missionaries who described such occasions with strong denunciations of idols and idolatry. In another letter, he wrote: 'I like it very very much and shall enjoy it very much more when I have a little home of my own ... So missionary life is not nearly as bad as I pictured it.'[4]

On 23 February 1911 James and Annie were married by Bishop White in Kaifeng. Strictly speaking the marriage was not legal. Without further inquiry, Bishop White simply assumed that he could perform marriages in China. However, the British consul asserted that except for a few individuals granted the right by special act of Parliament, no one had the legal right to perform a marriage between British subjects except the consul himself. Nevertheless, the North Henan mission did not object to White's claim at the time. A few years later, as relations between the NHM and Bishop White turned sour because of the latter's high-handed manner – as the Anglican 'Bishop in Honan' he claimed jurisdiction over the whole province, including North Henan – the Presbytery advised its missionaries not to be married by Bishop White.[5]

Two days after their marriage, James and Annie Menzies moved to a new station, Wu'an, where they arrived at night by lantern. For their honeymoon, they took a mule cart for a tour of their adopted home. They were to remain at Wu'an for three years, until they were transferred to Zhangde in late 1913.

Wu'an was a 'problem' station. It was the most northerly county town (*xian*) in Henan, located in a mountainous area near the Shanxi border. The missionaries considered it a backwater because it was some distance from Zhangde, the prefectural city (*fu*), where they had their main station, and twenty miles from the railway station at Handan. The road passed through valleys of yellow loess soil worn down by millennia of cart tracks until they formed a canyon many feet deep. In reality, Wu'an was a fair-sized city, with a population of fifty thousand, that 'had a flourishing trade and a large number of rich people and gentry ... 20,000 men from the county were engaged in business in other parts of China and had some of their prejudices rubbed off. Women appeared to have more freedom to move about and mix with men than did their sisters else-where in Honan [Henan].' Wu'an was famous all over China for its native medicines.[6]

The Wu'an station was established in 1909 when David Yuile, a wealthy Montreal businessman, offered to endow a new station by contributing $4000 a year for two evangelists and their expenses. This, Yuile hinted, would be raised to $6000 when a doctor could be found. FMC secretary R.P. MacKay was so carried away that he offered Yuile a station that 'he might call his own and appoint to it two evangelists and a doctor and thus have an entire station and develop it as he himself might desire.' Unfortunately, Yuile died one week later; his widow, who shared his plans, offered to donate $4000 a year for three years and $10,000 for a memorial hospital.[7]

This promise, the official historian Margaret Brown wrote, was 'one of Dr. MacKay's extremely rare errors of judgement ... Mrs. Yuile was to learn that a new station cannot be set up at the drop of a hat, especially in China, and under the rule of Presbytery. Land had to be bought – a time-consuming process in China –, materials had to be purchased and brought in, sometimes from great distances, buildings had to be erected, and someone found who could oversee the work.' The story of Wu'an, Miss Brown concluded, 'provides a classic example of the disastrous results of shaping policy to meet the desires of people thousands of miles away.'[8]

Mrs Yuile was impatient to see the work under way, and so the mission was assigned the two new men of 1910, James M. Menzies and Dr Frederick Auld. When she insisted that Murdoch Mackenzie, the re-spected pioneer, be sent to Wu'an to establish the work, Presbytery, the governing body of foreign missionaries, felt that would mean sacrificing existing work for a new venture. Instead, they designated Rev. J.H. Bruce, a younger man who knew the city from his evangelistic tours, and his wife to supervise construction. Mrs Yuile also expected that both Menzies and Dr Auld would be stationed there immediately, but Dr Auld was assigned initially to Zhangde for language study. Presbytery patiently explained that it was necessary to set aside two full years for language study, and that without a grasp of the language Dr Auld could do neither construction nor medical work.

The fate of the Wu'an hospital was tragic. Dr and Mrs W.J. Scott were sent there in 1911, about the same time as the Menzies arrived. Dr Scott's father was editor of the *Presbyterian Record*, which assured that the station received considerable publicity in the church papers. The Scotts stayed less than a year, however, as he developed eye troubles and had to return to Canada. Dr McMurtry replaced him for only a few months before he too had to leave in poor health. Dr Auld subsequently refused to leave Zhangde for Wu'an because of the possible effects on his wife's health. (Actually, Margaret Brown confided, the Aulds 'wanted the comforts and companionships of the big central station rather than the hardships of a more isolated one.' W.H. Grant, the clerk of the mission, commented on Mrs Auld's attitude: '"Has the heroic in Missions passed away forever?" flashes upon me.')[9] In any event, no doctor was allocated to Wu'an until 1915.

'Certainly Wuan did seem to collect trouble ... The Mission now began to feel that appointing anyone to Wuan was a prelude to their return to Canada. Was it merely a strange coincidence?'[10] After Dr Scott's departure, a windstorm blew down 900 feet of the compound wall. An enquiry revealed that $15,000 had been spent on Wu'an. Three missionary residences, a dispensary, and an out-patient clinic had been built, but the main building had not been started, and the money had run out. R.P. Mackay seemed more concerned with Mrs Yuile's feelings than with the reality of the field. 'Generally, people seemed to feel sorry for themselves when sent to Wuan,' Margaret Brown concluded.

Located in this quiet backwater, with two couples as foreign companions, James and Annie did not feel sorry for themselves. Since the station was under construction outside the west wall, they lived in a Chinese mansion that dated back to the Ming dynasty (1368–1643). Unlike the Anglican mission, which paid for furniture and living expenses, the North Henan mission granted only a house, free of rent. 'All our furniture consisted of a roll-top desk which I had taken out from Canada and some furniture which I designed and was made by local carpenters,' Menzies recalled. 'We had straw-mats on a brick floor over rafters. Boxes with a square Chinese table and chairs comprised our furniture.'[11] However, they did not need to spend too much time house cleaning, since Wu'an was such a dusty place that everything would be covered with thick yellow dust in a few days.

By the time they moved to the compound at the west gate, Annie was pregnant. This was the fall of 1911, the moment when the Chinese revolution overthrew the Qing dynasty. The political situation throughout China became more and more dangerous after the Wuhan uprising in October. By November the British and American consuls ordered their nationals to evacuate the interior. The Methodist mission in West China was forced to evacuate 149 Canadians because of a 'recrudescence of Boxerism,' but that turned out to be a local situation rather than a national emergency.[12]

The NHM decided to hold on to the main stations along the railway, Zhangde and Weihui. 'Things have remained quiet at all our stations while fighting and killing were going on all round about and we did not know what day might bring confusion to our own district.'[13] For this fragile peace, the Canadians could thank Yuan Shikai, a powerful warlord and local hero whose ancestral home was at Zhangde. During the course of the revolution, Henan was under the tight control of Yuan's Beiyang Army. Nevertheless, the revolution did cause great anxiety among the Canadians.

Amidst this turmoil and confusion David Menzies was born, and named after his grandfather who had been born during the 1837 rebellion in Upper Canada. He was known as Laddie, a happy, sweet-tempered child, a joy and delight to his parents. 'We had a suitcase packed and I had the back gate to the compound oiled so it would not squeak if opened,' James recalled. 'There was great excitement in the city and all night long soldiers paraded the city walls with lanterns and fired off gas pipe cannon to inform the countryside that they were ready and on guard ... One night, a few nights after Laddie was born we started out from Wuan for Liao Chou [pinyin Liaozhou] in Shansi [Shanxi]. Once and twice I and the muleteers had a bad time passing a camel train with your mother and Laddie in a mule litter but beyond excitement no one got hurt. Those were adventurous days.'[14]

Except for this disturbance and a few bandit raids, the Menzies' life at Wu'an was peaceful. They had hoped to go to the North China Union Language School in Beijing to learn the language, but Presbytery objected since the Beijing dialect was quite different from the colloquial of Henan. As a result, James and Annie studied with a private teacher, a local Confucian scholar.

The old-fashioned language training adopted by the NHM made learning the language difficult. Of the first generation of missionaries, few became masters of the tongue. One who did was Donald MacGillivray, the gold medallist in Hebrew. Jonathan Goforth 'worked just as hard and just as faithfully at the language as did MacGillivray, but the contrast in progress was painfully evident ... Had he been of a less optimistic and hopeful disposition, he would have become utterly discouraged.'[15] Hugh MacKenzie, the business manager, wrote after three years that he had not yet passed his first-year examination, and he concluded, 'I shall never become a ready Chinese speaker. I am more fitted however for the office and the desk than for the platform.'[16]

Menzies's biblical Hebrew helped a little, but his battle with the language was not easy. In 1913 he wrote his parents: 'The greatest headache is to study the language. It is so interrupted that I make no progress whatever. I am so far behind the others that I am ashamed. I have not passed my second year exam yet.'[17] Menzies worked so hard that his eyes hurt and he had migraine headaches. Nevertheless, with his skill at visualizing blueprints learned at SPS, he was attracted to the written characters, the ideographs that combine 'pictures' and ideas. By the time he was appointed to Zhangde, the language was no longer a worry for him. Years later, even Bishop White praised him as one of the few Canadian 'experts' on the Chinese language.[18]

Menzies's interruptions were partially caused by the 'extracurricular' responsibilities he took up voluntarily. A YMCA activist, he naturally carried his interest in student work to his new field. The circumstances were very different, though, for modern education in North Henan was still in its earliest stage. Besides supporting his mission's participation in the YMCA in Kaifeng, Menzies tried to start his own work among students in local schools. After only a month in the field and still unable to speak the language, he helped set up a YMCA for students at Huaiqing. 'Just now I am much interested in getting YMCA work started among the students in the city. Mr. Mowatt is interested in it and we are working together. I can not do much because I cannot speak the language. But when we are with the Chinese, he interpreted what they say to me and what I say to them. We hope to get something definite done soon.'[19] Later, at Wu'an, he also ran a lower primary school and a Sunday school of thirty children, most from non-Christian families.

He also took on the bookkeeping for the station. Even though Wu'an only had three missionary families, it was a demanding job keeping track of construction materials and workmen's wages. Fortunately, Menzies had learned bookkeeping from his father, who had instructed him in business-like accuracy and detail.

The most time-consuming job was helping supervise the building projects. Since the NHM did not have its own architect, buildings were designed and supervised by missionaries who happened to have some background in construction and carpentry. This meant they were called away from their regular evangelical or medical work to supervise construction. Between 1900 and 1910, the NHM built three main stations and three substations, with twenty-six foreign residences, four hospitals, and several boarding schools.[20] Gradually, some people felt they needed a professional architect/builder. They asked Menzies if he would consider that position, but he turned them down, saying God had called him to be an evangelist.[21] However, he did take up engineering responsibilities at Wu'an until the mission recruited James B. MacHattie, a Scottish-trained construction engineer, in 1912.

'Dr. Scott supervised the building,' Menzies wrote. 'Though still a language student, I did a great deal of supervising too, for Scott knew next to nothing about building.' Until this time, foreign residences in North Henan were copies of Ontario farmhouses, two rooms front and two rooms back with a central hall, upstairs and downstairs, a total of eight rooms. Menzies thought this design was inefficient, and so he designed a six-room house with a sliding door that created a large space for gatherings.[22] The Chinese workmen needed careful supervision in order to understand and follow the blueprints correctly. 'We have to superintend all the work and show them how to do any new thing we ask them to do. Of course, they are not entirely novices for many of them have helped build foreign houses before.'[23]

His most important project was sinking the deepest well in Wu'an. City wells had to be deep to reach good and sufficient water, but village wells tended to be shallow and few in number because of primitive well-digging techniques and equipment. Many villages shared a single well. As Menzies reminisced:

> There was no good water at the west gate of the city and all the water for drinking and food had to be bought from water barrow men who brought it by wheel barrow from the east side of the city, a good mile away. People of course tried to use the local surface wells which were alkali and the workmen building the houses and hospital were all with sore lips and a greenish scum about their mouths from using only a little local water when they could not get sweet water that was bought. I drilled a deep well at Wuan with a big bamboo bow cased with a pinch cedar casing which I designed and taught Chinese carpenters to make. I also installed a pump operated by a big iron flywheel all imported from the Peking Syndicate coalmines 150 miles away. That was quite a job, one that had never been done before in that part of the country. I had to devise original methods to drill the well past great round boulders and drive the casing down.[24]

In 1948, when their daughter Marion Menzies returned to North Henan, she found the well was still in good condition and well used.

The years at Wu'an gave Menzies a good preparation for his missionary career. His Chinese was still not perfect, but he had acquired the courage and confidence to preach to a Chinese crowd. In addition, he had started learning about Chinese history and culture, which formed the basis upon which he would build his interest in archaeology and ancient culture.

Zhangde

By 1914 James and Annie Menzies had two children: David, nicknamed Laddie, born to the guns of revolution in 1911, and Marion, born eighteen months later at their summer home at Beidaihe. In those troubled times, Wu'an was far from the railway, therefore isolated and dangerous. Always anxious to accommodate missionary families, the Presbytery transferred them to Zhangde, the oldest, largest, and most comfortable station in the mission. Zhangde was on the Beijing-Hankou railway line. The Menzies family was to grow during the Zhangde years between 1914 and 1917. Frances was born in 1915. Laddie died suddenly in 1916, when Annie was already pregnant with Arthur Redpath (named after his mother's brother). The Chinese considered him a replacement for Laddie and so called him Bao Bei, 'Precious.' When Annie carried three-month-old Bao Bei to Canada in 1917, her Canadian relatives could not say the Chinese name properly and so they nicknamed him Bobby. He was called Bobby until he went to school.[25]

James and Annie brought another member of the family from Wu'an, their amah named Shen Dasao (literally, Mrs Shen, a term of respect for women), who was to remain their faithful servant and friend for twenty-five years, including three years in Canada living at the farm of the Menzies grandparents. Marion wrote an affectionate tribute to Shen Dasao in her memoirs. She was an 'uneducated, bound-foot woman who had a native capacity to learn and adapt.' When Annie was pregnant with Marion, she enquired about a nursemaid for the children. Shen Dasao, who was from Huaiqing, was anxious for the job. Although she was 'about Mother's age,' she had had several children, all but one of them having died. Her husband was elderly and cared for their son. 'When she came to Canada with us in 1917, she learned to speak English. Her sentences often contained a mixture of Chinese and English. I recall she once complained about her bread-making – a newly acquired skill – "Tai

Tai" [meaning Lady or Mistress] the hops [yeast] mei yu "hop" la
[haven't risen]. In her mind hop meant "to jump up" so hops logically
meant a jumping up agent.' Shen Dasao was a strict disciplinarian and
the Menzies parents could trust her implicitly with the children. Sometimes at the beach at Beidaihe, she would call the children to come just
to show the other amahs how obedient they were.[26]

The Menzies family moved to Zhangde in early 1914. Zhangde was the
most important of the three prefectural cities in North Henan. By the
beginning of the twentieth century, thanks to the development of the
railway and mining industries, it had become a commercial and manu-
facturing centre, with light industries such as cotton spinning and flour
milling. Unfortunately, the limited modernization in this region increased the sufferings of the people as well, for during the civil wars the
railway increased the ease of transporting troops and arms. Although the
Canadians were protected by their British status, they were caught between fighting army units several times, with their work interrupted and
lives placed in danger.

Since the seven counties (xian) of the Zhangde prefecture were adja-
cent to the neighbouring province of Shandong, the city had been the
goal of the Canadian mission pioneers in 1888. But it was not until 1894,
with the 'gunboat diplomacy' of British consuls and the personal intervention of Li Hongzhang, the 'foreign minister,' that they were able to
buy a property just outside Zhangde city. By the time of the Menzies'
arrival twenty years later, the station was well established. The compound
was located on Zhuzhong Street outside the north gate of the city wall.
Protected by a high brick wall, it was a world of its own. Besides several
foreign residences, there was a church that seated three hundred people,
the Binying Boys' boarding school, the Sanyu Girls' boarding school, a
hospital for women (the hospital for men was inside the walled city), and
a dozen Chinese buildings.

There, the Menzies became neighbours to the mission's most famous
evangelist, Jonathan Goforth. After his unsuccessful attacks on 'heretics'
at Knox College and within his own mission, he had moved towards
fundamentalism. There is considerable scholarly debate whether American Fundamentalism – which took its name from a series of booklets
called The Fundamentals published after 1910 – was primarily theological:
premillennialism taught (and teaches) that the end of the world was
approaching, when Jesus would return to 'rapture up the saints' in the
Second Coming. Other scholars emphasize that Fundamentalism was a
temperament, a belligerent tone of religious war. In any event, Goforth

was the most influential figure in transplanting this North American-style fundamentalism to China, through the Bible Union of China, which translated and printed 500,000 copies of *The Fundamentals* in China.

Increasingly, Goforth felt estranged from the North Henan mission, especially the younger men such as James M. Menzies, a civil engineer influenced by the social gospel and higher criticism. Goforth asked Presbytery to release him from the mission to enable continuation of his God-given task of the evangelization of all China, not just North Henan. This was granted in 1911, but for several years he was half in and half out of the mission, living also at the mountain resort of Jigongshan and making extensive crusades throughout China. He became famous for his campaigns among the soldiers of the 'Christian general' Feng Yuxiang, a warlord who controlled Henan at various times and reputedly baptized hundreds of his soldiers at a time with firehoses. In 1918 Goforth severed his formal relations with the mission and left North Henan to 'traipse through China with his wife and five children like "gospel nomads."' Since he had already left Henan, spiritually if not physically, Goforth did not become an influence on young Menzies, nor indeed did they have any notable clashes.[27]

Although the senior missionary at Zhangde, Murdoch Mackenzie, was equally conservative, he had the opposite temperament from Goforth. A hearty Scotsman who seems to have been the nicest of the Henan pioneers, he too was a graduate of Knox College and had arrived in 1889. Conservative in theology and mission policy, he was more flexible and tolerant than Goforth. He came to love the North Henan peasants and enjoy rural evangelism. Margo Gewurtz, a historian of the NHM, calls Mackenzie 'the accountant of souls' for his meticulous parish registers of baptisms and enquirers.[28] Despite differences in age and theology, Mackenzie and Menzies became friends and partners on rural evangelical tours.

The 1911 revolution brought down the Qing dynasty, but it failed to establish a functional new political order. Nonetheless, the new Republic made many missionaries feel optimistic, especially as new laws proclaimed religious freedom. Even in North Henan, changes were easy to notice. 'The Revolution has not only taken off the queues and stripped off the long gowns and loose clothes of many Chinese, but it has created a great demand for Western hats, caps and clothes.'[29] The demand was so great that the Chinese congregation at Weihui floated a joint stock company for the manufacture of Western clothes.[30]

More important were changes in the attitude of officials and local gentry. After the Boxer Uprising, they had been forced to respect the foreign 'barbarians'; now after the Revolution they began to show sincere friendliness. For conservative and anti-foreign North Henan, this change was remarkable. Proud and lofty prefectural officials received missionaries with dignity and even visited mission stations to witness sewing machines and model kindergartens. This interest in Western things helped the Canadians take up more responsibility in North Henan's modernization, especially in education.

Although the missionary role in China's educational modernization has been recognized as a lasting contribution, it has been assumed that the missionaries were the initiators and the Chinese passive recipients. With its emphasis on evangelism and its policy of 'first the Church, then the school,' the conservative NHM was far from being the initiator: instead, it was pushed into educational modernization by changes around it. As late as the 1930s – thirty years after the government abolished the Confucian examination system – the old-fashioned traditional schools (sishu) were still the norm in rural education. They were usually housed in abandoned temples and had one teacher drilling the village boys in the millennium-old curriculum of the so-called Four Books and the Five Classics. Modern, Western education made only limited advances. The provincial government established the first modern schools in 1902 and the first school for women in 1906. Much later came a university in Kaifeng, as well as specialized technical schools.[31]

In its drive for modern schooling, the local Christians and provincial authorities sought help from the missionaries. The mission's response was neither enthusiastic nor unanimous. Among the older missionaries, the opposition to non-evangelical activities was still strong. The younger missionaries, restless to broaden the scope of the mission, received encouragement from the larger ecumenical movement. After the 1910 Missionary Conference in Edinburgh, the Association of Missionary Societies of the United States and Canada called upon missions to cooperate in developing a coordinated, unified system of Christian schools in China, an alternate, private system from kindergarten to university.[32]

It was in this context that the NHM moved to build its educational enterprise. The first high school was at Weihui, the Muye High and Normal School, headed by Robert A. Mitchell, the first male educationalist of the mission. At Zhangde, the Sanyu Girls' Boarding Primary School was upgraded to a junior middle school, the only one in Zhangde.[33] James Menzies was given responsibility for the boys' boarding school.

Begun in 1896, with a Confucian scholar teaching the Classics and missionaries teaching English and the Bible, by 1915 it had been upgraded to the Xianying Lower and Higher Primary School, with Menzies as the principal and Wang Qiuxian vice-principal. The students came from the city and surrounding villages, from mostly poor Christian families who could not afford to pay the tuition fees. The NHM waived the tuition fees, but the families had to pay for the students' food. The regulations were strict: students had to attend church on Sunday; they could not go beyond the compound gate without permission; and in the spirit of competition, student records were made public at the end of each term.[34]

Menzies remained principal for only one year, then was appointed an evangelist to a large country district. He was disappointed by this change, since he felt drawn to student work. However, as a junior member, he had to defer to the Presbytery. While on trial in his new rural assignment, Menzies was called to organize a province-wide evangelical campaign focusing on students and gentry.[35] This was something new, organized by the YMCA. In 1914, Sherwood Eddy, a leading figure in the North American Student Volunteer Movement, came to Beijing, where he conducted a successful student campaign and delivered stirring speeches to missionaries and students. When the NHM invited Eddy to extend his meetings to Henan, the YMCA asked the mission to appoint a secretary to work full time preparing for the meetings.[36] As a result, Menzies was appointed executive secretary of the Student Evangelistic Campaign in Henan.[37]

Ten years after Menzies had organized YMCA campaigns at the School of Practical Science, he was doing the same thing at Zhangde. Scheduled for October 1915, the campaign had the goal of interesting students in Christianity and organizing them into Bible study classes. One secret of its success was that it invited speakers well known in student circles.[38] Menzies invited Dr William Wesley Peter of the YMCA Lecture Bureau in Shanghai, who had conducted a well-known, nation-wide public health campaign. He gave five lectures in North Henan, with a total attendance of 3500 people. The result was remarkable, the mission secretary wrote, for Peter's 'vigorous manhood, lucid statements of important facts, along with his innumerable models and maps, made a lasting impression on all who heard him.' As a result, the Weihui Civic Board of Health was formed.[39]

Another speaker was Donald McGillivray, who had left North Henan to work at the Christian Literature Society in Shanghai. He was an outstanding linguist and writer who was chosen as the successor of Timothy Richard, the leading missionary reformer with the Society. At Weihui, McGillivray gave three speeches on Christianity and its relations to patriotism, social progress, and the life of the individual. As a 'local son' of North Henan, McGillivray was particularly welcomed. The mission secretary reported that the 'audience, consisting exclusively of educated men, listened on the three occasions, the attendance varying from 450 to 750. The attention was close and at times intense. Dr. McGillivray spared not himself at all. His style was fervid and highly literary. His addresses were coloured with numerous local and classic illustrations and brightened with many modern ideas and recently assimilated new terms.'[40]

The campaign allowed the NHM to strengthen its ties with local officials and gentry. The officials were enthusiastic and attended the meetings as chairmen and honorary guests. At Weihui, three squads of soldiers were assigned as the guard of honour when the *Daotai* invited his foreign guests for an elaborate foreign dinner, 'which in style and sumptuousness would tax many a European gentleman to surpass.'[41] In evangelistic terms, the campaign was also a success. The local school authorities removed the restriction on religious activities among the students.

MacGillivray's 'cultural Christianity,' which stressed patriotism, social progress, and personal life, impressed the students and teachers. 'At the conclusion of the second and third addresses, nearly one hundred men, the great majority of whom were teachers and Middle School students, signed cards enrolling themselves in classes for the investigation of Christianity. On Sunday morning eighty of these men gathered in the city chapel where refreshment was served. Dr. Auld's phonograph acted as orchestra, and then after some singing, and a short address, and a clear explanation of our plans, the men were divided into some 15 Bible classes to meet once a week for study.'[42]

After the campaign, the Weihui station put on record: 'We are greatly indebted to Mr. Menzies and Mr. Hu for the vigorous way in which they carried through the general arrangements.'[43] Menzies was a skilled organizer, and he loved to work with committees. By 1926 he was on the following NHM committees: Education, Cheeloo University Field Board of Managers, Students, Staff and Recruits, Summer School, Men's Bible School, Roll Book, Reports, and Maps and Survey.[44] In 1916, as executive secretary of the Student Evangelistic Campaign, he took over the YMCA work in Kaifeng when Mr Wheeler was on furlough.

In early June 1916 Laddie died suddenly of scarlet fever at their summer home at Beidaihe before James was able to arrive from Henan. The next day he escorted the coffin to North Henan to be buried in the mission's small but expanding cemetery. On the train he wrote his parents, 'A sad hearted son sits in the corner of a Chinese baggage car writing this brief note to you. A little coffin lies before him, all that remains of Laddie.'[45] The pain was so great that Menzies could not get over it for a long time. His letters were full of deep grief and self-criticism. He tried to focus on his work, but many times he could not control himself. 'Today there is a meeting in the city for students and I have to speak on the little subject of science, philosophy and religion,' he wrote to Annie, 'but I am at my wit's end. All day yesterday I tried to think out my subject but could not. The whole place is full of the dear little Laddie, calling out to me, "come on Daddy."'[46]

During his first term in North Henan, James Menzies came to know Confucian scholars, school teachers, students, and local gentry – the educated classes. His message, demanded by the audience, was the gospel of patriotism, progress, and ethics. This pattern was interrupted in 1917, when he came to know and appreciate the lowest classes of society, the peasants. He did not live among them in North Henan, but ten thousand miles away on the battlefields of France during the horrors of the First World War.

Chapter 6

Somewhere in France, 1917–1920

The Great War Comes to North Henan

In August 1914 the First World War broke out in Europe. Although China was able to stay out of the conflict until 14 August 1917, it was affected by the struggles among the Powers. In November 1914, on the basis of the Anglo-Japanese Alliance, Japan sent a large naval and army force to occupy the German concession territory at Qingdao (old spelling Tsingtao) in Shandong province. The Chinese government could do nothing but acquiesce in the Japanese occupation.[1]

While still officially neutral but hoping for better treatment after the war, the Chinese government in late 1916 surreptitiously agreed to a British scheme that brought it closer to the Allied side. This was the Chinese Labour Corps (CLC), also known as 'the coolie corps,' which eventually sent about 92,000 Chinese to France as non-combatant workers. This little-known episode was strategically important in the British war effort. As casualties escalated, the CLC released regular Allied soldiers from manual labour, such as digging trenches and building roads, and other logistical tasks. It was also a strange story of culture shock as illiterate Chinese peasants were shipped across the Pacific in crowded troop ships, put into sealed train cars from Vancouver to Halifax, and then re-embarked in crowded ships to be dropped into war-torn France. Alvyn Austin has sketched the conditions in France, where almost 'every Allied camp had its "Chinese Johnnies" cleaning the latrines, laying railroad tracks, and mopping up the battlefields.' According to one missionary, the Chinese worked under adverse conditions, 'winning golden opinions for themselves here for their capacity to do work and for their unfailing cheerfulness under all circumstances.'[2]

At first, the British War Office planned to raise Chinese workers in Hong Kong, a British colony, but North China soon attracted their attention, since 'Coolie workers from northern China, especially those from Shantung province, had long enjoyed a reputation for hard work and stout constitutions.'[3] Besides, the British had a deep-water harbour at Weihaiwei near Qingdao on the Shandong peninsula that could be used for recruiting and transporting labourers. In late 1916 T.J. Bourne, a former engineer-in-chief of the Pukou-Sinyang Railway, was sent there to 'enrol' labourers. To limit its liabilities and distance itself from a quasi-legal diplomatic problem, the British War Office instructed its agents in China to use the term 'enrolling,' rather than 'recruiting,' Chinese labourers; if they were recruited as soldiers, the War Office assumed unwelcome responsibilities for the welfare of the men and their families. Enrolment, by contrast, implied an element of voluntarism, since China was technically neutral. The contract was designated a commercial transaction between an agency called the British Emigration Bureau and each individual labourer.[4]

The Canadian missionaries in North Henan were registered as British subjects when the British Legation in Beijing in 1916 issued a formal and urgent call to all missionaries of military age in North China to join the CLC as officers. They were assured that 'the labour battalions are not to be employed under fire and the work is purely non-combatant,' which implied that missionaries could continue their religious activities among the workers. This would give 'an opportunity of serving their country to any missionaries or others who might have conscientious scruples as to fighting.'[5]

Nevertheless, many Canadians did have conscientious difficulties with any active participation in the war. In 1914 Robert A. Mitchell, principal of the Henan mission's high school, wrote: 'It is a terrible thing that the nations professing faith in the Prince of Peace should be doing their best to destroy one another. It is hard for us to speak of the advance made in Western countries through Christianity with this example before our eyes.'[6] Appalled by the news of atrocities, another wrote: 'China may be able to teach the nations of Europe some lessons shortly ... Chinese industry, temperance, organizing capacity, economy, endurance and patience, may well cause some of China's detractors to pause and ask which Continent has most to learn from the other.'[7]

Murdoch Mackenzie, in a private letter to R.P. MacKay, secretary of the Board of Foreign Missions (formerly the Foreign Missions Committee), summed up the dilemma of 'our workers in Honan':

Years ago they had listened to the voice of the highest King, and in obedience to His command had come to China. They studied Chinese for the express purpose of making Christ and His great salvation known to the Chinese people in north Honan. In many spheres they had rendered whole hearted and cheerful service to their Divine Master. An opportunity, such as does not come often in an ordinary lifetime, has now led them to ask whether their lives, and all the knowledge they have gained of Chinese, may not be turned to account in the struggle now being waged. Britain is about to put forth its maximum effort. The weightiest issues for our Empire and the World depend on the result. No one worthy of the British name would shrink from considering the question of duty at such a time. It has been taken up seriously by all our brethren, and their response is only that which was expected of them.[8]

Eventually sixteen of thirty-two male missionaries from the North Henan mission – all the younger men – would join the CLC and leave North Henan. Their wives and children waited out the war in Canada.[9] This was a heavy burden for the mission, as the work painfully built up over twenty-five years was 'practically suspended.' The work of evangelism and the five-year Forward Movement, 'in which the Chinese Church should take a leading part,' was cancelled. Medical work was 'completely stopped' when all six male doctors and their Chinese medical assistants departed, leaving only two female doctors, Jeannie Dow and Isabelle McTavish, to take care of the missionaries' health.[10] Three of the four hospitals had to be closed. The mission's woes were compounded by the forces of nature: the drought of 1916–17 was followed by torrential rains and floods that wiped out the fall harvest and left hundreds of thousands homeless.

James Menzies was the second man from North Henan to apply, after Dr Percy Leslie, who had to resign from the mission to do so. In December 1916, Menzies wrote to the British Legation at Beijing offering his services:

I have been seven years in China as a missionary ... My qualifications are, (1) graduate in engineering of the University of Toronto, with postgraduate work in astronomy and geodesy. (2) I am a licensed Dominion Land Surveyor ... [and] a junior member of the Canadian Society of Civil Engineering. I have spent several years in survey work in Canada, both in the subdivision of land and in the geodetic survey of Canada. (3) I am a graduate in theology of Knox College and have spent my time in China in evangelistic work, two years among the students and gentry of the province of Honan. During these years I have had supervision of Chinese workmen in the erecting of buildings and other work.[11]

Menzies passed the obligatory examination in Chinese, with 'good' in written and 'very good' in colloquial, and his offer was promptly accepted.[12]

Since James and Annie had already served a seven-year term, they were due for a furlough, normally a year-long period of rest with only mild requirements of itinerant speaking in Canadian churches. This was now impossible. Menzies did not mind postponing his own furlough but he was worried about Annie and the children, Marion aged four, Frances two, and three-month-old Arthur. How could she look after them on the long journey home under wartime conditions and then in Canada for the unforeseen future? As usual Shen Dasao, the Chinese nursemaid, came to the rescue. She begged to accompany them to Canada; according to Marion, 'Shen Dasao was beloved by all of us.' This resolved everything; in their peripatetic three years in Canada, she was always there to look after the children and cook when Annie went on deputation tours.[13]

As James Menzies wrote to his son Arthur in November 1945, at the end of another world war,

> Then I went off to war and you were carried home in a market basket with a little collapsible top of blue grey heavy silk set up like a top on galvanized iron wire. I took you all down to Shanghai in March [1917] and saw you off on the boat for Canada with Mrs. Arthur and her children. I remember after I got you all on board, I found I had time to rush up town and get a big bunch of flowers for mother. We had had such a scramble with you all and with the baggage that I had not dared take time before. Then I found after you had gone that I had missed the last good boat to Tsingtao [Qingdao] and was going to be late reporting for duty. So I took a little Japanese fishing boat that was leaving at once and after four days I arrived in time to report for duty on the proper date. That fishing boat I remember had only raw fish and cold rice with some pickles. I also tried to learn Japanese chess.

He concluded with his characteristic interest in archaeology: 'Many years after in a Tang dynasty grave, northwest of Chang-te, I found a red clay jar of the same shape with the same kind of chess men in it.'[14]

After a fearful voyage across the Pacific with submarine drills every day, Annie, the children, and Shen Dasao arrived at the farm of David

Redpath Menzies and his wife Jane McGee at Staples. David was eighty years old and Jane sixty-seven, but they opened their hearts and home to their boisterous grandchildren. Fortunately, Annie's family, the Sedgwicks, were only a short drive away at Windsor. With financial help from David, the Menzies family rented a house at Leamington, half-way between, where James had attended high school. 'It was during our year or more in Leamington,' Marion wrote, 'that I began to understand and appreciate belonging to an extended family.' There were Menzies and Sedgwick cousins, since Annie had five sisters and a brother, also named Arthur. 'I was also much impressed by having grandparents and even a great grandmother, Mary Ann [Scott] Wright. She had a distinctive English accent and a proud carriage with snowy white hair.'[15]

The Chinese Labour Corps

Canada's connection with this unique venture has been little known. Some years ago Margo Gewurtz and Peter M. Mitchell, founders of the Canadian Missionaries in East Asia Project, wrote a pair of important, complementary papers on the Chinese Labour Corps. Gewurtz concentrated on the recruitment of missionaries, who 'became the critical element in a scheme the British considered of great importance to their war effort.' Mitchell examined their recruitment and transportation across Canada, conducted under strict wartime secrecy that suppressed almost any mention of these events in Canadian or American newspapers, including the church journals. This account of James Menzies's experiences, reconstructed from the NHM records and his personal letters, is the first eyewitness account of the CLC to be published.

The Chinese workers were enrolled mainly in Shandong, Hebei, and Henan by native labour agents and brought to Weihai and Qingdao, where they were processed by British officers. Gillies Eadie, a North Henan colleague, ran the War Emigration Agency at Qingdao, the centre of operations. 'He handled all the paperwork, kept all the accounts and oversaw the distribution of some twenty million dollars a year. He was responsible for seeing that the Chinese in France and their families in Chihli [Hebei], Honan and Shantung received the money due them ... Thus, in large measure was entrusted to two Canadian missionaries, Eadie, and at war's end, [J.A.] Mowatt, "the good name of the Empire in Shantung."'[16]

The CLC recruiting agents were primarily Chinese who were skilled at raising contract labourers for the warlord armies, for large state projects such as building roads and railways, or as overseas workers. They would tour the villages and negotiate with the headmen who made some squeeze from each transaction. They picked up a few village idiots who looked strong but could not pass the medical exams, and not a few were returned from France.[17] Most were semi-skilled or skilled young peas- ants, such as carpenters and blacksmiths, who had been displaced by recent social conditions. Certainly, most were attracted by the pay, ten cents a day and twenty dollars cash paid to their families on embarka- tion, and the fact that they were not soldiers. After the medical exams at Qingdao, they were put onto steamships and shipped 'practically as freight' in contingents from 300 to 3200.

Just as Annie's life was made easier by Shen Dasao, James Menzies took a Chinese servant from North Henan as his batman. Xiang Er (Lucky Boy) had helped Menzies for years, travelling on evangelical tours and looking after his old white horse named Bucephalus, after Alexander the Great's steed. Years later Menzies recalled, 'Lucky was always very careful to keep my buttons shined and my shoes polished and to wake me early in the morning to be ready for parade. He also made my bed, washed my sheets and packed my baggage neatly in my bedding roll ... He looked after me so faithfully all through the war in spite of danger and hardship.'[18]

In March 1917 Menzies boarded the S.S. *Protesilaus*, a 9500-ton ship leased from the Blue Funnel Line, the major British shipping company. There were over three thousand labourers, the largest CLC contingent, which was organized into two battalions and eight companies, then further subdivided into groups under a 'head man.' Menzies's company had 382 labourers. The ten officers, all British subjects working in China, were under the command of P.V. Jackson, formerly of Jardine Matheson, whose only credentials seemed to have been supervising Chinese labourers in South Africa in 1903–4. His assistant was an insurance agent from Shanghai; the doctor was from the British Lega- tion in Beijing. Others included a teacher from Beijing, an assistant engineer in the Department of Public Works of Shanghai, a printer at the British American Tobacco Company, and two agents of Standard Oil. Most were unmarried.

The only missionary, Menzies complained to Annie, 'It has been rather a shock getting back into the old life again. Of all the filthy language, the drinking and smoking, I will not attempt even to let you get the slightest intimation. Not even my old experience prepared me for this.' Being the only one who spoke fluent Chinese turned out to be a disadvantage when an officer resigned at Yokohama and Menzies had to take over his company as well.[19]

The farmers' sons from the flat North China plain had never been on a ship on the rough Pacific. Just out from Yokohama, they ran into 'quite a gale ... The boat went up and down like a seesaw. I cannot say I was not sick but I stuck to my job. I tell you it was fun getting about the decks. I could not get a Chinese to move. Everyone was in bed, hanging on for dear life. It puts the poor Chinese out of business for a long time.'[20]

Although the British refused to identify the CLC labourers as military recruits, they were governed by strict military discipline. 'To say that we had been busy would not be exaggerating the truth,' Menzies told Annie.

> From morning until night and some nights all night, we are at it. We start at 6 a.m. Get the men lined up for 7 a.m. breakfast and see them all fed, 3000 and more ... Then we have our own breakfast at 8 a.m. and after that see all the bunks are tidied up and swept. Then at 10 a.m. the Captain, Doctor and the orderly officer for the day come around and inspect. Then at 11:30 we have the men come up one by one for *congee* or what we call *hsifan* [pinyin *xifan*]. At 12:30 we have our own dinner and after dinner we have such little jobs as vaccinating the whole ship or giving each man 12 numbers and seeing that they are properly sewn on all the proper garments ... I have had a big job in my hands managing these coolies. I have had to cuff and throttle them into order.

In order to prevent chaos, the labourers were prohibited from drinking, but in such confined conditions problems were inevitable. 'Oh it has been a great job,' he wrote. 'Knowing Chinese as I do and then my temperament seems to get me first to any row or fight.'[21]

The secrecy was so strict that not even the officers were informed about the route. This posed a problem, because James hoped to meet his wife and parents for a brief reunion while traversing Canada. He was unable to send even a 'coded' cable, as he explained: 'I will not be able to wire anything very clearly. You may have to guess what the message means for many German Americans might be glad of the opportunity to wreck either train or ship with so many persons on board.' The *Protesilaus* docked at Vancouver in May, and after a brief stay at Ivan Head army camp, the CLC battalions were put on special trains with barred windows and armed guards to travel across Canada by night.[22]

With special permission, Menzies did leave his company at Toronto, took the train to Windsor to see his family, and then rushed to Montreal to rejoin the train. He left his parents with 'broken hearts' and a daughter suffering from an 'unknown Chinese fever.' R.P. MacKay, who was in an awkward, ambivalent position concerning the missionaries abandoning their work, reported: 'We had a hurried call from Mr. Menzies ... He ran over to Windsor to see his family and had to leave one of the little ones in poor health. Naturally he was anxious. It was also distressing to say good-bye to the old people. Nevertheless he is brave and under a sense of duty.'[23]

At Montreal, the CLC embarked on two ships, with Menzies as senior officer in charge of Battalion 12 on the *Corinthian*. With the greatly increased responsibility and authority, Menzies began to feel his importance. Though a even-tempered man, he complained, 'Life among these Chinese is trying because so many misunderstandings arise and everyone comes to me for everything all the time.' He was often called upon to settle disputes among the men, and between the men and the officers. He showed no hesitation in using his authority when he had to discipline a British officer for insubordination.[24] For the most part the voyage was peaceful and comfortable, and Menzies was in a cheerful mood. 'Everything has gone harmoniously. As yet no hitch of any kind has occurred. The crowd has been ideal. There has been no drinking and in all as pleasant a crowd as one could wish ... The number of sick is very small, except for mumps ... We get along fine and have the best of discipline.'[25]

Menzies also noted the escort ships. 'They have been all around us all day. They go like the wind and are such fine boats that you simply enjoy seeing them go.'[26]

The CLC contingent disembarked at Liverpool, where they were detained because of an epidemic of mumps. Here Menzies began to taste the privations of war, 'living in a tent, sleeping between camel's hair blankets, and living on locusts without the wild honey for a diet.' However, he felt the sacrifice was worthwhile: 'Were it not that I am convinced that I am needed to look after these men; I should be wishing myself back home. The feeling that I am doing something keeps me satisfied whatever the cost.'[27] After a few weeks, the Chinese were sent by the Directorate of Labour to France, where they were allocated to various branches of the British Army.[28]

Menzies's life in the next two years is difficult to trace because of the military censorship: his letters were always addressed from 'somewhere in France.' Nevertheless, he wrote regularly to Annie and the children, and sent birthday greetings to his parents, and these letters presented a censored version of events. In November 1917 he was promoted from lieutenant to captain, one of the first missionaries to be promoted. 'So you see dear, your lover is up one or rather two notches higher in the world. You will address me then in future as Capt. J.M. Menzies.'[29] With this promotion, he was given his own company, Number 108, which had five hundred men. They built roads, prison camps, and temporary military structures. As trench warfare turned the region into a sea of mud, Menzies complained, 'The mud is deep. Oh so deep that I shudder when I think of the possibility of our moving off into a muddy field with tents and no floorboards.'[30]

From this time onward, for the rest of his life, Menzies was plagued with migraine headaches. 'Well we were just on the road when I could hardly stand for a sick headache. When we got to our new camp, I managed to get the camp settled in a few minutes and then I bowled over. I was awfully sick. Oh, so sick all day and the next that I could hardly move. I could not lift my head except to vomit and I had eaten nothing for nearly two days.'[31] In these difficult moments, the only person who could comfort him was Xiang Er.

The British authorities had little concern for the CLC's welfare, for 'the food was poor, the hours long, the work extremely hard, and the danger of death from enemy action always present.'[32] As a missionary who had spent seven years among the educated urban classes of Henan, Menzies maintained a paternal attitude towards his men. 'It takes some looking after to govern 500 men and get them all fed, washed, clothed, worked, rested, tried, punished, amused, paid, doctored and all the other 101 things that it would take too long to mention.'[33] When the English officers had turkey at Christmas, Menzies made sure the men had *jiaozi* (dumplings) as their holiday treat. He participated in the recreational activities organized by the YMCA and set up an amateur Chinese opera troupe that staged operas for the men. He had an innate sense of fairness and often protected the men from unfair treatment or discrimination; he once court-martialled his chief English non-commissioned officer for beating a Chinese labourer.[34]

As a missionary, Menzies was concerned with his men's spiritual life. Although a few missionaries with the CLC met opposition when conducting religious services, such as George Ross who wrote bitter letters to the FMB,[35] this was not the case for Menzies. Like the other Henan missionaries, he saw his role in France as a continuation of his mission in China. He wrote R.P. MacKay: 'I have had service with my men every

Sunday and one of my interpreters is an ardent evangelist. He has men about him always. Of course we do nothing about baptizing or anything like that for there is the danger of men thinking that it pays to be a Christian.'[36]

In the same letter, Menzies stressed the importance of the CLC and the necessity of having missionaries take care of the Chinese labourers:

> They are the best labourers in France by far. We are constantly releasing men for the front. The [local] women are doing light work and the Chinese the heavy, so that none but old men are left on labour work ... The Chinese much less than we understand the war. The bloodshed is horrible to them. The wholesale waste is insane to them. All their thoughts of us are turned upside down by this war. We are needed to counteract all this ... I heard a missionary not of our mission say, 'I would try to get out of here at once, were it not for the fact that the Chinese would be misunderstood without us.' For the sake of the Chinese, we are needed in France. I am afraid that through misunderstandings, our work in China would be handicapped if it were not for the missionaries here.[37]

In February 1918 Menzies was transferred to the Corps Headquarters at Dieppe as a technical officer. This was an important change, as it freed him from the confinement of his company and allowed him to roam the British front in France and Belgium. He no longer had to travel on foot, since he had a motorcar and chauffeur, and officer's rest houses in which to spend the night. As a technical officer, his duty was to settle troubles in the CLC camps, but the scope of his work was much broader than the official definition. In a letter to his parents, he described the kinds of work he was assigned:

> I have to quell riots at times. I have to show coolies the reason why they should have their hair cut. I have to advise engineers on how to employ Chinese to advantage. I have to investigate cases of all kinds from stealing to murder. I have to translate petitions and to interview interpreters. I have to examine officers on their knowledge of Chinese and to lecture to officers on Chinese characteristics and how to handle Chinese. I have to teach Chinese, and make out and translate proclamations and orders. All these and hundreds of other things fall to my lot from day to day. From time to time we go out to distant places and are attached to officers commanding important posts such as Base Commandants or Labour Commandants of Army Corps.[38]

Yet, amidst the carnage Menzies remained a man of optimism. On May Day 1918 he wrote to Annie: 'I am sitting at a table under an apple tree in an orchard on the top of a hill. The weather has been very fine. The sun is just beginning to get down behind the church spire and the birds are warbling their vesper hymns. Over the hedge a calf strains at its tether to get some tender blades of grass while the smell of burning wood comes from the kitchen ... And yet there are those other sounds. The sound of swarming bees, that is as near as one can come to the sound of aeroplanes.'[39] And to his parents: 'Poppies grow in Flanders fields in wild profusion. As the timothy gets high, the sun shining through the upright green stalks on the red poppy stars, looks some-times like a glorified Stars and Stripes ... All are so wonderfully beautiful that you stop to wonder if there is a war on.'[40]

As the trench war dragged on, Menzies's optimism evaporated. His sense of duty in his early letters was replaced by images of death and waste. 'What do I think of the war? I think that if we as a nation put the energy into peaceful pursuits, we would accomplish many wonderful things. We would free the world of disease of starvation and all plagues. If men were as heroic as in peace time, we would have a world full of heroes.'[41] At Christmas 1918, he wrote his mother: '[M]any and many a time I snuggle down in my rough blankets with your quail feather pillow under my head and weep tears of lonesomeness.'[42]

Armistice

The Great War came to an end on 11 November 1918. Menzies cel-ebrated the armistice coping with a group of Chinese labourers who were on strike and refusing to work. 'This is the first day of peace. It has been a wonderful day. No bloodshed. No death. It is the beginning of the great new era ... When evening came, I spent from 6 p.m. till midnight standing over a gang of Chinese who would not work. They were unloading hay and should have finished at 8:30. They did not finish till 11:30. I had no supper for I would not leave them. It was raining, a fine rain. This was the way I celebrated peace, standing over Chinks who were just moving sufficiently to make it impossible to say that they were not moving.'[43]

For Menzies and the CLC the war would not be over for another year or more. The Chinese non-combatants were considered cheap labour and were assigned the task of 'mopping up' the mess of four years of conflict. In other words, the British government broke its contract with both the mission societies and the Chinese workers. According to the original understanding, they had come to France to release British subjects for active service, and with the coming of the armistice, they should have been repatriated immediately. Unfortunately, the British Army was vague about the conditions for their release. As a result of their forced detainment in France, some Chinese protested with riots and strikes that meant more trouble. Several Chinese workers were court-martialled.

Menzies and his missionary colleagues tried to put pressure on the British authorities for their own repatriation. In May 1919 the North Henan mission sent a formal request to the British Minister in Beijing: 'Our men went to France in response to a very definite call, to set free for the trenches British subjects whose places the Chinese labourers would take. In view of this circumstance we gladly agreed to "carry on" as best as we could in their absence. Now that the war is over, we shall be deeply obliged to Your Excellency if you see your way to use your utmost endeavour to prevent the following members from being detained in after-war service.'[44]

R.P. MacKay brought the issue before the Canadian government through the Office of Chaplain Services and the Department of External Affairs, both of which refused to intervene. The Foreign Mission Board was told: 'The missionaries in question are officers of the Imperial Army and are, consequently, not within the jurisdiction of the Canadian authorities. Further, white officers, qualified and capable of commanding yellow men are very scarce and the services of the gentlemen in question are still urgently needed with the Chinese troops. You will appreciate the fact that it is not every officer who is suited for the command of yellow troops and these particular officers, on account of their special qualifications could not be easily replaced ... I do not feel justified in embarrassing the War Office by asking for the immediate release of the officers named.'[45] The phrase 'white officers commanding yellow men' was a common trope in the official correspondence.

The Canadians were partially responsible for their own problems; they were too important to be released. Of the sixteen North Henan men who served in the CLC, fifteen had been promoted to captain and four to company commanders, a record unmatched by their British counterparts.[46] When Menzies was transferred to the Provost Branch as staff captain in May 1919, he received a letter stating he was 'indispensable to the Chinese Labour Corps.'[47] Major Martin wrote: 'This officer has been attached to me as DAPM Chinese since 28th May 1919 and has during this period done exceedingly good work, and by his untiring energy has succeeded in bringing about a most satisfactory state of discipline in the Companies working in 3rd Area. Captain Menzies is exceedingly thorough in all his work, tactful and full of sound common sense and I am greatly indebted to him for his work while attached to this area. He is always most successful in his dealings with the Chinese who appear to be ready to listen to his advice as he thoroughly understands their character.'[48]

After the armistice, the British officers were allowed to visit their families in England, while Menzies and the other Canadians could only wander about France or Britain on short leaves. Menzies complained, 'I have been endeavouring to get released from the army but so far there is no success. I came only to assist in the war and to make it possible for the release of men for the trenches by having Chinese do their work. Now that the war is over and others are being released, one naturally expects to get home. The men who came from England have two weeks every four months with their families, while those of us who come from overseas are never allowed to get leave to Canada. They say we may be here another year but we will hope for something better than that.'[49]

As the situation in Europe improved and contingents of Chinese labourers were repatriated, the Canadian officers were allowed to bring their wives to France for a visit. In September 1919 Annie Menzies went to France, leaving the three children at Staples with the Menzies parents and Shen Dasao. She remained for several months in England, staying with her Sedgwick aunts, and she and James had a 'second honeymoon' touring England, Scotland, and Belgium during his leaves. Meanwhile, Christmas at Staples was 'bleak,' according to Marion. 'Grandfather cut a leafless little bush and decorated it as best he could for our Christmas tree. I remember thinking it a very poor show, but then he was 83 and hadn't had children around for many years.'[50]

James Menzies was honourably discharged in February 1920. Only then was his war finally over. The three years with the CLC constituted Menzies's only spell of military life. He welcomed it with enthusiasm and a strong sense of patriotism, but ended with a critical view about war. Did he think his war experience was helpful for his evangelical mission back in Henan? He did not elaborate, but his letters did opine that the care missionaries took of the Chinese labourers would enhance the reputation they already enjoyed among the Chinese. In addition, the work with the Chinese labourers in France provided Menzies with his first opportunity for extensive contacts with the rural classes. They were quite different from the students and gentry whom Menzies had known during his first term in Henan. These new experiences became valuable assets for Menzies when he tried, during his second term in North Henan, to win souls for God among the peasants.

Chapter 7

Rest and Return, 1921–1927

Home Is the Soldier

In February 1920, a few days before his thirty-fifth birthday, Captain James Mellon Menzies was given an honourable discharge. His war was over. It was three years since he had left North Henan and fifteen months since the armistice. His nerves were shot; he suffered from migraine headaches and needed a rest. After his batman and companion Xiang Er left France with the last Chinese Labour Corps (CLC) contingent, Menzies packed his kit bag and returned to Toronto. Recognizing that he had served a full seven-year term in Henan before joining the CLC, the Board of Foreign Missions granted him and Annie an extended furlough that lasted until August 1921.

While James was in France, Annie and the children had moved to Toronto after his eighty-three-year-old father David had rented out the farm at Staples and retired to Edmonton, where his eldest son Robert and daughter Margaret Judge were both pursuing successful careers. David had become moderately wealthy in land in Ontario and Alberta and often supplied his wandering son with a few luxuries such as a cottage at the seaside resort of Beidaihe. None of the family's moves would have been possible, though, without the constant attentions of Shen Dasao, who had learned to speak English and become a part of the family. She remained with the children for the three months that Annie was in Europe in 1919.

'We were a happy family,' Marion, the eldest at six-and-a-half, recalled in her memoirs, giving a glimpse of the family during this period. Father brought home a French porcelain doll dressed in the height of Parisian fashion, but some eighty years later she remembered being upset that he did not bring any chewing gum, a habit she had acquired in Canada. Frances was five and Arthur, who had been a baby in 1917, was a robust three-and-a-half-year-old. In a household of females, he had become a character with his pageboy haircut, constantly rebelling against Mother's strictures to act like a little gentleman. Father gave him a cast-iron steam engine complete with a cow-catcher in front, which he would energetically push around the rented house in Toronto.

'Daddy was more remote,' Marion continued,

> because of his three years in the army and later because of his work as a missionary and his absorbing interest in Sinology. But when we gathered together at meals, outings, special occasions or holidays, we knew he loved us and was interested in us ... Our father shared his interest in history and interesting places with us. He made them fascinating by his ability to talk to us so a child would understand. He was strict – often angry, for he had migraine headaches, but I remember only once that he hit me ... [with] a flyswatter to our legs. When we were young our father did not write to us on a regular basis, leaving this to mother, but when he did write they were letters to remember.

Mother was the opposite, a loving, affectionate, beautiful woman who never ceased reminding the children that she was 'an English lady' descended from the landed gentry. 'We had lots of hugs and kisses. We were surrounded by her love. She also disciplined strictly, expecting immediate compliance with her wishes. She never hesitated to take the back of the hairbrush to our bottoms when we were very naughty ... Those were the days when corporal punishment was thought to be one of the best ways to punish a child. Our mother had a good sense of fun and planned happy times for us. She loved to sing and taught us all to sing too.' Annie was an excellent seamstress and just before they left Toronto she copied a dress she saw in Eaton's window for Marion, with a Menzies red and green tartan skirt and a green velvet tunic. 'I thought it looked like a medieval pageboy's tunic'; it remained her best dress for several years. Annie loved singing, and when they stopped at Tianjin, thanks to Father David's generosity they were able to purchase a piano, which they had shipped by railroad from Tianjin to Zhangde.[1]

After a reunion of the Menzies clan in Alberta, James and Annie, the three children and Shen Dasao sailed in August 1921 from Vancouver on the *S.S. Monteagle*, along with their friends Rev. Andrew Thomson and his family. Little did they realize that, except for Christmas and summer holidays, this was to be the last occasion when they would live as an intact family for the next seven years. Since September was the beginning of the school year, Marion was immediately escorted to Weihui, the central station some seventy miles south on the railway line, where the mission had established a small school for the children of missionaries. The following year, Frances, who had been in frail health, and Arthur, not quite six, joined her there.

After the Great Famine

The whole world had changed since 1917. James Menzies and his family arrived back in North Henan to find a demoralized, confused mission and a destitute countryside crawling with bandits and agitators. The 1920s were a pivotal period in China, when Christian missions were caught between the forces of virulent nationalism and civil wars among contending warlord armies. These were the forces that would shape Menzies's work, life, and thought until 1927, when the mission was forced to 'evacuate' – the common euphemism – ahead of the Northern Expedition.

The North Henan Mission never fully recovered from the crisis caused by the First World War, when the younger, idealistic generation of men had joined the Chinese Labour Corps and their families had returned to Canada. Educational and medical work was entirely suspended, the hospitals and schools were closed, and the Forward Campaigns were cancelled. Rev. T.A. Arthurs was the only one who died in action, but several of the CLC men never returned to China.[2] After the war, contributions in Canada for foreign missions declined and the Board of Foreign Missions (BFM) was forced to cut its grants to its far-flung missions. As a result, it became increasingly difficult for the North Henan Mission to take up new responsibilities outside its narrowly defined evangelism.

One cause for the declining income was the lack of interest in foreign missions in Canada prompted by the growing critique of cultural imperialism. Another was the negotiations that would create the United Church of Canada (UCC) in 1925. Many loyal Presbyterians were reluctant to contribute to a mission that would be given to the United Church after church union. The Methodist and Congregationalist churches entered Union as a corporate body, but the Presbyterian church, because of its government of presbyteries and elders, allowed each member and each congregation to vote whether to join the United Church or not. As a result, the Presbyterian Church in Canada was split; two-thirds joined the United Church, while one-third remained as the continuing Presbyterian Church in Canada. The North Henan missionaries voted to join the UCC with two exceptions: Jonathan and Rosalind Goforth, who were now working independently and no longer considered as members of the mission. The North Henan Mission passed to the United Church along with the Presbyterian missions in South China, Shanghai, Korea, India, Trinidad, and the Canadian West. The Methodist missions in Japan and West China and the Congregationalist mission in Angola also were incorporated into the United Church, making it the foremost supporter of foreign missions in Canada. The only significant Presbyterian foreign missions remaining were in Taiwan, with small missions in India and British Guiana (now Guyana) and new ventures launched by Goforth in Manchuria and among Koreans in Japan. Since the Methodist missions in Japan and West China and the Congregationalist mission in Angola also were incorporated into the United Church, it became the paramount supporter of foreign missions in Canada.

By September 1921, when the Menzies returned to North Henan, the district was just recovering from the grip of one of the worst famines in modern Chinese history. Far back in ancient history, the Chinese had built sophisticated dykes and irrigation canals, but by modern times the Yellow River was no longer tamed as nature's blessing: now it was 'China's sorrow,' alternately flooding and drying up. The monsoon rains had failed in the summer of 1919 and the situation deteriorated when icy winter winds blew in from the Gobi Desert. By the next summer, the new crops simply blew away with the loose sandy soil and the people were reduced to eating bark, roots, and grass mixed with ground-up stones. The 1920–1 famine was exacerbated by overpopulation as well as the civil war then ravaging the countryside. Altogether some twenty million people died across the North China plain.

Protestant missionaries had been involved in famine relief ever since Timothy Richard in 1877,[3] and the North Henan Mission itself was initially inspired by Jonathan Goforth's reading of accounts of famine conditions in 1888. By 1920, the missionaries were respectable members of the society and the Henan provincial government called upon them to undertake relief work. In Canada, the churches organized a large fundraising campaign with heart-rending eyewitness accounts in the newspapers. The missions called upon the Canadian government to play a leading role in the fundraising campaign, as the United States government was doing. Altogether in North Henan, the Presbyterian mission and affiliated churches distributed 11,000 tons of grain, both food and seeds, and $800,000 (Mexican silver) to help 1,212,316 destitute people.[4] They even carried out epidemic prevention, offering one 'cash' (copper coin) for every dead louse brought to the depot. The Anglican mission in Kaifeng also distributed tons of grain.

This relief differed in several respects from that provided during nineteenth-century famines. With a Chinese president and Canadian vice-president, the mission relief committees worked with the government in catering to the needs of all local Chinese, not working as an alternate system that benefited Christians only. The NHM adopted a new policy of providing make-work projects for the victims rather than merely distributing relief. These projects would construct amenities of permanent value rather than temporary relief. As a result, thousands of male and female workers built several miles of gravel roads. For example, the road from Wu'an to the railroad station at Handan, Hebei, was known years later as the 'Christian Road.'[5]

In 1921 the China International Famine Relief Commission (CIFRC) was established as a permanent organization for famine prevention. Through the 1930s, it remained one of the main organizations for rural reconstruction, carrying out comprehensive conservancy projects on a national basis and supporting scientific agriculture and education.[6] As one of the few missionary engineers in China, Menzies was called upon to take part in this noble cause.

His engineering work with the CIFRC started in the spring of 1923 when he was sent to Shanxi to supervise the digging of an irrigation canal. The problem in the mountainous region was lack of water. The canal was to divert water from the Yellow River to the terraced farmland. For this labour project the workers were paid in grain. Menzies remained in Shanxi for two months. Nothing is known about the project, but the local officials showed their gratitude with a banquet. When the customary huge fish on a platter appeared, the host barely touched the delicacy with his chopsticks, and ate none. Not having eaten fish for a long time, Menzies helped himself, only to discover it was a wooden fish covered with decorations. It was another lesson in Chinese customs; Menzies lost face, as he failed to recognize the convention of dressing up a replica to disguise their poverty.[7]

Two years later, in the spring of 1925, Menzies was called upon again to supervise the building of dykes along the Yangtze River, one at Hankou and one on the Han River. The CIFRC chief engineer, O.J. Todd, recommended Menzies:

As an assistant engineer, Mr. Menzies will act as my representative in Hupeh for the present, to make such alterations in plans and specifications, and wages of men in wet places as the conditions of the work seem to require. This is done to facilitate the work and prevent delays. Mr. Menzies will use his judgement in these matters and in case he finds local officials at Shih Show [pinyin Sishou] or Tsu Kow [pinyin Zuzhou] acting in bad faith, will have authority to recommend to you such action as seems to him justified by the circumstances. That may be going so far as to suspend the work.[8]

Shishou was a remote place, 300 miles upriver from Wuhan, where the dyke was 25 feet high and 2 miles long, protecting an area of 300,000 acres of flat and fertile rice paddies that had flooded for six continuous years. Over 2000 peasants with picks and shovels and wicker baskets did the work. Menzies wrote: 'We live in a mat shed put up on the dyke ... It rains here about every third day and is cold. Colder it seems to me than it is in Honan, although that is much farther north. The country is very flat and wet. The bottom of our dyke is only five and a half feet above the level of the Yangtze ... This place is dead, although it is a county town and has a local magistrate. It takes nearly 8 days to get a letter from Hankow.'[9]

Menzies also used his map-making skills to draw up an evangelistic map of North Henan, with detailed information about each village, the population, churches, and number of converts. This was one of the first modern maps of North Henan. Railway companies had conducted geological surveys, but these only covered the narrow strips alongside the railway lines. Yuan Shikai's army had also made a military map. Using the information from these surveys and local gazetteers, Menzies made his own surveys when his work allowed him to visit cities and towns outside his immediate neighbourhood. Since there were over ten thousand named villages in North Henan, it was a huge job to put all of them on one map. Although the complete map was never printed, smaller maps of Wu'an, Shexian, Zhangde, and Linxian districts were printed. Years later, Menzies managed to complete a draft of his map, which he mounted on six scrolls like Chinese paintings. He hung these on the walls of his study in Toronto as a reminder of the villages he had visited and the churches he had helped found.[10]

Engineering was a far cry from street-chapel evangelism, but it was part of a larger mission to solve China's rural poverty often called rural reconstruction. In age and temperament, Menzies was between the older conservative Henan missionaries who had gone out in the 1880s, such as Murdoch Mackenzie and the mission clerk Harvey Grant, and the younger enthusiasts recruited after the First World War, such as Dr Robert McClure. 'Doctor Bob,' whose father Dr William McClure had been among the original Henan Seven of 1888, was a flamboyant surgeon sent to replace Dr James R. Menzies, James M. Menzies's colleague in the early years at Huaiqing, who had been murdered by bandits. Although Bob McClure was born in the United States during the Boxer evacuation, he grew up in the Henan mission, where he learned to speak the peasant dialect fluently. He was one of several second-generation missionaries who became key members of the mission. He launched several innovative social programs, such as a rural medical system.[11]

James M. Menzies's interest in rural reconstruction was an indication of his progressive approach toward evangelism. He felt that secular work was essential to promote the missionary enterprise in China, whether it be canal building, mission schools, or archaeology. Something of his idealism shines through in a light-hearted story he wrote for his children and published in the *Honan Messenger*, the mission's monthly newsletter. An update of the story of the widow's mite in the New Testament, it centred on a beautiful statue of the Buddha, something that most missionaries still regarded as a symbol of 'idolatry' rather than a work of art. The temple priests scoured the countryside collecting bronze for a statue, and the faithful contributed coins, implements, jewellery, vases, and mirrors. But the priests rejected a single copper cash offered by a poor little slave-girl, her only possession: 'Do you think the great Buddha wants to have anything to do with a slave-girl like you, or would accept anything so mean as a single cash picked up from the dirt?' When they cast the bronze statue, it turned out to be streaked and ugly; they melted it down, only to produce one uglier than before. They realized their ingratitude, and accepted the girl's coin. When they added it to the molten bronze, lo and behold, they cast 'the most beautiful and perfect image of Buddha that the monks had ever seen, and there, all glistening and unmelted was the little slave-girl's cash just over the Buddha's heart.'[12]

A Year in the Life of a Rural Evangelist

Between 1921 and 1932, James Menzies's main activity was rural evangelism, itinerating from village to village, visiting the congregations, and preaching the gospel in the countryside. As he wrote in 1949, 'Most of our missionaries had been in the war and the older men had remained on the mission field while we were away. They took furlough as soon as we got back and for a long time I was alone in Changte [Zhangde], a field of 3 million people, to supervise 40 congregations and 100 schools ... The strain of trying to establish a Chinese church through cooperating with untrained Chinese leaders was very heavy ... I had no regular hours; missionaries as a rule do not and [I] got my only relaxation in my Chinese studies.'[13] By this time, the patterns of evangelical work in North Henan were well established. They help us to understand how Menzies and his colleagues spent their time and delivered the gospel to North Henan peasants.

North Henan was essentially a rural mission, and as such its evangelistic activities were largely determined by the peasants' yearly work cycle. The mission year started in late August or September, when the peasants had a short break between planting and harvesting after the hot season had passed. In accordance with Presbyterian tradition, at this time the Presbytery of the NHM would meet to decide the budget, the stationing and work of each individual, and the forward movements for the next year. Until 1927, Presbytery was composed of Canadian male missionaries, both ordained ministers and professionals, with a few women as non-voting observers (even concerning their own work). Meanwhile the Chinese Synod, composed of pastors and elders, would meet separately. As the Chinese church became increasingly assertive, it participated in the mission's decisions, particularly concerning schools and evangelistic campaigns. While Presbytery was meeting, the station schools were being inspected and cleaned for the school year.

As autumn advanced, after the harvest the missionaries and local evangelists would tour the country congregations to baptize converts and record catechumens, to revive the spirits, and to prepare for mass evangelistic campaigns. The most important event was the autumn rally held at each of the three main stations. Zhangde had sixty rural congregations and, Menzies reported in 1922, '1500 Christians from all over the field met together for 8 days. Conferences were addressed by speakers from different missions as well as our own. The meetings, 4 times a day, arranged from 500 to 1000 in a big mat shed put up by the Chinese who met all the expenses, except the travel of the speakers.'[14] The Chinese were sociable, delighted to gather in large companies to listen to Bible stories, watch entertainments, and eat communal meals. The rallies brought Christians from many congregations, including some from the deep countryside who had only this one opportunity each year to see the city and its lively life.

As October blended into November, the winter wheat was planted, and thereafter the peasants had a few months with no farm work to do. For the missionaries, this was their busiest time. Accompanied by Chinese colporteurs and evangelists, Menzies and Murdoch Mackenzie would make month-long tours of the countryside and organize evangelistic campaigns. They travelled in springless mule carts that 'banged, rattled and bumped over the road so as to nearly knock the riders to pieces.'[15] Whenever possible, Menzies rode his old horse or a bicycle; otherwise, he walked. He described one tour in 1926 to his father: 'I have just returned from a long trip to the North East of Changte ... I came home here on the 16th and was to have gone out today, but was not feeling well. So, I am delaying till tomorrow. My boy and things went today. Dr. Mackenzie is to be with me for a week and we expect to have ordination of elders and deacons in two places. He went today. I will go on my bicycle.'[16]

Beside itinerating tours, the missionaries also organized winter campaigns carried out by the evangelistic bands. Consisting of Chinese evangelists, local Christians, and one or two missionaries, these bands were like traditional theatrical troupes that travelled from place to place. Riding in carts and rickshaws, the band visited each district, setting up a table at marketplaces and religious fairs. They were well equipped, for the carts were loaded with bedding, food, literature, tents, and musical instruments. When they arrived at their destination, they would set up their tent and play music: not the deafening, discordant Chinese drums and gongs that could be heard far away, but an exotic foreign tune played on a harmonium. Sometimes, they brought a special attraction, the magic lantern, which they would set up after dark to show pictures of the Life of Jesus or scenes of Canada, which were equally exotic to the isolated Henanese. They would stay in a place for a week or ten days, during which they conducted door-to-door distribution of tracts and held singing meetings for men and women three or four times a day.[17]

As one of the few evangelistic missionaries at Zhangde, Menzies was a member of the evangelistic band and chair for a few years.[18] He celebrated his mother's birthday in 1922 with the band at the city of Tang Yin. 'Your birthday has come round again and finds me this time in bed in the countryside with a very bad sick headache,' he wrote.

> We are having a series of evangelistic meetings in a large tent ... Our band is a large one this time, five Chinese from other stations, two from Changte and some local Christians. Mr. [Andrew] Thomson is here from Taokou and

Miss [Minnie] Shipley and Annie are looking after the women ... We will finish here on Tuesday night when I am due to leave immediately for similar meetings at Hwaiking. Naturally being away so much, there is a lot of work left undone at Changte station. So that when I return, I am overwhelmed with work ... [T]he good Doctor [Murdoch Mackenzie] is no business man and that will still largely devolve on me.[19]

A Henan winter, although there is seldom snow, can be harsh, with cold dry winds blowing up dust storms. 'It has been very very cold this last two or three days. There has been a very high wind blowing the dust on the road to the tent just outside the north gate. The dust on the road is up to your boot tops and in potholes a great deal deeper.' Menzies had poor circulation, which affected his feet and legs, and so he asked his brother to send him 'a pair of heavy Mackinaw socks; long ones up to the knees and a pair of strong oil tanned soled moccasins ... I want them for walking. Perhaps they should be hob nailed.'[20]

Travel in summer could be equally difficult, and even dangerous. Back in 1913, when Menzies was a young missionary, he had his first experience of rural travel. When heavy rains destroyed the railway bridges and turned the roads into rivers, he almost drowned while crossing a swollen river.[21] By the 1920s a few missions purchased motor vehicles, but the conservative and frugal NHM was never enthralled with this idea. When a family friend sent a cheque to buy a Ford car, Menzies explained that 'purchasing a car, training a chauffeur and experimenting on our roads, from almost every point of view seemed inadvisable.'

Menzies's real dilemma was his conscience. At the time, the mission was cutting expenses to deal with the reduced grants from Canada, while trying to continue its famine relief work. He wrote A.E. Armstrong: 'I was somewhat embarrassed by this cheque. As you know we have cut our expenses, so much so that it has hurt everyone. At such a time to spend money for a car or to run one would be flaunting extravagance in the face of those to whom you were not giving even the reasonable support in the master's work. Do you see the moral problem?'[22] The only motorcar the mission ever owned was a van that Dr Bob McClure bought from the Americans in Zhengzhou and used as an ambulance for Huaiqing Hospital.[23]

The build-up to Christmas, when the mish-kids returned from school, was a time of socializing for the whole mission, climaxing with a party where each child, Canadian and Chinese alike, received a present from a dressed-up Santa Claus. The church was decorated with festive evergreens and red banners, while every missionary home had a Christmas tree – imported, since Henan did not have many pine trees – with decorations brought from Canada, and carefully wrapped for next year. Being Scottish, the Presbyterian mission also celebrated New Year's Day (Hogmanay) with a 'watch-night service' on New Year's Eve, a solemn evening of prayer and re-dedication.

The Chinese New Year, one or two months later (in February or March depending on the lunar calendar), was the major holiday for the Chinese people. Many non-Christians used this holiday time to attend one of the sacred mountains or temple fairs. The missionary pioneers had found that these fairs were most productive venues, since many pilgrims were already on a spiritual quest to seek something better. Menzies and the evangelistic band followed the pilgrims to the Xun Xian (old spelling Hsün-hsien) fair at Fuqiu (old spelling Fu-chü) Mountain, the largest in North Henan, which lasted from the Lantern Festival to the first of the second month (March or April). Marching in groups carrying banners, an estimated 30,000 pilgrims from as far as Shandong, Hebei, and Shanxi crowded into the little city and mountain inns. The Xun Xian fair maintained a strong religious tradition among the local people, an eclectic mix of Daoist and Buddhist elements, even attracting some Christian converts. The Canadians were interested in these fairs as a way to infiltrate the existing local religious sects and proselytize their followers who, once converted to Christianity, became zealous helpers and evangelists.[24]

Spring comes early in North Henan; it is warm by April and hot in May. The monotonous yellow is replaced by a sea of pale green. With the change in the weather, the peasants return to their lands. For the mission, this meant winding down the rural evangelical campaigns and returning to the drudgery of station work. In June, as the weather became subtropical, the mission sent the students and teachers home and closed the schools. Except for a skeleton staff crew who stayed to carry on the summer theological training class, everyone would decamp for one of the summer resorts.

Like the other missionary families, James and Annie Menzies would start planning for the summer at Christmas time. The North Henan folks had their choice of several resorts. Jigongshan (old spelling Chikungshan) in the mountains of southern Henan, where Jonathan Goforth had his base of operations, had a reputation for its conservative (or 'fundamentalist') Bible studies and Pentecostal revivals among the missionaries. Further afield was Guling in Jiangxi province, where James had wooed Annie that summer long ago. Northeast of the mission on the salubrious northern coast of Hebei was Beidaihe (old spelling Pei-tai-ho), overlooking the sparkling salt-water beach on the Bohai gulf. The wealthier Henan missionaries owned cottages there, while the single women would pool their resources and rent one for the summer.

In 1912, one year after arriving in China, James Menzies bought a cottage at Beidaihe from a retired British missionary for $2600, a 'princely sum' for a young missionary whose annual salary was only $1200. Marion was born there a year later. Built by S. Lavington Hart, principal of the Tientsin Anglo-Chinese College, the house occupied one of the best lots at Rocky Point overlooking the American Beach. For two years Menzies used his carpentry and masonry skills to renovate the house, adding 'a large living-dining room surmounted by a wonderful tower bedroom and porch ... As the natural stone foundation of the porch was round, ten feet high in spots, to make a base level with the existing cottage, it looked like a tower with a screened top. We were convinced it was our personal castle.' Thus, the simple beach house was transformed into a 'modest establishment' named 'Hai Feng Lou,' or 'Sea Breeze Cottage,' which became one of the most visibile landmarks to ships at sea.[25]

'The sea is silver and the sun is shining brightly,' Menzies wrote in 1928. 'I look right from where I sit at a table in my room upstairs in the tower out to the sea. The water seems to be right below my veranda ceiling ... The bathing beach is right in front of our house and every morning and noon a boat or sampan is anchored out half way to the diving raft. It forms a rest on the way out for good swimmers.'[26]

Beidaihe offered foreigners a chance to 'escape from China in China.' The community included diplomats and language students from Beijing, merchants from Shanghai, and missionaries from all over north China. A gunboat anchored off shore provided protection in times of civil war or banditry. According to the treaty system, the residents organized themselves into an autonomous self-governing municipality, the Rocky Point Association, which was elected annually to represent the foreign community and to coordinate the hectic social schedule.[27]

'My happiest memories of my childhood in North China were of Bei Dai He Beach,' wrote Marion in her memoirs. Arthur recalled the day the family would pack their suitcases and take the train across the North China countryside:

I remember how our excitement would mount as we changed from the mainline to the spur line at P.T.H. [Pei-tai-ho] Junction, and began to recognize familiar landforms. Then there was the *Re Nao* [chaos] as every-one piled off the train at the station and began to bargain with donkey-men, rickshaw-men or cart-men about moving themselves and their luggage to East Cliff, Temple Bay or even our own Rocky Point. Through the village there were the familiar shops, and past the Assembly Hall we looked to see what friends had arrived. And finally we arrived at our house with its wide inviting veranda with a commanding view of the American Beach, the Danger Rocks, the Tiger Rocks and Baby Beach. And if we rushed upstairs to look out from the upper veranda, there was Lighthouse Point to the left and the Lotus Hills to the right. What a restful sound to hear the waves curling onto the beach and to smell the salt in the ocean air![28]

Each morning before breakfast the family went for a swim, except Shen Dasao, the beloved amah, who remained at the water's edge. Marion recalled that Mrs Shen kept a watchful eye for danger. 'She delighted in demonstrating her control over us to the other amahs. She would call us to come and we dropped our pails and shovels and came to her. The other amahs were amazed ... and Shen Dasao gained much face with her control over us with her colleagues.'[29] In addition to playing on the beach, the children took French and dancing lessons from a White Russian countess, but these were not as exciting as the camping trip to the mountains or the excursion to Shanhaiguan, the rocky promontory where the Great Wall meets the ocean. There were other activities, such as donkey polo on the beach or watching local craftsmen creating figures from Beijing opera out of rice dough or cricket cages out of sorghum sticks.[30]

For over twenty years, James and Annie Menzies repeated this annual cycle. After a year of intensive work among the Chinese, Beidaihe was their reward. Ruth Jenkins, a member of the Anglican mission in Kaifeng, recalled that the summer vacations were 'almost like going away from China for a breathing space and getting in touch with the life of the home-lands. It is almost entirely foreign – and the life is so entirely foreign, with picnics, sports, lectures, concerts etc. For missionaries who live in the interior, where all year they only see a small group of foreign-ers, it is very refreshing and helpful.'[31]

Chapter 8

Converts, Education, and Nationalism

Rice Christians and Pragmatic Peasants

When James Menzies returned to North Henan, he asked to be designated for educational work, as that was what he had been engaged in since his time at the School of Practical Science. He had spent his first term among the scholar gentry, but the three years in France had given him the opportunity to work at an intimate level among peasants. Presbytery in its wisdom assigned him to rural evangelism. His circuit was the hundreds of villages surrounding the walled prefectural city of Zhangde.

One of the perplexing questions of China missions has been why would a Chinese peasant convert to Christianity, which seemed antithetical to traditional Chinese values? James Menzies must have asked himself this question many times during the decade he spent touring the countryside.

The peasants in North Henan were mostly illiterate, though they shared the Confucian values of the upper classes, especially the ethical and family values inculcated through state proclamations. Popular culture such as puppet theatres, opera performances, and teashop storytellers offered a livelier world of tricksters, heroes, and gods.[1] In religion the peasants were pragmatic, worshipping whichever god was deemed more effective in bringing good luck, fat baby boys, health, and wealth. Publicly, Confucius and Huang-Ti, or the Yellow Emperor (the legendary emperor who has been regarded as the creator of the Chinese state), were at the top of the state pantheon, helped by a multitude of Daoist gods and immortals. Religious sects such as the White Lotus and Red Spears were common in the district, promising long life through vegetarian diets and *taichi* breathing exercises.[2] In this syncretic religious background, Christianity was seen as 'heterodox,' a set of 'evil teachings' that offended the traditional gods and sages. The anti-Christian tracts and posters produced by the local scholar-gentry reinforced that reaction to instil in the peasants a profound fear and hatred of Christianity.[3]

By 1921, when Menzies started his rural evangelism at Zhangde, over three thousand peasants and townspeople had converted to the Presbyterian church. Fortunately, we can understand their motivations as a result of a remarkable study of the North Henan Christian community, the only in-depth historical study of a Christian mission in China. This was a co-operative venture involving scholars from Canada and China. Margo Gewurtz of York University combed the archives in Canada, and – thanks to Murdoch Mackenzie's meticulous records of church lists and baptisms, including the wife's maiden name – compiled a list of 1500 converts between 1888 and 1947. In 1992 Song Jiaheng, the founder of the Canadian Studies Institute at Shandong University, took a group of graduate students from the Department of History to conduct oral history interviews at the stations and churches founded by the NHM. They interviewed local Christians, particularly the elders who had personally known the missionaries.[4]

Curiosity seems to have been the starting point for many peasants on their journey to the Christian community. The missionaries attracted large crowds out of sheer novelty, simply because the Chinese love to stop and watch street performers. They would gaze at the foreigners, commenting on their big noses and blue eyes, their strange clothes (Menzies always wore a black Western suit and clerical collar), and the foreign stuff they brought: sewing machines, flashlights, magic lanterns, and bicycles. A few did pay attention to what the foreigners were preaching, whether the sin and hell-fire oratory of the older generation or the emphasis on regeneration and good deeds of the social gospellers. The Jesus doctrine (as Protestant Christianity was called in Chinese) was not very different from their traditional ethical values. People do want to be good, Confucius stated, and Christianity said that if one did good and avoided evil, he or she would go to heaven. With this simple understanding of Christianity, some accepted the Jesus religion.

Perhaps most converts were initially attracted by Western medicine and 'miracle' drugs. China was a land of disease and epidemics, especially during famines, and in North Henan the Canadians were the sole practitioners of modern medicine. From its inception, the NHM had emphasized that medicine was the chisel that would open China. As the primitive clinics and dispensaries grew into modern hospitals, their fame spread. Many peasants had relatives who had been cured (or born) in the mission hospital, and some joined the church out of gratitude to the doctors. They had a sincere belief that God had cured them or they hoped for more medicine in the future. Realistically, for those who could not afford to pay, the services were free and better than those of the Chinese 'quacks' (Dr Bob McClure's word).

Some converts joined the church for employment. The Canadians in North Henan, who numbered about one hundred, employed a host of servants and workers of all sorts, male and female: amahs and biblewomen, gatekeepers, barrow-men, water coolies, household servants, cooks, catechists and preachers, school teachers, doctors and nurses, YMCA secretaries, and social workers. Thus, they offered a comparatively large labour market with better-paid work in the local communities. The largest employer was the Industrial School established for famine relief of widows and orphans at Huaiqing (old spelling Hwai-king). It grew throughout the 1920s and into the 1930s until it employed three hundred workers. They sold their handicrafts through 'Hwaiking shops' in Canada. In addition, each Canadian mission family had four or five servants, which meant at least two hundred servants, gardeners, and colporteurs. The four hospitals hired hundreds more; by 1937, the Huimin hospital at Weihui had a staff of ninety-two of whom eighty-five were Chinese.[5] Because the mission hired only converts, some accepted Christianity as the necessary trade-off. Indeed, many poor people became better off working for the mission and spread the gospel stories to neighbours and friends.

Another pathway to the church was the school system. The Chinese have always cherished education, and in the early twentieth century mission schools provided the only opportunity for poor peasants to give their children a modern education. At first, the mission provided everything including textbooks, meals, and lodging in the boarding schools, even a stipend to defray their parents' loss of the child's wages. This policy was severely restricted later, when financial aid became based on need. Poor Christians were given allowances, while non-Christians had to pay fees. This made it possible for the humblest Christian families to give their children at least a few years of primary education, an attractive luxury in a society esteeming education as a major pathway to social mobility.

Although the Canadians in North Henan were not known for interfering in local legal affairs, some converts were convinced that the church had political power to help them in lawsuits. After 1900 missionaries were viewed by many as a protection for the weak and poor in the local communities. This was summed up by a popular saying reported to the Shandong University historians: 'The religion of Jesus Christ is non-sense, people joined the Church only when they have law suits.'[6] Arthur W. Lochead was one NHM missionary who did occasionally interfere in cases of persecution; he was a good friend of the Jixian magistrate Kui Mao, who never failed to meet Lochead's requests. Even James Menzies once helped a convert get out of jail by speaking to the official in charge.[7]

The mission historian, and contemporary of Menzies, Margaret Brown recalled that though the whitewashed brick houses of the stations seemed modest by Canadian standards, to the Chinese they were citadels of capitalism. With its servants and charities, the mission seemed to have access to vast amounts of money. Even after the famine, poor Christians received help from the church, food and clothing and a sort of family allowance, a five-dollar reward to Christian parents who gave birth to babies.

Finally, Christianity had (and still has) a special appeal for peasant women, the most oppressed people in Chinese society. By organizing literacy classes and co-operatives, Canadian women and their Chinese assistants became pioneers of a female (if not a 'feminist') movement.[8] Since women were the principal recipients of the mission's charity, once their bodies and souls were taken care of, they became important building blocks of the new church. Without women, the church would have remained a religious sect of men (of which there were many in Henan); women brought in families, children, and grandparents. This emphasis on 'Christianizing the family' made the church different from other sects. Thus, it was able to draw from extended family networks, as can be traced in Mackenzie's lists of converts. In fact, women were the most devoted and faithful converts.[9]

From this scholarly analysis, it is clear that most North Henan peasants were attracted by the practical or material benefits available from the 'rich' Canadians. This was understandable, for they had to be practical in every aspect of their daily life in a hostile environment. A peasant would not risk joining the 'foreign' church if he was not convinced that the benefits were greater than the sacrifice.[10] It is naive, however, to conclude that all converts were 'rice Christians.' They may have come for the rice, but despite their initial motivation, they were confirmed in their faith as their spiritual life evolved. To use the metaphor of a traditional arranged Chinese marriage, in which conjugal love came after the wedding, the Chinese grew as Christians as their knowledge of Christianity increased. In other words, they may have converted for pragmatic reasons, but over time faith confirmed their decision.

It took years for the Canadians in North Henan to understand this pragmatic peasant approach to Christianity. Those engaged in rural evangelism had two general methods. The conventional method was concerned only with evangelism, preaching the gospel in public and approaching each individual as a potential convert. The younger missionaries who came after 1918 were proponents of a more flexible evangelism that took care of the converts' practical as well as their spiritual needs. They felt that social services were no longer peripheral or temporary, but were necessary to promote the evangelical cause and help the Chinese. Although Menzies was a senior missionary, in mission policy he essentially belonged to the generation who came to China in the 1920s and 1930s. He saw no conflict between saving souls and using his engineering training to fight famine. In addition, as an advocate for a 'respectable' Christian church composed of educated citizens of the New China, he pushed the NHM to upgrade its educational system.

The School Promoter

Modern education was slow to develop in North Henan. The warlord governments and local Chinese elites wanted a modern school system to replace the old-style Confucian schools, the *sishu*, which were still common in rural primary education as late as the 1930s. The NHM originally responded to the demand for schools reluctantly, as summed up in their slogan, 'first the church, then the school.' The mission school system should be based on the church. Schools were for the children of converts, to create a literate and intelligent Christian community and train church workers. They had no illusions that non-Christian students would bring their parents into the church.

The Chinese church was not satisfied with schools whose purpose was limited to training barely literate converts to read the Bible. They wanted schools whose graduates would become leaders of the church and the community. At Zhangde, leading Christians approached Menzies and the mission to open a high school. In 1923, with much fanfare, the boys' boarding school called the Binying Lower and Higher Primary School was upgraded to Binying Middle School, but without any financial support from the mission. The old building was too small, and Menzies and Murdoch Mackenzie 'put up a temporary structure out of broken bricks and mud, with the old iron off Mr. Griffith's home for a roof.' It was quickly filled with forty students.[11]

The NHM had traditionally supported the boarding schools financially, providing buildings, operating funds, and most of the teachers' salaries. When Presbytery (still only Canadians) refused to support the new high school, many local Christians blamed the missionaries. When a strike broke out among the students, Menzies explained that with the financial problems in Canada, 'there has not been enough money to carry on our work and the Chinese Christians cannot understand why. In all the 34 years in Honan, it has never happened before. We have seemed as financially strong as the Bank of England. Now we are continually saying that we have no money to carry on with. It is very hard. Annie has told you about the school strike. I fear that the teacher was responsible. It has been a very trying experience for it let me in for a lot of nervous excitement just when the doctors ordered me to keep quiet. I have not slept well for a long time.'[12]

Although he was displeased with the way the Chinese had forced the issue, Menzies was sympathetic with their aspirations for modernization. He wrote a detailed twenty-page letter to A.E. Armstrong, the assistant secretary of the Board of Foreign Missions, with a strong appeal for a new high-school building at Zhangde. 'With our 60 primary schools, we are graduating pupils who have nowhere to go. We cannot receive them all in our school here. You know the accommodation.'[13]

The problem was not just bricks and mortar, Menzies continued, but how to make higher education available to Christian children, particularly the poor.

There were 45 [who] entered middle school grade, of whom 5 had to drop out because they could not go on and pay the increased fees and expenses. For these 150 boys [including higher primary], only $125 gold was given as assistance to poor pupils of Christian parents. What I want to point out is that all the second year and a good part if not all the first year would not be able to go on to Weihuei where the standard of living [food expenses] is much higher due to the better off pupils going there ... We aim only at giving the opportunity to Christians and believe that it should be possible for every Christian child, however poor, to have at least a primary school education. At present not one of the children of Christians are at school. Some have been a year or two and then had to drop out as soon as they can gather grass for the fire or manure for the land. Others have never been. Yet I have known many to sell land, which means selling the future, and resort to all imaginable ways to send their children to school.

Mission schools were expensive, he admitted, but the very future of the Christian cause in China was at stake.

In our present financial crisis in the Church, I would slow down on every advance but let us not fail to reap the harvest that our pioneers sowed in tears of sacrifice and prayer. The Chinese are doing their utmost but it cuts to the heart to see the suspicion developing in their minds that we are not playing fair. This is becoming evident in the attitude of our oldest and most tried leaders. It hurts ... The pressure for the boys' [high] school is due solely to the growth of the Chinese Church and to the increased sense of responsibility on the part of the Christians for the education of their children.

Finally, Menzies urged the mission to restructure its education policy. By this time, the NHM supported four professors at Cheeloo University (pinyin Qilu), even though it sent only two or three students there each year because the mission had so few high school graduates. This was the bottleneck that blocked the development of Christian education.

The present situation is this. We have many primary pupils but we choke them off by not giving them any opportunity to go on for higher education. We have very few boys graduating and those only boys of the wealthiest Christians. Besides these, there are a number of well-to-do non-Christians and we send on to university only one or two or at most three a year and yet for these we maintain a staff of 4 professors and a not inconsiderable expenditure for equipment and maintenance ... I could not see how we can possibly do any more for higher education until we have done a great deal more for middle school education which when all is said and done is the back bone of the education work of the country.

The bottom line, Menzies concluded, was money: 'The Mission sees the need of $2,000 for our school here to provide for a higher primary and for lower middle and junior normal school to accommodate 400 pupils.' Then, to add a bit of personal pressure, Menzies reminded Armstrong that when he visited North Henan a few years earlier, he had promised a new school building. The Chinese Christians 'quoted again and again what they considered was your promise when you were here regarding the new Boys School building.' Menzies's appeal was successful, and the new Zhangde High School became one of the best in North Henan.

James Menzies's interest in education was shared by his wife, Annie.

Unlike most married women in the mission fields, who went to China after they were married in Canada, she had gone out as a single woman who expected to serve her term as a missionary – until James's unexpected proposal changed her goal. At least in her first term, marriage meant that she became one of the wives whose role was to take care of their husbands and children. Missionary wives were not numbered among the 'full missionaries,' the men who were supported by the BFM and the single women of the Women's Foreign Missionary Society. Nevertheless, they played a critical, if unsung, role in the missionary enterprise, not just by providing a domestic home and social occasions that freed their husbands for evangelistic work. The role of missionary wives is a topic that demands further study.[14]

Annie found her own niche outside the gate of the mission compound at a nearby village called Zhuzhong (old spelling Chu-chung) or Bell Casters' Village. Relations between the mission and the village had been tense since the headman had forbidden the villagers to have anything to do with the foreigners. Annie Menzies decided to take Frances and Arthur to break the ice when she visited the women in their homes. Arthur recalled many years later, 'The village women, who had bound feet, sat on their *kang* beds trying to sew in the poor light of windows covered with oil paper. Their hands were chapped with the cold. Mother gave them cream for their hands and taught them to knit gloves with half fingers.'[15] In time she started a school, held in the village temple, for thirty boys and girls of Bell Casters' Village. A Montreal congregation became interested in this project and paid the salary of a teacher.

From her little school, Annie expanded her work among the women and elders, and organized 'clubs' for mothers, girls, boys, and old people. She played music and started a public bathhouse where the children could take a free, warm bath. The mothers also could bathe for one penny, perhaps their first bath with soap and warm water. Annie's village school continued until 1927, when it was destroyed during the Northern Expedition.[16]

Mission and Nationalism, 1927–1928

Appreciation of Chinese culture did Menzies little good when violent nationalist movements swept China like a bonfire. For two decades, the Chinese seemed to have been open to the Christian message. Missionaries had helped organize educational, medical, and social services, and the 'Christian warlord' of Henan, Feng Yuxiang, became their friend in the 1920s. After the Great Famine, the Canadians became a type of 'new gentry' in the local society.[17] R.P. MacKay, secretary of the Board of Foreign Missions in Toronto, was convinced that the missionaries' heroic sacrifices would eliminate the Chinese negative impression about the West. Ironically, their elevated status was a product of China's weakness, which could not withstand the nationalist, anti-warlord, anti-foreign, anti-imperialist, and anti-Christian movements that started with the May Fourth Movement of 1919.

Despite President Woodrow Wilson's eloquent rhetoric about self-determination, the Versailles peace treaty that ended the First World War did not return to China the ex-German territory in Shandong seized by Japan in 1915. Instead, it allowed the Japanese 'protectorate' to continue. As a result, the Chinese government refused to sign the treaty on 4 May 1919, a day remembered thereafter as a 'Day of National Humiliation.' Students and intellectuals rose spontaneously throughout the country to inaugurate the May Fourth Movement, which proved to be both a renaissance of Chinese culture as well as an anti-warlord, anti-imperialist political struggle. From the beginning, this New Culture Movement led by leftist intellectuals in the large cities ushered mass nationalism onto China's political stage. Disillusioned with politicians and militarists, these Western-influenced intellectuals took the nation's fate into their own hands and advocated radical changes that would shake the foundations of the nation. Liberals, nationalists, or communists, they re-evaluated China's ancient culture, contrasting it with Western concepts and tried thereby to build a new nation based on 'Mr Science' and 'Mr Democracy.' They rejected familiar Chinese hallmarks such as Confucianism and foot-binding as 'feudal' and 'unscientific' relics.[18]

Though iconoclastic, the New Culture Movement did not reject Christianity at first. Many leaders such as Hu Shi (old spelling Hu Shih) and Chen Duxiu (old spelling Ch'en Tu-hsiü) defended Christian missions in the name of religious freedom and modernization.[19] However, in 1922 a huge YMCA-sponsored World Student Christian Federation conference at Qinghua University in Beijing published a large compendium of maps and statistics called *The Christian Occupation of China.* This title quickly raised the anger of young radicals. Middle school and university students organized protest marches in many cities, including Zhangde, and denounced the YMCA and the Christian church for aiding world capitalists in robbing the poor and oppressed.[20]

Another anti-Christian protest, the Movement to Restore Educational

Rights, occurred in 1924 in response to the publication of the Burton Commission's report, *Christian Education in China.* Consisting of Western educators and theologians, Chinese Christians and missionaries, the commission had started a survey of mission educational work in 1922. Ernest D. Burton, professor of theology at the University of Chicago, was the chairman and Edward Wilson Wallace, a Canadian Methodist who had established a system of mission schools in West China, was the secretary and author of the final report.[21] It proposed that the missions unite to create a Christian system of education in China, parallel to but separate from the state system. It would be more efficient, more Christian, and more Chinese through the integration of mission schools and colleges. For patriotic Chinese, the primary function of education was to create new citizens for the New China. The mission schools, beyond Chinese control, seemed to work against the goal of a unified, national system of education. Thus, the members of the Movement to Restore Educational Rights attacked mission schools for serving the cause of imperialism and creating a nation of 'denationalized' youth. Students from mission schools and colleges played an active role in this movement and forced the closure of a number of schools.[22]

At first, North Henan seemed immune to this student agitation. Indeed, the Canadians seemed more worried about mission finances than student nationalism. By 1925, however, they were forced to react when North Henan was galvanized by the May 30th Incident, another day of humiliation. British police in Shanghai fired on a demonstration on behalf of Chinese workers mistreated in Japanese-owned cotton mills, provoking nationwide protests, strikes, and boycotts by students, workers, and merchants. Hong Kong came to a standstill for two years when all workers returned to their villages. In Shanghai, it was six months before public anger subsided after the municipal council paid an indemnity of 75,000 *yuan* to the families of the killed students.[23]

The May 30th movement sparked demonstrations and strikes throughout Henan. In the north, the British-controlled Peking Mining Syndicate and the Canadian Presbyterian mission were the only foreign intrusions and therefore the prime targets. In July the local Chinese Communist Party organized a general strike at the Jiaozuo mines, bringing the syndicate to a standstill. With the support of the provincial government and military warlords, the strike lasted eight months until March 1926, when the company accepted the workers' demands.[24]

These anti-Christian campaigns caused a decline in religion among educated Chinese, greatly affecting the work of Christian missions. It became increasingly difficult to deliver the gospel to educated Chinese who came to 'worship' only science and nationalism. Battered and disappointed, many 'old China hands' among the missionary force retired from China. Those who stayed believed they could meet the new challenges by adapting their gospel to changing Chinese conditions. James Menzies was one. Sympathetic to Chinese aspirations, yet confined to rural evangelism, he became increasingly restless with the conservative policies of his mission. He was no longer comfortable with the mission's paternalistic attitudes and felt drawn to progressive approaches to missions. He increasingly believed that his own effective role was not among the peasants but in a Christian university, where he could help train future Chinese Christian leaders.

The Evacuation

The dangers of Chinese nationalism burst like a thunderstorm on a sunny summer afternoon, catching the Canadians by surprise.[25] In 1925, in the wake of the nationwide demonstrations after the May 30th incident, radicalized students organized student unions in government and mission schools and coerced every student to join, since no one wanted to be accused of not loving his or her country.[26] At Weihui, the educational centre of the NHM, the high-school students went on strike, refused to take their final exams, and enforced a boycott of carts and rickshaws entering the mission compound. At Zhangde, the agitation was so violent that even the pastors in the summer theological class went on strike.

Facing this nationalist fire, the North Henan mission decided on a passive non-provocative response; they went on summer vacation. By July the situation was so dangerous that the remaining Huaiqing and Weihui missionaries appealed to the local military commander, who told them it would cost 30,000 *yuan* for 'protection.' Realizing the danger of the situation, they handed the mission property over to the magistrate of Weihui, who accepted responsibility and sent escorts to guard the missionaries. As soon as the missionaries left, a 'gang of students' called on the magistrate and asked why he had let the foreigners leave without making it 'uncomfortable' for them. The magistrate said he was 'acting according to international treaties' and 'had the authority of the President and the Provincial Governor.' When he asked the students what authority they had, one drew out a revolver. The magistrate had to escape through the back door while his men persuaded 'the school boys not to get excited,' that 'the whole matter would be explained without any trouble.'[27]

Like most of his colleagues, Menzies was clearly on the British side, which angered both Chinese students and Christians. He explained: 'Everyone dislikes seeing people killed. But one must recognize that thousands of people are killed, murdered, carried off by bandits every month, because the Chinese do not enforce the law. These students were killed while trying to *mob* a police station in order to release persons arrested. Chinese seem to think that because they were students, they should be allowed to do as they please ... This has been used as propaganda against the British and we are being persecuted for the enforcing of the law, the one thing next to Christianity that China most needs.'[28]

From Menzies's commonly held perspective, the main cause for these anti-Christian movements was the communist agitators recruited by the Comintern then working in concert with Sun Yat-sen's Nationalist Movement in planning a mass campaign to unify the country. 'The students are all under the power of the so-called Students Union, which is used by the Russian Bolshevik agitators to stir up all kinds of trouble. They went all over the country trying to force strikes of all in the employ of foreigners, especially the British. They took British goods out of stores and destroyed the cheaper things and appropriated the most valuable.' It was not just the ignorant, Menzies concluded, as now the students were 'telling the people that we are tyrants, trying to steal their country ... So, now we have not only the conservatism and suspicion to deal with, but also this new opposition of the students. The Russians are behind this. Bolshevism is anti-Christian while China is non-Christian. So, our fight is doubly hard.'[29]

This nationalist movement put Chinese Christians in a difficult situation. They might be Christians, but they were first and foremost Chinese citizens. Nationalism was patriotism: if they did not oppose the Canadians, they would be accused of not loving their country. Some NHM missionaries proudly displayed their British identity by flying the Union Jack. This agitated not only the students but Chinese Christians as well.[30] As a result, some congregations broke their ties with the 'imperialist' missionaries and formed independent churches. The independent church at Jixian issued the following proclamation:

The English in accord with unequal treaties have forced their way into interior China to preach, in so doing casting aside the very spirit of the Christian religion. Then recently when the Shanghai murder cases occurred, not only were the English missionaries unable to imitate Christ in opposing violence and supporting the truth, in behalf of the sovereignty of China; but they even supported the Government of their own country by asserting that in the Shanghai massacre the Chinese were to blame. Such behaviour on their part truly cannot but make men suspect that they are the thin edge of the wedge of imperialism. We are the defenders of our country, and opponents of imperialism.[31]

The Canadians were caught off guard by this sudden outburst. As one reflected:

Led by the school boys, China has given herself over to an exhibition of anti-foreign feeling and activity that seems *hard to believe*. It has swept through the whole country like a prairie fire. The spirit of friendliness seems to have given place entirely to suspicion, denunciation, and in many places open hostilities. After what we have been accustomed to for years, the present situation seems unnatural and impossible ... We know that the charge was laid and the fuse set some time ago. Some people have been talking for a year or more about the anti-foreign sentiment spreading throughout China; but there was no evidence of it in our little corner of Henan, so I would not believe it till I was forced to do so.[32]

As the hot summer of 1925 ended, North Henan calmed down. The Canadians extended their vacations until late August, when they returned to the field. They managed to revive the evangelistic and medical work, but they did not reopen the boarding and high schools since the anti-foreign hostility made many missionaries doubt their value. Although the student strikes, demonstrations, and boycotts had ended, the spirit of nationalism – 'China for the Chinese' – continued to grow. By October the Chinese evangelists and workers at Huaiqing staged a strike, demanding improved working conditions and better pay.[33]

In the spring of 1925, Sun Yat-sen, the Christian leader of the Guomindang (GMD, old spelling Kuomintang, KMT) or Nationalist Party, died at Beijing and his reputation and power passed to his heir, Chiang Kai-shek, head of the Whampoa Military Academy. In July 1926, Chiang launched a Northern Expedition, sending the GMD armies from the movement's main base around Canton to conquer the warlords controlling Central and North China. Three months later they reached the Yangzi River. The GMD was united in a Common Front with the Chinese Communist Party (CCP), and sent professional agitators ahead of the army to provoke strikes and anti-foreign agitation. A climax occurred in March 1927, when six missionaries were killed at Nanjing, prompting the British and American governments to send gunboats upriver to shell the city. The consuls ordered all their nationals – some eight thousand missionaries – to evacuate the interior for the coastal cities. Once again, China teetered on the brink of war with the foreign powers.

Even in the quiet backwater of North Henan, the situation turned tense. To prepare for the expeditionary armies, the local CCP organized the peasants, who took control of several counties.[34] The Canadians in Henan did not plan on leaving, just as they refused to evacuate during the 1911 revolution; the people seemed friendly and the Canadians were willing to rely on the goodwill of the local officials.[35] In April the situation deteriorated when the Beijing–Hankou and Longhai railroads became battle zones between contending armies. Reluctantly, the Canadians decided to evacuate.

After they left, there was a bloody engagement between the local Guomindang army led by Marshal Feng Yuxiang, who had been such an 'old friend' of the missionaries, and the Manchurian troops under Zhang Zuolin. This was followed by a rebellion of Red Spears, a secret society across North China. The mission properties were occupied by one army or another, and some were destroyed or looted. For nineteen months, until the end of 1928, the Canadians remained in exile. Most took early furlough in Canada, while some found temporary work in North China, Manchuria, Shanghai, Korea, Japan, Taiwan, or India. Menzies and his family evacuated to Beijing, where he taught in the North China Union Language School.

The anti-Christian, nationalist movements of the 1920s destroyed the basis for accommodation between the missionaries and the state that had developed since the Boxer Uprising. During the 'mass movement' of the early 1900s, some Chinese embraced Christianity not only for their spiritual needs but also for national salvation. They invited missionaries to participate in China's modernization by opening hospitals and modern schools and introducing Western institutions and knowledge. In the 1920s, however, in the name of national salvation, Christianity was denounced as 'unpatriotic' and 'unscientific ... Mission schools were criticized for 'denationalizing' their students. As Philip West has observed, by the end of the 1920s the debate over science and religion 'was so clearly won by science that the one error Chinese intellectuals, including Christians, have tried to avoid is the charge of being unscientific ...

Being scientific became linked with being patriotic.' With science as the new god, the tides of secularization rose high and Christianity lost its appeal for many intellectuals and students. As the philosopher C.K. Yang wrote, the students waved off religion with 'defiance and even contempt.'[36]

Nationalist agitation was not limited to big-city students and intellectuals; even the North Henan peasants asked the Canadians, 'Are you Christians or imperialists?' The declaration of the Jixian Christians was the strongest statement. Although they were Christian followers of Jesus, they resented the missionaries' arrogance, particularly when the latter sided with the imperialist rhetoric after the May 30th incident. Thus, they drew the line between the 'defenders of our country' and the 'thin edge of the wedge of imperialism.'

In early 1926, the United Church pressured the Conference of Canadian Foreign Mission Boards and Societies to adopt a conciliatory resolution. 'They do not desire that the legal rights of Missions and Missionaries in China should in future rest upon existing treaties ... and in particular upon the so-called toleration clauses in those treaties dealing specifically with missionary work; and they desire that their future legal rights and liberties should be those freely accorded to them by China as a sovereign power.'[37] This resolution could have become the basis for an equal and cooperative working relationship, but the NHM, conservative and frightened, was not ready to abandon the previous protections until definite replacements were guaranteed. In reply, Harvey Grant wrote: 'We shall not venture an opinion on extraterritoriality in its broader issues, but approve of the deletion of the present tolerance clauses on condition that there shall be definite and clear safeguards in the new treaties for our residence, holding of mission property and work in interior China.'[38]

While the Canadians were in exile, the Chinese Christians reorganized the church in North Henan. The congregations that had proclaimed their independence were now forced to stand on their own feet, financially and otherwise. For the first time, the Chinese synod proclaimed its authority throughout the field. In October 1927 the Church of Christ in China (CCC) was founded in Shanghai as a the national body of Christian churches, mostly Presbyterians. Another national organization, the National Church in China (NCC), which included Methodists, was founded at the same time. The United Church of Canada agreed to join the CCC on behalf of its missions, and thus the formerly Presbyterian mission in North Henan became part of the same church as the Methodist West China mission.

These events led to considerable reorganization of the North Henan field, which was divided into twelve congregations and two presbyteries, Zhang-Ci (Zhangde and Cixian) in the north and Wei-Huai (Weihui and Huaiqing) in the south. Zhangde, Menzies's station, the largest city in North Henan, was chosen as the headquarters for the Chinese synod. In order not to provoke the issue of national sovereignty, the CCC suggested that the foreign missionaries should wait to return to their stations until they were 'invited' back by the local church.

Once the Canadians returned, there was a power struggle between the Chinese synod and the mission, with control of mission funds as the main issue. The mission wanted to continue the old practice in which it controlled all funds from Canada and granted money to the Chinese church for specific purposes. The synod demanded that the mission should give block grants and that they, the synod, should determine the use of the funds. Since both sides refused to compromise, the mission simply stopped transferring funds to the synod, forcing them to close several schools.

The Chinese received the Canadians with hostility, telling them to stay at home and read the Bible. The struggle lasted for over a year until a few radical leaders were expelled by the synod and the general assembly of the CCC was called upon to reach a compromise. The Canadians were 'invited' to return by the Chinese church, of which they were equal members, and their work was to be 'supervised' by the synod; the Canadian funds were to be 'granted' to the synod and dispersed according to joint decisions.[39]

Chapter 9

The Waste of Yin, 1914–1927

'Old Bones'

James M. Menzies and his family left Zhangde during the evacuation of 1927. In July 1928, when he returned for a brief inspection, everything was in ruins. The mission station had been occupied and reoccupied by the army of Feng Yuxiang, their erstwhile 'friend,' the Christian general. Before this, Margaret Brown wrote, 'soldiers of various armies had visited the mission stations out of curiosity or for medical treatment ... but for more than twenty years none, no matter what faction, had never [*sic*] harmed anything. It remained for the Nationalist Army to set a precedent.'[1]

'It was a great heartbreak to see things all smashed up,' Menzies wrote to his parents. 'Clothing, dishes, food stores and utensils that were of any use were all gone ... Where once we had a restful place in a weary land, now all is destruction.'[2] Menzies's personal tragedy was not the piano and rosebushes destroyed, but the 'whole of one's lifetime of gathering together: books of which I had nearly 5,000 and into which I had put nearly all my spare money were wilfully destroyed.' These were local histories or county gazetteers (*Xianzhi*), some of them rare editions dating to the Ming dynasty, which Menzies collected for his interest in Chinese history.

Worse, the soldiers had dumped his precious archaeological artefacts into the courtyard and crushed thousands underfoot. 'I was gathering materials for a description of ancient Chinese life and manners. I had a lot of pottery, true, much of it was broken, but then it was enough to show the shapes of old vases and sacrificial vessels. I had also a considerable amount of stone-age implements and then there was a great many fragments of oracle bones. All these were destroyed. One of the first things I saw as I was being led around by the soldier to see our house was a broken vase over 3000 years old, old as David in the Old Testament. It was smashed in a hundred pieces on the sidewalk.'[3] Menzies claimed that he had collected 50,000 oracle-bone fragments by 1927.

To understand how and why Menzies amassed this astounding collection, we must retrace his continuing education, this time as a scholar and archaeologist. The previous chapters have outlined his mission work and his concern for indigenizing Christianity within Chinese culture. This chapter concerns the mind of a scholar learning the way of the Chinese heart. 'Some of us,' he wrote, have to 'school ourselves in Chinese thought, and ideas, so that we know something of the soul and mind of China as well as the outside form.'[4] Working in the 'still watches of the night,' Menzies became the foremost non-Chinese expert in oracle-bone script, which meant going back through the earliest stages of Chinese writing to decipher its original meaning. A few details of James Menzies the collector have been told, but the whole story has never been presented.[5]

He started collecting as a hobby during his first term, before the science of archaeology had developed in China. He became so well known in the district that his fellow missionaries and Chinese alike called him 'Old Bones.' Collecting oracle bones and evangelism appear to be two very different things: indeed, the undercurrent of this and future chapters concerns Menzies's difficulties convincing his colleagues in the North Henan mission and the Board of Foreign Missions in Toronto that archaeology was 'real mission work.'

For Menzies, collecting fragments of an ancient civilization permitted him to act as a cultural interface, to negotiate a new basis of accommodation for the missionary enterprise in China. Menzies hoped that collecting and studying Chinese artefacts could help cross the cultural gulf between the Chinese and the missionaries. 'God seemed to guide me when He placed in my hands the discovery of the Oracle Bones,' he wrote.[6] He felt he had been called by God to act as their custodian, to protect and preserve these fragile bits of bone for future generations.

This strong religious motivation meant that he conducted his collecting activities according to a set of principles and ethical standards that set him apart from other collectors. He had no interest in sending Chinese artefacts out of China – as Bishop White was doing, aggressively – to be 'preserved' in the West. He bought from the peasants or simply picked up shards from the fields in order to study and learn from them more about the country's ancient traditions. He collected in China, for China, and intended to leave his collection in China.

Historical Background

The most ancient Chinese records that have survived speak of a succession of divine humans – the Nest Builder, the Divine Farmer – who taught the Chinese how to be human. At the dawn of time, the Yellow Emperor taught the Chinese how to be civilized. The last of these legendary rulers, Yu the Engineer, is credited with building dykes along the Yellow River to harness it for irrigation and with establishing the Xia dynasty (2205–1766 BCE traditional).

The Xia, which modern scholars have identified with the neolithic Erlitou site in southern Henan near Luoyang, were conquered by a warlike people known as the Shang about 1766 traditional / 1700 revised BCE. The Shang seem to have had bronze technology from the beginning – weapons, chariots, horse bridles and large ritual vessels – for the oldest Chinese bronze artefacts date about 1800 BCE. The Shang moved eastwards into Henan, where they established a succession of capitals south of the Yellow River. About 1395 (traditional) / 1300 (revised) the nineteenth Shang king Pan Geng led his people and officials north of the river to a place called Beimeng, which he renamed Yin. Yin was a lavish ceremonial city with a large palace and ancestral temple complex. It had an estimated population of 100,000, a huge number considering the time.

The Shang capital remained at Yin for over 250 years until the dynasty was conquered by the Zhou people from the west, who burned the city; the devastated site, known to historians as the Waste of Yin, was abandoned and gradually silted over. A walled city named Anyang was built a short distance away during the Warring States period. The city's name was changed during the Northern Wei dynasty to Xiangzhou, and under the Jin in 1192 C.E. to Zhangde (known to Menzies and his generation as Changte). Since 1949, the name has reverted to Anyang.

It is significant that Pan Geng divined with the tortoise to select the *feng-shui* of the city of Yin. Three thousand years ago North Henan was a marshy plain with thousands of turtles and subject to frequent flooding and silting. Of the 150,000 oracle bones discovered at Yin, some 30,000 are the plastron (lower shell) of turtles; most are scapulas (shoulder bones) of cattle and sheep, although spatulas (ribs), leg bones, deer antlers, and human skulls were also used. They were used by court diviners on behalf of Shang kings to address questions to their deity *Shangdi* (Lord-on-High) and their ancestors. The bones were dried for several years in the summer sun until they were brittle. When they were ready for divining, a small pit was gouged on the bone, and a red-hot poker was applied to the pit. The heat formed a lopsided Y-shaped crack, with one straight line and another branching off to the left or the right. The direction indicated either an affirmative or a negative answer to the diviner's question. Afterwards, the diviner incised both the question and answer in 'oracle bone script' on the bone. Some bones had as many as one hundred separate divinations, questions and answers.

The information extracted from the bones is phenomenal, allowing scholars to recreate an intimate, almost daily history of the Shang kingdom for 250 years, a perspective that cannot be duplicated for some later periods of Chinese history. The divination ceremony was the heart of the king's activities. Of all the kings, Wuding, the twentieth Shang king (and second of the Yin period), left the most extensive records. He would arise before dawn and sit on a raised dais in the ancestral pavilion, surrounded by hundreds of officials and noblemen. He would down several *gu* (beakers) of wine, the better to commune with the ancestral spirits. He asked a variety of questions through the diviners' oracle bones, relating, for instance, to auspicious days for hunting and waging war, the potential weather for planting or harvesting, auspicious dates for weddings and funerals, and even such mundane concerns as the treatment of toothaches.

There were twelve kings at Yin. These became the historical figures that James Menzies spent his life trying to understand. He came to know their children and grandchildren, their wives and concubines, the ancestors who brought them good luck, and, above all, he learned about their god, *Shangdi* – the Protestant name for Jehovah God – the invisible Lord on High.

The Little Village

Menzies's artefacts came mainly from Xiaotun (old spelling Hsiao-t'un), or 'Little Village.' A generic village on the broad North China Plain, it consisted of a cluster of sun-dried mud-brick houses as yellow as the loess soil, with cotton and wheat fields radiating in all directions. It was located in the northern suburbs of Zhangde city, south of a bend of the Huan River, which meanders through North Henan and empties into the Yellow River seventy miles to the south. The village, now a huge museum and archaeological complex known as 'The Garden of Yin Ruins,' constitutes the largest and most significant Bronze Age site anywhere in the world.

The museum's official website states that the 'Yin ruins are the key cultural relics unit under the government's protection.' The 24-square-kilometre site stretches 6000 metres long by 4000 metres wide. 'The Yin ruins' general layout concentrates on the Xiaotun palace and ancestor's temple area. It's an open-styled ancient capital. Nowadays, this area has preserved many ruins such as the palace and ancestor's temple, emperors' mausoleum, tribes, family graveyards, caverns of oracle, casting yards for bronze vessel, jade-making workshop, and bone workshop and so on. All of them epitomize the essence of this unique culture and the fantastic capital city of the Shang dynasty.'[7]

The discoveries at Anyang were spectacular, upsetting all preconceived ideas of early Chinese society. Chinese archaeologists unearthed fifty stamped-earth foundations of temples and palaces, the largest of which measures 230 by 130 feet. Dozens of royal tombs, deep pits 35 feet below the surface contained chariots, bronze vessels, and hundreds of human and animal sacrifices. In the ruins of the palace, a thick calcified layer of charcoal attested to the story of the last Shang king, who perished in his burning palace when the capital was captured by the Zhou king in 1122 BCE (traditional 1045 BCE). The royal archives contained thousand of oracle bones and ritual vessels, inscribed with the earliest forms of Chinese writing. Shang and Yin are commonly used interchangeably in referring to this early Chinese culture. The oracle bones attest to a rich written language, primarily used for divination. This complex stratified urban society was a Bronze Age culture based on millet agriculture, bronze technology, and silk weaving.

It was a spring morning in the third year of the Republic of China, 1914, when Menzies first visited the Waste of Yin. In his own words:

Early in the spring of the year Chia Yin [Jia Yin] the writer was riding his old white horse along the south bank of the Huan River north of Changte City in the province of Honan. The ground had just been harrowed for cotton planting, and the farmers had thrown the freshly ploughed up potsherds and rubble to the edge of the fields. A number of potsherds of a very early date attracted the rider's attention, and led him on from sherd to sherd to a bend in the river where the debris disappeared, either washed away into the river through the centuries or buried in the drift of sand. Along the low sandy banks the willows were just putting forth their first, tender leaves and a number of half-clothed dirty children with baskets on their arms were stripping the trees for willow tea leaves. At the sight of a foreigner they gathered about me as I stood by a well examining a little pile of potsherds. 'What are you doing?' said the leader. 'Examining some broken potsherds,' said I. 'What for?' said he; 'Because they please me,' I replied. 'Do bones please you?' he ventured. 'Well, that depends,' I answered. 'But I can show you some dragon bones with characters on them.' Upon which I said that I was very much interested and off we went around the bend and up over a barren, sandy waste to a little hollow on the western slope white with powdered particles of bones. This was the Waste of Yin, the ancient capital of Wu I of the Yin Dynasty, lost in the centuries before Confucius and only known to have been 'North of the [Yellow] River.' About fifteen years ago a Chinese archaeologist named Wang I-jung [pinyin Wang Yirong] went into a Chinese drug store in Peking to buy some dragon bones for medicine. Among the fragments was a small piece on which were engraved small, delicate characters, which in some cases closely resembled the characters on the earliest bronzes in his collection ... He was the first discoverer of the bone fragments that have now become known as the Oracle Bones ...

The writer, then, was the first foreign or Chinese archaeologist to visit the Waste of Yin with a purely scientific interest in these objects. Many a subsequent day has he stolen away on his old white horse to tread the ruins of this old adobe city. Even Lo Chên-yü [pinyin Luo Zhenyu], the collector and publisher of the most famous Chinese collection [*Yinxu Shuqi*], who was in Changte once or twice in recent years, has only once visited the site of this ancient capital of China.[8]

The scene is captured for posterity with a precise surveyor's eye: the geometry of the furrows and fields, the mounds along the river, and the little cave on the western slope where the dirt was white with bone dust. Not only did he know what he was looking at, Menzies knew what he was looking for. He had only been at Zhangde for a month or two after his language training at Wu'an, and this may have been his first tour of the village. Yet he recognized that the shards were of a very early date and knew about 'dragon bones' with characters. The peasant boy, too, knew what Menzies was looking for. 'Do bones please you?' he asked slyly, as though he was used to outsiders wanting to buy dragon bones.

Although Menzies gave credit to Wang Yirong and Luo Zhenyu, he carefully and modestly staked out his claim: he was 'the *first foreign or Chinese archaeologist* to *visit* the Waste of Yin with a *purely scientific interest* in these objects.' He did not say what first attracted him to this place. He was not yet an archaeologist and therefore we must ask what knowledge prompted him to come to the conclusion that this 'was the Waste of Yin, the ancient capital of Wu I of the Yin Dynasty'? Clearly, he stumbled on the place by providence, and was shown bones by children in which he took a scientific interest; he did not claim to be 'the discoverer' that oracle bones came from Xiaotun, but rather that he was the first *scientist* to *visit* the site.

The story of Wang Yirong's discovery of the dragon bones in 1899 is famous, repeated in all books about Oracle Bones. Wang, too, knew what he was looking at when he actually saw the first dragon bone. Even if he could not read the inscriptions, he recognized that these scratches were ancient Chinese writing. As a scholar, Wang was part of the long tradition of antiquarian study of the development of calligraphy styles and inscriptions on stone and bronze monuments. As soon as Wang identified the script, a small group of scholars in Beijing began to collect and study these inscribed bones. By 1914, when Menzies surveyed the Waste of Yin, there already existed a body of knowledge both in Chinese and English about oracle bones and their inscriptions. This scholarship is summarized in the appendix of this book.

It is not clear how much Menzies knew of this scholarship, but from his response to the village boy's question, he was probably aware of local stories. In fact, the demand for bones in Zhangde was so great that an industry had sprung up to produce forgeries of oracle bones, bronze vessels, and pottery. As dealers and collectors came and went, people in Zhangde, from peasants to scholars, gained a good knowledge of the nature and value of these inscribed bones, called by the local people *zi gutou* (inscribed bones).[9] Menzies's Chinese teacher, steeped in local lore, must also have informed him about dragon bones and where they came from.

The person who should be given credit for 'identifying' Xiaotun as the Waste of Yin was Luo Zhenyu. He recognized the names of Shang kings on some inscribed bones and made inquiries among curio dealers. He published his discovery in 1910, and in 1912 produced the monumental *Yinxu Shuqi Qianbian* (The Waste of Yin Oracle Bone Inscriptions, Part One), which consisted of two thousand ink-squeezes of oracle bone inscriptions, selected from his collection of 20,000 to 30,000 bone and shell fragments.[10]

Zhang Kunhe, who studied archaeology under Menzies's personal supervision at Cheeloo University in 1932–6, provided the best evidence for Menzies's relationship with the Waste of Yin. In the article 'Ming

Yishi yu Qilu Daxue Jiagu Yanjiu' (James Menzies and Oracle Bone Studies at Qilu University), Zhang unequivocally stated that Menzies never called himself the 'discoverer' of the Waste of Yin:

> Now books on oracle bone studies use Menzies' works as reference. But some add critical notes saying that Menzies pretended to be the first discoverer of oracle bone inscriptions or the first identifier of the Waste of Yin. Both are wrong. In his book, *Jiagu Yanjiu* (Oracle Bone Study), Menzies clearly stated that the first discoverer of oracle bone inscriptions was Wang Yirong. The first to document and publicize oracle bone inscriptions was Liu E. Menzies admitted that he came into contact with oracle bones at a much later date. Even though he stated in his article that 'this is then the capital of Wu Yi of the Shang dynasty,' he never said that this conclusion was his own. In fact, he stated in his lectures that this conclusion was based on Luo Zhenyu's study ...
>
> Nonetheless, Menzies was proud of himself as the first person to frequent and investigate the Waste of Yin. He mentioned this often in his lectures. He said that Wang Yirong, Wang Xiang, Liu E, Duan Fang, [F.H.] Chalfant and [Samuel] Couling knew about oracle bones, but did not know that the oracle bone fragments available from dealers were from Anyang. After finding out the provenance of the oracle bones, Luo Zhenyu first sent his brothers to buy bones at Anyang. It was only in 1915 that Luo himself visited the place, more than a year after Menzies' visit to Xiaotun. Menzies also said that when Luo came to Anyang, his purpose was mainly to buy bones: he spent about ten minutes on the south bank of the Huan River, saying 'this is the Waste of Yin,' and then went back to his hotel and never came back. Luo's careless visit to the site led him to the wrong conclusion that 'the treasures at Huan Yang [south of the Huan River] were all gone.'[11]

To conclude, James Menzies stumbled on the site, but knew instinctively what he was looking at. He would have been aware, in an amateur way, of the newspaper reports of archaeological discoveries in Greece, Egypt, and the Middle East that were popular in the 1910s and 1920s. He was a civil engineer and Dominion Land Surveyor with surveying experience, better preparation for field archaeology than an old-fashioned Chinese antiquarian might acquire sitting in his Beijing study. Simply put, he was the first *scientist* to stay at the site for years to study the artefacts at the moment they appeared from the ground. This in no way diminishes his stature as a scholar and archaeologist, for his academic credentials rested on his achievements in oracle-bone collection and

Shang archaeology rather than with the technical question of who discovered the Waste of Yin.

The so-called dragon bones had been used in Chinese medicine as far back as the Han dynasty (206 BCE to 221 CE) to treat a range of illnesses. Called 'knife point medicine,' the use of powdered dragon bones was considered effective in healing cuts and surgical wounds, and 'dragon teeth' calmed the heart and soul.[12] When the Canadians arrived in North Henan in the 1890s, they found that during slow seasons villagers went out to pick up dragon bones, which they sold in the marketplaces. Those bones with characters incised on them were considered of low quality by Chinese doctors and thus had little market value. It was the usual practice to scrub off the inscriptions before selling them to drugstores. Only by chance did some inscriptions survive and find their way to Wang Yirong. The negligence of one peasant from Little Village gave the world a new understanding of ancient Chinese civilization.[13]

James Menzies: A Unique Collector

Practically every missionary family at Zhangde had an old Chinese jar or bronze mirror that they had bought as a souvenir or were given as a gift. Many of these have ended up in the Royal Ontario Museum (ROM). Menzies was the only serious collector of the North Henan mission. He lacked any independent income and did not have access to private or public funds. He was not, he stated repeatedly, a museum agent. Yet he managed to build up the largest private collection of oracle bones.

Unlike most foreign collectors at the time, Menzies did not collect for the international art markets. Instead, he gathered a personal study collection. Museum collectors want 'art' in perfect condition, but to Menzies a seemingly useless broken potsherd or bone fragment, covered with the original dirt, had more scientific value than an intact vessel with no context. However small, each artefact was a clue to the vast jigsaw puzzle of ancient China. He was attracted to beautiful jars and bronze vessels that the peasants or curio dealers showed him, but he could not afford them. Rather he collected what others thought were 'old trash' (*polan*), fingernail-sized fragments of bone with one or two characters.[14]

A survey of Menzies's collections, now dispersed in China and Canada, reveals they consisted mostly of broken pottery, tiny fragments of oracle bones, broken stone implements and jade disks, and a few bronze vessels. The Cheeloo University collection, now at Shandong Provincial Museum, consists of 29,457 artefacts including 8080 bone fragments, of which only 3668 had inscriptions.[15] Menzies built up his collections by placing academic value over artistic value. In the eyes of the world, his things were simply the waste from the Waste of Yin, but for serious scholars they were treasures of humanity's past.

As a self-trained archaeologist, Menzies tried to preserve the scientific context of the objects. Most collectors bought from curio dealers whose suppliers were usually tomb robbers, who washed off the earth and destroyed the context. Whenever possible, Menzies visited the site personally to record for each artefact a small note describing the provenance, the discoverer, objects found at the site, and other relative comments. To preserve the scientific value, he treated each shard with a glue mix to keep the earth crust intact, as he believed this might someday be valuable in determining scientifically the date of the artefacts.[16]

The description attached to one of the first objects he acquired, a bronze axe now in the ROM, is typical of his detailed third-person style:

> NB 1778, with crust, 3 perfect specimens, said to have been found on the south bank of the Chang [Zhang] River near the Peiking – Hankow Railway Crossing in 1915–16. Menzies considers these to be earlier than Shang II, 1311–1039 BC. This type is not common at the Anyang site, Yin Hsu [Waste of Yin]. These 3 axes were obtained by a man named T'ien, a resident of one of the villages just north of the Chang River. Menzies on visiting the site was not able to locate the find spot exactly or to obtain other axes from this site on the Chang River.[17]

In 1914, the Royal Ontario Museum in Toronto was opened to the public. Its dynamic director Charles Trick Currelly sent a letter to Canadian missionaries all over the world requesting them to donate or deposit ethnological artefacts. James Menzies responded by lending thirty-eight artefacts, stone implements, and potsherds from the Waste of Yin.[18] This was the first sign of Menzies's collecting instinct. By 1917 he was enough of a scholar to publish an important book, *Yinxu Buci* (Oracle Records from the Waste of Yin), which contains line drawings of 2369 inscribed bones. One indication of his ability, even then, to spot forgeries, was that only one example later proved to be a fake. Such accuracy was exceedingly rare among the early documentation concerning oracle bones.

Before *Yinxu Buci* came off the Shanghai press, Menzies joined the Chinese Labour Corps and was shipped off to France. In Toronto, the

Globe, published by his old friend J.A. MacDonald, and the *Presbyterian Record* hailed him as the 'discoverer of the Waste of Yin.'[19] Even in France, where he dwelled among ruins of a different sort, he was always collecting something, such as a box of potshards dug up in the trenches, which he sent to the ROM.[20] Menzies kept in touch with Currelly, and in 1921, when he was on his way to China, he deposited his second box of Waste of Yin artefacts on permanent loan to the ROM.[21]

As a collector, Menzies had frequent contacts with curio dealers, but he only trusted them for supplementary information. As he told Currelly:

I never depended for one moment on any man who offered an object for sale. He was always interested in the sale, while I was only interested in scientific truth to be learned. To me a broken fragment which I personally found on a site was a fact to be trusted, while a valuable object purchased from a seller was almost certainly not excavated in the place where he stated it had been found. His interest was in protecting knowledge of the site for himself, in case of other finds. A lifetime's experience of these things, and almost daily contacts with these dealers, taught me the very great value of a little evidence personally acquired at great effort. By means of these little beacon lights of fact, I was gradually able to make my way through the wilderness of false objects and misinformation that I found all around me.[22]

Menzies learned about the treachery of curio dealers when he was first starting to collect. He bought a number of large bones with inscriptions from a dealer at Zhangde, but quickly his study began to stink of rotten meat: the bones were all new ox bones, which spoiled in the hot weather.[23] From this experience, Menzies learned that tiny fragments were more likely genuine, while larger, intact, more spectacular, more expensive pieces might be forgeries. He wrote in 1917:

For the little pieces are practically all of tortoise shell, which was very precious in those ancient days and reserved for the king's sacrifices, while the larger, coarser animal bones were used for divinations of lesser import, just as some of the ancient Greeks wrote on sheep's shoulder-blades because they could not afford parchment. These tortoise shells were so precious that the diviner inscribed on them sometimes as many as one hundred inquiries, and the characters written were no larger than a grain of rice ... Each divination required the cutting of an oblong hollow in the underside of the shell and the production by fire of two cracks, one horizontal and one perpendicular. This generally has resulted in the tortoise shells being broken into very small fragments. It is, therefore, not the size of the fragments that is important, but the characters on them.[24]

Menzies's principle was to go directly to the source. 'My way of working,' Menzies explained to Currelly many years later, 'would have been the very simple one of going unknown in person to the site and gathering with my own hands among the debris about the mount of the excavations fragments of which I was personally sure. One fragment of a glass bead so gathered by him would have been worth its weight in gold. This is the kind of work I did in North Honan over a period of more than 25 years. It is very arduous, it is slow, and the results are not spectacular, but one learns the truth.'[25]

In 1954 he described to his son Arthur how he had acquired a particularly fine neolithic pottery jar: 'We have two or three pots in Royal Ontario Museum. Unfortunately with them as with most things in the museum, there is no scientific data as to where they were unearthed. My jar ... had a lid which the peasants broke in the finding and left beside the hole. I went back and recovered the 2 pieces personally. So, I know the find spot. It was about half way between Hou Kang [Hougang] and Hsiao Tun [Xiaotun] on the south bank of the river. I left a more beautiful example in Tsinan [i.e., Cheeloo] University museum.'[26]

As an evangelistic missionary, able to travel widely throughout North Henan, Menzies gained a knowledge of other ancient sites. In addition, his interest in *gu dong*, or old stuff, gradually became known inside and outside the church. With his amiable personality, he made friends with local people. His daughter recalled that it was not rare for him to be called away from the dining table to receive visitors with 'dragon bones' or other objects they found on their lands. On occasion, he was visited by country peddlers who had purchased some 'old stuff' on their buying and selling travels and knew Ming Mushi (Pastor Ming) wanted broken objects.[27]

Menzies built the bulk of his collection between 1914 and 1917, and from 1922 to 1927, while he was stationed at Zhangde. In *Jiagu Nianbiao*, Dong Zuobin, the chief archaeologist at Anyang, made an entry under the year 1927: 'Menzies bought a great number of oracle bones. From the third year of the Republic, Menzies was stationed at Zhangde as a missionary. Local people called him 'Ming Mu-shi.' According to the villagers, during the past ten years, Menzies secured a large number of oracle bones.'[28]

James Menzies was obsessed by broken objects. He used the term

'lover's eye' to describe his interest in ancient bones and potsherds.[29]
Once he came upon a farmer 'digging a hole to get some earth for filling
in a road,' and picked up some black potsherds from the mound. Later
he made two trips and 'got 50 pieces of one pot and stuck most of it
together.'[30] As a result, his houses – at Zhangde, Jinan, and Toronto –
were packed with boxes of mended pots and bones.

Annie Belle Menzies wholeheartedly – if a little woefully – supported
her husband's collecting and recognized its scholarly importance. She
herself collected the beautiful Song dynasty celadon porcelain and Qing
embroideries, including some from the imperial palace. However, she
was a practical housewife and chastised her husband gently: 'Do not buy
a lot of junk that no one will ever give you a penny for you have such a lot
of unsaleable stuff already. Take my advice and hereafter buy fewer but
better things, things that will have a good market when you want to sell
them. One or two good pieces instead of a lot of poor stuff even if it is
cheap.'[31] Everyone in the family became a collector under father's and
mother's tutelage. When he was eleven, in Beijing in 1928, Arthur
started his collection, which consisted of small embroidered accessories
such as fan cases, pipe cases, small panels, and decorations.

Chapter 10

Museums and Collectors

Many missionaries collected souvenirs that they used as object lessons when they spoke to people back home in Canada. A few became serious, systematic collectors of Chinese art. These included two notable Canadians, John Calvin Ferguson, president of Nanjing University, and Bishop William Charles White of the Canadian Anglican diocese of Henan, who both became benefactors of the Royal Ontario Museum in Toronto. Because Menzies's career became intertwined with Bishop White and the ROM with unfortunate later results, this chapter considers their relationship at the beginning. As questions have been raised concerning Bishop White's ethics as a collector of Chinese antiquities, it is instructive to contrast how and what the amateur historian/archaeologist Menzies collected compared to Bishop White, the museum agent.

The Royal Ontario Museum

Museums are assembled in bits and pieces over a long period of time. What a museum collects depends on many factors: the philosophy of its curators, the availability of 'museum quality' art, benefactors with deep pockets, and, most important, a network of hunters and gatherers. Toronto, 'the rich, imperialist, evangelical city of churches, headquarters of many mission societies, got the Royal Ontario Museum'[1] A steady stream of missionary collections flowed into the ROM: bound-foot shoes and idols from China, bark-cloth and fetishes from the South Seas, oil lamps from the Holy Land, and potlatch ceremonials from British Columbia. For years a baleful panda, courtesy of Dr Leslie Kilborn of West China, sat at the entrance to the mammalogy gallery.[2]

The impresario of the ROM was its flamboyant founder and director,

Charles Trick Currelly. He entitled his autobiography, modestly, *I Brought the Ages Home*, with an introduction by Northrop Frye, the eminent literary critic. Frye commented that Currelly's story was 'one of the most amazing ever to come out of Ontario.' He was a missionary in reverse, Frye wrote: 'A graduate of Victoria College in a generation when so many of its most brilliant graduates became missionaries, Dr. Currelly was a cultural missionary. His converts were Canadians and his gospel was preached by all the world.'[3] We might say more cynically that Currelly wanted to bring the whole world to Toronto in the form of decontextualized objects that would be rearranged according to the rigid taxonomies of ethnology and anthropology to preach the gospel of Evolution to the people of Toronto.

Currelly's meeting with George Crofts is one of the pious legends of the ROM. Late one afternoon in 1918, an immaculately dressed stranger presented his card, saying he was a businessman from New York City. Currelly brushed him aside, even though Crofts said, mysteriously, 'It is in my power to help you a good deal, but I'm afraid I couldn't give you the things for nothing, so I suppose there's nothing more to be said.' After Crofts left, however, Currelly realized that the stranger was 'the Great Unknown from China who sent to London most of the Chinese things that had come to Europe.' He raced to the hotel, where he found Crofts ready to board the train for the Orient. As a result of this chance meeting, 'we [the ROM] received over ten million dollars' worth of material, and were lifted by it to the position of one of the world's great museums.' Forty years later the scene had not dimmed: 'I feel that my meeting with Crofts was one of the two most important things that have happened to me and the museum, the other being my first meeting with [Flinders] Petrie [the Egyptologist]'[4]

By contrast, Currelly's account of his meeting with Bishop William Charles White in 1924 is parsimonious. 'While the flood of Chinese materials was coming in, I had a visit from a man who told me that he was Bishop White, the Anglican bishop of Honan. I soon worked it out that we had been students at the same time in Toronto. He presented us with a fine painting of about 1300 or 1400, a superb piece of drawing and in wonderful condition.'[5] Nevertheless, on the basis of this meeting Currelly appointed White as the museum's purchasing agent in China. This arrangement was kept secret, as Lovat Dickson explained in *The Museum Makers*, the official history of the ROM: '[C]uriously, in his annual reports, he [Currelly] does not acknowledge Bishop White as the source from which flowed year by year huge shipments of immensely valuable

Chinese artifacts. This may well have been at the bishop's own request. The church authorities in Toronto might not have been pleased to know that their bishop had been spending so much of his time in archaeological pursuits. It was not until ten years later in 1934 ... that his great contribution was openly acknowledged,' when White retired from Henan.[6]

White and Currelly stand out as the two major figures in the early history of the ROM. According to Dickson's evaluation, 'Currelly's contribution was unquestionably the larger; he covered the whole field of art and archaeology and had the supreme quality of the museum director, the ability to get the best out of all who worked with him. White was totally lacking in this ability; he had an unfortunate capacity for irritating his subordinates.' Dickson concluded,

> White's visit to Currelly in 1924 had been speculative, but it was in line with his ambition for wider fame. Currelly had the gift for igniting latent enthusiasms in those capable of serving his Museum. Though he did not much like White at their first meeting, he saw in him someone ideally placed to complete the work that Crofts had begun; and he became quite attached to him in the next ten years as they exchanged long and frequent letters. These letters make strange reading today, when ethical attitudes towards acquisitions make past practices seem heinous, the more so because they were written by a man of the cloth and a man who had begun his career as a missionary. What Currelly had been doing in Egypt twenty years earlier was what the bishop was then doing in China. The Museum's life, like that of all museums, even the great and world-famous ones whose collections had been built in the 19th century, depended on snatching these treasures while there was still time.[7]

What were those strong words alluding to? On 20 January 1926 Bishop White wrote: 'I was somewhat worried about what a dealer said today. He asked me not to let people [in China] see the good Shang bowl, and I gather there is criticism of the best things being bought by foreigners, and sent away from China. The present nationalistic feeling in China is really anti-foreign and it is going to hinder the exportation of Chinese antiquities.' To which Currelly replied, 'There is no doubt that a settled China would try to make it difficult to export the antiquities. I feel therefore there is all the more need to make hay while the sun shines.'[8]

After the 1911 revolution large quantities of Chinese art of superb quality began to appear in the art markets, acquired from impecunious scholars and officials who fared poorly after the fall of the Qing dynasty.

Much came also from accidental excavations by labourers engaged in railroad-building and road-widening projects, which opened ancient tombs and obliterated village temples. The constant civil strife throughout the early 1920s made it impossible for Chinese governments to protect the country's cultural heritage. In fact, corrupt officials and warlords were often involved in the pillaging.

With the assistance of Chinese dealers and their networks of grave robbers and stonecutters, Western collectors looted many major cultural sites throughout China, such as Dunhuang and Longmen. Just before 1910, the British Indian Government's representative Sir Aurel Stein and Frenchman Paul Pelliot visited Dunhuang and carted away much portable material, including the oldest printed paper in the world. In 1925 Langdon Warner of the Fogg Museum came back to Dunhuang for the frescoes that Pelliot had photographed but left intact. Warner viewed the Chinese as 'subhuman, uncivilized and unable to appreciate their past culture.' His self-proclaimed mission was to 'preserve' Chinese culture by procuring as many artefacts as he could. At Dunhuang, he cut out pieces of twelve frescoes, including the most important, which arrived at the Fogg Museum in pitiful fragments.[9]

The Guomindang regime in power during the 1930s proved incapable of radically changing these practices. The desecration of Longmen, Henan, had many villains. In 1934 Alan Priest entered into a contract with local bandits, who carved out a frieze he had chosen. He sent to the Metropolitan Museum of Art in New York fourteen pieces of a stone screen with statues, and six heads of Buddhist statues. The last shipment was smuggled out of China while the Japanese troops were raping and looting their way into Nanjing in 1937.[10]

Bishop White, The Museum Agent

Although Bishop White and James Menzies were timid souls compared with these notorious collectors, Bishop White was the bolder and more reckless in his collecting activities of the two. For a decade, 1924–34, he was the largest buyer in the curio shops of Kaifeng and as far away as Beijing and Shanghai. He sent literally tons of material to the ROM – The Bishop White Collection – which complemented the Crofts material, because 'Crofts had got very little that was B.C. and White very little that was A.D.'[11] From his first year of collecting, he sent in 'January 1925, 50 items, including more than 100 pieces; February, 26 items; April, more than 50 items, pottery and porcelain; May, 9 boxes, many pieces of bronze and pottery; 1 September, 22 articles; 15 September, 140 pieces,' and another 170 pieces by the end of the month.[12]

In 1924, when Bishop White was recruited as the ROM's purchasing agent, he was aged fifty-one and had been bishop for fourteen years. He had established a flourishing mission that was among the most progressive in China, with schools and hospitals at Kaifeng and at Zhengzhou and Guide along the railway line leading into and away from Kaifeng. As John Foster has commented, White's aim was to build an institutional church, 'but a Chinese Church armed with the Gospel, rather than a battalion of Canadian missionaries, was to be the means.' Already he could see, he told the Missionary Society of the Church in Canada that '[t]he day for direct evangelistic work by the foreigner in China has gone.'[13] In 1925, at the height of the anti-Christian, anti-foreign nationalist movement, White consecrated Rev. Lindel Tsen as his assistant bishop, the first Chinese bishop in the world-wide Anglican communion, who became his successor when he retired in 1934.

The story of Bishop White's collecting has been recounted in the biographies and histories of the ROM with varying degrees of frankness. It is clear that even Lewis Walmsley, his successor as Professor of Chinese Studies at the University of Toronto and biographer, was appalled by the letters between White and Currelly. In *Bishop in Honan*, the official biography commissioned by the Bishop White Committee of the ROM, Walmsley merely hints at the darker side. 'Secrecy played an important role in collecting, and valuable information was often obtained through hired spies and informants,' he wrote diplomatically. 'It required ingenuity, imagination, and diplomacy. It required too the mind of a detective to trace accurately the origin of artifacts, and even more to distinguish between genuine objects and forgeries. It demanded patience, insight and a quick alertness to what was happening in the Chinese archaeological world if one were to be first on the scene of each new discovery and procure its choicest treasures. Beyond that, it called for a man of position who could deal with unscrupulous officials.'[14] After 1930, the problem was not unscrupulous officials, but scrupulous ones.

Charles Taylor suggests a psychological pattern that went back to White's first encounters with 'idols' as a young missionary in 1898. Like many other missionaries at the time, White organized bonfires to burn 'all the idols and idolatrous scrolls, the charms and shrines, idolatrous prayer books and paper money' of new converts. 'Even allowing for the evangelical temper of the time, White's glee at the burning of idols seems excessive and fanatical. It may well have been that he was already starting to feel an instinctive *attraction* to the Chinese culture – an attraction which the young missionary could only suppress through acts of passionate destruction.' Be that as it may, White did not burn all the idols he confiscated: 'I brought home,' he wrote, 'the [idolatrous] scroll and one of the little gilt idols, and perhaps some day they may find their place in the mission.'[15] This combination of evangelical iconoclasm and clandestine collecting was to characterize Bishop White's first acquisitions when he arrived in Kaifeng.

In 1183 CE the Song emperor had granted a congregation of Jews permission to build a synagogue in the capital city, Kaifeng. This 'orphan colony of Chinese Jews' had survived until the last rabbi died about 1850. All that remained was the abandoned synagogue, a couple of stone monuments, and a stone baptismal laver. White brought Shanghai Jews to lecture the surviving tribe on the history of the Jewish nation, while convincing them that Christianity was the successor to Judaism – and thus would be the best custodian of their relics. In 1919 he purchased the ruins of the synagogue, hoping to move the stone steles to the cathedral. White sent a man to collect them, but he was imprisoned by the authorities for theft. After a long and acrimonious wrangle, White bought the stones outright 'with no condition as to their custodianship other than that they were never to leave the province.' They are still in the Kaifeng museum, but the stone laver and a rare Hebrew-Chinese scroll of Esther made their way to the ROM, and are now on long-term loan to the Judaica museum at Holy Blossom Synagogue in Toronto.[16]

By 1924, Bishop White was a learned Sinologue with a well-trained eye. He had read widely in the Chinese histories, but he was an old-fashioned Orientalist without any experience in serious, systematic collecting. He was powerful and ambitious, and his new-found goal was nothing less than to build his monument: the largest collection of Chinese art and archaeology in the world. His correspondence in the Thomas Fisher Rare Books Library of the University of Toronto reveals a who's who of Chinese art, from Père Teillard de Chardin to the Crown Prince of Sweden, as well as Chinese scholars. In particular, he turned to the two men on the spot, a curio dealer in Kaifeng named Lin and James Menzies.

Walmsley describes White's relationship with Lin the dealer as cordial and helpful. White came to trust his judgment: 'He knew the particular objects the bishop was seeking – perfect specimens of certain periods – and worked unceasingly to obtain them. The two men trusted each other as professionals and dispensed with many formalities such as the bargaining which usually preceded a deal. The dealer agreed to tell White the exact price he had paid and add the customary commission. He took responsibility for the genuineness of his goods and for securing them at a fair price. His ability to discover new finds also proved useful.' In other words, 'White was not able to visit the graves from which he obtained these treasures and thus was unable to find objects *in situ*; he was unhappy with the situation but unable to change it.'[17]

As for Menzies, Walmsley admitted, 'Dr. White also leaned heavily in his early years of study on the experience and knowledge of Rev. James M. Menzies, a Canadian Presbyterian missionary stationed at the strategic centre of Anyang.'[18] Bishop White would not have been pleased with that begrudging statement, for he never openly acknowledged the younger man's technical expertise. In fact, he carefully wrote Menzies out of all his published works. Menzies already had a debt of gratitude to Bishop White that went back to 1910, when the new bishop had released his first missionary deaconess, Annie Belle Sedgwick, from her contract and allowed her to marry the young Presbyterian Menzies. Bishop White played on Menzies's emotions, and the latter was more than willing to share his passion for oracle bones.

Especially in his early years of collecting, Bishop White frequently consulted with James Menzies on the authenticity of objects originating in the Anyang area. Menzies was an expert on forgeries, and warned White against Lin and other dealers who valued profits over friendship. The bishop on several occasions summoned Menzies from Zhangde to Kaifeng (a two- or three-day trip) to identify artefacts. More often, he sent rubbings or smaller items, especially oracle bones, by parcel for identification. As a result, there are very few forgeries in the ROM, except for some sixth-century statues that White purchased in Shanghai. To White's chagrin, Currelly discovered they were fake after the shipment arrived in Toronto.[19]

'Your parcel of bones came. All false.' Menzies wrote on one occasion.[20] This was after the bishop had been collecting cultural artefacts for eight years. In another letter: 'With regard to the bones ... they are all good but the black splinter which you thought had had a former inscription scraped off. It is a forgery by Lan Mao-kuang who has just died. So probably is your bigger piece.'[21] 'Your stone *ch'ings* have come to hand. They are undoubtedly false. The stone is old but that is all.'[22] Menzies didn't hesitate to disclose his trade secrets: 'The forgeries are getting harder to detect. Use a strong glass and a toothbrush and water on the inscriptions. When you have washed out the recent dirt or glue, you will find a rough edge and a white cut, while the surface of the bone is darker and more weathered.'[23] He also advised the bishop how to approach the local dealers: 'Do not ask for characters on the clay from Hsiao Tun [Xiaotun], none is inscribed and if you suggest it, they will inscribe them for you and spoil the pieces. For scholars doubt clay vessels on the least pretext, a false inscription is apt to make them cast doubts on the whole lot. Clay things are so easily manufactured.'[24]

The Antiquities Law

Pressured by scholars such as Li Chi and Rong Geng, in May 1930 the Nationalist government in Nanjing passed China's first cultural-relics protection legislation for the 'preservation of all antiques and ancient relics of the country.' It declared that all antiquities and relics underground belonged to the state and that valuable antiques in private collections had to be reported to the government authorities. The law stated explicitly that 'exportation to foreign countries is strictly prohibited.'[25] This legislation had little effect because of corruption, political instability, civil wars, and the Japanese invasion. As a result, China continued to be the big game for foreign collectors.

James Menzies approved the protective legislation and sought to abide by its regulations. Once the Academia Sinica started excavating Xiaotun, he stopped collecting artefacts from that site. He did continue to purchase other antiquities, however, until he left North Henan in 1932, because ancient bronze and pottery artefacts were found throughout Henan. Thus, while Li Chi and his colleagues were excavating at Xiaotun and Hougang, Menzies was still able to buy Shang bronzes and pottery from local peasants. In 1932 a local peasant found a pit of Shang bronze and pottery in an old brick kiln, near the Zhangde railway station. Menzies bought the cheap things and Bishop White bought up the rest.[26]

Bishop White was indignant about the new law, which he felt had been brought about by 'the present selfish and narrow anti-foreign attitude' of the government.[27] He actively sought to evade its restrictions and continued to procure objects that he *knew* had been obtained illegally and to ship them to Toronto. Indeed, some of his most spectacular objects were sent between 1930 and 1934. One coup was a 50,000-volume Mu Library that had belonged to the Chinese secretary of the German embassy, purchased by White and John Calvin Ferguson, another important Canadian collector. Another was the Elephant Tomb east of Xiaotun, right under the Chinese archaeologists' noses, in 1934. This burial site of an important Shang prince eventually enriched the ROM collection with over one hundred bronze and pottery objects, many of which were decorated with an elephant's head motif. [28]

Bishop White's collecting naturally attracted attention. On one occasion, he was accused of possessing 'national treasure' by Feng Yuxiang. When the bishop denied holding the 'treasure,' Feng's troops seized it in transit, and the general issued a proclamation stating that 'if such an offence as that committed by Bishop White should be repeated, in the event of future troubles protection would be withdrawn from the Christian Missions.'[29] To avoid further embarrassment, White sent his 'goods' to Shanghai, and then arranged ocean transportation to Toronto. When inspection at the Kaifeng railway station tightened after 1930, his limousine driver would drive to Lankao, a small station nearby, to send the objects to Shanghai.[30] White also packed artefacts in the luggage of missionaries who were returning to Canada on furlough, since foreigners' baggage was not inspected by Chinese customs. In fact, this became the prime way to smuggle small artefacts out of China after the government cut off the mail channels.

Postscript on Collections

On the eve of his retirement from Henan, in May 1930, Bishop White published his first book on Chinese archaeology, *Tombs of Old Lo-yang*. It was a lavish book, privately printed by the best press in Shanghai, with 200 pages of text and 200 full-page, glossy-paper plates illustrating almost 600 objects from a series of Zhou dynasty tombs near Luoyang. This was meant to be his entree into the new world of scholarship that awaited him when, as the title page declared, he took up the office of 'Sometime Bishop of Honan, Associate Professor of Archaeology (Chinese), University of Toronto, and Keeper of the East Asiatic Collection of the Royal Ontario Museum.' Another more murky image is suggested by a letter to James from his wife: 'How are you progressing in your work? I am ever so anxious for you to get something out. It seems such a shame for you to have covered so much ground and done so much work and for other people to put it into print.'[31]

Put into the context of White's relationship with Menzies and the ethics of collecting, *Tombs of Old Lo-yang* is very revelatory. It is dedicated to Currelly: Menzies is merely mentioned as one of 'many others who have helped greatly.'[32] Even Bishop White's staunchest admirers admitted he was ambitious and ruthless, that his methods of collecting were somewhat unsavoury. By 1934 White had been collecting thousands of objects for a decade and not a word about his collecting activities had appeared in public, in either the ROM reports or the church press. His ambition now was to be recognized as the person who collected, catalogued, researched, and published the largest and best collection of Chinese art in the world.

Even Bishop White admitted his scholarship was thin, as he said with mock humility: 'There is nothing much that is original in this book – it is simply a record.' He had never visited an archaeological excavation and he had no way of knowing the provenance and legitimacy of these objects except the word of the curio dealer Lin and the authentication of James Menzies. In 1931 (after the antiquities law) White wrote, vaguely, that 'very beautiful things had been coming to light,' although 'many passed into the markets and in time were scattered and the knowledge of their origin lost.' He continued: 'The local people who had anything to do with the excavations are naturally very reluctant to talk about the matter, since their doings might well be called into question, but two of them, including an intelligent artisan who actually took part in the work, have produced such evidence that we cannot but accept as a fact that the [bronze] bells [dated 550 BCE, the year after the birth of Confucius] and certain articles hereafter described were from the burial chamber of what we designate as Tomb VII.'[33] On this basis, he described in minute, technical detail the construction and contents of the tombs as well as the dating and inscriptions. Not only was White vague about the provenance of these objects, he never mentioned where they were – in Toronto in the vaults of the Royal Ontario Museum.

Bishop White's collecting activities did not end with his retirement in 1934. He designated Rev. Canon I.H. Wei (Wei Yiheng), 'my close friend and colleague for over twenty-five years' and diocesan secretary of the Henan Anglican church, as his agent. Working through the same dealer, Lin, Wei continued to purchase the best finds in the province. In September 1934 Wei wrote to White: 'I sent you two boxes of things I bought for you ... Among the things bought one comes from Anyang, which Mr. Lin said was what you have wanted some years. I know that you would like to get things from Anyang tiger pit and I shall hereafter look out for them and buy them for you whenever possible.'[34] A year later, Wei did get several valuable objects from the tiger pit near Xiaotun, but the parcels were confiscated by the Shanghai Customs. Only under pressure from Rev. George E. Simmons, treasurer of the Anglican mission, did the

Shanghai authorities return the parcels instead of sending them to Nanjing for government inspection.[35] These and other items were taken to Canada in 1937 by a Miss Howard, as Wei reported to Bishop White: 'These things I am asking Miss Howard to bring to you, as she will be leaving in about three weeks I think. I am also asking her to take the two boxes from Shanghai containing the two animal masks, that were bought some time ago, the little animals from tombs, one made from pieces of stone and the other of mother of pearl. I think it would be best if you could help Miss Howard get these things through the customs. Miss Gibberd suggests that she need not open the trunk containing these things until she gets to Toronto.'[36]

Bishop White's final effort to 'save' China's cultural treasures occurred in 1947 when he returned to Kaifeng after the Second World War. Henan was in a desperate situation. The countryside was destroyed and Kaifeng was filled with tens of thousands of refugees. Using his old connections, White managed to buy and to export a number of artefacts. As Lewis Walmsley wrote, 'Before he left Kaifeng, Bishop White's absorbing interest in archaeology reasserted itself. He knew of the many recent discoveries of ancient grave sites and their rich caches of treasures and he was able to procure for the Royal Ontario Museum a number of first-class bronzes dating to the second millennium B.C.'[37]

Even if Bishop White could never acknowledge the help he received, by 1927 James Menzies was generally recognized as the outstanding non-Chinese authority on oracle bones and bronze vessels from the Little Village, the major Shang site in China. That year, although Menzies had evacuated from Henan, Charles Trick Currelly again approached him to act as the museum's purchasing agent in China. 'Chinese material has poured at us at such a rate that the European sinologues who have been here say that ours is much the best and largest collection in existence,' he wrote, without mentioning names. 'One of the best known authorities stated that we have at least sixteen times what New York has.' Currelly suggested the conditions for an arrangement:

> I should like you to deal with us in the following manner, if you will deal at all: sell us your things at what they cost you, and then charge us a fee for getting them, and another fee for packing them or having them packed. You will appreciate some time this position of a missionary not making profit but charging a fee ... Regarding your own collection, would it not be best to turn it right over to us by sale, with the understanding that you had all the rights in the use of it for scientific purposes? I think you would get

more satisfaction out of it as the Menzies Collection in Toronto than in any other way.[38]

It is quite clear that Currelly was not interested simply in Menzies's scholarship or his skill at detecting forgeries: Currelly was also interested in what he was already calling 'the Menzies Collection.'

James Menzies kept to his principles: *buzuo maimai*, 'no business.' He did not sell his collection to the ROM nor did he accept Currelly's offer to become its agent. Menzies's explanation was that his purpose as a collector was providential. He did not want to build a museum in Toronto. He needed the freedom to collect what he thought was significant, and for that purpose his collection must be with him *in China*. It was not until 1960 – when Menzies and Currelly were both dead and Bishop White retired – that the ROM finally acquired 'The Menzies Collection' from his widow and children. George Crofts sent spectacular objects and the Bishop White Collection material made the ROM a world-class museum; the Menzies Collection of Chinese archaeological artefacts (including 5000 oracle bones) made it unique.

The Ethics of Collectors

Though they decry the imperialist tactics of nineteenth- and early-twentieth-century collectors, Canadian apologists for the Royal Ontario Museum, and indeed most major museums throughout the world, seemed content with the standard line: Bishop White preserved artefacts that otherwise would have been destroyed in China's troubles. As Lewis Walmsley put it, with 'every new railway thrust across the North China plain, every new industrial enterprise near an old city, some ancient tomb or archaeological treasure was uncovered. Frequently these were ruthlessly despoiled, and their valuable contents destroyed, scattered, or sold, often for a pittance, on the black market.' This line of argument thus concludes that by keeping these perfect museum-quality specimens safe in Western museums, White (and others with similar methods) helped preserve a part of China's ancient civilization and, at the same time, made a great contribution to the West's understanding of Chinese culture.

As for the ethics and legalities, Walmsley skirted these issues: 'White's career as a museum collector had started and ended at precisely the right time in Chinese history ... He did succeed, after the laws restricting export had been passed, in shipping abroad a small quantity of material not included in the government classification of material permitted to pass customs, because of loose supervision. However, the great period for collecting in China was now at an end.'[39] It was not 'loose supervision' that enabled White to export prohibited artefacts after 1930; it was illegal manoeuvres.

Foreign museums and their agents in China, buying from the curio market or through direct contracts with grave robbers and stonecutters, faced clear-cut ethical issues. As Warren I. Cohen wrote, 'The dealer [acted] as "fence" for stolen goods, the collector as purchaser of goods known to be obtained illegally, as smuggler of objects a weak nation was trying to retain.'[40] This is definitely the case for Bishop White, no matter how little he understood these ethical issues. Legally and illegally, Bishop White sent thousands of artefacts, large and small, ancient and modern, to build a collection that would enable 'the average Canadian to gain a knowledge of the life of the Chinese people and to appreciate with understanding the story of their remarkable civilization – "to catch an intimate glimpse of the common life of China over a period of 4,000 years."'[41] A remarkable cause, but accomplished by the wrong means!

After the establishment of the People's Republic of China, Bishop White was denounced by Bishop Francis Tseng, his student and successor in Kaifeng, for using the cloak of religion to plunder China's treasures. Bishop Tseng accused Bishop White of growing rich by illegal profits. 'He had been a robber of graves and a robber of souls.'[42] Walmsley explicitly denied this charge: 'The bishop had received no commission from the museum and had made no profit. He had purchased most of the articles on an open market at current prices. Most Chinese officials at the time had had little interest in their nation's antiquities; they sought only profit from what to them were little more than useless objects.'[43] This statement is not quite true, and blaming corrupt officials does not help the bishop's case. As with other sensitive issues, Walmsley gave no evidence (the biography has no footnotes) to substantiate his statement.

Though it does not contradict Walmsley's conclusion, my research places White in a different light. White went to China as a poor missionary, but he retired a rich man. While he was collecting for the ROM, he was also collecting for himself, and we do not know how he distinguished between his public purchases and his private collection. Despite a general rule that prevents museum agents from making private deals, White did not hide his personal collection from the ROM. He sometimes packed his own things in a box of museum artefacts. For instance, he informed Miss Greenaway, the museum secretary: 'I have enclosed three or four of my personal articles, which are designated with a "W." Among these is a mirror, which I have not dared to include in the Museum list, for it was so costly. I paid M$2400 [Mexican] for it.'[44] After 1934 White sold parts of his personal collection to the ROM for $35,282 Canadian, to be 'payable in sums not less than $5,000.00 yearly, with interest at 5% per annum from January 1st, 1934.'[45] At that time this was a large sum of money.

James Menzies was also accused, though more mutedly, with stealing China's ancient treasures. How did he fare from an ethical point of view? It is true that on several occasions he did send some artefacts to Canada. In 1934 his wife Annie took her collection of Song ceramics back to Canada. He also asked friends to take things to Canada: 'I am sending with Miss Cleverley a large flowerpot or jardinière that I hope you will like. Inside it are a clay jug, a pottery glazed pillow stand and two plates ... [Y]ou may give one of the plates each to the girls on their birthdays.'[46] A year later, he wrote his wife: 'Those paintings I sent home, especially the fragment of a Tang Dynasty head are really good. They will need to be handled very carefully and should be mounted between two sheets of glass. The dates are between 700 and 900 AD. They came from Tun Huang [Dunhuang] and belonged to the private secretary of the governor of Kansu [Gansu]. Do not tell Mrs. Mitchell for I gave them no inkling what was in the parcel.'[47]

Unlike Bishop White, Menzies was sensitive to Chinese nationalism and the concerns of Chinese scholars for the preservation of their cultural heritage. If White collected for Canada, Menzies collected primarily for personal and academic benefit. A comparative study will highlight this point. On only two occasions did Menzies receive payment for parts of his collections, but the money was so small it would not have even covered his expenses. The first was for the potsherds he sent the ROM from France in 1918; the second was from Cheeloo University. While he was teaching archaeology there, he set up a study museum in the library, using artefacts to show different stages of Chinese history, including 259 fine articles from his personal collection.[48] Some were classified as 'first class national treasures.' In November 1937 the university authorities decided to transfer two special pottery wares from the museum to the university treasurer's safe to avoid attracting attention from the Japanese.[49] A year later, while Liu Shuming, the president of Cheeloo, was visiting the United States and Canada, he negotiated with Menzies to buy his artefacts that were on loan to the museum for $3000

Chinese, approximately $1050 Gold.[50] This was the largest amount Menzies ever personally received. After 1937 China was in constant warfare for over a decade. The collections that Menzies left in China were dispersed into several parts and taken over by the state after 1949. Menzies did not get a cent for them.[51] After Menzies's death in 1957, 85 per cent of the artefacts sent back to Toronto by the North Henan mission treasurer in 1948 from Tianjin on the eve of liberation were finally acquired by the ROM. All proceeds ($40,000) went to the Menzies Fund, administered by the University of Toronto to promote Chinese studies in Canada.[52]

Menzies remained a poor missionary from beginning to end. Before 1936 he spent much of his savings in collecting. After that date, he and his wife managed a simple life with occasional outside income from inherited properties. When he returned to Toronto in 1949, he had to borrow money from his children to buy a house.[53] He wrote to Arthur, then a rising diplomat in the Department of External Affairs, 'Everything is very expensive; so that I hesitated to order anything [books] ... The price of clothes is prohibitive. I have enough summer clothes even if they are not new. A pension of $780 with dues taken off does not go very far these days.'[54] Meanwhile, he was living among 'treasures,' having turned his little house at 62 Tilson Road into a miniature museum with Shang bronzes, oracle bones, and Song porcelains.

Menzies took upon himself what he considered his call from God to study ancient Chinese culture, especially ancient Chinese religion, for the evangelical cause in China. As his name became known in China as a scholar of oracle bones, he made friends with eminent Chinese scholars such as Rong Geng (old spelling Jung Keng), Ma Heng (old spelling Ma Hang), and Dong Zuobin (old spelling Tung Tso-pin), who were pushing the Nationalist government to protect the country's cultural antiquities. From his long professional association with these people, Menzies fully understood the suspicion and even hostility that Chinese scholars held towards foreign collectors. As a result, he made known that his collection was for scholarly purposes only and would remain in China. He once wrote White, 'I am foolish perhaps in keeping all my things here or moving them to Tsinan [Jinan]. But I want my things for study and proof purpose.'[55] Menzies did not regard himself as the owner of his collection, but merely the custodian of China's national treasure and monuments for the purpose of Christian missions. In other words, he collected in China, for China, and to that end he kept the bulk of his collection in China.

Chapter 11

Interlude, 1927–1928

The North China Union Language School

In the spring of 1927, as the Guomindang's Northern Expedition escalated tensions, the British consul general in Tianjin ordered the evacuation of all British nationals from the interior of China. The three Menzies
children – Marion, aged fourteen, Frances, twelve, and Arthur, ten –
were attending the school for missionaries' children at Weihui, some
seventy miles from Zhangde, where James and Annie were stationed.
Marion remembered the evacuation vividly. The children were taken to
the train station, where they waited for a day and a night, sleeping on
camp cots and surviving on porridge. When the train arrived, it was filled
with refugees and the only available place was a boxcar. Previously used
to carry horses, its floor was inches deep with manure. 'In shovelling the
manure we came across two hand grenades. Mr Flemming gingerly
picked them up one at a time and threw them out the sliding doorway.'
Their father James Menzies met them at the Zhangde station and took
them home, where they helped pack his library of books – 'we counted
5,000' – into the clothes closet. The next day they left Zhangde, and as
Marion recounted, 'I never returned to our home there.'[1] After 1930,
the three children attended the Canadian Academy at Kobe, Japan.

At Tianjin, the Menzies family was met by Hugh Mackenzie, the
mission's business officer, who took them to a barracks in the British
Concession already overcrowded with missionary refugees. With almost
a hundred missionaries, the North Henan mission was medium sized
compared with British and American missions, some of which had several hundred adults and children. Altogether, eight thousand missionaries evacuated from the interior and huddled behind the barbed wire of

the treaty ports. The NHM personnel were scattered. A skeleton staff remained in Tianjin ready to return to North Henan; some went to Korea or India; Dr Bob McClure went to help out in a Taiwan hospital. After spending the summer at Sea Breeze Cottage at Beidaihe, James Menzies moved to Beijing, where he obtained a part-time position lecturing at the North China Union Language School while he prepared his second volume on oracle bones.

This forced exile lasting until August 1930 provided unique opportunities. For over a decade, isolated in the interior, Menzies had been pursuing his studies in early Chinese culture and archaeology during his spare time. Most of his missionary colleagues viewed his 'hobby' as an irrelevant waste of a missionary's time. His stay in Beijing offered the first chance to meet and associate with Chinese academic colleagues. Menzies also had access to books on archaeology and ancient history in the city's university libraries. The exile gave him the time to prepare several studies for publication that he had written over the years. However, his busy but quiet life in Beijing was interrupted by a dispute over his status between the North Henan mission and the Board of Overseas Missions of the United Church of Canada.

The North China Union Language School (NCULS) was one of the few missionary-training institutes in China. When Protestant missionaries arrived in China during the nineteenth century, they knew almost nothing of its culture and language. They were expected to learn the language by osmosis, by living and working among the Chinese and working with an old-fashioned Chinese teacher. The NCULS was a joint enterprise established around 1910 by British and American Protestant missions in North China, the YMCA and YWCA, as well as the American and British legations, the British Chamber of Commerce, and the American Association of North China. Later, the China Medical Board funded by the Rockefeller Foundation also became a supporting organization. The school used the Direct Method, also known as the Phonetic Inductive Method, based on the Beijing dialect. Experienced Chinese teachers conducted most of the teaching. Besides language study, courses were also given in English on missionary methods and Chinese culture, including Ancient and Medieval Chinese History, China's Modern International Relations, the Chinese Government System, Chinese Philosophy, Educational Work in China, Social Conditions in China, the Chinese Point of View, and Work for Women and Girls in China.[2]

By 1920 NCULS had expanded into a large-scale language-training institute with twenty foreign and eighty Chinese teachers. There were

250 students registered, representing twenty-four mission societies, five legations, and twelve foreign business firms. As a joint venture, the school depended on the supporting societies to supply student fees and the salaries of the foreign teachers. For several years its requests for aid from the NHM had always met with polite refusal. The NHM already had financial and personnel commitments to the Christian Literature Society in Shanghai and to Cheeloo University in Jinan, and some members resented proposals for new commitments to interdenominational organizations. Such was the attitude of William Harvey Grant, the long-time clerk of the Presbytery and an influential senior evangelist, who wrote to the board in 1922 that '[s]ome seem to look upon this mission as the happy hunting-ground for workers.'[3]

The principal of the NCULS, William B. Pettus, was one of the best-known people in Beijing. He was attracted by Menzies's mastery of the Chinese language and his scholarly interests, and decided to make a direct appeal to the NHM to appoint Menzies to the school. Menzies was delighted by this recognition and welcomed the invitation. In fact, he had become increasingly dissatisfied with the narrowness of rural evangelism as he began mulling over just how to put his special knowledge of Chinese archaeology to better use. He sought a path uniting two objectives: training missionaries to have an open mind to Chinese culture, while also helping to educate a generation of capable Chinese church leaders.

In December 1927 Pettus went to Tianjin to discuss the matter with the NHM's executive committee. He emphasized that Menzies's appointment would benefit both the school and that Menzies would work

along the following lines:
1. To study archaeology and prepare for publication the results of his studies. 2. To give the results of his studies in courses of lectures both to elementary and to advanced students. 3. To conduct seminars and lead groups of students in the investigation of China's past, thus developing a larger group of missionaries and others able to do original work along these lines. 4. The long experience that Mr. & Mrs. Menzies have had in mission work fit them well for taking a part in introducing China to young missionaries who come to our school for their preparation.[4]

Menzies's interest in Chinese culture and archaeology was well known among the mission's supporters in Canada. Three years earlier, A.E. Armstrong, who became the assistant secretary of the Board of Overseas

Missions (BOM) of the United Church of Canada, had encouraged him to write a book on ancient Chinese culture. 'It was suggested that you collect material for a book that would add to knowledge concerning archaeology and other subjects. It might not be wise to issue it for a few years, but I hope you are storing up some material on which you can draw. In that connection, if you have time, I would like to hear from you as to whether you are following up the volume you did publish showing cuts of bones found in "the Waste of Yin."'[5] Initially, the BOM supported Menzies's assignment to NCULS, but the board changed its position under pressure from the NHM.

There were several factors behind the mission's opposition to Menzies's appointment to the NCULS, even though the exile from Henan meant that an exceptionally large number of North Henan missionaries were studying there at the moment. Foremost was money, for the mission was chronically in debt. 'The members of our Executive here are quite unanimous about this,' wrote Harvey Grant.[6]

Moreover, the NHM always had felt that language training in Beijing was of little use in Henan, since the local peasants could not understand the Beijing accent. That was why they continued to prefer language lessons with private Chinese teachers and senior missionaries with a strong Henan accent. 'Our Mission has already placed itself on record as believing that a period of six months is ample time for our students of the language to spend in the Language School' to lessen the danger of their acquiring a 'foreign' Beijing accent.[7]

Having raised these criticisms, the NHM attacked the school and its management. 'This dissatisfaction is not confined to the members of our Mission, but is felt by several Missions in North China,' Grant claimed.[8]

When the North Henan mission received the request from Principal Pettus, the committee asked Menzies how his teaching would contribute to the work of Christ in China. Menzies replied that he could do more at NCULS than in North Henan because of the school's role in 'fitting new missionaries for the field' by initiating them into a method of study and to the 'heritage of China.'

My work will be along four or five lines. (a) A share in the general lectures to students along a variety of lines, too numerous to mention: missionary methods, history, characteristics of the people, literature, art, language, proverbs, a library, etc. (b) The conducting of special courses for more serious students. This will include the fields in which I am best qualified: early history, the development of language, the original religion, early

Chinese culture, oracle bones, bronzes, archaeology, the root meanings of words, the Classics. (c) Linked up with both will be serious study leading to publication of papers, such as I have long longed for the opportunity to do. The completion of the program I laid down in the preface to my 'Oracle Records from the Waste of Yin' (1917). A dictionary of the earliest characters, a history of early man in China, his culture, language, and religion. (d) Some public lecturing. (e) Last but possibly most of all a general help to [the] missionary student.[9]

Neither Pettus's request nor Menzies's letter convinced the North Henan mission-in-exile, but it did accede to Menzies's temporary appointment in principle without any financial responsibilities: 'The Mission has been well aware for years past that Mr. Menzies desired an opportunity to pursue lines of work that his position in the Mission did not afford him and he is still cherishing this desire. His fellow missionaries desire to give him all the liberty possible in this connection and accordingly are recommending to the Board that he be permitted to accept the invitation of the Executive of the Language School. However, it cannot recommend the Board to assume responsibility for financial partnership in the Language school.'[10]

In January 1928, when Pettus's request arrived at the BOM in Toronto, A.E. Armstrong, always a supporter of Menzies's appointment, was not pleased with the negative comments from the field. He requested that 'the Mission amplify its opposition to our taking any financial responsibility for the Language School by giving us its reasons for dissatisfaction. I think personally the Board will not oppose Mr. Menzies taking up the work in the Language School.'[11] Further, Armstrong questioned the mission's traditional language training: 'It would seem to be an ideal method of teaching language to have new missionaries together with good teachers and good equipment rather than to have them with individual teachers in a Mission Station where there would not be the encouragement of a large group.'[12]

The following month, February 1928, Pettus visited Toronto during a tour of North America and met with the BOM. As Armstrong informed Grant, '[W]e are all the more of the opinion that the Mission should seriously consider, perhaps along with other Missions, making the School satisfactory rather than withdrawing from it. We think there is some responsibility resting upon us to co-operate in a Language School where our missionaries get their further equipment for service in the Field.'[13]

While waiting for information from China, the board matched Grant's comments by conducting a survey of North American missionary societies. The result was positive. Armstrong was confused. 'The information we gathered from other Boards does not tally with the sentiment you express regarding the present management, but I shall not make further comment upon it until the official statement arrives.' But, Armstrong indicated, the board felt 'that the information that has already come hardly warrants our refusing to pay Mr. Menzies' salary, if he is to be attached to the Language School staff.'[14]

Since James and Annie had served a full seven-year term in Henan, they were due for a furlough in 1928, and so the BOM decided to postpone its decision until he returned to Toronto. Struggling to complete his second book on oracle bones, Menzies was informed of the board's positive response and the mission's conditional support for his appointment. This led him to believe that indeed he would be appointed to the language school when he returned from furlough.

Around the World

Under the protection of the Manchurian warlord Zhang Zuolin, Beijing remained relatively immune from the fighting of the Northern Expedition (1926–8). However, pressure from the Japanese persuaded Zhang to abandon the capital and retreat back to Manchuria. On 2 June 1928 he left Beijing with his staff in a luxury railcar; two days later, he was killed as a bomb destroyed the railway car approaching Mukden. Beijing was peacefully occupied by the Shanxi warlord Yan Xishan on behalf of the Guomindang (GMD). Since the GMD power base was in Nanjing, Chiang Kai-shek transferred the national capital there, downgrading Beijing (old spelling Peking) from 'Northern Capital' to 'Northern Peace,' Beiping (old spelling Pei-p'ing).

It was a wonderful time to be in Beijing as the city relaxed after the threat of war. The Menzies children attended the Peking American School, which was open to children of many different backgrounds, foreigners, Eurasians, and Chinese. They also picked up 'a colourful smattering of Chinese swear words and expressions' from the rickshaw coolies. This was an enriching experience, Marion remembered, and prepared the children for the next school year in Canada. With his interest in history, James Menzies took the children to the famous temples and historic sites of Beijing, including the Summer Palace and the Great Wall, where he would delight them with stories that he told in a way they could understand.

The Forbidden City had remained in the hands of the former Qing emperor Puyi until 1924, and had just been opened to the public as a historical museum; James took them there several times. Picking over a pile of rubble near the Altar of Heaven, James – ever a collector of broken things – took a few pieces of dark blue glass tubes that had once formed a screen, and later had them made into brooches for the girls. He also found a couple of glazed roof-tile ends with dragons in relief.[15]

In the fall of 1928, James asked the children, 'How would you like something that no-one can ever take away from you?' This, Marion wrote, 'was the way he introduced us to the idea of taking a trip around the world. We were very proud of our father. We knew some of his weaknesses, but we loved him and he loved us.' The idea had originated when James had experienced the looted compound in Zhangde after the Northern Expedition. He wrote to his parents that he had been a 'fool' to invest his money in houses and collections that could be destroyed by China's undisciplined soldiers. In contrast, 'knowledge gained from education and travel could not be taken away.'[16] His elderly parents were sympathetic, and sent a large cheque for $5000 to cover the additional expenses.

On 23 November 1928 James and Annie Menzies and the three children left Beijing for Tianjin, where they boarded a German ship, the S.S. *Coblenz*. Shen Dasao, who had been with them for fifteen years as a member of the family, stayed behind since the children were grown. In Hong Kong, Annie felt 'like Alice in wonderland,' and told her parents that she had 'behaved something like Shen Tasao did when Lucy took her to her first movie.' They sailed south to Manila, where the lush grass was 'so thick and lovely. You do not know how we get starved in Honan for a bit of green grass.'[17] From Singapore they took the train through the Malay States, 'miles and miles of rubber trees and rice fields,' to Penang and on by boat to Rangoon, Burma. They spent two months in India, sightseeing from Calcutta to Darjeeling, including Agra, where they saw the Taj Mahal by moonlight. James was fascinated by Buddhism and its transfer from India to China, and so he took them on a pilgrimage to Bodh Gaya, where the historic Buddha had attained enlightenment. After leaving India, they zigzagged up the Persian Gulf, stopping at a dozen ports, and on Easter Sunday they arrived at Basra in the country then known as Mesopotamia, a British protectorate now known as Iraq.

Since the children were out of school, James and Annie insisted that they keep a diary about the places they visited. Marion, aged fifteen, dutifully kept a daily record as far as Damascus, where she ran out of steam. The trip was such a momentous event in her life that, seventy years later, she devoted fifty pages to it in her memoirs. Looking back, two things stood out. Almost every stop they made was part of the British Empire, from Singapore, Malaya, and Burma to India, Mesopotamia, Palestine, Egypt, and Cyprus. 'Another feature of the period was the extent and the strength of the missionary movement ... As a missionary family we were welcomed by the missionary communities, put up at minimum cost and given the missionary perspective on the local scene. In exchange, Father and Mother talked about their missionary experience in China.'[18] In Delhi he was invited to address the Missionary Association.[19]

James Menzies himself wrote nothing about the trip, and yet his voice comes through in the children's diaries: didactic, precise, highly visual, filled with vivid historical stories. Typical is Marion's description of Ur of the Chaldees, just being excavated by Sir Charles Leonard Woolley. This was the birthplace of the Bible's Abraham about 3000 BCE. Among the spectacular discoveries was the so-called 'ram in the thicket,' a gold and ivory statuette that seemed to confirm the account in Genesis 22:13. 'It was [a] brick dome covering a large pot four feet deep which held the body and was set into the ground. Then we saw the courtyard where the recent finds had been made of the 74 women victims with the 4 harps and their many gold jewellery. Then we saw many other excavations ... Not far away in front of us was Ur Junction and the rest house and the R.A.F. tents. All the rest was desert sands except for a few men carrying bundles and some goats.' Ever the collector, picking through the excavation's 'discards,' James found some old pottery figures, and the guide gave Annie a little pot as a souvenir.[20]

At every place, James Menzies would seek out the local experts, the missionaries, museum directors, archaeologists, and native teachers who knew the ancient local history. He would share his interests in Shang archaeology and learn from them about the ancient peoples and religions that had flourished there. In particular, he wanted to comprehend the chronology of the Bronze Age to gain an international perspective for his own studies. In the Middle East, he planned their route to include every archaeological dig at Baghdad, Babylon, Damascus, and Baalbek.

The Holy Land was their principal destination. James had written ahead a long time before to reserve accommodation at the English mission in Nazareth, where they stayed for two weeks. 'This gave us time

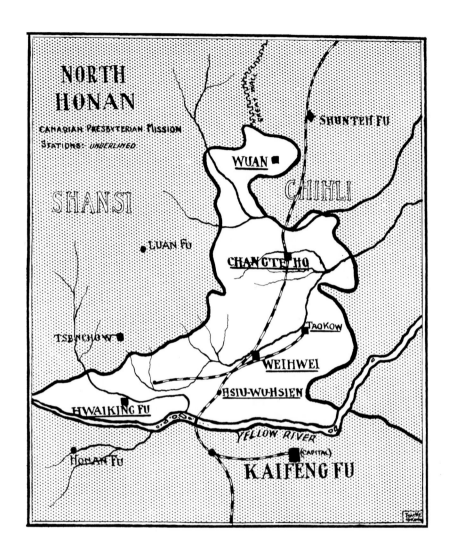

A map of the Canadian Presbyterian mission in North Honan (Henan), originally published in Murdoch Mackenzie's *Twenty-Five Years in Honan* (1912). The
Menzies were stationed at Wuan for language studies 1910–13, and then transferred to Changte (Zhangde, now called Anyang).

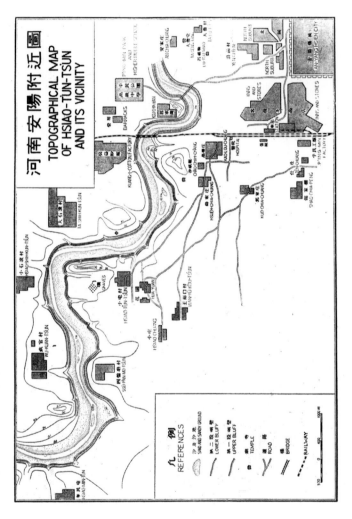

Map of Changte/Anyang drawn by James Menzies. The Canadian mission was located in the north suburbs of the walled city (southeast corner). The Waste of Yin was located near Hsiao-t'un (Xiaotun), 'the Little Village' (top of map), south of the bend in the Huan River. A modified version of this map, minus the Chinese characters, appears in Bishop William Charles White's *Bronze Culture of Ancient China*.

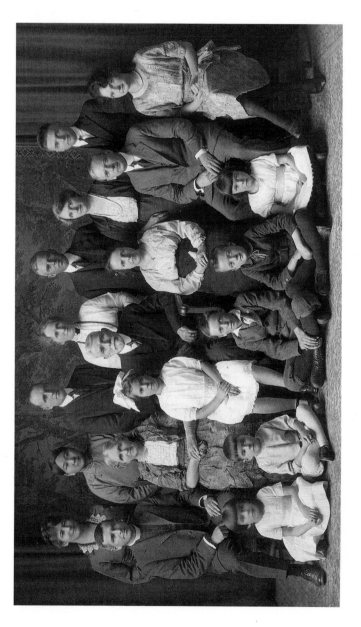

Three generations of the Menzies family at a reunion in Edmonton in 1921, just before James and Annie Belle Menzies returned to China for their second term. Annie Menzies, Shen Dasao, and Jack Judge are in the back row. James Mellon Menzies is seated at left in the middle row, beside his parents, Jane and David, who have James's daughter Marion between them. James's sister, Margaret Judge, is seated beside her father. Frances and Arthur are in the front row left.

James Menzies, the student activist. The Student Volunteer Movement conference, such as this one at Niagara-on-the-Lake in 1908, inspired his dedication to foreign missions, with a sense of student fun. James Menzies, John Thompson, and George Bryce.

In 1910 James Menzies attended the Edinburgh Missionary Conference with his sister Margaret. Afterwards, they visited relatives in Ireland, where this photograph was taken on 22 July 1910.

James Menzies, the bachelor missionary in his study at Wuan in 1911, when he first arrived in North Henan. The collegiate air of the room, with its tennis racquet and framed pictures, was typical of missionary residences in inland China.

Bishop William Charles White with the first members of the Anglican mission in Kaifeng, Henan, 1910. From the back row: Bishop White and Canon G.E. Simmons; Mrs Jones, Mrs White, Mrs Simmons; Annie Belle Sedgewick (white blouse) and Miss Robins; Maude Sedgwick, Annie's sister. Bishop White graciously allowed Annie to marry James Menzies and join the Presbyterians north of the Yellow River.

James and Annie's wedding in Kaifeng, 8 February 1911. Annie's sister Maude was the maid of honour and Canon Simmons the best man.

Staff Captain James Menzies of the Chinese Labour Corps. He joined the CLC in 1917, just before his book *Oracle Records from the Waste of Yin* was published, and remained 'somewhere in France' until he was demobilized in 1920.

The faithful amah, Shen, Shen Dasao (literally, Mrs Shen), was an 'uneducated, bound-foot woman who had a native capacity to learn and adapt.' She remained with the Menzies family from 1912 until 1936. When James went to France with the CLC, Shen Dasao accompanied Annie and the children, Marion, Frances, and Arthur, to Canada, where she learned to speak English without an accent. This photograph was taken in 1919 at the family farm near Windsor.

Frances, Marion, and Arthur Menzies ride donkeys in front of their house at Zhangde in 1923.

In 1912 James Menzies purchased a small cottage at Rocky Point, in the foreign resort at Beidaihe. He enlarged it, adding a tower, verandahs, and a circular stone wall. Hai Feng Lou (Sea Breeze Cottage) became a prominent landmark for ships at sea. The children's fondest memories of China were the summers spent at Beidaihe.

Frances, Arthur, James, Annie, and Marion Menzies at the ruins of Capernaum. In 1929, James Menzies took his family on an around-the-world trip to visit archaeological sites in India and the Middle East. He was hired by an American dig near Jerusalem as a field surveyor, which gave him experience in scientific archaeology.

The Waste of Yin, the site of the ancient capital of the Shang dynasty (1400–1040 BCE), much as it appeared when James Menzies first saw it in 1914. It was located a short walk from his station in Zhangde. Menzies was the first scholar to visit the site and collect fragments of oracle bones. This photograph, taken in 1935, shows Arthur (seated), then aged 18, at the bend in the river.

Starting in 1928, the Waste of Yin, or Anyang, was excavated by the Academia Sinica under the direction of Li Chi, a prominent archaeologist, until excavations were halted by the Japanese invasion in 1937. This photograph may depict the spring of the 1931 season, when the entire site was 'carpet-rolled' down to the mud-brick foundations. The trio in front seem to be a Chinese scholar and a missionary couple, who resemble James and Annie Menzies themselves.

After the Academia Sinica completed their excavations at Anyang, they covered the site to prevent erosion of the fragile mud-brick structures. This photograph, taken in 1935, shows Arthur Menzies (left), Bill Roulston, and a Chinese driver standing in the corn field that had been planted over the tomb of a Shang king.

James Menzies beside a prehistoric dolmen in Shandong province, 1935. He conducted archaeological investigations of neolithic and Bronze Age sites while teaching archaeology at Cheeloo University from 1932 to 1936.

In 1935, when Arthur was 18, James Menzies took him to visit the historic sites of North China. While climbing Mount Tai, the sacred mountain, James experienced muscle spasms and had to be carried down in a sedan chair. For this photo, the bearers stepped aside to let Paul Rumball, a teacher at the Canadian Academy in Kobe, and Arthur pose.

James Menzies taught archaeology at Cheeloo University in Shandong in the mid-1930s. He created the archaeological museum from his own collections of oracle bones and other ancient artefacts (although the skeleton suspended from the ceiling was not part of Menzies's collection). During the Anti-Japanese War, 140 boxes of artefacts were buried on the Cheeloo campus. This one collection, now in the Shandong Provincial Museum, consists of 29,457 archaeological specimens, including 8080 oracle bones and 8000 bronze vessels.

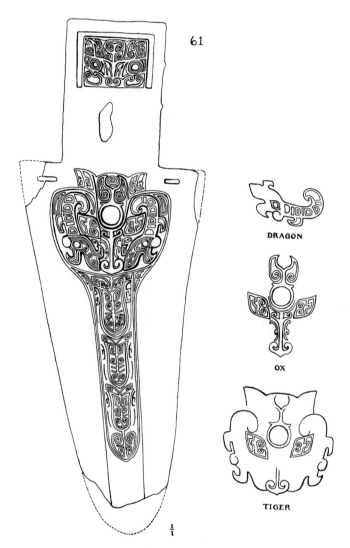

With his training in engineering drawing, James Menzies became skilled at deciphering the complicated ideographs on the oracle bones and intricate designs, such as this bronze *ge* (*ko*), sometimes called a 'halbert.' His doctoral dissertation *Shang Ko* (1942) was a monumental study of the characteristic weapon of the Bronze Age in China, 1311–1039 BCE. This drawing of a Bronze Ko with 2 Lashing Slots was published without credit in Bishop White's book, *Bone Culture of Ancient China* (1945).

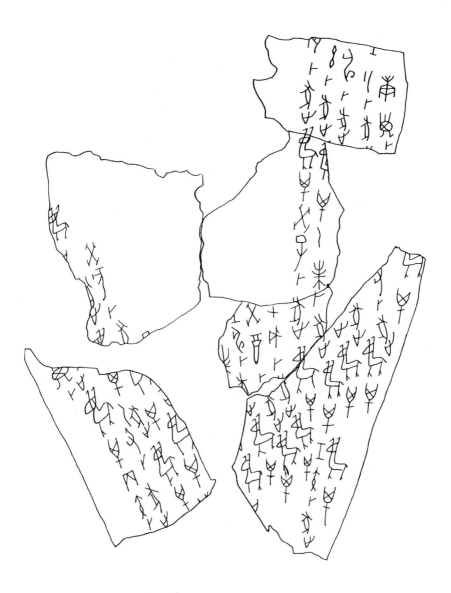

James Menzies became an expert at matching fragments of oracle bones that had been broken and dispersed into several collections. This drawing shows how one bone was reconstructed from six different pieces. The scratches are the oldest form of Chinese writing, and consist of divinations to the supreme deity, Shangdi, 'the Lord on High.'

James and Annie Menzies and their grandchildren, 1953: Norah (left) and Kenneth (third from left), children of Arthur and Shelia Menzies, and Patricia and Gordon, children of Frances and Ervin Newcombe.

James and Annie Menzies in Toronto in 1952, still in love after forty years of marriage. He died on 16 March 1957; she died five years later.

All of James and Annie Menzies's children retained an active interest in China. After graduating in social work, Marion returned to China to aid in the post-war reconstruction under the United Nations Relief and Rehabilitation Administration. This photograph was taken in April 1948 at the end of a trip with Marion Stanley into the Communist Liberated Areas in North China. The translator Han Xu (top left) was later Chinese ambassador to the United States.

Arthur Menzies joined the Department of External Affairs in 1940, and then completed the general exams for a PhD in Far Eastern History from Harvard University. In 1946 he was appointed head of the Far Eastern Section, where he remained until 1950, and was thus involved with the intricacies of Canada's policy during the Chinese revolution. From 1976 to 1980, he capped a long and distinguished career by serving as the Canadian ambassador to the People's Republic of China.

to familiarize ourselves with the town and its old-fashioned tradespeople ... We just got there in time. The flowers were out. The whole hillsides were covered.'[21]

They stayed for a month in Jerusalem at the Suisse Pension Almazie. James took the children to the sites mentioned in the Bible and explained their significance from a large red book, *Peakes Commentary on the Bible*. 'He made it come alive to us so that I carried that feeling all through my life – the feeling that I had walked on sacred ground.' During their stay, James learned about an excavation conducted by the American School of Oriental Studies, whose field surveyor had fallen sick. 'Father, who was a qualified civil engineer and Dominion Land Surveyor, was asked if he would agree to replace him. Father thought this offer would give him real "hands on" experience in the excavation of an archaeological site in company with professionals who had experience and the latest technology. So he signed on for four months.'[22]

While Menzies was learning archaeological fieldwork, Annie Menzies and the children continued their world tour, planning to arrive in Edmonton in time for the school year in September. They left Jerusalem at the beginning of June and visited Egypt, where they boarded a ship that took them to Lebanon, Syria, Cyprus, and on to Istanbul. Even though James was not with them, they visited archaeological sites along the route. After a stop at Athens, they continued leisurely through Italy for two weeks and then took the train to Paris. They had the special excitement of flying over the English Channel in a small twin-engine plane, which cost 500 francs each. In London they stayed with their mother's Sedgwick cousins. They had left Beijing in November; nine months later, on 30 August 1929, Annie and the children arrived in Edmonton.

Looking back, Marion wrote, 'It is evident that all three of us children lost a year of schooling during the academic year 1928–29. This put us all a year behind our contemporaries, say, at the Canadian Academy in Kobe, Japan. However, we were privileged, under the guidance of a father, interested in world archaeology, and Biblical historiography, to get a real feel for what we saw and to record and express ourselves about our experiences in our diaries ... But in residue, this world-wide experience and exposure gave each of us a strong personal memory of widely different historical cultures, yet a sense that all these regional, cultural, and religious differences could be pulled together in a modernized and caring world order.'[23]

Archaeology as Mission?

There was a happy family reunion when Annie and the children reached Edmonton. James's sister, Margaret Judge, lived there with her husband, Uncle Jack, an engineer who had been James Menzies's fellow student at the University of Toronto and was now in charge of road building for the Alberta government. He was a warm-hearted and affectionate uncle. Annie and the children moved in with grandfather David Menzies, now aged ninety-two, and grandmother Jane, aged eighty. David was 'a bright, alert, erect man with white hair and a trimmed beard, and such a kindly face.' He was pleased to see his grandchildren again and asked many questions about their world tour. Sadly, the happy reunion lasted only two weeks. David broke his leg in a fall and died of a blood clot. His last words to Marion were 'What are the boundaries of the Levant?'[24]

James was recalled to Canada and left Palestine as soon as he could leave the archaeological excavation. W.F. Badè (1871–1936), the head of the dig at Beth Shamesh, was so impressed that he asked the Board of Overseas Missions to loan Menzies to the dig for a year, but the BOM naturally turned him down.[25] James did not arrive in Edmonton until October, three weeks after the funeral of his father.

A rude shock awaited him when he stopped at Toronto to pay a visit to the Board of Overseas Missions. Unintentionally, it seems, the board had misled him, raising false hopes that he would be appointed to the North China Union Language School after his furlough. According to Hugh Mackenzie, the mission treasurer in Tianjin, 'The conclusion that I came to from seeing the correspondence that passed between the Board and the Mission, was that the Board seemed quite ready to take on this added responsibility.'[26] Unfortunately, the board changed its position under pressure from North Henan. A.E. Armstrong informed Mackenzie that the board had 'simply [been] courteous to Principal Pettus,' but at no time did they contemplate 'paying Mr. Menzies' salary, should he go to the Language School.'[27]

In December 1927 the mission had raised objections to the possible secondment of Menzies to the NCULS, disliking particularly any new financial responsibility. Harvey Grant had never raised any objections to Menzies's scholarly studies in archaeology, but considering the mission's conservatism, this may have been a hidden reason. It came into the open in November 1929 when the BOM reviewed the situation: 'In view of our objection to additional expense ... and in view of our difficulty in recognizing archaeology as definite Mission work, we request the Sub-

Executive to endeavour to hold Mr. Menzies for our Mission work in Honan.'[28] Some members of the board 'could not concede that archaeology could be interpreted at all as missionary work.'

A.E. Armstrong conveyed the decision to Menzies: 'therefore that we are not warranted in making a grant from the funds which the people give us for missionary work to enable a man, however devoted a missionary he may be, to spend his time in archaeology.'[29] The mission did not officially oppose Menzies's appointment to Beijing on the grounds of archaeology; rather they refused to make a financial contribution. The board could not endorse archaeology as mission work and refused to act against the mission's will. At this same meeting, the board asked him to return to China within a month since he had spent almost a year in his round-the-world tour, which, some suggested, he had taken with a view of leaving the service of the NHM.

James Menzies, a quiet thoughtful man, was deeply hurt. He felt betrayed by his colleagues in North Henan and his supporters in Toronto. He did not usually put his deepest thoughts into writing, but to defend himself he wrote several long letters to Armstrong and the BOM. These letters, a rare outburst of emotion, clarified his life and mission with passion. They are worth quoting at length.

His colleagues did not understand the importance of his 'hobby' of archaeology, Menzies felt, and therefore did not recognize his value as an evangelistic missionary. 'Except the time spent in YMCA work in Kaifeng and as Secretary of the Forward Evangelistic Movement in Honan, I have been doing mission work that had to be done but which was not the kind of work I would have chosen for myself, nor for which I was best fitted, either by training or natural aptitude.'

In other words, he had been engaged in work among the illiterate peasants when he would rather have been working among the students and intellectuals of the New China. Nevertheless he had given his best: 'To the carrying out of these tasks I have given no half-hearted endeavour nor have I been unsuccessful in the judgement of the Chinese church or of my fellow missionaries. I have never counted the number of Christians I have baptized but I should not be ashamed if they were counted. I have had more than my share to do with the organization of the Chinese Church and the Board of Education in North Honan ... What more do you want? Is not that task enough for any man? Yes, it is and more.'[30]

As to spending his furlough on personal interests, Menzies called Armstrong's statement

[a] gross misinterpretation of the motives. I was not holidaying ... I was working for what I believe to be the extension of the Kingdom of God in China. It was for this reason that I decided to return via the mission fields in India, Mesopotamia and Palestine. If I am to have any share in the training of missionaries or in the larger missionary outlook of the work, I wanted to know how the rest of the world were progressing and what lessons they had to teach us in China where all missions seem to be in the same disorganized chaos. Added to this general outlook was my particular interest in original cultural foundations in the countries where mission work is seeking to erect a Christian Church and the newer archaeological methods of determining what these cultural foundations are. This I knew could not be learned in any postgraduate school, but must be learned on the ground. It was therefore in preparation for the work I presumed would be mine in the future, a work which would link my Chinese research work more closely with the work of missions to the Chinese.[31]

Menzies defended his interest in archaeology with thoughtful arguments. The seventeenth-century Jesuits had won converts by science and technology, and among modern Protestant missionaries, few had done greater service than 'Robert Morrison who spent so much time on his dictionary, James Legge who spent so much on his translation of the Classics, S. Wells Williams on his dictionary, W.A.P. Martin in the Imperial University, and with due deference to our own Dr. [Donald] MacGillivray's work in the Christian Literature Society.'[32]

'What conception does the Chinese mind have of the Gospel we preached?' he asked. 'Some things that to us are the logical outcome of our teaching do not seem to follow for them at all. Now part of the blank wall of impasses which has arisen is just here ... What do they understand when we speak of God? It is certainly not exactly what we understand when we say God. What of Salvation, Eternal Life, or belief in Jesus or any other term we choose. There is a great gulf there that has not been bridged.'[33] This cultural gulf could only be bridged by efforts on both sides. 'It will not be solved satisfactorily only by Chinese coming to the West and studying in our universities and theological colleges. Some of us have got to cross the bridge from our side and school ourselves in Chinese thought and ideas, so that we know something of the soul and mind of China as well as the outside form.'[34]

In December 1929, while the BOM was debating the legitimacy of archaeology, Menzies was invited to give a speech to the Archaeological Institute of America at its annual meeting in New York. He entitled it

'Archaeological Significance of the Oracle Records from the Waste of Yin, China.' Impressed by his presentation, the Harvard-Yenching Institute asked Menzies to put his observations into a proposal to excavate the Waste of Yin.[35] George H. Chase, the dean of the Harvard School of Graduate Studies, invited Menzies to spend a year at Harvard to study field archaeology in order that he could lead the proposed expedition. John Leighton Stuart, the president of Yenching University in Beijing, offered him a scholarship to complete and publish his studies.[36]

For Menzies, these offers were precious opportunities. Either could have made his life different. Yet, bound by his loyalty to the mission, he was not ready to accept a 'pure academic' position. He wrote Armstrong: 'Personally I am only interested in archaeology as a means to an end not an end in itself and while the Harvard-Yenching Institute is linked with a Christian university, I would be expected to put in all my time on definitely and purely scientific work. This to me is just as much a dilemma as the other and I am not prepared for it.'[37]

Menzies's most eloquent statement of his life's purpose was a speech he gave when he was summoned to attend the Board of Overseas Missions in April 1930. He emphasized the urgency of the task of evangelization. 'The great tendency of the educated Chinese today is to look down on religion and missionaries as relics of a bygone age, a hang over from a superstitious age. As one of my parishioners wrote to his wife, "All religions are superstition, but if you must have a religion, then keep on attending the Christian Church. It is a high-class superstition."'[38] This anti-religious attitude did not just influence the intellectuals. 'If it were only the educated that were affected, we would not need to care. But in China where education is reverenced, the whole mass of the people follows wherever their educated leaders lead them. In our ordinary preaching we feel this dead wall of opposition, the opposition of a conservative past, but more than that, now the opposition of the modern anti-God atheism, which fits hand and glove into their old agnosticism of Confucius and is far worse than any heathen religion.'[39]

A knowledge of Chinese culture could give missionaries the means to convey the gospel message in a way that the Chinese could understand, but it would also equip them with the most efficient weapon to combat the anti-religious and anti-Christian tendency of the educated Chinese. Menzies argued that the best way to inculcate Christianity in modern nationalist China was to refute the intellectuals' assertion (by such as the philosopher Feng Youlan and the author Hu Shi)[40] that the Chinese were a philosophical and not a religious people.

By going back to ancient Chinese history, Menzies had discovered the name of 'God' on Shang oracle bones: *Shangdi*, the same name as the Protestants used to translate 'Jehovah, God Almighty.' He felt that the concept of *Shangdi* showed that the Shang people had been 'god-worshippers,' countering the argument that the Chinese had never worshipped a monotheistic God. Menzies was not the first to make this connection, for it goes back to the Jesuits, who were troubled by the contradictions between the biblical chronology of early human history asserting that the universe was created in 4004 BCE and Chinese mythology. Without any evidence, the Jesuits sought to reconcile the issue by arguing that before Confucianism 'perverted' the ancient Chinese religion, the Shang Chinese had worshipped a monotheistic 'God' who bore a strong resemblance to the Hebrew Jehovah.[41]

Not content with explaining his archaeological interest, Menzies gave the BOM a lesson in Chinese religious history:

> For sixteen years now I have been attacking this problem from an angle that has not been undertaken by any other missionary or Chinese Christian. In 1914, I discovered the ancient capital of China, 1400 B.C. and there the oracle bones which are the turtle shells and bones used to inquire of God through the medium of their ancestors. The results of the study of these religious documents, of which there are thousands, are startling for missionary work. I cannot do more than to say that in the earliest time of which we have record, the Chinese believed in a personal spiritual being called *Shangti* [*Shangdi*] or God. The idea of Heaven as God does not appear on the bones and this impersonal idea of Confucius' time came into being only with the Chou [Zhou] dynasty in 1000 B.C. and was amplified as the dynasty went on. The great moral factor God of the earlier religious life had been largely set aside. They introduced manufactured heroes called Yao, Yu and Hsun who are never mentioned on the Bones. Now Sir, you may not realize that this all cuts right at the root of such teachings of modern Chinese scholars who would say that the Chinese are not religious and have never believed in God. It is not true.[42]

Finally, Menzies explained that his collection of oracle bones was not merely an academic hobby. He felt called by God to use his special skill and knowledge to serve His cause in China. The study of these bones 'has in the last fifteen years carried me into the heart of the great literature of the Chinese people. It has been a study which the Chinese recognize as peculiarly Chinese. It has given me contacts with some of the greatest Chinese scholars and I believe, has given me a peep into the soul and mind of China ... This is what has been called Archaeology. No doubt to your committee this archaeology seemed divorced from Mission work, but to me the crossing of the great gulf of misunderstanding between the Christian world and the Chinese people is the most important task that faces the missionary forces in China.'[43]

The Board of Overseas Missions was so impressed by Menzies's speech that it revoked its earlier decision. Armstrong informed the North Henan mission that 'Menzies made an impassioned statement to the Board which reversed the attitude expressed in the action of the Executive last autumn, and expressed sympathy with the idea that a missionary is making a valuable contribution to the cause of Christianity when spending part of his time in special research such as Mr. Menzies has been engaged in. The Board decided to ask Menzies to return to Honan for regular work under the direction of the Council with the understanding that he continue his research studies, leaving it to him as a matter of conscience to see that it does not interfere with his evangelistic work.'[44]

This compromise ended the immediate crisis of the North China Union Language School, but left no one satisfied. The North Henan mission accepted the decision reluctantly. As for Menzies, he no longer thought that rural evangelism was the best way for him to serve the missionary enterprise. His mission was to build a new basis of accommodation for the missionary enterprise using scientific methods and archaeological discoveries. This new mission work will be taken up in the following chapters.

Chapter 12

Marking Time, 1930–1931

Zhangde Revisited

Four months after his impassioned plea for the recognition of his unique scholarly gifts, James and Annie Menzies left Edmonton with the children and turned their faces to an uncertain future. James's migraine headaches were getting worse.

Sailing through the Inland Sea of Japan, they stopped at Kobe to drop the children at the Canadian Academy, a school sponsored by a number of missionary societies, including the United Church of Canada, and representatives of the English-speaking business community. The school was run according to the Ontario Department of Education curriculum with qualified Canadian teachers. Entering Form Four (Grade 12), Marion, aged seventeen, was a plump young woman with her mother's sunny disposition but a mediocre student. Frances was fifteen and Arthur, with the same stocky build as his father, at thirteen was just entering high school. The Canadian Academy attracted children of all denominations from all over East Asia. Marion recalled that 'some students were part Scandinavian and part English or Japanese. One could not live in a dormitory and attend classes without a growing sense of being of one family – being enriched by our multiple heritages and cultures ... During my two years there our parents encouraged us to be involved in sight-seeing trips, to attend concerts given by visiting international celebrities such as Fritz Kreizler [*sic*], Efraim Zimbalist, and Renée Chemet.'[1]

James and Annie continued on to Tianjin, where they were welcomed by their old friend Hugh Mackenzie, the mission treasurer. James was bitterly disappointed by the board's decision to turn down the North China Union Language School offer, but Mackenzie warned him that some of the NHM old-timers could not accept even the compromise BFM decision. Now, after a three-and-a-half-year absence, what would going 'home' to Zhangde mean?

The North Henan mission was in disarray: twenty out of the ninety-six missionaries evacuated in 1927 had left the field permanently. The decline in missionary numbers coincided with a Depression-caused drop in contributions to foreign missions in Canada. Mission field programs opened in the optimistic years had to be closed or curtailed, including both evangelistic campaigns and secular work such as that in schools and hospitals. The new Chinese government regulations stated that recognized mission schools could not teach Christianity even outside school hours, causing some missionaries to feel that mission schools were no longer evangelistic agencies. Each mission-supported school from kindergartens to universities had to decide whether to hobble along as a second-rate non-accredited institution for training Christians only or to try to attract a higher-class, non-Christian segment of the population by foregoing overt proselytizing. In addition, the Chinese church in North Henan was demanding an increasingly larger share in making decisions concerning money and the allocation of missionaries.

When James and Annie arrived at Zhangde, they found their house was in much the same condition as in July 1928, when he had visited during the evacuation. He had retrieved the vandalized books and archaeological fragments from the ashes, but the house was ruined and the furniture destroyed. It had been unoccupied for three years and the accumulation of broken plaster and wind-blown sand added a further forlorn touch. It was a sad beginning to a supposedly revitalized missionary effort.

Except for his 'special studies,' which occupied more and more of his time, the year in Zhangde seemed like a waste. Menzies threw himself into the familiar rural evangelism and was active in rural reconstruction programs initiated by the Chinese churches. He tried in good conscience, as the BOM had asked, but his heart was not in it. Zhangde was a small city in the interior that lacked a culture of learning: there was no well-equipped library, no learned society. The few scholars were products of the traditional examination system, and in fact most were failed candidates, familiar with the Confucian classics but ignorant of archaeology.

James Menzies was not a letter writer. Throughout their married life, Annie took the responsibility for communicating with family and friends, writing loving, instructive letters. James's letters were special, such as one he wrote on Christmas Day 1930 to the children at Kobe. It captures the contrast between his rural congregation and his intellectual interest in archaeology and shows how he tried to bring the two together. As he told the peasants the story of the birth of Jesus, he described the long winter journey that Mary and Joseph took from Nazareth to Bethlehem, just as he and his family had travelled that road himself the year before. 'How the wind would be cold and how no one had any winter clothes like the people in China or Canada,' he told them in the universal language of weather. Retelling the story to his own children, James reminded them of the time they had spent at Nazareth, Jerusalem and other sites mentioned in the scriptures, and closed with paternal gratitude that Frances and Arthur had decided to join the church. 'Mother and I have been thinking about it for a long time but we wanted you to do it of your own free will because Jesus calls you and because you hear his voice. Just like the sheep in Palestine follow the shepherds and each day you must listen to his voice.'[2] Also evident was his longing to share his research with scholars of his own calibre.

Previous chapters have discussed the transformation of James Menzies from a rural evangelist to a missionary collector. This chapter initiates an examination of his re-education as an archaeologist. This process was exceedingly slow: it took almost two decades before he was recognized as a scholar. Although it is now difficult to trace this process, several distinctive features should be noted nonetheless.

The Skule of Practical Archaeology

In Canada James Menzies was recognized as an archaeologist and the 'discoverer' of the Waste of Yin, whereas in China he was considered a collector of oracle bones and scholar of that most arcane study which Chinese scholars call *jue xue*, a subject few can master.[3] Chapter 10 examined the unusual efforts Menzies made in collecting artefacts with limited resources. But collecting was only the first step. To Menzies and other archaeologists, the objects were merely tools to study ancient Chinese religion and culture. The next step was to understand 'what the turtle said,' to comprehend the ideas that the Shang people conveyed in those primitive chicken scratches to the all-powerful god *Shangdi*.

Menzies's training as an engineer and a theologian did not prepare him for this cultural aspect. As soon as they were discovered in 1899, oracle inscriptions became a highly specialized academic discipline. To be competent in this field, he needed not only fluency in reading ancient Chinese (quite different from the modern, spoken colloquial).

He also needed a sound foundation in the Chinese Classics and a knowledge of epigraphy (the development of ideographs,) a sophisticated discipline developing since the Song dynasty (960–1279 CE). By the 1920s oracle studies had expanded from palaeographic study of inscriptions to include oracle-bone periodization, forgery identification, reconstruction of fragments, and Shang-Yin history and culture, with scientific information from oracle inscriptions cross-referenced with the historical records.[4] These skills were not easy for erudite Chinese scholars and posed a huge obstacle for a foreigner.

Menzies's earlier Western education helped somewhat. The personal discipline developed during his early studies in ancient Hebrew, Greek, and Latin at Knox College sustained him during the four years studying Chinese in North Henan, but those language studies also turned his mind to linguistics and the art of deciphering archaic inscriptions. The School of Practical Science had trained his eyes to see and his hands to draw. Those hours spent 'practising' engineering drawing, with their precise measurements and three-dimensional perspectives, paid off in his thousands of drawings of oracle-bone inscriptions. His summers as an apprentice Dominion land surveyor in the Canadian bush had taught him how to identify what lay under the ground, the substrata below the surface. In his re-education as an archaeologist, he was putting into 'practice' the 'practical' lessons he had learned at 'Skule.'

Menzies started to draw as soon as he found his first dragon bone at the Waste of Yin. Like other collectors, he tried ink rubbing, a delicate process that needs special dexterity, which at this point Menzies had not yet acquired. As a skilled draftsman, he copied the inscriptions on paper. This was difficult, for he could not yet understand the characters. As he explained candidly in the preface to *Oracle Records from the Waste of Yin* (1917): 'The drawings were made as the pieces were secured, and in his ignorance some were drawn upside down and some sideways, while scratches not belonging to the characters were also reproduced. As gradual increase in accuracy came, disgust with former blunders caused him after a year and a half to place the whole collection in his chests and begin anew, with the result that after three entire corrections of the manuscript and many corrections of the proof from a fresh comparison with the objects themselves, the present volume is presented to the public.'[5]

Menzies made the 2369 drawings for *Oracle Records* during his first two years at Zhangde, from 1914 to 1916. The Kaifeng Commercial Press initially refused to undertake the work because of its difficulty and the low profit. They did agree, however, to print the pages if Menzies agreed to 'purchase the paper, fold it, plan it, and prepare the medicated paper transfers for the lithograph stones.' That was an interesting job, he recalled years later, that required new talents. 'First we collected the pieces that when assembled made a suitable balance page and then these were outlined on a preliminary volume of sketches. This was the second time the whole collection of oracle bones had been drawn and arranged under their proper numbers. When the final copy was made on the medicated transfer paper, all errors had been eliminated and only certain slips in drafting the ancient bone script remained to be corrected. This was done on the lithograph stone itself. Many and many an hour I bent over those stones with erasing knife and brush in hand making the characters clear and correct.'[6]

While James Menzies was scraping away at the lithography stone, Annie was expecting the birth of their fourth child. Arthur was born just before the first two hundred pages rolled off the press. In early 1917, James took the printed pages to Shanghai for publication by Kelly & Walsh. 'The job may not be perfect in appearance,' he wrote thirty years later, 'but there are no errors in transcription and of the hundreds of false inscriptions which found their way into my collection, only one was included in the book. After 30 years of work on the bones I am still proud of my work.'[7]

A Circle of Scholarly Friends

In 1914, when James Menzies providentially came upon the Waste of Yin, archaeology still meant digging up ancient treasures to acquire perfect museum-quality specimens. Institutions in Germany, France, Great Britain, and the United States sent archaeological and ethnological teams to conduct piecemeal 'excavations,' some of which (such as the looting of Dunhuang described in chapter 10) were little more than plundering expeditions. By 1930, when the government instituted the cultural antiquities law, archaeology had become a science. It was introduced into China by both foreign scholars and Chinese students who had studied abroad.

Among the important discoveries of the 1920s was the neolithic Yangshao Culture (5000–3000 BCE) in southern Henan, characterized by hand-moulded 'painted pottery' of red, black, and grey clay with decorations in red and black. The excavation was conducted by Dr Johan Gunnar Andersson, a distinguished Swedish geologist originally engaged by the Chinese government as an expert adviser on surveying China's mineral deposits. His book *Children of the Yellow Earth* (1934) conveys his excitement when, as chapter titles put it, 'We Discover the First Prehistoric Villages,' which the 'Doubting History' scholars doubted even existed.[8] The discovery of the Yangshao culture pushed the origins of Chinese civilization 4000 years earlier than the historical records, but the succeeding discovery of fossilized proto-human remains in a cave at Zhoukoudian near Beijing were dated to 250,000 years ago. In 1929 a Canadian professor at Peking Union Medical College, Dr Davidson Black, named them *Sinanthropus Pekinensis*, Peking Man, on the basis of several teeth and skulls. These pioneering efforts prefaced the formal beginning of modern archaeology in China, the excavations at Anyang by Li Chi (pinyin Li Ji) and the Academia Sinica.[9]

During his first term at Zhangde, Menzies's letters do not mention either Western or Chinese colleagues. To make up for his lack of professional training, he found his first teacher in the printed word. He was always buying books, so much so that Annie was surprised when he came home without one. He told Arthur in 1941, 'I have bought no books and am trying not to. Your mother says it is the first time in 30 years that I have bought no books.'[10] Once he became absorbed in archaeology, he read only publications relating to his field. He indulged in light reading only when Dr Isabelle McTavish prescribed it to relieve his migraines: 'Well I have read very few novels since coming to China. I had too much else to do. But now I am doing it as medicine. It takes my mind off my work, lifts me into another world and so gives me a rest.'[11]

As a result of his thirst for knowledge, Menzies built up an extensive library in Chinese and English, numbering five thousand volumes by 1927, most of which were lost, as noted earlier. Later, while he was teaching at Beijing and Cheeloo, he accumulated many more. He left most of his books at Cheeloo when he returned to Canada in 1936, taking only those he needed for immediate research. Nevertheless, when the Canadian portion of his library was transferred to the Royal Ontario Museum in 1960, it was valued at $5000.[12]

James Menzies was not a bookish recluse, and he and Annie had a great gift for friendship. As an 'English lady,' Annie created a gracious, restful home, filled with flowers from her garden, sending to Holland for tulip bulbs 'so I shall hope to have lots of nice flowers in the house from Xmas on.'[13] In Beijing, and later in Jinan, their home acted as a social haven for the students on weekends and special occasions. Annie was a memorable hostess who served high tea and conducted Bible studies.

She was particularly attentive to the North Henan students, who felt she and James were *laoxiang*, hometown people who spoke the Henan dialect. Besides, the students could practise their English with Shen Dasao, more a companion now that the children were gone, who spoke English with no trace of an accent.[14]

During the 1920s, as *Oracle Records* spread Menzies's scholarly reputation, he established a network of friends and colleagues in Chinese archaeology, art, and epigraphy. When Menzies taught at the North China Union Language School in 1927–9, Beijing/Beiping was experiencing a golden age of exchange, respect, and appreciation between Chinese and foreign scholars. In 1929, when Menzies made his proposal to Harvard University, he included a list of references: his peers who were able to judge his work. It was a remarkable list. Even though not complete (Gu Jiegang and other members of the Beijing academic circle were missing), it comprised practically the entire generation present at the creation of Chinese archaeology. By drawing the connections between these men, we can see the cross-fertilization among missionary orientalists, American museum-based archaeologists, Harvard professors, Chinese antiquarians, and young, Western-educated scientists that brought forth the discipline.[15]

The first group on Menzies's reference list were connected to the NCULS. These included:

1 William B. Pettus: From 1911 until Pearl Harbor (1941), he ran this key institution, which trained many missionaries, career diplomats, and business persons in North China, instilling not just the language but also Chinese culture and history.[16] He probably knew everyone in Beijing's political, intellectual, and social elite.
2 Lionel Charles Hopkins (1854–1952): A long-term resident of Beijing, he had already retired to England when Menzies arrived in 1910, but they corresponded extensively. Hopkins arrived in Beijing in 1874 as a student interpreter in the British consular service and became a self-professed 'Sinologue' with special interests in early China. He wrote copious articles for the *Journal of the Royal Asiatic Society of Great Britain and Ireland*, and some nine hundred of his purchased oracle bones (including many, many forgeries) were donated to Cambridge University Library.[17]
3 James Henry Ingram: He compiled an etymological analysis of the thousand characters of *Baller's Mandarin Primer*, which was the school's textbook. For each character, he listed the standard printed version,

the ancient seal script, the Mandarin pronunciation, and an English translation, followed by an explanation of the character's historical origins, semantic content, radical, and components.[18]

4 Arthur de Carle Sowerby (1885–1954): Sowerby was a renowned naturalist and curator of the Natural History Museum at the Tientsin Anglo-Chinese College. Born in Shanxi province of missionary parents, he led an early Smithsonian expedition to Shanxi and Gansu in 1908, collecting natural and ethnographic specimens. The same age as Menzies, he had also enlisted with the Chinese Labour Corps in France during the First World War. Moving to Shanghai, he edited *The China Journal of Science and Arts*. He wrote *A Naturalist's Notebook in China* (1925) and numerous articles, including one on 'animals in the Shang pictographs,' thus overlapping Menzies's interests.[19]

Menzies was part of this group only temporarily in the late 1920s, but they remained academic colleagues for years afterwards.

During 1928, two first-class research centres were founded in Beijing, the Harvard-Yenching Institute and the Academia Sinica. James Menzies was eventually connected with both and counted many of their staff members as special archaeology comrades.

The Harvard-Yenching Institute (HYI) was a consortium of six Christian universities in China and Harvard in the United States. Substantially funded initially by the founder of Alcoa and later by the Rockefeller Foundation, its goal was to train Western and Chinese Sinologists to provide leadership for intellectual cooperation between the West and the East. Harvard was naturally considered to be at the first level, while Beijing's Yenching University was at the second, the only China institution then allowed to conduct graduate work. The other five participants – Lingnan, Nanking, Fukien, West China Union, and Cheeloo universities – were required to have competent teachers, adequate libraries, and research facilities: however, they were not initially allowed to conduct graduate work in related fields.[20]

Since James Menzies was sending his references to Dean Chase at Harvard, it is not surprising that many on his list were connected to Yenching University. Yenching was then only ten years old, created in 1919 by a merger of four church colleges. Its first president was the famous missionary educator John Leighton Stuart (1876–1962), who remained in that post for twenty-seven years until appointed U.S. ambassador. As Dwight Edwards wrote in the official history, 'Yenching University and Leighton Stuart are synonymous terms.'[21] Stuart was born in

Hangzhou of Southern Presbyterian mission pioneers who founded schools for boys and for girls. Stuart rebelled against what he called the 'theological concepts of a bygone age' embedded in his narrow upbringing, but after a crisis of faith, he returned to China as a teacher at the Union Theological Seminary in Nanjing, moving to Beijing to help establish Yenching.[22] Within a decade Stuart transformed Yenching from a fledgling to the third top university in China, surpassed only slightly by the government Peking University (*Beijing Daxue*, or *Beida*) and private Tsinghua (*Qinghua*) University.[23]

Another prominent faculty member on Menzies's list was Lucius Chapin Porter (1880–1958), dean of Yenching and executive secretary of HYI. He was born at Tianjin to American Methodists and educated at Wisconsin's Beloit College (which his grandfather had founded), with graduate work at Yale, Berlin, and Jerusalem before returning to China under the American Board for Foreign Missions. He taught at North China Union College from 1909 to 1918 and spent the rest of his professional career at Yenching. He was the author of *China's Challenge to Christianity* (1924), 'an articulate apology for liberal Christianity in China.'[24]

Yenching was planned as a bicultural university, but that mainly meant that students were expected to become bilingual, as compulsory courses were taught in both Chinese and English. During the nationalist 1920s, Yenching began a policy of 'Sinification,' hiring more and better-qualified Chinese professors and establishing an Institute of Chinese Studies. William Hung (pinyin Hong Ye or Hong Huilian, 1893–1980), the Chinese dean of arts and science from 1923 to 1927, was instrumental in the development of Chinese studies. Born in Fujian and raised in Shandong, where his father was a Qing official, he received the classical literati education followed by a few years at the Anglo-Chinese College in Fuzhou, where he accepted Christianity. From 1915 he attended Ohio Wesleyan University and then did graduate work at Columbia and Union Theological Seminary in New York. In 1923, he returned to China with his Chinese-American wife (who spoke no Chinese) as head of the department of history at Yenching. After eight years in the United States, the transition was difficult, for Hung continued to 'live a style of life that was decidedly American.' He was not liked by nationalistic students of that era who considered him 'a fake Chinese.'[25] Hung resigned as dean in 1927 to devote his time to Chinese scholarship, which brought him into Menzies's orbit. He was instrumental in founding the Harvard-Yenching Institute, enlarging the university library and editing the famous *Harvard-Yenching Sinological Index Series*. 'It was under his leadership that several disciplines in Chinese studies, including history, philosophy, literature, archaeology, religion and art, became Yenching's flourishing programs with strong research emphasis and institutional support, drawing national as well as international attention in only a short period of time.'[26]

Menzies's closest colleagues were two leading scholars on oracle and bronze inscriptions, Rong Geng (old spelling Jung Keng) and Ma Heng (old spelling Ma Hang). They had helped him recruit the Manchu teacher Zeng Yigong to prepare the ink-squeezes for the second volume of *Yinxu Buci*. Ma Hang (1881–1955), four years older than Menzies, was director of the new Palace Museum and an authority on ancient coins and seals. Nine years younger, Rong Geng (1894–1983) was a graduate of Peking University and chairman of the Chinese Department at Yenching, where he specialized in bronze inscriptions, ancient history, and archaeology. In 1925 he published a five-volume etymological dictionary of every character contained in bronze inscriptions. Rong Geng was also a famous calligrapher of the ornate seal script, and his paintings are widely collected. Menzies always regarded him as 'the best man on inscriptions,' and often sent him archaic characters for identification.[27] In return, when compiling his book *Yinqi Buci* (Yin Oracle Bone Inscriptions), Rong Geng consulted only two people about Shang royal genealogy: the renowned Chinese scholar Guo Moruo and James Menzies.[28]

The next group on Menzies's reference list were four Canadian colleagues who shared a common interest in ancient China and who each made a significant contribution to Chinese studies. Charles Trick Currelly, director of the Royal Ontario Museum, and Bishop William C. White have been discussed in chapter 10. The third was John Calvin Ferguson (1866–1945), a renowned scholar reputed to have had 'the most valuable private collection of Chinese art objects in China.' Born near Napanee, Ontario, he joined the American Methodist Episcopal Church (North) in 1886 before Canadian churches had missions in China. Ferguson was the founding president of Nanking College, forerunner of Ginling (pinyin Jinling) University, and administrator of *Nanyang Kunghsüeh* (pinyin *Nanyang Gongxüe*, or Southern Public School), which became the famous technical Nanyang University. He was an adviser to the Qing government on educational reform and remained close to government circles after Chiang Kai-shek established the national capital at Nanjing. Ferguson wrote one of the first histories of Chinese painting in English (1927) and several other surveys of Chinese art. In 1934 he donated his collection to Nanking University, which built a special building to house it, 'the first instance in China of a collection of this kind being donated to an institution for public exhibition.'[29]

The other Canadian in Menzies's circle was Davidson Black (1884–1934), professor of anatomy at Peking Union Medical College (PUMC), who identified Peking Man. After graduating in medicine at the University of Toronto in 1906 with a speciality in neuroanatomy, his interests shifted to palaeontology and human evolution. His study of fossil skulls led him to believe that humans originated in Central Asia, and in 1919 he was hired to establish the department of anatomy at PUMC, the most renowned and favoured of China projects underwritten by the Rockefeller Foundation. In 1926, when two human teeth were discovered at Zhoukoudian, a series of deep caves near Beijing, Black began a large excavation that uncovered more teeth and skulls, which confirmed his contention that Peking Man had been a pre-human hominid. In 1932 he was the first Canadian elected a Fellow of the Royal Society, but he died two years later at the age of forty-nine.[30]

Several of these men, Chinese and Western, were philologists and epigraphers steeped in ancient texts who considered Menzies their equal, but in the new field of scientific archaeology Menzies was still the student. His reference list included several archaeologists and anthropologists. Among the former were two whom he regarded as his teachers: W.F. Badè, head of the dig at Beth Shamesh, where Menzies worked as a site surveyor, and Clarence F. Fisher, curator of the Egyptian section of the University of Pennsylvania Museum of Archaeology from 1914 to 1925, whom Menzies met in Palestine in 1929.

Prominent also on Menzies's list were the following:

1 Berthold Laufer (1874–1934), curator of Asiatic Ethnology and Anthropology at the Field Museum in Chicago from 1908 to his death. Of German origin and Swiss training, he was multilingual, a polymath in academic publications, and a phenomenal collector for the Field Museum. Menzies met Laufer at the museum during his furlough of 1928–30.[31]
2 Arthur W. Hummel (b. 1884), with whom Menzies would become particularly close. Once a Congregational missionary in North China, in 1928 Hummel was appointed the first chief of the Library of Congress's new Orientalia Division. In the late 1930s he edited the famous *Eminent Chinese of the Ch'ing Period (1644–1911)*, published in two volumes (1943–4) and still considered an essential reference

work on that period. Hu Shi stated that *Eminent Chinese* was 'the most detailed and best history of China of the last three hundred years that one can find anywhere today.'[32]

3 Throughout the 1920s and 1930s, the curator of Asian art at the famous Freer Gallery of Art, part of the Smithsonian Institution in Washington, DC, was Carl W. Bishop (1882–1942), born of missionary parents in Japan. With a master's degree from Colombia University in Anthropology, he became the leading expert on human origins in East Asia.[33] Menzies also visited Bishop in Washington during his furlough.

Taken as a whole, Menzies's list was impressive for its inclusion of such a range of eminent Western and Chinese scholars in a variety of disciplines related to the suddenly blossoming field of ancient Chinese society and culture. Yet more impressive are the indications that these men of international academic stature were coming to regard Menzies as one of their number. Chinese scholars and a few knowledgeable foreigners dealing with oracle studies had taken increased notice of him since the appearance in 1917 of his first collection of reproductions, the *Oracle Records from the Waste of Yin*. The reception accorded his address to the Archaeological Institute of America in December 1929 demonstrated the widening of that appreciative audience. It is not easy to go beyond that, as Menzies was not a letter writer until his retirement in the late 1940s. The Menzies Family Papers contain only a few letters that he wrote to or received from academic friends whose names appeared on his reference list. Thus, it is difficult for us to describe his relationship with these people in detail. However, his modesty and honesty make it safe to assume that all who appeared on his list knew him personally. Most were in Beijing in 1927–8, and there is no doubt that he consulted directly with them concerning their own particular specialities. Sufficient notices appear in their writings and correspondence to indicate a growing reciprocal regard for Menzies as a Shang/Yin expert.

Chapter 13

Next Stage, the 1930s

Oracle Records

As already noted, following Menzies's address to the Archaeological Institute of America in December 1929 Dean Chase of Harvard asked him to prepare a proposal for a joint international excavation of the Waste of Yin under the auspices of the Harvard-Yenching Institute. Although never published, this detailed, nine-page proposal was one of the most important documents that Menzies ever wrote. He believed the HYI would act differently than a museum since it was interested in promoting Chinese culture in China and the West. As he wrote to Leighton Stuart, 'To my mind the work must be undertaken on a far more permanent basis than has been attempted. I also feel that the task is much more important than has been realized and that much more systematic work must be undertaken.'[1]

Before we examine Menzies's proposal in detail, let us review the purpose of his research. As early as 1917, he had written that his aspiration was nothing less than 'an extended work on the dawn of history and the development of civilization in China.' He planned a series of books under the title 'Prehistoric China.' The first, on oracle characters, would 'throw a fresh light into the dim origins of Chinese religion and culture.' The second would be a dictionary of the 'life-history of each character through the five most distinct forms ... with excerpts from actual inscriptions in each case.' Volumes three and four would turn from epigraphy to culture with 'a dissertation on the early religion of the Chinese race as shown on the fragments [of oracles] and the other objects collected ... [and] a dissertation on the earliest culture period in China with corroborative evidence from stone, bone and pottery objects.'[2]

These aspirations were recorded in his 1917 publication, *Oracle Records from the Waste of Yin*, the first book on oracle inscriptions by a foreign scholar. By this time thousands of bones had been dug up at Xiaotun and six other books had been published, making 5154 inscriptions available to scholars. Menzies's 2369 drawings of bone and shell inscriptions increased that number to 7523. Thus, he provided one-third of the known oracle inscriptions. His book was also the largest and proved to be the most accurate contribution to date.

Menzies's goal proved too ambitious for an amateur scholar who spent most of his time in rural evangelism. It was not until the Beijing spring in 1928 that he could return seriously to his studies. After settling in at the North China Union Language School, he started to work on his second book, *Yin-hsu Pu-tzu Hou-pien* (Oracle Records from the Waste of Yin, Part II; pinyin *Yinxu Buzi Houbian*), with Zeng Yigong, a young Manchu scholar, as his assistant. By this time, Menzies had acquired the skill of making ink rubbings. The work was tedious and slow. The bones, thousands of years old, were very fragile and brittle and had to be handled with extreme care. First they were cleaned with a paintbrush and impregnated with shellac, which strengthened them while leaving the carved character crevices uncovered. Broken bones and shells had to be glued together with celluloid.

Menzies took about 20,000 oracles to Beijing and by the time he left for Canada in late 1928, he had made a further 2819 ink rubbings. These were divided into nine volumes, with one inscription on each page. The first six volumes contained rubbings of tortoise shells; the other three were of animal scapulae.[3] In a letter to his parents, he described his work: 'As for my book, well it is not yet done and cannot be finished before I return to Canada. I have worked hard on it but there was a great deal to do and it took a lot longer than I expected that it would ... I had hoped that the summer would see me further on but it is slow work. I will not have completed rubbings of all the bones, much less finished the text of it all. It is Chinese work and could not be done in Canada. So, it will have to be left here in China until I come back.'[4]

Dated 30 December 1929, Menzies's proposal to Dean Chase listed fourteen reasons why the scientific excavation of Anyang was an emergency salvage operation. 'The site is gradually being ruined. The most damage was done early after 1900 when bones were being sold in large numbers. The whole site has been pot-holed ... Some of the early pits have been carried down to a depth of 30 feet or more to water level. This "pot holing" is disastrous for the proper excavation of the site.'[5] Properly excavated, the site would furnish scholars with scientifically excavated artefacts to understand Late Shang culture, language, religion, geography, and royal genealogy, as well as fostering comprehenson of the incised white pottery. It would provide concrete evidence for Chinese culture before the Zhou dynasty, when written records begin. 'There is evidence from the bones that this culture differed in many respects from the later "Confucianism" of the Chou [Zhou] dynasty. It is even possible that the Chou people who came from the west were not so cultured as the Shang dynasty people. A proper excavation would clear up this problem ... It is usually considered that the Chinese people came from the west along the Yellow River basin to the great plain. [The finds at the Waste of Yin], combined with the find of Prehistoric man near Peking make it reasonable to conceive of Chinese culture as *developed in the east on the great plain.* In the quest for the origins of Chinese civilization, the finds at the Waste of Yin would provide the relationship between Shang culture and the Neolithic painted pottery culture.' The proposed excavation would also help corroborate the Chinese Classics, Menzies concluded, disproving the 'Doubting History' school of thought prevalent at the time. 'There is no more fundamental piece of work that can be undertaken by a western foundation looking toward the promotion of Chinese studies than the excavation of the Waste of Yin.'

Menzies's proposal stressed the importance of cooperation between Western and Chinese scholars. Their different knowledge and skills would make the excavation a success: 'The Westerner would have an archaeological advantage while the Chinese the language and literary advantage and both of these are essential in an excavation where the oracle bone records are so important.' At the same time, he viewed the project as 'a training field in archaeological technique and method for Chinese as well as Westerners and an opportunity for 'Western scholarship and science of archaeology' to 'materially aid Chinese studies both for Westerners and Chinese alike.' As for the ownership of the finds, he proposed, 'the custody of the objects excavated would probably be left with the excavations so long as they were not removed from China and were available to all Chinese scholars for study.'

Turning from the theoretical to the practical, Menzies drew a map of Xiaotun, the Little Village, and 'a considerable area, on both sides of the river.' Based on observation, he stated, '[t]here are low mounds on the river banks extending from the railway west for almost three miles. These points may indicate successive sites of cities. Most of the site is flat in loose soil with no stone or bricks apparent. The buildings may have been entirely of beaten earth.'

For a while, the Harvard-Yenching Institute seemed interested in Menzies's project. Dean Chase asked the United Church to grant Menzies a leave of absence to enable a year in Beijing working on the publication of his collection while making arrangements for the larger scheme. John Leighton Stuart further suggested that he spend 'a period of study at Harvard in the technique of this sort of research before returning to China.'[6] However, no matter how well the proposal was written, it was doomed from the start; by this time, Chinese scholars would never have accepted the international nature of the proposal. He did not know that a group of highly trained Chinese archaeologists, led by Li Chi and the Academia Sinica, had already started the excavation of Anyang. When he learned of this in February 1930, it 'was somewhat of a surprise to me,' he wrote.[7]

The Academia Sinica

Standing in contrast to the Harvard-Yenching Institute was the second Beijing scholarly institute founded in 1928, the Academia Sinica. It was a Chinese-government scientific academy specifically established to foster a national intellectual culture. One of the key figures was Li Chi (Li Ji, 1896–1979), famous as the 'father of Chinese archaeology' and the head of the important archaeology, department of the Institute of History and Philology within Academia Sinica. Born in Hubei, Li Chi had a traditional education before attending Harvard University, where he received a PhD in archaeology in 1923. He returned to China and began working on Neolithic sites such as Xiyincun (Xiyin village). He met Carl Bishop, whom he considered to be 'one of the few Americans in Beijing who impressed me as honest and sincere.' Bishop hired him on behalf of the Freer Gallery to join the field team to do some archaeological excavation. Li Chi stated two conditions, in order that his work would not be 'unpatriotic': that the excavations be done in cooperation with a Chinese learned body; and that he 'be excused from any obligation to export the artefacts from such digging – [the] hint being that studies of such finds be done in China.'[8]

While James Menzies was on his way to Palestine in the spring of 1929, Li Chi was entrusted with the excavation of Anyang, considered the most extensive and most precious site of China's prehistory that could be dated accurately according to the ancient records.[9] The Academia Sinica had already conducted one preliminary excavation in August 1928, one month after James Menzies had visited Zhangde to survey the ruins of his home after the Northern Expedition. A young scholar named Dong

Zobin (old spelling Tung Tso-pin) was dispatched to reconnoitre the Waste of Yin near Anyang. Dong's main qualifications were that he was a native of Henan and 'was intellectually alert, although not an antiquarian even in the traditional sense.' He met local gentry and curio dealers at Zhangde and visited Xiaotun at the bend of the Huan River. Mainly he purchased oracle bones. He found that every home in the village had some *zigutou*, small fragments that the curio dealers had rejected, which they sold to him at one hundred fragments for three silver dollars. Larger pieces cost four to five dollars each, which Dong considered exorbitant.[10]

In the last three weeks of October, after the harvest, Dong conducted the first excavations at Anyang. He dug trenches in the cotton fields between Xiaotun and the river, uncovering 785 pieces of inscribed oracle bones, 70 per cent of which were tortoise shells and the rest scapular bones of cattle, plus an additional thousand fragments of uninscribed bones. After Dong's preliminary dig, Li Chi took over the leading role in the Anyang field excavations, which continued until the Japanese invasion of 1937.

When Li Chi wrote his record of the excavation, *Anyang*, he revealed how little knowledge he had of the site beforehand. He noted that his early understanding consisted of three principles:

1 The site at Hsiao-t'un (Xiaotun) was evidently the last capital of the Yin-Shang dynasty.
2 Although the size and scope of the remains were uncertain, an area where inscribed oracle bones were unearthed must have been an important centre of the capital site.
3 Together with the inscribed oracle bones, there might well be many other kinds of artefacts found in the underground deposits. These might have coexisted with the inscribed oracle bones, or be even earlier, or possibly later, depending of course upon a number of depository conditions.[11]

Li Chi had excavated other Neolithic sites and was better prepared than Menzies for archaeology. Yet comparing their preliminary understanding of the actual site, Menzies had a better sense of the dating and function of inscribed oracle bones, the relation between the earlier Painted Pottery culture and the Shang, and the importance of the 'low mounds' on both sides of the river.

Inevitably disputes arose during the excavation over the ownership of excavated objects, first between the Academia Sinica and the Henan provincial government, and then between Li Chi and Carl Bishop. Since the Freer was financing the excavation on an 'experimental basis,' it expected to share the finds. But the contract stipulated that the excavated objects were national treasures that must remain and be studied in China. In June 1930, the Freer withdrew from cooperation with the Academia Sinica. According to Li Guangmo, son of Li Chi, the main reason for this was the conflict of interest; the Freer was interested in collecting and Anyang in no way served this purpose.[12]

If Menzies had been at Zhangde in 1928–9 and if the soldiers had not trampled his oracle bones and trashed his library, he could have saved the archaeologists a lot of time. But he was not. Consequently, they spent the two seasons in 1929 duplicating his work: surveying the site to provide a detailed topographical map; noting the mounds and depressions that indicated pounded-earth foundations; digging exploratory trenches to ascertain the stratigraphy and dating of Shang and pre-Shang layers; and cataloguing the oracles and ceramics. Menzies returned to Zhangde in September 1930, and the following spring Li Chi returned for the fourth season at Anyang.

We do not know the exact nature of Menzies's involvement with the Anyang excavations of 1931–2. The site was less than a mile from his home, and for fifteen years, whenever he was in Zhangde, he would take his evening walk in his 'adobe city' beneath the sands. The residents of Xiaotun called him Professor 'Old Bones' (*lao-gu xian-sheng*) and treated him as a friend, and invariably their conversation would come back to his favourite topic, oracle bones. Li Chi was a colleague from his Beijing days who would have welcomed him as a resident expert – after all, certified Dominion Land Surveyors were a rare commodity in rural China – and would have consulted him on the stratigraphy separating the Shang period and the earlier Neolithic culture. We know that Dong Zobin, the young enthusiast in charge of transcribing and drawing the oracle inscriptions, did consult Menzies concerning tricky points in royal Shang genealogy.

Li Chi's history of the excavations, *Anyang*, was not published until 1977, forty years after the last dig, but in it he gave a gracious tribute to Menzies. Citing him as one of the earliest oracle-bone scholars, he wrote: 'A pioneer in this field was the author of "Oracle Records from the Waste of Yin," Mr. James Mellon Menzies, the Canadian missionary. Menzies was first sent to Changte Fu in 1914, and after the First World War, was again stationed there from 1921 to 1927. He was thus in a position to learn, *in situ*, about the unearthing of oracle bones by the native diggers on his frequent visits to Hsiao-t'un [Xiaotun]. This fortunate combination of an appropriate appointment and an inborn instinct for archaeology prepared the way for his special contribution to the oracle bone studies among the small community of scholars.' In a footnote, Li Chi noted that although Menzies's lecture notes from Cheeloo University 'were never published, they were widely read and quoted.'[13] As a more lasting tribute, Li Chi named a fossil animal discovered at Anyang after Menzies. The *Elaphurus Menziesianus* is an extinct form of water buffalo or elk with magnificent backward-turning antlers that were sometimes used for oracles. Its nearest living relative is the strange Père David's deer, which survives only in captivity.

The fourth season in the spring of 1931 was the most ambitious yet undertaken. Li Chi made the decision 'to excavate the Hsiao-t'un [Xiaotun] site in its totality by the carpet rolling method,' that is by systemically digging down to the lowest strata, a depth of three metres or more, to trace the architectural foundations. The official field report stated: 'The excavated area is more than fourteen hundred square meters. With the exception of the exposure of a large area of pounded earth, the discoveries included a large number of circular caches, twenty-five huge underground dwelling spaces, and eighteen burials ... In the storage cells of E16 were found some very valuable artefacts: bronze spearheads, bronze halberds, moulds for bronze casting, carved bones, together with pot-sherds and a great number of inscribed oracle bones.'[14] Menzies had left Zhangde in May 1932, thus missing the excitement of the discovery of the royal tombs under those mounds that he suspected were there from the beginning.

Although his proposal for the Harvard-Yenching Institute did not have an immediate result, it nonetheless symbolized his transition from a rural evangelist to a recognized scholar. It should be stressed that his transition did not mean he had a 'change of heart.' He remained committed to the missionary cause in China to his last days. The transition was essentially a change of approach. The social gospel that he had learned at Knox College was concerned with not just individual salvation but also the social environment. As an expression of this social agenda, the overseas missions established schools and hospitals and pursued other efforts such as rural reconstruction. The success of these initiatives relied upon professional experts in educational, medical, and social work.

Menzies's transition was a reflection of this larger trend, even though his conservative colleagues in North Henan had difficulty recognizing archaeology as a legitimate part of missionary work. In the early 1950s, he reflected: 'While I have counted 1,000 persons baptized and many more prepared for the catechumens, yet perhaps my work on the bones permeated deeper into Chinese life than my work among the schools and churches of North Henan ... When one starts from the premise that God is the God of the Chinese and was so recognized by them, Christianity no longer becomes a foreign religion in the eyes of the Chinese and you have a firm foundation for your Christian preaching.'[15]

A New Environment

In late 1931, Menzies received an invitation from Cheeloo University at Jinan (old spelling Tsinan), the provincial capital of Shandong, to teach history and archaeology. He passed it on to the mission council without expecting much. In January 1932 L.J. Davis, the associate president of the university, formally asked the council to release Menzies, pointing out that the North Henan mission 'owed' the university a professor. Cheeloo had recently received money through the Harvard-Yenching Institute that would enable it 'to undertake what we hope will prove valuable research work in the history and archaeology of China and in other lines. Now we want Mr. Menzies to come to the University to specialize in archaeological research ... What Mr. Menzies has already done seems to mark him as a man splendidly fitted to lead in archaeological research.'[16]

This time the mission council accepted the invitation and the only 'opposition' came from the Chinese synod, which petitioned for Menzies to stay at Zhangde. In May the BOM asked the synod to reconsider and support this decision. 'We appreciate very much your confidence in Mr. Menzies and your desire to have him remain at Changte that he might continue his work with the Synod and the Mission. We feel, however, that Mr. Menzies' talents are such as to justify our concurring in the call of the University to Mr. Menzies and of the Honan Mission Council's recommendation that he be located at Tsinan [Jinan] ... Mr. Menzies has peculiar gifts which can be utilized to enhance the prestige of the cause of Christ in China and he can make a real contribution to China in the area of history, archaeology and folk-lore.'[17] The years of searching for a suitable venue for his talents and dedication seemed to have ended.

In the spring of 1932, the Institute of Chinese Studies at Cheeloo University proudly reported: 'After two year's strenuous work looking for competent specialists and seeking the co-operation of outstanding scholars in this province, we have succeeded in inviting to the Institute Mr. J.M. Menzies who has specialized on oracle bones and the ancient history of China.'[18] For James Menzies, the move to Cheeloo was recognition that his interest in archaeology was a legitimate pursuit, not a hobby. The president made this clear in his invitation: 'We want Mr. Menzies to come to the university to specialize in archaeological research ... He would be given considerable liberty in the selection of his main lines and in the arrangement of the details of his work ... The Harvard-Yenching funds will make possible the employment of writers to assist him and we hope to be able to establish relationships with Chinese government archaeological agencies, which will give him a share in excavation work.'[19] This had been Menzies's dream for twenty years.

The summer of 1932 was one of those bittersweet reunions for the Menzies family. The children, who had been attending the Canadian Academy at Kobe, came to Haifenglou, 'Sea Breeze Cottage,' at Beidaihe. Marion, who celebrated her nineteenth birthday that summer, had completed the Ontario Grade 13 examinations and was thinking about her future. Frances was seventeen, and Arthur fifteen. By now, with James's building alterations, including a round tower that served as his study and a broad stone terrace with a ten-foot-high foundation wall, Sea Breeze Cottage was the most visible landmark at Rocky Point.

After spending the summer with the children at Beidaihe, James and Annie Menzies returned to Zhangde to pack up their household, including the piano and dozens of tin-lined crates containing over 20,000 pieces of oracle bones, broken potsherds, bronze vessels, and other archaeological objects. Marion sailed for Canada, while the two younger children returned to Kobe.

A 'Canadian' University in North China

Cheeloo (pinyin Qilu) University, formally known as Shantung Christian Union University, was considered the top of the second rank of the thirteen Christian universities in China. It had been established in 1902 by an amalgamation of several colleges founded in the nineteenth century. However, the university did not have a permanent location until 1911, when it settled down at the campus in Jinan. It also adopted a new name, Cheeloo, which had a suitably archaic resonance, since it combined the names of two dukedoms that had dominated Shandong at the time of Confucius (about 500 BCE), Qi (formerly Ch'i) and Lu.

The founders had a high ideal: a great university in the birthplace of

Confucius that would radiate Christian influences throughout the country, just as Confucius had done 2500 years earlier. It was seen as an evangelical institution rather than a first-class educational institution. As the charter stated: 'The aim of the United Colleges shall be first and foremost the furtherance of the cause of Christ in China.' Cheeloo also had a unique distinction in that it was the only Christian college with Chinese as the language of instruction, which dissuaded many ambitious, non-Christian students whose major academic goal was to learn English.

A report on 'Religious Life in Cheeloo' asserted that it was 'thoroughly Christian.' Two-thirds of the students (62 per cent) at Cheeloo were Christians, compared to only 31 per cent at the prestigious Yenching University.[20] Bible classes were organized and well attended; and even the Fundamentalist and 'Sentimentalist' camps found their followers on the campus.[21] This strong religious atmosphere appealed to Menzies, who proudly wrote, 'Cheeloo stands away highest in the % of Christian students in regular university classes.'[22]

Eventually, thirteen Protestant missions – five British, six American, and two Canadian – supported the university financially or provided professors.[23] By 1917 it had 303 students at a time when the total enrolment in all Christian colleges was 1500.[24] It attracted praise from Christian leaders such as Robert E. Speer of the North American Student Volunteer Movement, who wrote: 'That institution has led, and leads still, the higher education of the whole Empire ... It has been uncompromisingly and avowedly Christian, and has never graduated a man who was not a Christian.'[25] Through the 1920s Cheeloo was recognized as a leading Christian institution of higher education and its model of ecumenical cooperation was emulated by the others.

The Canadians joined Cheeloo comparatively late, in 1915, and were never more than minor players among the predominantly English and American staff. Yet they did perform a key function as the 'hyphen in the Anglo-American missionary alliance.'[26] The invitation to join with Cheeloo came at the right moment for the North Henan mission. They had been negotiating a cooperative college with the Anglicans at Kaifeng, headed by Bishop William C. White. Confidentially, the mission clerk, Harvey Grant, reported to the Board of Foreign Missions (the mission was still under the Presbyterian Church in Canada) that 'Presbytery is at present carefully feeling its way in regard to Union Higher Education. Our relations to Bp. White have always been cordial, but his high-handed dealing with some of our sister Missions who are labouring at Kaifeng does not re-assure us, or encourage us to enter into closer union ... The outlook seems more hopeful in other directions.'[27] The 'other direction' was Cheeloo.

The North Henan mission became a supporting member of Cheeloo, even though the Board of Foreign Missions had second thoughts. In a letter to Robert A. Mitchell, the leading educationalist, R.P. Mackay wrote, 'Whilst I usually approve of proposals looking toward co-operation and economy, on the other hand I am not sure that it is best for Honan in the long run. You are acquainted with the policy in Canada of having a theological college related to each university in order to interest and capture students ... If the Honan students are educated in some other province, and the flavour of a theological college is not felt within the area of our own Mission, one feels that a considerable amount of influence will be lost.'[28]

As a sponsor, the NHM was required to share in the operating expenses and to contribute three professors, one each in Arts, Theology, and Medicine. It took years to reach that quota. The first was Dr William McClure, who had already retired when the invitation came in 1916. He had served for thirty years in Henan and was appointed to Cheeloo for a short-term service. However, the good doctor stayed twenty years, well into his eighties.[29] Theologian John Donald MacRae was the second Canadian. As president during the troubles of 1927, he rescued the university, but had a nervous breakdown soon afterwards and had to return to Canada.[30] The third was Harold Harkness, a Canadian who had been working with the American Presbyterians. He remained at Cheeloo until 1930, when he resigned to teach at McGill University, creating the vacancy filled by Menzies.[31] In 1920 the Augustine church in Winnipeg raised $50,000 to build the Augustine Library, and continued to make an annual contribution for its maintenance. When James Menzies came as professor of archaeology, he established a teaching museum based on his collections, assuring that Cheeloo became the centre of oracle studies in China.[32]

In 1924 the North Henan mission performed a uniquely Canadian compromise; they helped the university obtain a Canadian charter. The English missions had sought a charter in London, but British laws did not apply to an educational institution outside the Empire. If the charter was based in the United States, Americans had to constitute a majority of the governing board. Perhaps, it was suggested, a Canadian charter might be secured. A committee headed by A.E. Armstrong of the Board of Overseas Missions negotiated with Canadian authorities. They, however, raised the eternal federal/provincial constitutional issues: provincial governments control education, while the federal government handles foreign relations.

In May R.P. MacKay wrote to Mackenzie King, the prime minister, stressing the importance of Cheeloo for the evangelical cause in China and the need for Canada to assist. Besides, he hinted to the prime minister, there might be a precedent to the constitutional difficulty: 'Whilest there is no exact precedent for such a bill, the Dominion Government has passed an act incorporating Queen's Theological College, which act affects the rights of the provinces in regard to education in Canada. Perhaps that might be interpreted as a precedent for the proposed bill.'[33] In due course the federal parliament passed the Act of Incorporation, which received royal assent on 19 July 1924. The terms were generous, since they did not require any changes to the existing structure and authorized Cheeloo 'to grant such credentials and degrees, as are in accordance with the laws of China.'[34] This Canadian charter enhanced the value of Cheeloo degrees, making it also easier for Cheeloo graduates to study abroad.

By 1928 Cheeloo lost its pre-eminent position to the expanding, well-endowed big-city universities, such as Yenching in Beijing, Ginling in Nanjing, and St Johns, the elite Anglican school in Shanghai. Part of the problem was Cheeloo's early decision to offer all courses in Chinese. This became a handicap in the changed atmosphere, when English was increasingly in demand. Then, too, Jinan was geographically isolated in the North China plain, halfway between the Beijing/Tianjin and Shanghai/Nanjing axes. The cultural status of Qi and Lu were long gone and the birthplace of Confucius was no longer China's cultural centre.

Cheeloo's internal problems also strained denominational and institutional loyalties. The College of Theology was split in 1919 over the fundamentalist/modernist controversy, and the Presbyterian students withdrew to establish a conservative North China Theological Seminary at Weixian.[35] There was also endemic conflict between Medicine and Arts. For a long time, Arts had been by far the dominant faculty, but that changed with the sudden expansion of the medical college with money from the Harvard-Yenching Institute. Some suggested that Cheeloo should be downgraded to a junior college except for medicine. The medical school felt that they were being dragged down by the low standards in Arts.

In May 1929, when the Guomindang government published its educational regulations, Cheeloo attempted to register for accreditation. The provincial education commissioner, unfortunately, turned out to be a radical nationalist who put the university through a gruelling trial. Among the criticisms of the university, the following were significant:

> In the first place they objected to the presence of the College of Theology on the campus, as such institutions could not be registered. Secondly, they said that the library, which at that time had 24,000 volumes, was inadequate. Third, they insisted that a second foreign language should be offered in addition to English. Fourth, they pointed out that an institution desiring to be registered as a university must have at least three faculties, whereas Cheeloo, not counting the theological faculty, had only two. Fifth, they declared that some teachers in the Arts and Science faculty were below par. Sixth, they pointed out that two-thirds of the membership of the Board of Directors must be Chinese and not merely a majority.[36]

Menzies's tenure at Cheeloo corresponded with that institution's struggle to deal with these new conditions.

During the 1920s, Christian colleges were accused of 'denationalizing' students. This was not just political propaganda. They emphasized a solid education in Western learning – 'Science and Religion' – often taught in English by professors who were not fluent in Chinese. They neglected Chinese language and culture. The government universities and institutes such as Peking and Tsinghua universities and the Academia Sinica attracted the best scholars, were increasingly nationalistic, and provided leadership for the New Culture Movement. A demarcation line came to be drawn: students who wanted to work 'for God or for gold' (i.e., a career in the ministry or in business) chose the Christian colleges; those who desired to study Chinese culture went to government universities.

Professor 'Old Bones'

At Cheeloo, Menzies quickly became beloved by the students, who nicknamed him 'Professor Old Bones' because oracle bones were his life and work and practically his only topic of conversation. The four years at Cheeloo (1932–6) were the happiest and most productive of his life. He was doing what he wanted to do and he was surrounded by colleagues and students, with libraries of books and museums of objects. He produced important papers during this time, which even if not published, circulated as handwritten copies among leading scholars. He also pioneered new fields of study, such as piecing together fragments of oracle bones dispersed through several collections and published in different books.

There was a bittersweet feeling, too, perhaps a foretaste of things to come, when one of his colleagues appropriated some of Menzies's oracle rubbings and published them on his own. In personality, Menzies was a slow talker, shy, and often withdrawn because of his migraines. As a writer, he was too much a perfectionist to publish anything that was not exact. He weighed each word the same way he drew each inscription, methodically and scientifically. He spent years drawing and redrawing the *Oracle Records from the Waste of Yin* and never did publish part 2. Arthur Menzies comments that his father was a brilliant researcher but not a popularizer like Bishop White. As copies of his rubbings circulated, several showed up in works published by others: the rules of scholarly 'borrowing' were looser at that time than they are now.

Cheeloo was located in the south suburb of Jinan, Shandong. It was a pretty, tree-lined campus designed by a Chicago architectural firm in 1911. Like Yenching and the Peking Union Medical College, the architecture was deliberately 'oriental.' Even though the structures were built of reinforced concrete and blue bricks, with electric lighting, central heating, and indoor plumbing, they were capped with the sweeping curves of Chinese tiled roofs. One student wrote: 'The campus is very broad. It is full of beautiful flowers and trees especially the little park in the centre ... When spring comes the trees are shooting their beautiful leaves while the roses are blossoming. It looks like an Eden's Garden!'[37]

The Menzies moved into a foreign house near the medical college, and were delighted to discover that their neighbours were the famous novelist Lao She (sometimes spelled Lau Shaw), whose real name was Shu Sheyu (1899–1966), and his wife Hu Jieqing (1905–2001), a noted writer, poet, and painter. Born in an impoverished part of Beijing, Lao She was a Manchu whose father, a guard soldier, died during the Boxer Uprising. He worked his way through teachers' college and became a Christian as a young man. He spent the years 1924 to 1929 in London teaching Chinese at the School of Oriental and African Studies while he immersed himself in the novels of Dickens, Conrad, and Tolstoy. He has been called 'the Mark Twain of China' for his gentle humour, subtle nuances, and remarkable insights into personality. He found humour in everyday life.

When Lao She returned to China in 1930, he was hired to teach at Cheeloo. He became fascinated by local reminiscences of what had transpired in that city during the last phases of the Northern Expedition in May 1928, when the Japanese and Chinese had clashed so savagely, forcing Chiang Kai-shek to alter his line of march. By a 'bitter irony,' Jonathan Spence wrote, the novel Lao She wrote about the 'Jinan incident' was destroyed when the Japanese bombed the press. Instead of rewriting it, he wrote *Cat Country* (*Mao Chengji*), published in 1932. '*Cat Country* was a transparent satire, presenting the story of a space traveller who lands on Mars to find the country of cats [China] being invaded by a tough nation of small people [the Japanese]. The narrator details the bitter social and political divisions that separate factions of the cat people, preventing them from focusing any unified front against the aggressor ... At the end of Lao She's chilling novel the remaining cat people tear each other to death while the enemy soldiers watch.'[38] In 1936 Lao She published his most famous novel, *Luotuo Xiangzi*, which was translated in a bowdlerized translation as *Rickshaw* and later as *Camel Xiangzi.*

The two families soon became good friends. Lao She introduced Menzies to a more worldly – and decidedly leftist – circle, the members of the Writers' Association. His wife, who taught school and attended classes at the university, introduced Annie Menzies to her wide circle of women friends. 'I went out calling on some of the Chinese teachers' wives,' Annie wrote home. 'A few of them are very nice. It makes such a difference when they have had some education and have been brought up in a nice family ... Mrs. Mitchell thought I might be lonesome by myself. But I am not. Wednesday afternoon I had eight Chinese women in for a tea party. We played games for about an hour, then had tea and after that I gave them a short Bible lesson.'[39]

Zhang Kunhe, an archaeology student of Menzies, recalled that 'Cheeloo University had a strong religious atmosphere. Foreign teachers organized Bible study groups in their homes every Sunday and invited their students to attend ... It was very difficult to refuse. However, Prof. Menzies ... never organized such activities nor asked about our religious belief. By chance all the students in his "Oracle Bone Study" course were non-Christians. His attitude made us feel comfortable.'[40] He continued: 'After class, we many times took our questions to Prof. Menzies at his home ... Mrs. Menzies was much easier to associate with. When Prof. Menzies was not at home, she usually received us. Her Chinese was very good and sometimes had jokes with us. Once she said to us, "Is it true that you call foreigners *yangguizi* [foreign devils]? You should not call Mr. Menzies and me foreign devils."'[41]

The Institute of Chinese Studies

The foreign-mission establishment's answer to the new government's education accreditation system was the Harvard-Yenching Institute (HYI). Its mandate was to promote first-class Chinese studies in China and the United States.[42] Since Cheeloo was one of the five junior partners, it received a large infusion of money from the HYI, including $150,000 for the medical school and a further $200,000 from a restricted fund.[43] This aid came at the right time. To meet the government regulations for registration, Cheeloo upgraded its Chinese library and established the Institute of Chinese Studies. James Menzies was the foreign director, and the professors included Shu Sheyu (the novelist Lao She, Literature), Qi Shuping (Chinese Classics, Bronze Inscriptions), and Wang Xiantang (Shandong Epigraphs, Local History).[44] In 1934 Cheeloo appointed a new president, Dr Liu Shuming, a Shandong native and graduate from Cheeloo and Harvard returning to help save his alma mater. He felt that the Institute of Chinese Studies was the hope for strengthening the arts program, and accompanied Menzies in representing the university at the HYI's meetings.

As foreign director of the Institute of Chinese Studies, Menzies was responsible for its external relations, including attending meetings of the Harvard-Yenching Institute and writing the Institute's annual reports. Each of the affiliated universities was required to produce a detailed annual report about its finance, curriculum and number of students enrolled, and research projects and publications.[45] The Cheeloo reports had always arrived late or incomplete, and in 1933 it came within 'a hair's breadth' of losing the HYI funds. When Menzies took over, he worked to change HYI's negative views. His prompt and detailed reports and letters presented a clear picture of the Institute's progress. In 1934 he received a friendly letter from Serge Elisseeff, director of the HYI, assuring him that the HYI desired to 'co-operate with Cheeloo more closely and give help in any way possible.'[46] Menzies was also a member of the HYI's undergraduate committee for several years.[47]

Under Menzies, the Institute's efforts in research and teaching produced substantial results and received positive recognition from the HYI. When Elisseeff toured the six affiliated universities in 1936–7, he was 'much impressed' by Cheeloo's library and its Chinese studies program.

[I]n contrast to three years ago, he found they now have a very important collection of valuable books. Acquisitions have been made systematically, and good selections have been made of the local histories which describe the counties of Shantung province. The Chinese Library now occupies two large rooms in the main library building. Professor Menzies' archaeological collection is displayed in a very systematic and up-to-date manner in four rooms there, each room representing a certain historical period, which enables the visitor or student to see the chronological development of Chinese bronze and ceramic handicraft. Many objects are of great archaeological value, and, while the collection is not large, it represents a good selection of objects of practically every historical period.[48]

As director of Cheeloo's Institute of Chinese Studies, James Menzies was in a delicate position. He had to negotiate the nuances of Chinese nationalism in a Chinese-speaking world while also coping with the turmoil of the university's internal politics. The latter involved not only the animosity between the medical and arts faculties, but also the future of Christian higher education in China.

Menzies believed that Christian higher education was not an end in itself, but rather the means to, or a component of, a new evangelism: a living church led by well-educated Chinese who were aided by an indigenized gospel. This was far different from the mission-centred evangelism of foreign missionaries preaching a foreign religion dressed in foreign clothes. His opposition to using the HYI funds for purposes other than Chinese studies brought him into conflict with Cheeloo's Faculty of Medicine, which solicited outside funds for its recognized program of translating medical textbooks into Chinese. Dr. R.T. Shields, the American dean of medicine, brought the issue of HYI funds up with the Associated Boards for Christian Colleges in China (ABCCC) head-quartered in New York. Worried about intervention by such mission-related bodies outside of the university, Menzies wrote to A.E. Armstrong in Toronto, the Canadian representative to the ABCCC. Since most of Cheeloo's graduates would be working in interior China, Menzies wrote, they must be educated in Chinese culture: otherwise, they would be considered 'foreignized but not educated.' A university graduate would have a hard time being accepted by Chinese peasants if he (or she, such as public-health nurses) used Western terms and concepts. Students educated in Chinese culture were the hope of the Christian church because they 'have an intelligent grasp of their problems, can work on cooperation with all the other forces of society: governmental, educational, business, and philanthropy and take the same place as a minister does in the community in so called Christian countries.'[49]

The struggle over the HYI funds was symptomatic of the perpetual crises at Cheeloo and the competing visions concerning its future. Unlike Yenching, Cheeloo was dependant on the supporting mission societies, and thus fell into debt when they reduced contributions during the Depression. The gravity of the situation was clear in a cablegram the university sent to its Board of Governors in New York in March 1935: 'All current financial resources exhausted before May. Closure impending. US $20,000 needed to liquidate deficits.'[50]

The Association of Christian Colleges and Universities in China (ACCUC) and its parent body, the Associated Boards, in New York, added yet another layer to Cheeloo's byzantine bureaucracy. As far back as 1922 the Burton Commission on education had stressed that Christian colleges in China should coordinate their programs to avoid duplication and promote efficiency. The ACCUC organized a Council of Higher Education, which issued a 'Correlated Program' designed to achieve those ends. As a result, Cheeloo would concentrate on rural reconstruction, on preparing men and women to meet the needs of the villages and towns of North China. However, it would not be allowed to develop its own department of agriculture to compete with the already flourishing department at the University of Nanking.[51]

The ACCUC formulated its proposal with the best intentions. Since the arts college, the oldest Christian college in China, was dropping below standard, and most graduates were returning to rural areas, 'rural reconstruction' – a political rallying cry in the 1930s – provided one way to serve the Chinese nation. Although the new rural emphasis was well received by the Cheeloo Board of Governors in New York, the Board of Directors in Jinan was lukewarm, worrying that it would further lower the university's status. The issue became divisive when the medical college suggested that arts be either eliminated or transformed into a less expensive 'Rural College'. The alumni, students, and most of the Arts faculty accused the ACCUC of trying to make Cheeloo into a 'cow college.'[52]

The pressure from the Board of Governors in New York was not well received at Jinan. The new president, Liu Shuming, felt that Cheeloo was a Christian university with a distinct mission. It 'should be maintained as a University – i.e. all three schools should be carried on,' arts, science, and medicine. 'The closing of any one of these schools would mean a big loss in the life of the hundreds of graduates,' he concluded.

Liu's position matched Menzies's views perfectly, although they came from different perspectives. Liu Shuming was concerned about his alma mater's reputation and the unpopularity of the rural program among the Chinese faculty and students. He was an earnest Christian who had been a YMCA secretary before he went to study in the United States. After returning to Cheeloo, he preached in the campus chapel and supported religious activities. This may explain Menzies's unwavering support for him: 'President Liu Shu-ming ... was one of the 'Noted Professors' or 'Professors of Reputation' of international law in the National University of Peking ... He puts on no airs whatever, and has a real love for Cheeloo, which he considers has a real and important mission in China, which is the interior northern provinces.'[53]

Menzies felt that Cheeloo already had 'the real Rural Program,' which produced ministers, teachers, doctors, nurses, and community workers for North China. 'Our men have gone back to the country. They have been the corn of wheat falling into the soil and [they] died, so far as their advancement and gaining wealth is concerned, for the people.'[54] Of the 1419 graduates, one-half (715) had become teachers, while 587 were working in mission schools and 128 in government schools; 300 were medical graduates, mostly in mission hospitals; 65 ordained ministers; 114 social and religious workers; 66 businessmen; and 10 had gone abroad for graduate study. 'What better record could you want for real service in the country?'[55]

New York was not Jinan, Menzies reminded Armstrong, and the proposed rural program was not appropriate for Cheeloo. Rural reconstruction was recognized as a national problem and various levels of government had taken over responsibility for 'over 700 Rural Institutes in China, most of them government institutions connected with experimental farms, etc. We have a lot in Shantung and Honan ... The whole programme is being worked out as a national problem ... The problem is now long past the experimental stage. You people at home are always 4 or 5 years behind time. China is no longer in the state [it was] in 1931 or 32. Why our Cheeloo problem was just one of the manifestations of a trouble all over China?'[56]

Menzies was disturbed that the Associated Boards were blindly dismantling a fine Christian university. If the trustees in America and England truly wanted to be helpers of China, they must let the university decide its own future. 'No one who is not in the field and in the work can dictate details of policy to an institution that must live its life in the Chinese environment.'[57] For Menzies, the trustees in New York and London were just donors of funds, not policy makers. This was a radical view held by only a few foreign educators in China at the time. Besides, he concluded, the donors were getting good value, for Cheeloo was 'a school at which no money is wasted, either in budget or students' private expenses and living.'[58] The overhead cost for students in arts was $352 (Mexican), while at Yenching it was $991. The fees per student were $250, compared to $600 to $1000 at Yenching.[59] In fact, many Christians could not afford even these low fees. Many North Henan students were supported totally or partially by the NHM, which contributed up to $1000 a year in scholarships. 'Cheeloo deserves and needs better support from the Home Churches ... Any census of the church workers of today will show how much these missions owe to Cheeloo.'[60]

Finally, Cheeloo was 'thoroughly Chinese,' since it was one of the few Christian universities that employed Chinese as the language of instruction. 'You may get on with men poorly trained in Chinese, if they are to work in port cities,' Menzies told Armstrong. 'But if they are to work in the interior of China, they must be well educated in Chinese subjects or they are considered foreignized but not educated.'[61] In contrast, Yenching had a first-class Chinese department but most university courses were taught in English. As Menzies commented: 'In Yenching they are trained for an environment that is not found in country life in China. They dress and spend at a rate that cannot be supported by the country people.'[62]

Menzies never doubted his vision for Cheeloo. Even after he was detained in North America by the wars, he kept his concern. In 1940, while struggling with his PhD, he continued to write 'thought provoking' letters to the Associated Boards in New York, arguing for the 'maintaining and strengthening the University along the lines which it has followed in the past.'[63]

> Cheeloo should provide as broad an education as possible especially in those subjects which will best fit Christian students to integrate their Christian life into the essentially Chinese culture in which it must live. We all realize that Christianity is not essentially foreign to Chinese culture, but few seem to understand how essential it is to train adolescent students in a Christian atmosphere where Christian ideals and attitudes are placed before them in a favourable atmosphere. We may never have great numbers of students coming from our Church in North Honan, but I am very certain that if it had not been for the great similarity of 'Inland Chinese Christian Atmosphere' which pervades both Cheeloo University and our Church in North Honan, we would never have had the present indispensable Christian leadership in our Church ... With them Christianity is not something foreign but Jesus' Way of Life as natural in China as anywhere else in the world.

He trusted that in the Christian reconstruction Cheeloo would not be cramped into a second-rate institution, but would carry on its traditions of the past of providing the Christians of North China with the broadest education possible.

The North China country Christian does not live by bread alone. He is not only a farmer but a thinker as well. You might even call him a philosopher. He lives the same kind of life as the ancient philosophers who taught in the same environment. To him it is essential that he adjust his Christian way of life to the old Chinese philosophers' teachings which are the background of all Chinese thinking. It is therefore important that our Christian preachers and teachers be adequately trained in order to guide their parishioners 'into all truth.' Cheeloo has done this in the past and must continue to do it in the future.[64]

Chapter 14

Mature Archaeologist, the 1930s

Menzies's interest in oracle bones led to a unique mission theory that stressed cultural accommodation. The early Christian church had converted the Roman Empire by adaptation, which laid the foundations for Western civilization. In China, the Jesuits of the late Ming and early Qing followed the same policy, broad adaptation in non-essentials while retaining the purity of the Christian faith.[1] This tradition had been forgotten or rejected by the time Protestant missionaries arrived in China in the nineteenth century. They no longer stressed humility, patience, and adaptation. Instead, to many Chinese they epitomized the Westerner's arrogant air of superiority, exacerbated by the constant threat of military protection for their self-declared 'rights.' Out of his experience in North Henan, Menzies rebelled against the foreignness of this gospel with its Western houses, hospitals, church architecture, and 'compound-centric' culture. The conversion of China could be achieved only by adapting the gospel to the Chinese reality. His participation in Christian higher education and scientific archaeology would provide the means to develop a 'firm foundation' for Christian preaching. While the previous chapter dealt with his views and work with Christian higher education in the early 1930s, this chapter will deal with his final archaeological contributions during that same period.

Divinatory Inscriptions

Menzies was recognized as one of a dozen scholars who contributed to the first two of the three stages of evolution of oracle studies as a scientific subject. During the first stage, from 1899 to 1928, he assembled his collection of broken fragments, deciphered key oracle ideographs, and published *Yinxu Buci* (Oracle Records from the Waste of Yin) and completed a draft of its successor. In the second stage, 1928 to 1937, the Academia Sinica's excavations at Anyang marked the transformation of oracle studies into a science. It expanded from identification and publication to examination of divination methods, periodization, and the Shang calendar. In the third stage, Menzies was exiled in Canada because of the war. Oracle studies expanded in scope and depth, with important achievements in bone matching, forgery identification, and, most important, correlating information from oracle inscriptions with Bronze Age geography, human skeletons, society, economy, culture, and science.[2]

Menzies's work at Cheeloo was more sophisticated than his artefact collecting at the Waste of Yin. The early books of oracle studies were simply collections of rubbings with no explanation or transcription of the ideographs into modern characters. When Menzies was planning his second book he decided to include identification, etymology, and explanations. He did not, unfortunately, complete this project, but he did carry it out on a smaller scale in 'A Critical Study of the Divinatory Inscriptions from the Collection of Paul D. Bergen,' published in *Cheeloo Quarterly* in 1935.[3]

The identification and explanation of individual ideographs was painstaking, requiring knowledge of Chinese classics and the development of the Chinese writing system. Menzies's identifications were based on hundreds of bits of textual, phonetic, linguistic, and graphic evidence each of which independently was not conclusive. But by piecing together these fragments of evidence he was able to give rational and plausible explanations of unknown Shang ideographs.

Let us consider one Shang character: 且, the word for 'ancestor' that appears frequently in the oracle records. For a long time, scholars such as Bernhard Karlgren believed that the ancient Chinese had practised fertility worship and that this ideograph was shaped like a male genital.[4] Menzies challenged this view – which was the heart of his reconception of the nature of God in ancient China – by pointing out that it was 'imaginative' to identify 且 as the male genital. Rather, it was the Shang form for the character 祖, pronounced *zu*, which is in the shape of a grave: the horizontal strokes represent the surface and the vertical strokes resemble ropes linking the wooden frames surrounding a grave. This reading, Menzies explained, was based on comparative evidence from a number of sources: the *Shuowen Jiezi*, written during the Later Han dynasty (ca. 100 CE), the first dictionary to explain and interpret

Chinese characters according to the system of radicals and strokes, including some oracle graphs; the *Shang Shu*, 'History of the Shang,' in the *Book of History*; the *Zhou Yi* (old spelling *Chou I*, the Zhou *Book of Changes*), written by Wendi, first king of the Zhou dynasty (ca. 1050 BCE); the *Zuo Zhuan* (old spelling *Tso Chuan*), the *Tradition of the Zuo*, a commentary on the *Annals of Lu*; and the *Zhou Li*, the *Rituals of the Zhou* dynasty; as well as modern publications by Luo Zhenyu and Wang Xiang.[5]

In his reconception of the nature of religious worship of the Shang kings, Menzies came to believe that they worshipped an all-powerful, monotheist God named *Shangdi* (which he spelled *Shangti*). In his commentary on this Shang ideograph, he asked:

> Did the Shang people worship fecundity organs? They worshiped *shangti* who was their omnipotent god. He controlled rain, wind and season, sent down distress or good fortune, decided the win or loss of a war, and was consulted whether a city should be built. When the Shang people had a request for *shangti*, they worshiped their ancestors who were believed to live with *shangti* together in heaven. With their blood ties, the Shang people believed that their ancestors would act as helpful mediator between them and *shangti*. For this reason, we find that Shang people worshiped their ancestors, pleading for rain and assistance on the battle ground.[6]

Menzies's identification of 𩵋 as 祖 (*zu*) has remained the accepted etymology, even though some doubt his reasoning for the 'grave' symbol. Yan Yiping, a leading scholar, viewed Menzies's challenge to the fertility-worship theory as 'brilliant and remarkable,' one that represented a different approach to ancient societies. Menzies's 'Study of the Divinatory Inscriptions' represents his achievement in epigraphic study of oracle inscriptions and is still highly regarded by scholars. When Yan Yiping reprinted it in 1978 with his own commentary, he wrote that since Menzies's study was not available in Taiwan, he had made a copy in Japan.[7] This expanded edition is available in libraries around the world.

James Menzies had a phenomenal visual memory. He could visualize the broken edge of one fragment of bone and remember that it matched – scratches and all – a piece he had seen in another collection. After being buried underground for three thousand years, many bones had been broken during their excavation and shipping. As a result, pieces of one bone ended up in different collections and were published separately, and thus their value as historical documents was reduced. In 1918, by chance, Wang Guowei matched an important inscription, which contained the Shang royal genealogy, from different books, making scholars realize the importance of oracle matching. However, Wang's discovery was happenstance, whereas Menzies and his assistant Zeng Yigong established oracle matching as a specific field.[8]

Menzies's major contribution appeared in his article 'A Comparative Study of the New and Old Editions of Luo Chen-yu's *Earlier Compilation of Written Inscriptions from the Waste of Yin* and the Resultant Newly Discovered Historical Materials,' which was published in *Cheeloo Quarterly*, in 1933.[9] By comparing Luo's *Earlier Compilation*, published in Japan in 1913, with the new edition of 1933, published in Shanghai, Menzies was able to match sixty-five fragments into twenty-nine larger pieces, some of which contained important inscriptions. From rubbings in six books published by Chinese, Japanese, English, and Canadian scholars, he was able to reconstruct one whole bone with six divinatory inscriptions. With this new information he challenged Luo Zhenyu's view that *Tian Yi Shang* (Heavenly City Shang) was a mistake for *Da Yi Shang* (Great City Shang) (there is only one stroke difference between 'great' and 'Heaven,' the uppermost horizontal). '*T'ien* (*Tian*) *Yi Shang* as recorded in *Shang Shu* did exist. Luo Chenyu failed to realize this because he did not pay attention to bone matching.'[10]

Among the newly discovered historical materials were four inscribed human skulls that Menzies had purchased from peasants in 1915 or 1916. At first, he thought they were forgeries, but they proved to be the only human skull inscriptions discovered.[11] These particular inscriptions enabled Menzies to reconstruct the military campaigns of Zhou Xing, the last Shang tyrant, against the states to the east of Henan. King Zhou launched three campaigns against Renfang (the state of Ren), also called Yifang (the state of Yi), in southwestern Shandong, whose leader Renfang Bo, known as Bo Yi in the Classics, was considered a Confucian sage. Refusing to surrender, Renfang Bo fled to the eastern coastal region. One of the skull inscriptions contained the name Renfang Bo. In Menzies's reconstruction, the Shang campaigns were led by a general named You Hou Xi, the duke of You. For a long time, *you* had been interpreted as a pronoun, but Menzies identified it as the name of a state. After the Zhou conquered the Shang (1122 BCE traditional / 1045 BCE revised), the victorious Zhou king Wu chased You Hou Xi, who fled to Yan to organize resistance. Yan (old spelling Yen, as in Yenching University), Menzies claimed, later became the state of Lu. Since You Hou Xi was a brutal military man who controlled his subjects by terror, he was deserted by the people of Yan when the Zhou army arrived.[12]

Another important study completed by Menzies at Cheeloo was *Jiagu Yanjiu* (Oracle Bone Studies), his lecture notes written in Chinese, printed in the spring of 1933. This little book was Menzies's masterpiece, but because of its limited edition, only a few copies were available. Nevertheless, as Li Chi noted, it was widely read and quoted and is still recognized as an important work.

The first five chapters of *Jiagu Yanjiu* gave a brief history of oracle bones since 1899, when Wang Yirong found 'dragon bones' in a Beijing drugstore. This was first-hand information that Menzies had accumulated during the fifteen years when he was the self-appointed custodian of the Waste of Yin, and has been accepted as the authentic version, as Wang Yuxin wrote in *Jiaguxue Tonglun* (A Comprehensive Study of Oracle Bone Inscriptions). The only other collector of oracle bones who actually visited the Waste of Yin was Luo Zhenyu. He sent his brothers to collect bones, but he himself did not visit the site until 1915. 'However, Menzies ... spent more than twenty years at Anyang. His observation on the site was very different from the cursory inspection made by Luo Zhenyu. So, Menzies was able to get up-to-date information about oracle bone discoveries and circulation. He lived for years by the site and therefore his book *Jiagu Yanjiu* has *the most accurate, detailed, and authentic descriptions* on early oracle bone history' (italics added).[13]

Chapters 6 and 7 of *Jiagu Yanjiu* list the relevant books and articles (127 in all) published between 1903 and 1933, critically described in chronological order. Recognizing the significant contribution made by Luo Zhenyu and Wang Guowei, Menzies used them as to demarcate the development of oracle-bone studies as an independent field.

The last, most important chapter takes up half the book. It focuses on the genealogy of the Shang royal family, the eleven kings at Yin and their ancestors, their wives and myriad children, the backbone of late Shang history. Wang Yuxin commented that 'this chapter reflects the current achievements on the study of Shang royal genealogy. So, like Dong Zuobin's *Fifty Years of Study in Oracle Inscriptions* and *Sixty Years of Study in Oracle Inscriptions*, *Jiagu Yanjiu* is a critical review of the achievements of the early development stage of oracle bone study. As an important work on the history of oracle bone study, it helped and directed the research efforts in the next stage.'[14]

Here is an example of how James Menzies's mind worked at the microscopic level. By comparing the names listed in the oracle inscriptions with the names of the Shang kings recorded in *Shi Ji* (the Book of History) and other classics, Luo Zhenyu and Wang Guowei had been able to reconstruct the Shang lineage. The Shang had a distinct set of rules for royal titles: the honorific *fu* (father) was used by the reigning king to refer to his father or his uncles; *zu* (ancestor) was used for his grandfather's generation and earlier; and *xiong* (brother) referred to his elder brothers. These rules were also applied to queens.[15] Menzies regarded Wang Guowei as 'the greatest Chinese scholar of the last three hundred years,' yet he was not afraid to challenge the venerable scholar's identification of the names of two kings: Yang Jia (old spelling Yang Chia), the sixteenth king of the Shang, the last before the capital was moved to Yin (reigned 1408–1401 BCE traditional), and Wo Jia (old spelling Huo Chia), the thirteenth king (1490–1465 BCE). 'Lo Chen-yu and Wang Kuo-wei wrongly interpreted the character *chiang*, which was formed by the dropping horns of a mountain sheep and a man's mouth, as equivalent to the character *yang* for sheep. They also considered this as a homophone for the *yang* of Yang Chia. This identification has been generally accepted but is quite wrong and leads to much confusion in the genealogy of the Shang Dynasty.' Based on his own graph analysis and textual information, Menzies argued that the graph 𐐂 was not the name of Yang Jia, but that of Wo Jia, and that Yang Jia was inscribed as 𐐂.[16]

Here is Menzies's full reasoning, as taken from the draft of his doctoral thesis:

It is not difficult to see how the ancient form of the character *hsiang* [pinyin *xiang*, elephant] formed from elephant and mouth was copied by the early *li shu* brush script writers as *yang* [sheep]. And there is another error copied in the present text of the *Bamboo Annals* where under Yang Chia an original note says, 'an alternate name is Huo Chia.' Now the character *huo*, formed of a stalk of millet and a mouth, is also a wrong copy of late [1070 BCE] bone writing of the character *hsiang*. Mr. Wang Kuo-wei, perhaps the greatest Chinese scholar of the last three hundred years, did not fathom this when he edited the *Ancient Bamboo Annals*. The simple writing of Chiang Chia with a sheep's head and a man's body is found on Ch'ien-pien 7.40.2, 1.42.6, 1.43.1, 1.43.2, 1.43.3, etc. This is the script of Wu Ting's period [pinyin Wuding, the twentieth Shang king and the fourth at Yin, 1324–1263 BCE traditional], and Wu Ting would address his paternal uncle, the literary records' Yang Chia, as 'Father Chia,' and not by his full title, Yang Chia. This is an additional proof that Chiang Chia is the literary records' Wo Chia, and not Yang Chia. Since Wo Chia is of the fourteenth generation, he precedes Yang Chia of the sixteenth generation by two generations, and Wu Ting of the seventeenth generation would quite properly call him by his ancestral temple title Chiang Chia. It was customary for a grandson to call his grandfather by his temple title although at times the general term Tsu [zu], ancestor, was often used, perhaps before a permanent title had been finally chosen by the family. This use of tsu, ancestor, occurs on Hou-pien 1.27.7; 'Tsu Hsin [pinyin Zu Xin], one ox; Tsu Chia [pinyin Zu Jia], one ox; Tsu Ting [pinyin Zu Ding], one ox.' The person who holds the position in the Shang genealogy between Tsu Hsin and Tsu Ting is Wo Chia, so that this person named Tsu Chia can be none other than Wo Chia or Chiang Chia of the bone inscriptions.[17]

Roughly about the same time, the famous Chinese scholar Guo Moruo came to the same conclusion. His identifications of Yang Jia and Wo Jia became widely known through his book *Buci Tongcuan* (Annotations and General Discussions on Oracle Bone Inscriptions), which has been re-published several times. Menzies's lecture notes, *Jiagu Yanjiu*, were never officially published until 1996, when Qilu Press reprinted it.

Students and Colleagues

James Menzies was very generous with his research, willingly sharing his interest in oracle bones with his students and colleagues. His assistant, Zeng Yigong, the Manchu scholar whom he recruited in Beijing, became known in his own right as the first scholar to specialize in matching oracle bones. After Menzies left China in 1936, Zeng carried on 'the work which Mr. Menzies left for him to do.'[18] The first result was his book *Jiagu Zhuicun* (Matched Oracle Bones), published in 1939. Zeng also did important research in identifying duplications among the published inscriptions. It had been common for scholars to exchange rubbings, and so one rubbing might be published in different books, with resulting confusion. In his '*Yinxu Shuqi Houbian* Jiaoji' (Notes on the *Later Supplement of Oracle Bone Inscriptions from the Waste of Yin*), published in 1939 by Cheeloo University, Zeng listed over one thousand inscriptions published in Luo Zhenyu's *Yinxu Shuqi Houbian* and reprinted in other books.[19]

The eminent archaeologist Hu Houxuan wrote in his review of Zeng's books, 'Zeng Yigong is the disciple of Menzies. He has been diligently studying oracle bone inscriptions for years. Besides *Index of Shang Place Names in Oracle Bones*, he has two other books *Yinxu Shuqi Houbian Jiaoji* and *Jiagu Zhuicun*. The first is about identification of duplications of oracle bone inscriptions and the latter is about oracle bone matching.

These two tasks are what I have stressed in my study of oracle bones. I am very delighted to find that Mr. Zeng has achieved more in his study and published his results.'[20]

Zeng Yigong worked as Menzies's research assistant in 1927–8 and from 1932 to 1936, but Menzies gave him freedom to pursue his own research interests. In this sense Menzies was a true teacher, and his relationship with Zeng was a remarkable contrast to the difficulties he would have with Bishop White. In the preface to *Jiagu Zhuicun*, Zeng generously wrote: 'Before my teacher J.M. Menzies went back to Canada in the summer of 1936, he urged me to study ... oracle bone periodization, divination method, graph identification, and broken bone matching. For years I have not forgotten his teaching ... Now I use this book to remember his teaching.'[21]

For oracle inscriptions to be transformed into meaningful historical data, they had to be dated in accordance with the Shang royal genealogy, a process called oracle-inscription periodization. Menzies was a pioneer in this field. By combining Chinese epigraphy and the typology of Western archaeology, he made a breakthrough discovery in 1928 when he was compiling *Yin-hsü P'u-tz'u Hou-pien* (Additional Collection of Oracle Records from the Waste of Yin). By studying a set of more than three hundred oracle bones that he acquired in 1924, he was able to date them based on each inscription's size and type and the Shang royal names. He recorded this discovery in the unfinished preface to this book.

Menzies's work on oracle dating was carried on by other scholars, such as Dong Zuobin, who had conducted the first excavation of Anyang in 1928 and whose five-period theory, published in 1932, has been accepted by scholars. Dong was a self-taught scholar who participated in all the Academia Sinica's excavations at Anyang and became known for his achievements in the dating of oracles according to the Shang calendar. This calendar, which survives as the sixty-year cycles of heavenly stems and earthly branches, had to be correlated with each Shang king's reign and the dates of specific inscriptions. Dong's published work on oracle periodization was an important breakthrough, because it provided a chronological framework for the correlation of oracles, bronzes, and other associated artefacts from the same strata.

Unfortunately, Dong Zuobin seems to have 'borrowed' some of Menzies's ideas of oracle-inscription periodization, for Menzies wrote to Bishop White: 'Before Tung [Dong] ever went to Changte in 1928, I had already divided my bones into periods and settled most of the methods. Foolishly I spent a day with Tung and talked in 1930 ... Well, Tung has given it all back in this long paper and never mentions that he got the idea from me. In fact says it is his most important discovery and contribution!! I am glad to inspire these young chaps to new work. But you would expect them to mention it. He only mentions my name as possessing some of the bones he uses as proofs.' Menzies raised this issue again a few months later: 'Tung himself is here and says I was the one to first separate the periods, yet he begins his article with his discovery.'[22]

Menzies's periodization was rejected by some scholars, such as Chen Mengjia, who asserted that 'Menzies' periodic classification of these bones was all wrong, because he wrongly identified "Father Ding" as Wu Ding and "Father Yi" as Xiao Yi. In my opinion, these bones belonged to the period of Kang Ding, Wu Yi and Wen Ding.'[23] The whole matter was settled in 1981, when Li Xueqin, the leading scholar of Shang history, published part of Menzies's unfinished 'Introduction.' He wrote: 'As early as 1928 when Menzies was writing the introduction to "The Second Collection of Oracle Records from the Waste of Yin," he came to the conclusion that this group of bones belongs to the time of Wu Ding and Zu Geng. After 1960, in my study of some difficult questions I came to the same conclusion. I published my views in 1977 on the occasion of the discovery of the tomb of Fu Hao [a Shang princess whose spectacular tomb was discovered near Xiaotun].'[24] After Hu Houxuan passed away in 1995, nobody could challenge Li Xueqin on oracle-bone studies and Shang history.

Menzies had brilliant ideas on oracle classification and dating: the problem was that he did not publish them. What he left was an unfinished draft of *Additional Collection of Oracle Records from the Waste of Yin*, which he began compiling in Beijing in 1928. The criteria he used in his arrangement of over three hundred oracles excavated by villagers from one pot were the royal titles, the diviners' names, and the changes in the shape of the hollows on the bones. These were very important discoveries at the time. As noted by Wang Yuxin, an eminent scholar of oracle-bone studies, 'Menzies' oracle bone periodization efforts in 1928 [were] the result of a brilliant combination of Chinese epigraphy and Western archaeological typology methods. We could conclude, therefore, Menzies was ahead of other scholars of the time in oracle bone periodization.'[25]

Although this collection of oracle rubbings with its important 'introduction' was not published, Menzies made five or six copies, and it is interesting to trace how each copy circulated among the scholars. He gave one copy each to Rong Geng of Yenching University and Ma Hang of the National Palace Museum as thanks for their help. According to

Rong Geng, 'Five copies were made. Menzies kept three of them, while the other two were given to me and Ma Hang.'[26] Rong's copy was borrowed and studied by Ye Yushen, Guo Moruo, Dong Zuobin, Tang Lan, and Shang Chengzuo, the leading scholars in oracle studies.[27] The leading scholar Hu Houxuan stated that Menzies made five sets of rubbings and kept one, giving the others to Ma Hang, Rong Geng, Shang Chengzuo, and Zeng Yigong. Rong Geng gave his set to Yu Shengwu, who donated it to Tsinghua University. It is now kept at Beijing University. Shang Chengzuo's copy was lost during the war. As for the copy given to Zeng Yigong, his assistant, Hu said that Menzies took it back to Canada and gave it to the University of Toronto.[28]

The discrepancies between Rong Geng's and Hu Houxuan's stories were corrected by James Hsü when he edited and published Menzies's *Yin-hsü P'u-tz'u Hou-pien* in 1972. He quoted C.C. Shih (pinyin Shi Jingcheng), a professor at the Department of East Asian Studies of the University of Toronto and a long time friend of Menzies, who said that Menzies had made only four sets of rubbings in 1928, not five. The University of Toronto never received a complete set, nor did any Chinese scholar, since Menzies did not include rubbings of the fragile tortoise shells. He made only one set of shell rubbings and kept it himself. This, the only complete copy, was acquired by the Royal Ontario Museum after his death.[29]

My own research confirms that Menzies did not give a copy to Shang Chengzuo, a researcher at Ginling University in Nanjing. Otherwise, Shang would not have needed to borrow Menzies's book of rubbings from Rong Geng. This was confirmed by a letter Menzies wrote to Bishop White on 27 December 1933: 'Today I saw Shang Cheng-tsuo's *Yinqi Yicun* [Additional Oracle Inscriptions from the Waste of Yin], a collection of fine rubbings. They publish a large number of mine without any recognition whatever. When I made my rubbings I gave one set to Jung Keng [Rong Geng] of Yenching and one set to Ma Hang. They both helped me get my work done and exchanged rubbings but it was a definite understanding on their part that the rubbings were for their study and I was quite sure that they would not be published ... I am going to take the matter up with them both and see where Shang got the rubbings for no one else got them but these two men.'[30] If Menzies did make four sets of rubbings, and gave Rong Geng and Ma Hang one set each, keeping one for himself, one set is not accounted for. Zeng Yigong did not have it, as he tried to borrow a copy of rubbings from Jung Keng in 1939.

In 1936 Menzies returned to Canada for his regular furlough. The outbreak of war prevented his return to Cheeloo. Consequently his rubbings remained unpublished. In 1939, Menzies's assistant Zeng Yigong wrote him that Rong Geng and Yu Shengwu were going to publish the collection.[31] Chinese copyright law at that time stated that if an author failed to publish his work within fifteen years, his copyright would lapse. It is not clear what happened, but Rong Geng decided not to proceed with the publication. In 1947 he wrote: 'I was urged by friends to publish the rubbings, but I do not want to betray Menzies.'[32] In 1951 Hu Houxuan published 874 rubbings from Menzies's book in his own monograph *Zhanhou Nanbei Suojian Jiagu Lu* (Collection of Oracle Bones Seen in North and South China after the War). Under the new political situation in China, this breach of academic courtesy was no longer a problem. The publication of Menzies's whole collection had to wait until 1972, when it was edited by James Hsü and published by the Royal Ontario Museum.

Unfinished Business

These publications represent only part of Menzies's research efforts at Cheeloo. The annual reports of the Institute of Chinese Studies list at least ten research projects carried on by Menzies, some of which he completed, while others remained in process. These included:

1 'Introduction to the Study of Oracle Bones' (first draft, 1934).
2 'The Genealogy of Kings and Queens of Shang Dynasty' (printed, 1934).
3 'Later Collection of Oracle Records from the Waste of Yin' (ready for publication).
4 'A Comparative Study of All the Extant Oracle Bone Sentences' (in process, 1936).
5 'The Wars of the Shang Dynasty in the Oracle Bones' (research partially done, 1935).
6 'The Shapes of Shang Dynasty Vessels' (materials collected, 1935).
7 'The Early Art of China' (draft, 1935).
8 'A Dictionary Index of the Characters in the Oracle Records from the Waste of Yin' (card index completed).
9 'A Translation with Commentary of the *Oracle Records from the Waste of Yin*' (commentary incomplete).
10 'The Religious Conception of the Shang Dynasty' (in process, 1936).[33]

Their intricate and painstaking drawings and rubbings made these manuscripts too expensive to be published by the university, for the Institute of Chinese Studies had no funds other than the income from the Harvard-Yenching Institute. After paying salaries, it could only afford to publish the *Cheeloo Quarterly*, another journal, and a few course kits. As director, Menzies understood the situation and never pushed for special treatment.

He seemed to have found outside funding in 1936 when Lucius C. Porter, executive secretary of HYI, asked Menzies about his 'manuscript material on the Shang oracle bones and Shang dynasty culture generally. I remember that you have been working for some time on this material and wonder if you do not have it ready for publication. My thought is to present it, if the material is ready, as a special project to be considered by the Publication Committee of the Harvard-Yenching Institute at Cambridge.'[34] Menzies was delighted, and quickly submitted four studies that were ready for publication:

1 'Menzies' Second Collection of Oracle Bone Records from the Waste of Yin,' with rubbings of 3000 bone fragments, translation, commentary and index.
2 'Stone, Bone, Jade, Bronze and Pottery Artefacts from the Waste of Yin,' with photos, description, and interpretation of about 1000 objects.
3 'Menzies' First Collection of Oracle Bone Records from the Waste of Yin,' with rubbings, translation, interpretation, and index.
4 'The Culture History and Religion of the Shang Dynasty.'[35]

Porter replied enthusiastically that he would forward Menzies's memorandum 'to the Publication Committee with the request that they take favourable action on at least one of the projects.' As a result, Menzies stated in the Institute's annual report: 'An application has been made through the Executive Secretary for China Dr. L.C. Porter for stenographic assistance as well as for the Harvard-Yenching Institute to take over as a general project the publication of the "Second Collection of Oracle Bone Records from the Waste of Yin," which it seems is too large a project for the Sinological Institute of the University to finance itself. Two other major projects beyond the financial ability of the university were also mentioned.'[36] For whatever reason, Porter did not send the memorandum and Menzies's statement caused some confusion at Harvard, since the Publication Committee had 'never received any application of this kind.'[37] Menzies apparently never followed upon this opportunity.

Teaching

In addition to his own research, Menzies also established the first course in archaeology education at Cheeloo University. His 'Introduction to Archaeology' was given entirely in Chinese. This was a great challenge. Although he had spent decades studying oracle bones, he had little teaching experience and there was no textbook available. He inquired about archaeology education at Harvard, Yenching, and West China Union Universities.[38] For his courses, 'Oracle Bone Study' and 'Shang Dynasty Wars as Found in Oracle Bone Inscriptions,' he had to write his own textbooks. Unfortunately, the text on Shang wars was lost.

The students who took his courses were always fewer than ten, and so he conducted the lectures and seminars in his office. One student, Zhang Kunhe, recalled: 'Our classroom was Menzies' office. It was a big room on the third floor in *Kaowen* building, with two windows. Menzies and Zeng Yigong each had a big desk beside the windows. To the north there was a large lecture table. When we had class, Menzies had one side of the table and the rest of us sat on the other sides.' Zeng Yigong helped write oracle graphs on the blackboard.[39] Sometimes seminars were held in the museum established by Menzies with items from his own collection, where the students were shown artefacts from different periods. Menzies tried to give his students a solid introduction to archaeology in general, and a detailed examination of oracle studies. Sadly, none of his students became leading scholars: his best student died during the civil war.[40]

Shandong, like North Henan, was the heartland of ancient Chinese civilization, dotted with archaeological sites. Always curious about what lay below the ground, Menzies took his students to the excavations around Jinan such as the neolithic village at Longshan. Even though they did not have a chance to participate, they learned the techniques of surveying, stratigraphy, and artefact identification and conservation. Further, with the assistance of his colleagues, Menzies carried out a survey of archaeological sites in the province, and even applied to the HYI for special funds to carry out a cooperative excavation:

In Shantung province, the Provincial Librarian, who is charged with the custody of Provincial Antiquities, is keen on archaeological research and is very favourable to our participating in such work. Our present budget will not permit of our co-operating as more than observers. The province allows no funds for this purpose. These are provided by cultural foundations such as Academia Sinica, who naturally wish the work to be carried on by their own research fellows when they provide the funds. There are many sites in Shantung awaiting excavation but there is no hope of a private institution such as ours carrying on independent excavation. This must be done in co-operation with a government organ such as the provincial library or Academia Sinica. Should our institution carry out the preliminary field reconnais-sance and propose a definite undeveloped site with the funds necessary for the field work, it is quite possible that the necessary government co-opera-tion could be secured on the basis of their supplying certain personnel. If we were able to share in the field expenses of certain projects already proposed to be undertaken by the Shantung Library, we would be able to share with the Academia Sinica and Shantung Provincial University in these joint undertakings.[41]

After the HYI's failure to get a joint excavation of Anyang, it was not eager to engage in such a cooperative venture, and so turned down Menzies's second proposal. Nevertheless, Menzies and a British mission-ary, F.S. Drake, did carry out their field survey, which Drake published in the late 1930s. After 1949, archaeologists in Shandong had to repeat this survey, as Drake's publications in English were unavailable.[42]

The genealogy of the Shang kings seems irrelevant to evangelism. But for Menzies, archaeology was the way to serve the evangelical cause in China. His 'providential' discovery of the Waste of Yin was the formative event in his life. He believed he could find the religious foundations of Chinese civilization by studying oracle inscriptions, the religious docu-ments of the Shang people. He was convinced they had been worship-pers of the monotheistic *Shangdi*, or God. His change from rural evangelism to archaeology becomes understandable when put in the context of the missionary enterprise. Driven by China's needs, chal-lenged by Chinese nationalism, and pushed by the social gospel, Protes-tant missions eventually accepted – or at least tolerated – professionalism. An increasing number of missionaries became experts in medicine, education, science, and social services. Menzies became an expert in archaeology.

Motivated by his *Christian* purpose, Menzies made significant contribu-tions to Chinese archaeology. Assisted by Cheeloo University, he com-pleted and published several important research projects, which covered such topics as oracle-inscription identification, oracle-bone periodization, forgery identification, oracle-bone history, Shang royal genealogy, and religion. Some were pioneering works on matching fragments, while others helped shed new light on the rituals of divination and oracle-bone periodization. Most of his research was not published but circulated among scholars in the field. Li Chi, the excavator of Anyang, regarded Menzies as one of the few 'far-sighted' scholars, and commented that the 'fortunate combination of an appropriate appointment and an inborn instinct for archaeology prepared the way for his special contribution to the oracle bone studies among the small community of foreign scholars.'[43]

Menzies made Cheeloo a centre of oracle-bone collection and studies known throughout China. In 1940 the foremost archaeologist, Hu Houxuan, was attracted to Cheeloo because of Menzies's collections, even though Cheeloo itself was in exile in West China during the anti-Japanese war. After the war, in 1946, Wu Jinding, a student of Li Chi with a PhD from the School of Oriental and African Studies at the University of London, returned to head the Institute of Chinese Studies at Cheeloo. Wu was famous for the discovery of the Black Pottery neolithic culture at Longshan. For one brief moment, archaeological education at Cheeloo seemed bright, and James Menzies was its pioneer. He was not alone in broadening the scope of evangelism, but he was unique in approaching it from the perspective of Chinese archaeology and culture.

Chapter 15

Frustrating Exile, 1936–1941

The Winds of War

In June 1936 James Menzies wrapped up his projects and left China for his scheduled furlough. Always the adventurer, he travelled on the Trans-Siberian Railway, retracing the route he had taken on his first trip to China in 1910. He chose this route because he wanted to see the Chinese collections in European museums, but more importantly he wanted to see the Siberian landscape. For some time, he had been fascinated with the steppe peoples of Central Asia. As he stared out the train window with his remarkable vision trained by years of surveying, he speculated on the role that the rivers of Siberia had played in the cultural exchange between China and the West.

A warm welcome awaited him in Toronto. 'Home life in Toronto was a truly wonderful family experience,' Marion recalled in her memoirs:

> It was the first time we lived together for several years, not counting our home life on vacations from boarding schools. We ate breakfast and dinner together, attended church, had guests in, mostly missionary colleagues of our parents ... We took more adult appreciation of our father's study and interest in his Shang Dynasty oracle bones. Father guided our visits to the Royal Ontario Museum where we viewed that wonderful collection of Chinese artifacts ... Father had a wonderful way of telling stories and capturing our interest in artifacts he showed us to illustrate a point, whether part of a broken bowl or a small Shang arrowhead.

Marion concluded, 'In our home life we were drawn close to each other. This closeness remained with us all of our lives, though seas and continents might divide us physically.'[1]

By this time, Menzies was at the prime of his academic life. Twenty years after his 'discovery' of the Waste of Yin, he was a recognized scholar and professor of archaeology at Cheeloo, one of the finest Christian universities in China. Even though he was disturbed by recent events, he was optimistic about the future of Cheeloo, the Christian church in China, and his own role in both of them. He fully expected to return to Cheeloo for the autumn term of 1937, and so he left his museum and library there, bringing only those few books, manuscripts, and index cards needed for his immediate work.

On 7 July 1937 James and Annie Menzies had their luggage packed and tickets purchased to return to Cheeloo when Japan launched a full-scale invasion of China, the beginning of the eight-year Anti-Japanese War. There had been ominous signs before they went on furlough. Student strikes at Yenching and Cheeloo in late 1935 had been part of the national December 9th movement against 'a Japanese attempt to organize north China into an autonomous regime under Japanese influence.'[2] The invasion of 1937–8 was among the most brutal atrocities of the twentieth century. Its goal was to terrorize an abject people into submission. Everywhere, the Japanese burned villages, carpet-bombed cities, and raped women. By the end of 1937 North China was under Japanese control, and in January Nanjing fell in 'the rape of Nanjing,' in which untold thousands died. By the spring the Japanese had advanced up the Yangzi River as far as Wuhan.

Missionaries and converts were not free from harassment and even vicious attack. Worried about the safety of its missionaries, the Board of Overseas Missions postponed the Menzies' return. Tragically, this delay turned out to be permanent. Menzies was 'detained at home' from 1936 to 1951, when he finally accepted retirement. Other missionaries managed to reincorporate themselves back into Canadian life, but Menzies found that especially difficult. Deeply committed to his oracle bone studies, he only engaged in activities related to China. He wandered through North America, took a research position at the Royal Ontario Museum, obtained a doctorate from the University of Toronto, and then became a China expert with the U.S. Office of War Information in San Francisco and the State Department in Washington, DC. He had opportunities to settle down, but China was his home and he did not want to become 'less useful' in Canada. Nevertheless, as one of Canada's best China scholars, he made important contributions to Chinese studies in Canada through his research at the ROM and the University of Toronto, even though he failed to see his work published in his own country.

The Circle of Friends Is Broken

The war that brought the Menzies family together in Toronto shattered the world he had left in China. In retrospect, the 'golden age' of Chinese archaeology lasted only ten brief years, from 1928 to 1937, coinciding with the Academia Sinica excavations at Anyang. For a while it seemed that the excavation and study of China's ancient past could be achieved through 'internationalism' and 'sinification' of archaeology. As the foreign director of the Institute of Chinese Studies, James Menzies was at the centre of student and scholarly nationalism. By December 1937, his circle of friends (chapter 12) was broken, never to come together again. Some had died: Davidson Black, tragically young at forty-nine, and Berthold Laufer, the curator of the Field Museum. The rest had scattered.

Among the first victims of the Japanese invasion were the Canadian missions in Henan. In October 1937 the Japanese armies advanced down the railroad lines, capturing Zhangde and Weihui. A year later, in November 1938, Chiang Kai-shek ordered the dynamiting of the dikes holding back the Yellow River. The Anglican missions at Kaifeng and Zhengzhou came under Japanese occupation. By the summer of 1938, the North Henan mission stations had evacuated their territory; personnel temporarily resided at the mountain resort of Jigongshan for the fall and winter. In effect, the North Henan mission was disbanded, and it was not until after the Japanese surrender in 1945 that any Canadian missionaries could enter the district. Some remained close to the front, migrating to temporary refuge in southwest China, but many returned to Canada.

In October 1937, as the Japanese advanced towards Jinan, the capital of Shandong, Cheeloo University had three options: 'to close for the duration of the war, to remain in east China with the probability of frequent Japanese interference, or to flee to the unconquered interior.' The heroic story of the trek of the universities from 'Occupied China' to 'Free China' has been told frequently: how the students dismantled the libraries and laboratories and carried them thousands of miles, by whatever transportation was available, through the enemy lines to Chongqing, the wartime capital in Sichuan province, next door to Tibet. 'By June 1939 there were left in Occupied China only a few universities and colleges. Forty-seven institutions had moved to Free China and twenty-one had moved into foreign concessions in Shanghai or elsewhere.'[3] The migration of the schools was 'undertaken with high morale. It was accepted as a patriotic sacrifice to help keep the Chinese nation alive; it became a symbol of defiance of the Japanese who had deliberately destroyed the campus of Nankai University, and had billeted soldiers at Tsing Hua, Peita [Beida], and other schools.'[4]

Li Chi recounted in his monograph *Anyang* the sad trek of the Academia Sinica and the tens of thousands of oracle-bone fragments and an estimated 250,000 pottery shards from the Anyang excavations. The Academia Sinica had excavated Anyang continuously since 1928 and the thirteenth and fourteenth seasons in the spring and fall of 1936 were among the most spectacular. The archaeologists carried out 'in a systematic manner the carpet-rolling method of tracing the building foundations,' and discovered caves, caches, and neolithic semi-underground dwellings. In one pit were the first chariot burials, including human and animal sacrifices; in another, the 'crowning achievement and, popularly considered, the greatest success of fifteen seasons' excavations in Anyang,' the royal archives containing 17,000 inscribed tortoise-shell oracles, each neatly stacked for posterity, dating back to the earliest kings of Yin/ Shang. The fifteenth season in the spring of 1937 was to be the last.[5]

As a Guomindang government department, the Academia Sinica could not remain in Occupied China, but had to follow the national government to safety. In November 1937, after Beijing had fallen to the Japanese, a dispirited group of scholars gathered at a wayside inn near Changsha, Hunan, to decide what they would do during the war. Some – 'our talented younger archaeologists' – chose to leave for patriotic war duties, some wanted to stay with the collection. 'The main portion of the collections and the library of the Institute of History and Philology were, through the energy and historical insight of a few leaders, successfully transported to several destinations ... Needless to say, in the course of moving these national treasures, which included scientific records and equipment, there were overwhelming difficulties to overcome and inevitable losses suffered due to chaotic wartime conditions.'[6]

From 1938 to 1940, the Academia Sinica was based near Kunming, capital of Yunnan, where the artefacts were set out on shelves. It took half a year to complete the transportation to their next destination, a remote mountain village of Lizhuang (old spelling Li-chuang) in Sichuan, where they remained until 1945. Remarkably, the scholars continued to study the artefacts. These included Dong Zoubin, the self-trained archaeologist who had conducted the first Anyang excavation, who was in charge of the oracle bones. Lizhuang became a cosmopolitan place as the Institute of Social Sciences, the Dongzhi University from Shanghai, the National Central Museum, model farms, and other government agencies were settled there. When eminent scholars such as Joseph Needham, author of the monumental *Science and Civilization in China*, came to visit this out-of-the way place, Li Chi claimed, 'Li-chuang was one of the few places in free China where scholars could meet and discuss academic problems.'[7]

The Academia Sinica had no choice but to evacuate, but for the Christian universities the issues were more complex. At Yenching, where so many of Menzies's colleagues were professors, the president John Leighton Stuart asserted his extraterritorial rights and identified the university as an American enclave, which granted it certain immunity. 'Yenching raised an American flag on its high campus pole and dared the Japanese to touch the property of a non-belligerent nation ... The Japanese were treated with unfailing courtesy but were not permitted to enter the campus except by special arrangement.'[8]

'Though such a program might have seemed contrary to Chinese nationalism under other circumstances,' Jessie Gregory Lutz concluded, 'it inspired few protests from Chinese in Peiping [Beijing] and in fact was presented as a contribution to China's national welfare. Stuart argued that continuing operation in Peiping, Yenching expressed its faith that Chinese control would eventually return to the area.'[9] While cultivating a complex network of Japanese officials, Stuart played a clandestine role as a middleman because of his personal friendship with Chiang Kai-shek. He was convinced that 'trying to bring about real friendship between the Japanese and Chiang Kai-shek was the best protection for the university ... He made at least four extensive visits to the wartime capital at Chungking [Chungqing], bearing messages and inquiries from the Japanese authorities, and upon his return reporting Chiang's responses.'[10]

Riven by factionalism before the war, Cheeloo was split into two campuses: the official Cheeloo in exile as a 'guest university' at the West China Union University (WCUU) in Chengdu, Sichuan, and the rump 'cow college' in Jinan. As the Japanese troops advanced toward Jinan in October 1937, Cheeloo decided 'to suspend classes and send the students away, especially the women, before the railway lines were cut ... By November 6 there were no students left on the campus.' There was no fighting on 27 December when the Japanese occupied the city. The university was closed during 1938, but the hospital remained open, with few patients and five Western doctors, although the medical classes were transferred to WCUU. When the question arose whether to reopen that fall, President Liu Shuming went to Chungqing to confer with the chairman of the board of directors, H.H. Kung, China's minister of finance and Chiang Kai-shek's brother-in-law. There, Liu found 'an entirely different psychology.' He was led to believe that unlike the situation at Yenching, reopening Cheeloo in Jinan might be interpreted as collaboration with the enemy. In fact, he was informed 'that the government will list Cheeloo as a traitor institution and that will be the end of any future recognition or cooperation ... A compromise was worked out whereby some teaching could be done at Tsinan [Jinan] provided it did not duplicate work done in Chengtu [Chengdu], and provided it was confined to departments not registered with the government.' The College of Theology, the Rural Institute, and the Nursing School opened at Jinan in the fall of 1939; a 'Sub-Freshman Course' drew twenty students.[11]

Even in exile, President Liu Shuming aspired to make Cheeloo the leading institute of Chinese studies in Free China. He hired several important historians, including Gu Jiegang, a graduate of Columbia and Peking Universities,[12] Qian Mu, a specialist in neo-Confucian philosophy who celebrated China's 'national spirit' in the anti-Japanese struggle,[13] and Lü Simian, the author of *Xiaoshuo conghua* (Colloquy of Fiction, 1914). He even hired Hu Houxuan, who was to become the leading oracle scholar of the next generation. At the time he was a promising young assistant to Dong Zuobin at the Academia Sinica, making ink squeezes of the collection and registering the specimens.[14] It seems President Liu lured Hu with promises that after the war he would have exclusive access to the Menzies collection of oracle bones left behind at Jinan. Decades later, Hu recalled: 'In 1939 Mr. Gu Jiegang accepted Cheeloo's invitation to head its Sinological Institute. He then invited Qian Mu and me to be the institute's researchers. He told me that Cheeloo had Menzies' large collection of oracle bones, which I could study.' Hu's decision to join Cheeloo caused some tension when the Academia Sinica accused Cheeloo of stealing unpublished studies on oracle bones and Cheeloo threatened to take the Academia to court if it did not retract its accusations.[15] This expansion worried Serge Elisseeff, director of the Harvard-Yenching Institute, who repeatedly demanded that Cheeloo cut its research projects and give more attention to undergraduate instruction.

James Menzies's collection was his life and without it he was bereft. He knew that the Japanese sent 'anthropologists' in the wake of the military invasion to loot the local and national museums of art objects. He also knew that they were particularly interested in oracle bones and other objects from the Three Dynasties, the Xia, Shang, and Zhou. When Menzies left China in 1936, expecting to return the following year, he left various components of his collections at North China Union Language School in Beijing, at the North Henan mission's business office in Tianjin, and in the museum at Cheeloo, with some hidden around the campus. The story of the peregrinations of Menzies's collections is recounted in the Epilogue to this book, but suffice to say, they remained hidden during the war and emerged relatively intact afterwards.

Desperately, in 1938 Menzies negotiated an agreement with Cheeloo president Liu Shuming to donate the artefacts that he had loaned to the Cheeloo museum. Menzies remained the owner of the oracle bones and other archaeological specimens he had left at the campus. Several boxes were stored in the house of Dr William McClure, one of the respected elder missionaries, who remained teaching medicine at the university; others were hidden in attics and behind walls.

The Royal Ontario Museum

Unlike during his previous furloughs, James Menzies returned to Toronto in 1936 as a recognized scholar. Most retired and some furloughing missionaries took a small rural charge or a larger city congregation, thus integrating themselves back into Canadian society. Before Menzies arrived, the Council of Christian Higher Education in China had sent the Board of Overseas Missions a letter commending his work:

> Rev. G.W. Shepherd presented the need for a presentation, as a part of a program for rural reconstruction, of the elements of Chinese religion that might serve as preparation for Christianity, and stated that in his judgment the work done by Professor Menzies in the early religion of the Chinese would have great practical value in this field. It was pointed out also that such work would be significant in dealing with students. It was therefore
>
> Voted, to request Professor Menzies to devote a sufficient portion of his furlough to making available the results of his research in the religion of the Shang dynasty, together with its historical and cultural background, and further
>
> To request the Foreign Mission Board of the United Church of Canada to co-operate in providing full facilities for this work, particularly secretarial assistance.[16]

The Board felt honoured, and despite chronic lack of funds it supported Menzies's research on Shang culture as much as it could. Since he had left his collections and library in China, the only way Menzies could make 'available the results of his researches in the religion of the Shang dynasty' would be to affiliate with some institution where he could continue to study oracle inscriptions and publish his ideas. The Royal Ontario Museum was the ideal choice. He had been an associate of director Charles Trick Currelly and a friend of Bishop William C. White. The ROM had a superb collection of Shang artefacts with which he was already familiar because he had helped Bishop White to acquire and authenticate many of them.

However, Menzies lacked official academic credentials, and a PhD program at the University of Toronto was suggested. One month after his arrival in Toronto, at the age of fifty-one with two decades' experience in Chinese archaeology and four years as professor, he returned to his alma mater as a 'special student' in the Department of Art and Archaeology. In his application, Menzies stated his purpose was 'to make available in English work already done during the past 22 years in the culture, religion and language of early China based on the Oracle Bones and other archaeological material found at Anyang, Honan.'[17] Besides the Council of Christian Higher Education in China, others had urged him to publish his studies. Lucius C. Porter, executive secretary of the Harvard-Yenching Institute, wrote: 'I very much hope that in addition to preparing more oracle bones for publication, you are putting into English a comprehensive picture of Shang dynasty culture as you have worked it out from your original material.'[18]

The Royal Ontario Museum had changed in the six years Menzies was in China from 1930 to 1936. The original 1915 building, which housed four separate departments in cramped quarters, was dwarfed by the new addition that opened in 1933, a three-storey 'H' that more than doubled the ROM's size. The grand entrance was a city block long, facing onto Queen's Park Crescent at the junction of Bloor Street, one of the most visible locations in Toronto, near the provincial legislature, across the street from Victoria College, and surrounded by the University of Toronto. Built in Italianate style, as befitted a metropolitan museum, the lobby had a gold mosaic dome inscribed, 'That All Men May Know His Works.' In a little eyrie above the main door, where he could see everyone who entered the building, was the office of the director, C.T. Currelly. The ROM was Currelly's museum, and he had a warm personal relationship with each employee.

The new ROM had eighteen galleries to display the Chinese collections, practically the entire third floor. But the bulk of the collection of tens of thousands of artefacts rested in storerooms. Until Bishop White was appointed Keeper of the Far Eastern Collection in 1934, the ROM had no China specialist. His energetic efforts from 1934 to his retirement in 1948 transformed the great mass of objects into a world-famous collection arranged by historic period.

As early as 1932, while still in Henan contemplating retirement, Bishop White drew up a proposal for a 'department of sinology' at the University of Toronto. No university in Canada taught Chinese culture or language. His proposal gained the support of Henry John Cody, White's old teacher at Wycliffe College and canon at St Paul's church, who was both minister of education in the provincial government and president of the University of Toronto. White wanted something more grandiose than a mere department, envisioning an 'Oriental college or hall,' a 'School of Chinese Studies.' His memorandum stressed economic motives – promoting Canadian soft-wood exports to China, for example – and a political 'gesture of friendliness and sympathy.' Revealing his orientalist view, he added 'ethnological studies of the peoples of North China and their relationship with Europe.' A quasi-independent school would receive greater recognition. The combination was ideal, 'a university course and a laboratory for the study of Chinese life and culture.'[19]

By 1934 Bishop White's work in China was done. He had always been progressive in indigenizing the church, and now that the diocese of Henan was as stable as the troubled times would allow, he named as his successor Lindel Tsen, the first Chinese bishop in the world-wide Anglican communion. White was almost sixty, and a lesser man would have retired to his study. Instead, he started his third career: curator and associate professor of Archaeology (Chinese). By this time, as Lovat Dickson points out, his religion vocation 'was subordinated to another element in his nature, ambition for fame.' He wanted to be recognized as the scholar who assembled and interpreted the world's greatest Chinese collection.[20]

In October 1934 White gave his inaugural lecture at the University of Toronto on the subject of 'Chinese Culture Three Thousand Years Ago.' He was an inspired teacher and public speaker who took his audiences 'into another world ... His enthusiasm carried a contagion.' During the war, he would fill the museum theatre for his Friday afternoon lectures on 'A Pageant of Chinese Life and Culture,' with slides and pictures. He wrote five scholarly books in ten years based on the ROM collections.[21] In May 1943, at the depth of the Second World War, White's dream came true when the university established the School of Chinese Studies, with himself as director and the only professor.

Outside the classroom, there was an imperious 'impersonal' quality about Professor White, 'more Chinese than the Chinese.' He and Currelly, two autocrats under one roof, worked out a modus operandi: the Far Eastern department was at the farthest corner from the director's office, at the back of the third floor; they seldom saw each other. If subordinates questioned his authority, White kicked up 'all-out rows.'[22] Consequently, he staffed the school with former missionaries who could survive the compound mentality. Teaching Chinese was Ruth Jenkins Watts, one of White's missionaries in Henan before she married. Another of White's protégés was Francis Tseng, a Wycliffe student who would become Lindel Tsen's successor as Bishop of Henan.

Lewis Walmsley, his successor and biographer, put it diplomatically. 'The mutation of William C. White, bishop, into William C. White, full professor and head of the School of Chinese Studies, was not however accomplished without some stain and abrasion.' Essentially, White was an autodidact who himself did not have scholarly credentials and was out of his depth in the academic world of professors with doctoral degrees. 'In his department new ideas had to be presented as if they had come from the bishop himself.' Walmsley quoted one colleague: 'He was scared to death inside when anyone took exception to his views in this new speciality. Bishop White could not adapt himself to ... this modern world. He remained at heart a mediaeval bishop, like Archbishop Baldwin of Canterbury who maintained the right to crown Richard Coeur de Lion.' Meanwhile he was estranged from Canon Cody and the churchmen who felt he had abandoned Christianity altogether. 'He now talked incessantly about Chinese bronzes and bones, their dating and significance, but I never once heard him mention theology or the church.'[23]

Doctoral Student and Research Assistant

As required by the School of Graduate Studies, Menzies constructed his doctoral program with three fields: Chinese archaeology was his major, with 'the culture of early China' and 'early Chinese scripts' as his minor fields. His thesis committee was headed by Bishop White, the only member who knew anything about China. C.T. Currelly, the museum builder and archaeologist who was fascinated by the Bronze Age, was not especially knowledgeable about the Chinese Bronze Age. Widely regarded as one of the foremost archaeologists of his generation, Homer A. Thompson (1906–2000) was associated with the excavation of the Athenian marketplace, the Agora.[24] Thomas F. McIlwraith (1899–1964) was the first anthropology professor hired by the University of Toronto, in 1925, and founder of the department nine years later.[25]

At first, Menzies's studies went well because they served everyone's interests. For James Menzies, it was an opportunity to use his 'exile' in Canada to bring together the results of his studies while earning a doctoral degree. The ROM was pleased to have a recognized authority to catalogue and study its large collection of oracle bones, bronzes, and other artefacts from the Shang and Zhou dynasties. Bishop White was able to have Menzies's assistance again, but this time their relationship was quite different: no longer between equals but between supervisor and research assistant. This hierarchical relationship and personality differences would make Menzies's studies at the ROM extremely difficult.

During his first year, Menzies did most of his coursework with Bishop White. We do not know how or on what White instructed Menzies regarding Chinese archaeology, early Chinese religion and social institutions, and early Chinese epigraphy and literature.[26] There is no doubt that the student knew much more than the teacher. He completed his required coursework by May 1937. His original plan was to finish the thesis in China, but the Japanese war made it possible to complete the whole program in Canada.

During this year, Menzies donated his expertise to the ROM in identifying and arranging their artefacts. For years the ROM had tried to secure financial assistance from the Rockefeller Foundation, but to no avail. In 1938, it did receive a special grant from the Foundation that would subsidize Menzies as a 'research assistant' to help put the Chinese collection in order, properly labelled. Having no idea of settling down in Canada permanently, Menzies accepted the offer on a year-to-year basis. Currelly agreed, but hoped Menzies would 'remain at the ROM as long as possible during the five years that the Rockefeller grant in aid of research was available.'[27]

The Board of Overseas Missions was pleased at this arrangement, as it relieved them of financial obligations. It granted Menzies a leave of absence for 1938 and congratulated him on 'the high tribute' paid to his scholarship by the Rockefeller Foundation. However, it reminded him that his mission was in China: 'We are glad that you have no other intention than return to China when the way is open. We trust that your studies and research at the Museum while here will make it possible for you to continue to render even greater service to China and the Chinese in the future.'[28]

When Menzies started to catalogue the ROM's collection, he found many mistakes in the identification and arrangement of objects. Because of his lack of first-hand knowledge and reliance on information provided by the shady 'curio dealers,' White had made many errors in his arrangement of the artefacts. Diplomatically, Menzies tried to correct the errors, but found that his suggestions were not welcomed. He told A.E. Armstrong of the Board of Overseas Missions: 'When I first came, I spent most of my time on the museum seeing that everything was in its proper chronological order in the rooms. Often this took up considerable time in research. I took seriously the museum's place in Canadian life and threw myself into making sure that all was correct. Then difficulties began to arise. The results of my work are all in the museum itself but do not show my name ... I am glad, however, that Canada will have a better arranged and more reliable display than before I came. Much should yet be done but cannot be without causing friction. So, I have left that side alone since the spring.'[29] While Menzies's expertise was not well received at the ROM, his advice was sought after by American institutions that acknowledged him as the North American authority on oracle bones and bronzes. For instance, in 1940 he was invited by the Detroit Institute of Arts to organize an exhibit of ancient Chinese ritual bronzes and to write the introduction to the catalogue, 'The Appreciation of Chinese Bronzes.'[30]

When Menzies first submitted his thesis proposal, his plan was to write on 'The Culture of the Shang Dynasty,' which was to be essentially a summary of his studies of oracle bones and other aspects of Shang culture. When he was hired by the ROM to study its collection of Chinese bronzes, he was persuaded to change his topic to reflect the museum's collection. He proposed either 'The Ritual Bronze Vessels of Ancient China' or 'The Type Sequence of Bronze Weapons of Ancient China,' but the committee turned these down as 'too technical and specialized.' He was advised to choose a general topic such as the 'Contribution of Archaeology to the Understanding of the Life and Thought of the Shang Dynasty.'

As the first stage of his dissertation research he carried out a comprehensive study of the museum's Chinese collection:

I have carried out extensive researches in (A) The Bone Culture – the inscribed, carved culture objects made of bone; (B) The Jade and Stone Culture, even to a detailed study of the Field Museum collection formed by Dr. Laufer ... and the Art Institute of Chicago; (C) The Pottery Culture, which is so fundamental in all areas, especially the white pottery of which I lost so much; (D) The Bronze Moulds and metal technique, which I studied on the site of the foundry at Anyang. All these objects have an intimate relationship with the history, religion and thought life of the people, which form the great background of it all.[31]

Out of this research, Menzies planned to write two monographs, 'The Bronze Age Vessels and Weapons' and 'The Culture of the Shang Dynasty.'

Similar to the uncompleted research projects left behind at Cheeloo, these topics were too large to be done in a short time. In addition, Menzies's meticulous attitude made his scholarship and writing exceedingly slow. Bishop White could dash off a book in a year or so, but his writings were primarily descriptive. Like *Tombs of Old Lo-yang*, his monograph *Bone Culture of Ancient China* had 233 pages but only 46 pages of text; the rest consist of full-page line drawings with short, uninformative captions.[32] Menzies was shocked by White's passion for quick publication: 'The mere enumeration of objects which he considers Shang and the publication of drawings or photographs is worse than useless unless it is correct.'[33]

Another factor that affected Menzies's work at the museum was his status. His job description as 'research assistant' was not clearly defined. Bishop White took the term 'assistant' literally and was reluctant to recognize Menzies's academic contribution. However, he did take care of him in other ways that only made Menzies feel embarrassed. As he explained to Currelly in 1940, 'Bishop White and I have been friends ever since he married me to his first lady missionary twenty-nine years ago. He has been embarrassingly kind in so many personal ways, insisting on my spending my short holiday in his summer cottage at Niagara-on-the-Lake, and many, many other things. I am just sick over it all.'[34]

Menzies's complaint was that White was stealing his ideas without due recognition. This was common gossip around the ROM, but has only been hinted in print. Lewis Walmsley admitted in a private letter to Arthur Menzies that 'Bishop White picked Dr. Menzies' brains and did not give proper credit for information received.'[35] Yet publicly Walmsley could only say that their relationship was 'unfortunate. Both were considered experts but they were individuals of different temperaments. White, assertive, aggressive and dynamic, was relatively new to the field. Menzies, retiring and unassertive, was a scholar of the first order and a world authority on Chinese oracle bones. White, the propagandist and born popularizer was quick to publish. Menzies refused to express an opinion in print before every possible particle of evidence was assembled.

The conflict of personalities inhibited Menzies. As a result he created little in a field where he had much to offer.'[36] In what seems a gratuitous statement, Dickson commented: 'Menzies, a shy unassertive scholar who had given the Museum some fine early bronzes of the Shang period, and who had helped Bishop White with his knowledge and connections when he was making his first ventures in the archaeological field, could never have felt happy in his subordinate position under Bishop White. Fortunately Menzies' war duties kept him away from the Museum for much of the time.'[37] We should let James Menzies present his own case.

As stated, Menzies's first proposal for his dissertation was 'The Culture of the Shang Dynasty.' This topic had been approved by the committee of which White was the chairman. Perhaps unhappy with Menzies's slowness, White decided in 1940 to write a similar monograph, 'Outline of Ancient Chinese Culture.' This was too much for Menzies; for two years he had shared his research with White, understanding that the latter would not publish it himself. His letter to Currelly is worth quoting at length:

> The research work has been done and there only now remains the presentation of the results. False objects have been identified. Proper groupings of sets have been established. The bone, jade, stone, white pottery, and bronze moulds have been studied and identified.
>
> All these have been discussed with Bishop White during these years in Honan and in Toronto. He has used this material exclusively in his student classes this year in spite of my protest that he was using most of the results of my researches. I have no objection to classroom work only, but I do most strongly protest against his publishing the results of my researches in a monograph. I have assisted him in every way in his work and in the publication of monograph I and II, but I strongly object to assisting him to publish a monograph embodying many of the results of my life's work. In a primitive society you may force a slave to work for you, but you cannot force him to cut his own throat.
>
> Bishop White states that he is merely enumerating the objects in the Museum collection, but he forgets that the identification of these objects as Shang dynasty depends entirely on my own personal observation and the word of a dealer, Mr. Lin in Kaifeng ... But is the word of dealer scientific evidence? Not until I was able to say this and this and this did come, and this and this did not come from Anyang or Hsün Hsien [Xún Xian] or elsewhere, could we be sure whether these statements were true or not. Much of this corroboration work I did in Kaifeng on my visits there, and the rest of it

has been done here in the Museum. He calls this simple, but it is the result of my life's work ...

Bishop White is head of the department and what he says goes. The thing he is interested in must be done. A dozen times a day and often for long stretches of time, he would question me on the objects on which he was lecturing to his classes. His lectures were often held in the library, where I was working in the gallery or in my room, and I could not help hearing him, and never once did I hear him acknowledge any of the information given. Your own son is a member of the class and you can learn independently from him. Well, I finally turned and told him that I objected to his publishing this book, and that I could not understand his asking me these things when his avowed purpose was to publish them. I told him this was inhuman, for he seemed to take an unholy delight in forcing me to tell him what he would then pass off as his own. Often after questioning me he would say that what I said merely confirmed his own opinions, and when he has written them down and repeated them to his classes, he has quite convinced himself that they are his own ... Today again, March 15th, he was asking me questions about stone knives and stone sickles. I told him what he asked: the only alternative was another row ... So long as I was putting eggs into his hat, I was persona grata; but as soon as I begin to put eggs into my own hat, then trouble begins.[38]

After laying out the above complaints, Menzies asked Currelly for freedom to complete his research work for publication by the museum. He continued:

I must, however, insist on unhampered freedom to go on under the general direction of the Museum to produce in my own way the kind of book the Museum wants. I am either competent to do so or else I have been employed under a misunderstanding. I should never have submitted to the classification of 'research assistant' if by that was meant that I was employed to assist Bishop White to publish a book on the Shang dynasty culture over his name.[39]

Menzies asked the museum to give him permission to publish two monographs in its Museum Studies Series, 'Bronze Age Vessels and Weapons' and 'The Culture of the Shang Dynasty.' If funds were short, he would combine the two into a single monograph entitled 'Bronze Age Culture of China.' To stress his dissatisfaction, he told Currelly that he was prepared to give up the ROM altogether and return to China. 'I will not be pumped any longer; and in spite of the permission that the Foreign Mission Board has given, I am prepared to resign at once and return to Cheeloo University, where I will publish my work under the Harvard-Yenching Institute in Cheeloo, of which I am still Director.'[40]

No information is available on how Currelly responded to this crisis of early 1940. From the Menzies family papers we know that Menzies was allowed to combine the two monographs into 'The Bronze Age Culture of the Shang Dynasty.' Desiring to leave something concrete for the museum, he pushed himself to the limit. He spent the summer of 1940 making drawings of artefacts and felt terribly guilty when he could not see his son Arthur, who was sick in Ottawa.[41] In a letter to A.E. Armstrong, he described his frustration: 'The result of my difficulties is that the more I pushed myself and tried to make some real contribution to the Bronze Age of China, the more tired I got and for the last two months at least I have been having a great many headaches, caused not by food but by worry. My work is not finished and I am not at all fresh for work. I need a rest but cannot get one because I must leave some result of my work. I tried hard to get finished. I told Dr. Currelly that I would finish by the end of the year, but I am not finished and not nearly done.'[42]

Menzies felt uneasy being away from his mission field and in early 1941 seriously contemplated dropping out of the PhD program.[43] Then there was the personal animosity between him and Bishop White. His protest deeply hurt White, who, as his biographer wrote, decreed 'that no one [could] correct anyone in a position of authority even when it was obvious that the man was wrong.'[44] White never forgave Menzies for his 'rebellious behaviour' and would eventually make him pay for his actions. To get Menzies out of the way, White took the drastic step of cancelling the Rockefeller grant. He explained his decision to the BOM: 'Since no further word has come from him [Menzies], we assumed that he would automatically revert to his Mission Board on January 1st. I reported this in my letter to the Rockefeller Foundation last month, but since I knew that Mr. Menzies' work was not completed, I expressed my personal hope that his Mission Board might possibly be able to allow him facilities to enable him to clear up the work in hand ... We are very anxious to be free from this financial obligation ... [as] we have only two years of the grant left for application in other directions.'[45]

Sympathetic with Menzies's situation, the Board of Overseas Missions took him back on its payroll, advising him to complete his work and get ready to return to China. Menzies felt uneasy using mission funds for his museum work and even A.E. Armstrong tried to relieve his conscience.

'You need not have any qualms of conscience about the F.M. Board having carried you for about one and a half years when the Museum was having the benefit of your services. If the Executive Committee of the Board is satisfied, why should you worry? It is frequent practice for the Board to carry a missionary on furlough salary for post-graduate study purpose. The time seems to have arrived now, however, when your return to China in the early future should be considered and arranged if advisable and feasible.'[46]

It is remarkable that Menzies was able to carry on his work against so many odds. In April 1941 he completed the draft of his thesis, 'The Bronze Age Culture of China,' the result of five years' effort and the largest research project he had ever undertaken. The first part was a general study of Shang culture that showed his special expertise on oracle-bone inscriptions. The second was a detailed study of *ge* (old spelling *ko*), the typical weapon of the Shang armies, a short, sickle-shaped sword with a long, thick handle, shaped like a tomahawk. The completion of this draft fulfilled Menzies's formal obligation to the ROM, but his ordeal was still not over. When he submitted his draft, over one thousand pages long, his committee rejected it on the grounds that it was 'too broad.' He was advised to revise part two on the Shang *ge* and resubmit it as his dissertation. There must have been serious problems between Menzies and his supervisors, as this was the second time they had rejected his thesis topic.

After all the years of hard work, Menzies was exhausted physically, mentally, and spiritually. Except for a brief holiday at Lake Couchiching, he spent the summer of 1941 revising *Shang Ko*. By September, the BOM had already booked tickets for him and Annie, but the thesis committee still would not accept the dissertation. This time the problem was structure and presentation. In a letter to Arthur, he wrote, 'I am apparently so anxious to be trustful and fair that I do not make a clear presentation. I can do better in an address, but on paper I really do make a mess of things.'[47]

On 7 December 1941, the Japanese attacked Pearl Harbor, a tragic day in world history that gave Menzies the needed extension to revise his thesis. With the help of archaeologist Professor H.A. Thompson, he restructured the dissertation, but then Bishop White became 'annoyed at what he called a change in outline.' Menzies asked Thompson to 'straighten' the matter out.[48] Accordingly, Thompson wrote to White: 'For the general scheme here outlined I admitted joint responsibility with Menzies, since it is the result of repeated discussions between us. It is patterned, I should say, on several of the more recent and most effective studies of comparable material in the field of classical archaeology and was further recommended to me by the satisfaction with which I myself had used it in a similar study.'[49] At the same time, Thompson stated his dissatisfaction with Menzies's writing style. 'As for the English and the internal composition of the work, I again recorded my dissatisfaction but was inclined to leave them to the responsibility of the writer.'[50] After writing this letter, Thompson resigned from the committee.

Since Menzies's monograph had been financially supported by the ROM, it demanded the copyright and right to use the study as it pleased. On 15 October 1942, the museum, represented by White, signed an 'agreement' with Menzies. 'We are of the opinion that copies of the MS of the results of this work should be deposited in the Museum of Archaeology for such use as the Museum may require.'[51]

Two weeks later, the committee approved the revised dissertation, *Shang Ko*, with a begrudging, unfriendly assessment: 'In view of your probable departure for China it was considered desirable to conclude all the arrangements necessary for you to obtain the degree, including acceptance of the thesis and the final oral examination ... Those members of the Committee who had examined the thesis do not wish to put themselves on record as satisfied with the present form of the thesis. It was agreed that the material was adequate and that the value of the work done justified the Committee in recommending its acceptance.'[52]

On 10 November Menzies successfully gave his oral defence before the committee.[53] He was congratulated by his former supervisor, Professor Thompson: 'I have just heard from Prof. McIlwraith of the good showing that you made at your oral and of the final outcome. Please accept my warm congratulation. I also wish to emphasize again my admiration for the tenacity and courage with which you have seen this thing through. Let me express my appreciation, too, of your readiness to cooperate with an adviser so ill-equipped.'[54]

At the age of fifty-seven, James M. Menzies became a Doctor of Philosophy. However, he may have lost more than he gained. He failed to make his studies of Shang culture available in English as he had hoped. The monograph, 'The Bronze Age Culture of China,' was a strong piece of scholarship but too academic for a ROM publication. Financed by White's supporters and under his control, the Museum Studies Series was intended 'to make available to the public, in popular form but without sacrificing scientific accuracy, an interpretation of the history, culture, and processes of development that lie behind the objects in the Museum collection.'[55] Until 1955 the only works published by the Museum Studies Series were written by Bishop White. As for Menzies's PhD thesis, the ROM did not publish it until 1965, seven years after his death, as one condition for the transfer of his collection to the museum.

Meanwhile Bishop White published two books based on Menzies's draft dissertation that he had rejected in 1941. The first was *Bone Culture of Ancient China* (1945), primarily concerned with oracle bones. The second was *Bronze Culture of Ancient China* (1957), whose title reflects Menzies's 'The Bronze Age Culture of China.' It is hard to know to what extent White used Menzies's monograph, but by comparing White's books and Menzies's monograph, one can clearly see the words are White's but the ideas and the research (the scholarly apparatus behind them) belonged to James Menzies. Even the unattributed line drawings are his.

Menzies's term at the ROM ruined his thirty-year-long friendship with Bishop White. This unfortunate alienation of the two best China scholars of Canada at the only university department of Chinese studies not only destroyed Menzies's career but was also a scholarly tragedy, for it damaged the School for Chinese Studies at the University of Toronto. Although admirable, Menzies's commitment and perseverance in completing his PhD turned his one-year furlough into permanent exile. By sticking to his work despite repeated urgings for him to return to Cheeloo either in Jinan or Chengdu, he lost the opportunity to publish at least some of the researches he had left unfinished.

Chapter 16

American Interlude and Postwar Hiatus, 1942–1947

Pearl Harbor

Pearl Harbor changed everything. Until then, the way to China was still open. If James and Annie Menzies had chosen to return to China in 1938–41 as they hoped and planned, they could have joined their colleagues at Cheeloo in exile at West China Union University in Chengdu, Sichuan. The journey was long and hazardous, either trekking across no man's land from the end of the railroad line in Occupied China or via the 'back route' up the Red River from Hanoi into 'Free China.' Or they could have gone to Jinan itself, where a small number of faculty were bravely trying to operate a rump college consisting of the Rural Institute, theology, and nursing. There, James would have been reunited with his collections, his notes, his library, and unfinished projects. But they did not go and Pearl Harbor closed all possibilities until the end of the war.

The widening Second World War that brought the Allies into the Sino-Japanese conflict further shattered the circle of friends that James Menzies had left in 1936. Some were in Occupied China, some in Free China, and others were unaccounted for. Some did patriotic war work for the Nationalists, while others were with the Communists. Allied nationals in Occupied China had been considered neutrals, but at dawn on 8 December 1941 (the Asian side of the international dateline) they awoke to find themselves 'enemy aliens,' enemies of the Japanese state, which included Americans, British, Canadians, and White Russians. The process of rounding them up and interning them in 'concentration camps' was slow but inexorable. By mid-1942, there were internment camps scattered throughout the Japanese empire: in Japan itself, in the colonies of Taiwan and Korea, and in the territories in Indonesia and the

Philippines that had been captured during the military offensives of December 1941.

There were about twenty camps in Occupied China. A very few individuals were not interned, such as Dr John Calvin Ferguson, the Canadian art collector and adviser to the Chinese government, who remained outside the camps 'because of his advanced age and great prestige,' and died a few weeks after the end of the war. Regarded as a possible emissary between the Japanese government and Chiang Kai-shek, John Leighton Stuart, the president of Yenching University, was incarcerated in a private house for four years.[1]

The Japanese authorities were particularly anxious to get their hands on the Christian universities that had hitherto defied them by claiming immunity behind an American flag. At Yenching University, they rounded up twelve Chinese faculty members suspected of having patriotic sentiments, including William Hung (Hong Ye), the former dean and Menzies's friend, who spent five months in a Japanese prison.[2] The Japanese did not intend using the schools for education but rather meant to vandalize them, then use them for latrines and barracks as visual evidence of the downfall of the West's prestige and position in Asia.

At Cheeloo, the Japanese shut down the hospital, suspended classes, and locked the campus. Most American and Canadian faculty members were repatriated, while some of the British and Canadians were interned at Weixian.[3] Weixian was the most famous internment camp in China, for its 1500 residents included missionaries, university professors, business people, entertainers, and two hundred children of the Chefoo Schools run by the China Inland Mission.[4]

In contrast, James Menzies was exiled at home preparing for a career that had disappeared. He threw himself into the final revisions of his doctoral dissertation as a way to cope with the news from China. At least he knew that his collections of oracle bones at Cheeloo were safe. His North Henan colleague Andrew Thomson knew someone who knew someone behind the lines. One crate of 'first class national treasures' was stored in the university's vault, while another was put into the loft above the foreign children's school. The others were buried at various places around the campus. One advantage of the Japanese closure of the university was the end to further searches for buried treasure.[5]

On 10 November 1942, Menzies defended his dissertation and became a Doctor of Philosophy. He was fifty-seven and Annie two years older. What was he to do? The United Church, which had supported him all those years after the Rockefeller grant at the museum had run out, now urged him to take up paid employment as a local church minister. That, he felt, would be a waste of his expertise.[6] He was not welcome at the Royal Ontario Museum, where Charles T. Currelly had refused to stick up for him against Bishop White, and there were no teaching appointments at the University of Toronto, where Bishop White was head of the School of Chinese Studies. He was invited to join Cheeloo in exile in Sichuan, but the Board of Overseas Missions decided, against Menzies's will, to postpone his return because of budgetary problems. As time passed, Menzies became worried. 'I am beginning to be restless again,' he wrote to his son Arthur. 'What would you suggest as a task where I could earn bread and butter if I cannot go to China at once?'[7]

By 1942 the three children had grown up and moved away, pursuing their own careers. Marion, who was twenty-nine, had graduated with a BA from Victoria College, then taken the Bachelor of Divinity course at Emmanuel College, the United Church theological seminary. Following in her parents' footsteps she had always expected to go to China as a missionary and was devastated when a 'lady doctor' turned her down, deciding that her 'stoutness was caused by glandular imbalance and that an overseas appointment would only exaggerate it.' She recalled, 'This was a very hard thing for me to accept and also for my parents.' Instead, she went on to acquire an MA in social work. As she wrote, she'd progressed from being 'a grade C student at Vic to a good B student at Emmanuel, [and] I rose to become an "A" student in Social Work. The older I got, the smarter I became, so it seemed.' She moved in 1939 to Montreal, where she worked in family welfare among the poorest of the poor.[8]

Frances, the quiet one, aged twenty-seven, had graduated with a diploma in social work, also expecting to become a missionary to China. She worked as a social worker for three years in Timmins, a mining town in northern Ontario, and in 1942 returned to Toronto to attend the United Church Training School for Professional Church Workers. She worked for the Big Sisters of Toronto from 1943 to 1945.

Arthur, aged twenty-six, was beginning his diplomatic career at the Department of External Affairs in Ottawa. After graduation from Victoria College in 1939 and a summer of Chinese language study, he took graduate studies at Harvard in Far Eastern History under the legendary John King Fairbank, the most influential expert on Sino-American relations. He wrote the Canadian Foreign Service exam, and in July 1940 was hired to help process the 60,000 passports now required as the United

States clamped down on cross-border traffic. He was given leave to complete his MA and the general examinations for a PhD, which he did not finish before being appointed to Ottawa in May 1942 as a third secretary.

War Work

On the morning after Pearl Harbor, 'December 8, 1941, a Monday,' John King Fairbank recalled, 'the ACLS [American Council of Learned Societies] phone was jammed with government agency requests for names of Japan and China specialists, preferably male between twenty-one and thirty, field-experienced and fully fluent.'[9] As early as the summer of 1941, the United States government had established a new agency, the Co-ordinator of Information (COI), to gather secret intelligence and spread propaganda world-wide. Its research and analysis branch was a separate group, with staff recruited mainly from universities. One of the first was Fairbank himself, who had access to the scholarly departments of Oriental studies throughout the country, still pathetically small in both number and size. The U.S. Navy was also recruiting Japan and China specialists. As a result, most young, capable American scholars in East Asian studies were put into war service.

At the beginning of the war in the Pacific, the Canadian Department of External Affairs had only a handful of officers with appropriate background and academic training. Dr H.L. Keenleyside, who had served several years as counsellor in the Canadian legation in Tokyo in the early 1930s, was an assistant under-secretary in charge of the American and Far Eastern Division until 1946. Herbert Norman, son of United Church missionaries in Japan, had his doctorate from Harvard in Japanese studies and became recognized as one of the foremost Western historians of Japan. Posted as a Japanese language officer in 1939 to the Canadian legation in Tokyo, he was interned in December 1941. After repatriation in August 1942, he was assigned to a communications intelligence unit in Ottawa. After the war, he was initially attached to the staff of General Douglas MacArthur, Supreme Commander for the Allied Powers (SCAP) in the occupation of Japan. Later he became head of the Canadian Liaison Mission to SCAP. Arthur Menzies was posted in November 1942 to work with Herbert Norman in the communications intelligence unit. He returned to External Affairs in January 1944 and became head of the Far Eastern Section in May 1946. He was posted to Japan in December 1950 to replace Norman as head of the Canadian Liaison Mission to SCAP.

When the DEA opened an embassy in Chongqing, China's wartime capital, in 1943, the ambassador was a former Liberal politician, Major General Victor Wentworth Odlum. He knew nothing of China. DEA consequently hired Chester Ronning, principal of Camrose Lutheran College in Alberta, as a cultural attaché and first secretary. Ronning was another 'mishkid' (his parents were Norwegian American Lutheran missionaries in central China) who had returned to China as principal of a high school during the 1920s. He had a charismatic, loquacious personality and cultivated friendships with Communist leaders like Zhou Enlai. During the civil war and the crucial first days of the People's Republic of China, Ronning became an actor on the world stage and a leading voice at DEA for diplomatic recognition of the PRC.

Arthur Menzies was a senior member of this cadre of 'mishkids' at External Affairs. 'The names of several others are well known – Chester Ronning (though not raised by Canadian parents), Ralph Collins, and John Small, to mention only those who, with Arthur Menzies, would at one time or another act as chief Canadian diplomatic representatives in China,' wrote Peter Mitchell, professor of Chinese history at York University and the grandson of Robert A. Mitchell, James Menzies's colleague at Cheeloo. 'The common denominator that runs through the careers of all these men cannot be found in their style or specific views but in their acute interest in China. The implications of this interest provide at least a partial explanation of why China became central to Canada's Pacific policy in the post-war years.'[10]

By 1942, the reservoir of Japan and China specialists in the United States had dried up and the Co-ordinator of Information (COI) started to recruit in Canada. In June the COI was reorganized and its Foreign Information Service branch became the Office of War Information (OWI). The work of the OWI was divided into three 'theatres': Europe, the British Commonwealth, and the Far East. George E. Taylor, an academic, was chief of the Far East section. On 3 April 1943 he wrote to Arthur Menzies at External Affairs in Ottawa: 'We are recruiting a new Bureau of Intelligence and Research for our radio operation in San Francisco. This letter is to inquire whether you would be interested in such work.'[11] Arthur turned the offer down, and instead recommended his father.

James Menzies did not seem to meet the ideal specifications for war work. He was twice the suggested age, his speciality was narrow, academic, and ancient, not applicable to the war effort, and after six years' absence he was out of touch with events in China. But he did have specialist knowledge of Chinese geography gained from his map-making efforts as a young missionary and his archaeological travels. Besides, he was a trained Dominion Land Surveyor, even if his surveying skills were a little rusty, and an excellent cartographer and artist. The United States Army Map Service also contacted Menzies, asking him to translate Chinese place names in its translation bureau.[12]

After consulting the Board of Overseas Missions, James Menzies accepted the Office of War Information job although it meant relocating to San Francisco. At least it provided an opportunity to use his professional knowledge, even if it also meant not returning to China until the end of the war. In late October 1943, James and Annie packed up their rented house in Toronto and took the train to San Francisco. Once again, like many of his generation, Menzies was involved in the second war in his lifetime. During the First World War, he was an officer with the Chinese Labour Corps and now he joined the United States war effort as the 'China Regional Specialist in Operation Intelligence.'

The OWI's San Francisco office was concerned mainly with radio propaganda on the Voice of America. As Menzies confided to A.E. Armstrong: 'We broadcast regularly to the Far East in most of the languages and dialects of the Pacific area ... In turn we monitor and record all the propaganda put out by the enemy from Hsin King in Manchuria to Singapore in the South in all the languages used by them. This propaganda is analyzed daily and in part our programs take into consideration what has been broadcast by them.'[13] According to Arthur, James also endeavoured to maintain contact with Chinese scholars in Free China such as President Liu Shuming of Cheeloo in exile and Li Chi of the Academia Sinica.[14]

As a senior China specialist, Menzies was concerned with policy and intelligence work. Every morning, after meeting with the Chinese writers, he planned the scripts for broadcast and advised on the content. Sometime his work was as simple as correcting the notion that peasants in North China ate rice when actually grains formed their staple diet. Other times, it concerned delicate political problems such as the conflict between the Guomindang and the Chinese Communist Party. He was also expected to respond to specific inquiries concerning Chinese geography and culture and to prepare background studies and intelligence reports on social, political, and military situations. When the OWI began to send men and women overseas to China, it set up a training school in Berkeley run by William B. Pettus, Menzies's friend from Beijing. The North China Union Language School had managed to survive under the initial Japanese occupation because it had been incorporated as the

California College in China. After Pearl Harbor, Pettus was interned and repatriated, and in 1942 he reopened the CCC at Berkeley.[15] Menzies lectured there seven hours a week on Chinese thought, area studies, and radio interception in East Asia. During his one-year stay at San Francisco, he trained over one hundred officers for the OWI's China operations.[16]

In November 1944 the OWI headquarters in Washington 'borrowed' Menzies to assist its China section, a temporary arrangement that became permanent in February 1945 when Fairbank left for China. Menzies liked this change, as he wrote to Annie: 'John King Fairbank who is the Deputy Director for Far East, asked if I could remain on [in Washington] ... I would like this place from the point of view of work and friends. People here know the Far East and China and one respects their ideas even when I disagree with their policy. The work here has more to do with all our relations with China: Radio, Press, Books, Film strips, Army, Navy, State Department, and Outpost Training ... There are many more people you know.'[17]

Annie Menzies joined her husband and they lived in a two-room upper-storey flat in Takoma Park, Maryland, on the outskirts of Washington.[18] One of Menzies's closest friends in Washington was Arthur W. Hummel, head of the Orientalia Division of the Library of Congress, who was compiling his mammoth *Eminent Chinese of the Ch'ing Period*. James and Annie spent many evenings at the Hummels, which gave him a feeling of still being part of Chinese intellectual life. One memorable evening, the guest of honour was Feng Youlan (old spelling Feng Yu-lan), a Harvard professor whose 1931 book *A History of Chinese Philosophy* remained the standard textbook at American universities into the 1970s. Born in 1895, Feng grew up in the May Fourth generation and was a leading advocate of the 'doubting history' or 'non-religious' theory.[19] He and Menzies had quite a debate. As James wrote to his son Arthur:

Feng said ... that Chinese were human creatures like the other peoples of the world, with the same emotions, desires and ideals. This is where he introduced his point of view that the Chinese people sought to achieve the super moral values of religion without religious observances. He says that knowledge and philosophy in the Chinese sense are different. Increase of knowledge is needed to make specialists such as engineers, doctors, and all kinds of useful arts. But philosophy is only concerned with the man himself, apart from his occupation or speciality. Chinese philosophy attempts to bring man directly into contact with what he called super moral values. Moral values he described as those that concerned man's relations to man.

The super moral values were those that concerned man's relations to the universe. The difference between moral and super moral was the difference that Western theology made between the love of God and the love of man.

Menzies thought Feng's presentation was a paradox.[20]

In Washington Menzies was given important tasks such as preparing directives for the OWI's China operations, distributing material to government and military agencies, and supervising the radio program at San Francisco. As his seniority increased, so did his salary. When the OWI's functions were taken over by the State Department, his annual salary was $5905, the most he ever earned in his life.[21] In contrast, as a missionary on furlough, his stipend had been $800.

Hope Deferred

As the Pacific War seemed to be drawing to a close in early 1945, James Menzies prepared to return to China. Cheeloo and the North Henan mission were still in exile in Sichuan, but they sent similar invitations to him to return as soon as possible when the war ended. However, Menzies felt bound by his commitment to the Office of War Information and only after the Japanese surrender in August 1945 did he write to the Board of Overseas Missions: 'With the signing of the surrender and the declaration by President Truman of V.J. day, the war comes to a close and I am at liberty to terminate my work with the Office of War Information ... Mrs. Menzies and I would if possible like to keep together and travel out as soon as possible. However, if this would cause any extended delay, we would be willing that I should go ahead and she follow as soon as possible afterwards. Do you wish me to place my resignation in the hands of the OWI administration at once to be effective Oct. 15th (one month's notice is expected)? I naturally am anxious to save the mission Board as much as possible and not to come back on Mission salary before it is necessary.'[22]

A.E. Armstrong had long championed Menzies's special gifts and now recommended an early return to Cheeloo, but he also warned him not to resign from the OWI immediately. The Board of Overseas Missions was having difficulty arranging transportation for the dozens of its missionaries who were desperately needed for the reconstruction of the war-torn countries of Asia. By this time, the United Church had missionaries in West China, North Henan, and South China, in Japan, Taiwan, and Korea, in Angola and Trinidad, and every one was clamouring to go to their respective fields.[23] For a year, civilian transportation across the Pacific was hard to secure, and by the time the board resolved this problem in the fall of 1946, it was too late.

In June 1946, in Washington, James Menzies suffered two attacks, first a cerebral hemorrhage and then a coronary thrombosis. These were usually fatal for men of his age, but for the moment he remained optimistic of a quick recovery. As he wrote to Arthur, 'I could do a job in China but in Canada there is no outlet of my special knowledge except private publication.'[24] By this time General Marshal's mission to China had failed and the civil war between the Guomindang and the Communists had broken out.

During the summer of 1947, Menzies came to Toronto to meet the board, then returned to Washington with the hopeful but not very useful advice from A.E. Armstrong not to look for a permanent post in the States.[25] In November Cheeloo University, back on its campus at Jinan, again invited them to return as soon as possible. Menzies pushed the board: 'Mrs. Menzies and I have read with interest and appreciation the letter from Dr. H.P. Lair and the repeated invitation to us to return to Cheeloo.' Despite the worsening situation, he and Annie looked 'forward and thank God for this opportunity to complete our life work in North China where our hearts have continued to be during all the years since we first went to Honan in 1910.'[26]

Frankly, the board was not willing to take responsibility for his health. They considered him an old (at sixty-two), sick man who might have another heart attack at any moment. To support his application, Menzies asked his family doctor to 'certify' his physical condition. His report, though optimistic, cancelled all plans of ever returning to China. 'Generally, he [Menzies] has made good progress in the past few months. He is able to carry on his normal activities, and I am sure that he would be able to do 60% to 70% of the usual day's work in China.' But the doctor's approval was conditional; Menzies should do 'no more than 6 hours of work daily' and avoid 'emotional strain and all strenuous activities.'[27]

James resigned from the OWI after he fell ill, but he and Annie remained in Washington until June 1949, when they bought a house and moved to Toronto. With remarkable patience and perseverance, he waited. He maintained his good spirits, trying to find ways to redeem the time. To prepare for his future work at Cheeloo, he studied the advances in archaeology made by Chinese scholars during the war, such as Li Chi at the Academia Sinica and Hu Houxuan at Cheeloo in exile. His good friend Arthur Hummel granted him special privileges to borrow rare

Chinese books from the Library of Congress for use at his own home.[28] As he told his son, 'Whenever I get interested in things of this sort, I am better in health and sleep well even if my days are longer and I do not get a rest after lunch. This all makes me hope that I will not find the work at Cheeloo too difficult or too trying.'[29]

Memoirs of a Mishkid

In a season of disappointment, James and Annie were proud of their children, who had all become involved with China's post-war reconstruction. They had always been fascinated with the country of their birth, even though they had left China in their early teens, first for the Canadian Academy in Kobe, then for Victoria College and the University of Toronto. Their father's stories had imbued them with his own deep interest in and respect for the great cultural achievements of the Chinese over a recorded history of some five thousand years. The family's trip around the world in 1929, when they stayed for several months in the Holy Land, had given them an international perspective and a lasting interest in world affairs, ancient and modern. Now it was their turn to tell him stories of their adventures in China. Through them, James was able to get up-to-date information about the political and military situations, which kept him in touch with China during his long convalescence. Privately, they could also make inquiries through personal and official channels about the Menzies collections of oracle bones.

Marion, the eldest, wrote her life story in an affectionate, gentle style, entitled simply *Memoirs of a Mishkid*. In September 1945, feeling restless with her job at Family Welfare of Montreal, she visited her parents in Washington, where she heard that the United Nations Relief and Rehabilitation Administration (UNRRA) was looking for personnel to send out to China for post-war relief work. 'I thought that with my background in China, my ability to speak Mandarin Chinese at street level and my university training and six years of experience as a social worker, I could make a meaningful contribution.' Five years after she was rejected by the United Church doctor, Marion joined the UNRRA staff, sailing for China from Newport, Rhode Island, in January 1946. The trip took two and a half months, with a one-month layover in Manila. At first, in Shanghai, she was assigned as executive assistant to the Chinese Liberated Areas Relief Association. The 'Chinese boss,' a Mr Li, was 'a well educated man and a real Communist Party man' who had studied in

France and been on the Long March. 'We got on well together.' She would practise her Chinese with him, while he spoke in English. By the autumn of 1947, the situation had worsened because 'the Guomindang sabotaged supplies [of food and medicine going to needy people in the interior], terrorized homeless people and spread civil war. UNRRA had to close its welfare department and recall its personnel.'[30]

Marion was selected as the representative of World Student Relief to inspect the educational institutions in the 'Liberated Areas' controlled by the Communists, 'to find out what had happened to the students who had been blacklisted by the Guomindang and fled' there. Travelling with a male acquaintance, she took books donated by the School of Chinese Studies at Berkeley. She spent four months in the Communist areas in Shanxi province mainly. 'Wherever we went on this trip I felt at home and comfortable with the people. At no time was I afraid,' she recalled many years later. 'We were treated with great courtesy and as honoured guests. We were provided with padded blue cotton garments similar in style to those worn by our hosts and guides. In the last half of our trip, our guide and interpreter was Han Xu, who later became China's Ambassador to the United States. While Arthur was in China 1976–80 as Canada's ambassador, he met Han Xu who was a senior official in the Foreign Affairs Ministry of the People's Republic of China.'[31]

Marion left China in early 1948. Like her father, she took the long route home, via the Suez to Geneva, to present her personal report to the World Student Relief office. While there, she was recruited by the World YWCA to go into Prague, Czechoslovakia, to find out what had happened to YWCA personnel after the Soviet invasion. It was 'a scary experience,' she recalled, since she did not know the language and everyone was in hiding. She stopped in Paris, London, and Scotland, where she went sightseeing at Menzies Castle. At each stop, she stayed with a worldwide network of professional men and women who worked for international Christian organizations. She visited her parents in Washington, who asked her to buy them a house in Toronto, stipulating that it could not cost more than $10,000; even at that price, James had to cash in a life insurance policy and borrow money from Arthur to make the down payment.

When Marion returned to Toronto, instead of staying with her mother's relatives, the Sedgwicks, she bunked down in an attic room of the United Church Training School, which she had attended a decade earlier. There she met James Hummel (no relation to Arthur Hummel in Washington), 'a tall handsome man in his early thirties, with an open beautiful face and laughing brown eyes. He was never too well-dressed, partly because he was a poorly-paid teacher on an Indian Reserve, and in part because he was partly crippled by rheumatoid arthritis which left him with a dropped wrist, crippled fingers and a flat-footed walk.' He drove a 1927 Model A Ford, which he called 'Ford Jabok.' They gradually fell in love and were married on 1 October 1949, when Marion moved to the 'teacherage' at Moraviantown, northeast of Chatham, Ontario.

Frances, two years younger than Marion, followed in her sister's footsteps, first to the School of Social Work, then to China. She too had always presumed she would become a missionary, but the war intervened. While working with Big Sisters in Toronto in 1945, she married a United Church minister in training, Ervin Newcombe. They passed the physical exams, and were accepted as missionaries to North Henan. On New Year's Day 1947 they arrived in Shanghai, where they were greeted by Marion, who was working with UNRRA. After language study at Weihui, the main station in North Henan, they were assigned to Zhangde, where Frances had been born thirty-one years earlier.

Five months later, their stay in North Henan was curtailed by the civil war. 'In that fateful summer of 1947, the communists moved down the railway lines,' wrote Alvyn Austin in *Saving China*. 'At Weihui the mission "acquiesced under severe pressure" to let the Guomindang army install a big-gun emplacement in the compound because of its strategic position. Consequently, when communists attacked the city, the battle swirled around the mission compound ... At Changte [Zhangde], the fighting came a week or two later, and the Canadians vacillated about whether they should move out. One group caught passage on a U.S. military plane, while four more flew out on the last American plane on 6 May.' On 16 June, the North Henan Presbytery held an emotional meeting to disband the mission 'forever.'[32]

Frances and Ervin Newcombe were evacuated first to Zhengzhou, the major railway junction south of the Yellow River where the Canadian Anglicans had a station, then to Kaifeng, the mountain resort at Jigongshan, and finally to Shanghai before they settled in the West China mission in Chengdu, Sichuan. Ervin was appointed principal of the Canadian School after the retirement of Lewis C. Walmsley, the beloved headmaster who had trained several generations of 'mishkids.' Frances and Ervin left China in June 1950 'after four and a half rather frustrating years in China, over-shadowed by the Communist Revolution.'[33] After China, Ervin was appointed principal of a teacher training school in Trinidad. They were on the 'left' wing of the United Church and devoted their lives as intellectual social activists to fighting against social injustice.

The Far Eastern Desk

Arthur Menzies also wrote a brief memoir, in the Victoria College alumni newsletter. 'I had a satisfying career,' he concluded, 'advancing fairly quickly at the beginning because of the post-war expansion of the [Department of External Affairs] service, and getting a series of interesting and challenging assignments. So far as I was able to help in some measure to promote understanding between Canada and other countries, I feel amply rewarded.'[34]

He was too modest, a family characteristic. Arthur joined External Affairs in 1940, before he completed his MA at Harvard in Far Eastern Studies, spending the summer processing passports in Toronto. After returning to Harvard to complete his MA and general examinations for a PhD, he was assigned to the passport office in Windsor for eleven months before being transferred to headquarters. In Ottawa, he was assigned to the general duties of a Third Secretary. He married Sheila Skelton, a high school English and history teacher, whom he had met while he was at Harvard and she at Radcliffe. She was the daughter of the late Oscar Douglas Skelton (1878–1941), one of the truly great men of twentieth-century Canadian government, one of the 'Makers of Canada.' Between 1924, when Skelton joined the civil service in Ottawa as the under-secretary of state for external affairs, and his death from a heart attack, he created the modern, professional Canadian civil service. In particular, he shaped the diplomatic corps as a well-educated cadre of 'generalists,' who could serve anywhere, anytime, on the world stage. Arthur met 'O.D.' when he was first hired, and but marrying his daughter brought Arthur – and by extension, James and Annie – into one of Canada's most distinguished families. From his marriage to Sheila in 1943 Arthur came to love her mother Isabel as his own.[35]

Arthur served in communications intelligence from November 1942 to January 1944, and then took over the Far Eastern desk for a little over a year. His first overseas posting, in April 1945, was to help open a legation in Havana, Cuba. On his return to Ottawa one year later, he was appointed head of the Far Eastern section of the American and Far Eastern Division of External Affairs, where he remained until late 1950. Thus, at a crucial moment in world history, Arthur Menzies was active in shaping Canadian policy towards Asia at a time when Canada cannot properly be said to have had a positive Far Eastern policy. These were the years of the American occupation of Japan, the birth of the United Nations, the Chinese civil war, the 'Liberation' of the People's Republic of China (PRC), the uncertainty concerning diplomatic recognition of the PRC, the Korean War, and the start of the Cold War. At the same time, Canada's immigration policies were changing to allow Chinese to enter Canada for family reunification, the beginning of the process that has changed the multicultural make-up of the country over the last fifty years.

As a diplomat in Ottawa, Arthur often received confidential communications from missionaries in China, such as one report from North Henan critical of the Communist take-over that the writer sent to selected missionaries and to Arthur at the DEA.[36] Arthur would pass the information on to his parents, who were thirsting for news of what was really happening in China. From time to time, he was able to advise them about the diminishing possibility of their return to Cheeloo.

Arthur was also able to perform a unique service for his father by helping achieve the transfer of the various components of the oracle-bone collections in China to appropriate institutions. This story is told in the Epilogue, below. The point to be made here is that James Menzies always insisted that he was collecting in China for China and that his collections should remain there to be studied by Chinese archaeologists and epigraphers. 'How I would have liked to finish my work in Cheeloo,' he wrote to Arthur in April 1947, 'if it only meant handing things over to the university in a proper way, so that archaeology would have its settled place in the curriculum of studies.'[37]

Arthur did not, however, have anything to do with another six boxes of artefacts that had been stored in the attic of the mission's business office in Tianjin. When Hugh Mackenzie was about to close the office and evacuate the city, not knowing what to do he shipped the boxes to 'James Menzies, c/o the United Church of Canada, Board of Overseas Missions, Toronto.' James had a mixed reaction to the arrival of the crates. He was happy that they would be safer in Canada than in China during the civil war. At the same time, he was disturbed by the uncertain future, his own and that of his adopted homeland, China. 'Do not ask what I am going to do with the things. I do not know yet,' he wrote to Arthur.[38] 'I would store them just as is in Rawlinson's [warehouse] until I know what our future is to be. I still hope to go out to China when Cheeloo has a place for me to work whether in Hangchow or elsewhere.'[39] Too dispirited to deal with them, Menzies left them in storage in a Toronto warehouse for six years (1948–54).[40]

The Long Wait

Incapacitated by coronary problems, separated from his collections, waiting in Washington, James Menzies took solace in writing letters. He had never been a letter writer, leaving that to Annie, but now he wrote long, emotional letters that stated and restated his life's work. He wrote to the Board of Overseas Missions, to friends and relatives, and maintained a weekly correspondence with Arthur. Thus, we can document his last years more clearly than other, more scholarly periods of his life. Father and son shared a special relationship that went back to 1935, when Arthur was finishing at the Canadian Academy and they spent the summer rambling through the archaeological sites of North China.

James Menzies was deeply concerned about the sufferings of the common people caught in the civil war. He was not happy with the way in which foreign aid to China was managed through UNRRA, because its relief work did not benefit the people in the greatest need. He was particularly worried about military aid given directly to the Guomindang government by Western countries, especially the United States and Canada. When Canada in 1946 extended a $60 million loan to the Guomindang regime to purchase Canadian military equipment including 150 airplanes, Menzies wrote his son, who was uneasy about External Affair's support of an unpopular regime. China did not need more weapons because it had too many wars, he wrote. 'I am sorry about the military supplies going to China from Canada ... The only danger Marion would meet was the bombing from Nationalist planes. So you see the problem becomes very real and personal to us.'[41]

What China needed, according to James, was well-administrated economic aid. With his knowledge of 'rural reconstruction,' he proposed a 'silver plan' to solve the problems of China's agricultural economic base. To his way of thinking, the economic crisis was caused by the monetary policy of the Nanjing government, which prohibited the open use of silver and printed too many paper notes. This destroyed the people's trust in the currency, causing hyperinflation and holding goods from circulation. To free China from this financial mess, silver should be rehabilitated as legal currency. It had always been a stable medium of exchange for the peasants and small merchants, and if sufficient silver were put into the hands of the common people, the nationwide financial crisis would be alleviated. This was the area where Western countries should intervene, he concluded.[42]

Son Arthur thought that his father's silver plan was 'out of date.' James responded: 'You say I am out of date in a modern world, but the world in China is not modern ... American policy did not get far in China. It held a hot China bowl but when it dropped the bowl, the bowl broke into fragments and will be very hard to put together again. It can never be done without greater understanding and without realizing that in China the only important person is the peasant.' He continued to explain: 'To my mind $300,000,000 in silver, sent in $20,000,000 a month and widely distributed in inland China, would be worth many times the same amount spent either in expensive American reconstruction equipment or in Chinese military expenses and supplies. Something is needed to facilitate the easy exchange of goods within China. That is much more important in limbering up trade and supplying local desperate needs than the importation of food and rehabilitation supplies from abroad. I do realize that railways are a desperate need, but the confidence in an adequate exchange medium such as silver is a much greater need at present.'[43]

To what extent James's 'traditional' view influenced his son, and thus Canada's China policy, is difficult to assess. Although Arthur was head of the Far Eastern section of the Department of External Affairs, he remained an outsider among the policy-making mandarins who focused Canadian foreign policy on Europe and the United States.

Where James and Arthur differed most – the missionary father and the diplomat son – was in James Menzies's concern for the survival of Christianity under a Communist government. When the Guomindang failed to retake Manchuria and North China from the CCP forces, this issue came to haunt mission societies in the West. The Board of Overseas Missions of the United Church held the clear position that communism was the enemy of Christianity. In June 1947, A.E. Armstrong wrote, 'Corrupt as the National Government is, if I had my way I would back them up to the limit and inflict a crushing defeat on the Communist forces. Theirs is a reign of terrorism and they are thoroughly anti-Christianity.'[44]

James Menzies did not share the political radicalism of James Endicott or other 'sympathetic observers' of the Communist Revolution,[45] but he found the board's policy too narrow, too pessimistic. He maintained that if Christian missions wanted to remain in China, they must be neutral from Cold War politics and focus on 'serving the people.' Marion had expressed a similar viewpoint when she had written that missionaries 'should not evacuate if they can manage to stay ... [as] to leave in front of the communists is looking as if the mission is identifying itself with the KMT [Guomindang].'[46] James fully concurred.

Menzies was deeply troubled by the decision to disband the North Henan mission and abandon the church. China had always been a land of troubles, he told Armstrong, and the missionary enterprise had faced nationalism before. 'Much of the trouble that is reported so vociferously in the press is the same kind of trouble that has been going on in China ever since I went there 36 years ago. Of course I do not mean that there is no trouble or difficulty. I am well aware of reliable reports which expect more clashes between the central government troops and the communists in the north. Nevertheless our mission stations have weathered a great deal of trouble in the past and will do so in the future provided they minister to the needs of the local populace.'[47]

On another occasion, Menzies wrote:

These are days of fierce testing in North China. In other parts of China peasant life may easily slip back into prewar ways ... but in North Honan, Shantung and most of North China, it is among the country villages that the most revolutionary forces are at work. Let us hope that the Church in Honan may find a way, not only to live, but also to grow in the midst of it all ... The seed has been well planted and is rooted in Chinese village life. The storms will blow, some plants may wither but if we can only carry a little of the water of life to the remainder, I am sure we shall see a harvest. Christianity in China is now seeing the fruition of work already done. If the last 100 years missionary work had been left undone, the world would be very different today and its problems grow more difficult with each tomorrow.

Using a homely metaphor, he concluded: 'The great lump of the world's dough seems little changed but the yeast is in the midst of it working secretly and the little leaven will leaven the whole lump.'[48]

Seemingly naive in the light of *realpolitik*, Menzies's optimism about the future of Christianity was the result of his understanding of the Chinese and their culture. He thought the Chinese spirit of compromise – the Doctrine of the Mean or Middle Way – would bring about the will of the people for peace. 'Surely in Shantung, the home of Confucius and Mencius, in the cradle of Chinese civilization the Chinese people will find a way to live in harmony.' As for the Communists, thinking back to those he had known in Beijing and Jinan, they were nationalists first and Communists second, and therefore bound by the Chinese cultural tradition. 'The Communists being Chinese first and knowing the usefulness of education and their own inability to provide adequate facilities for wide training, may well connive at the continued existence of the universities in Peiping [Beijing], Tientsin [Tianjin], Tsinan [Jinan] and Kaifeng. They may well allow students to filter into these colleges, knowing full well that they will come out better fitted to take part in the reconstruction of China whether the administration be under the Kuomintang or the Communist party or something in between.'[49]

Given this mindset, Menzies's desire to return to China at the height of civil war becomes understandable. After half a year's recuperation, he was well enough to return to Cheeloo, which was then returning from Sichuan to its campus in Jinan. In January 1947 Jesse H. Arnup, new secretary of the Board of Overseas Missions, wrote to Wu Keming, the president of Cheeloo, saying that Dr Menzies would return in the summer.[50] After wandering in North America for years, Menzies eagerly awaited the day of departure. To his disappointment, the medical board refused to pass him as physically fit. Sympathetically, the BOM authorized his return on condition that 'you and your wife and family are agreeable to your going to China and assuming whatever risks may be involved in view of the serious illness you have had and therefore your physical condition.'[51]

Menzies was grateful and accepted the condition without hesitation. In reply, he wrote:

> Your letter of March 27th arrived yesterday at noon and made me very proud to be a missionary of such an understanding and sympathetic Church and its Board of Overseas Missions. Your letter came in answer to many prayers and after much prayerful consideration of all the problems involved. Now that my anxiety over my future is solved ... [m]y wife and my family Marion, Frances and Arthur are all most willing that we should return to China and assume whatever risks may be involved in view of my serious illness and the possibility of my having a recurrence of my illness. A man's life is always in the hands of God, wherever he is located and his last resting-place is where God calls him in the end. My eldest son rests in Changte, Honan, and I should be honoured to rest there too. The Board may rest assured that my wife, myself and my children are all and each of us familiar with the situation as it is in China today and also with the condition of my own health. We are all grateful for the Board's consideration and understanding and trust that this decision for me to return to China may result in a furthering of the extension of the Kingdom of God and of His Church in that land.[52]

James confided to Arthur, 'I believe you understand that this going back to China is merely the completion of our life's task. We understand the risks involved and do not underestimate them. We shall not hesitate to supplement our salary with any funds needed to lessen the physical strain. There will also be mental and emotional strain arising out of the chaotic conditions in China, but these will be compensated for by the knowledge that we are placed where we can help fill out our life task. We shall plan to spend at least one full term of 6 years and perhaps more if God gives us the strength, for the Board might not be willing for us to return after the next furlough.'[53] Unfortunately, once again fate would cast this last opportunity aside.

Chapter 17

The Last Stage, 1948–1957

The University of Toronto: A Final *Démarche*

On 21 January 1948, while all these problems were swirling around, a letter dragged up again the turmoil of James Menzies's relationship with Bishop White. It came from Sidney Smith, president of the University of Toronto, informing him that, in view of Bishop White's imminent retirement, a committee had been set up to choose his successor and restructure the School of Chinese Studies. Would Menzies be 'interested in the Headship of the new department'?[1] This was a hopeful letter, but the events it unleashed were cruel, deeply wounding Menzies and saddening his future.

In 1945 Bishop White had published *Bone Culture of Ancient China*. Not only did it primarily deal with Menzies's speciality, oracle bones, it was based on the first draft of Menzies's thesis, which White had rejected and then forced Menzies to relinquish the copyright to the museum to use in whatever way it saw fit. This was apparently that appropriate use of his lifetime's research. Despite the wartime restrictions on paper, *Bone Culture* was a sumptuous book, printed by the Museum Studies Series of the ROM in five hundred numbered copies. It follows the same format as *Tombs of Old Lo-Yang* (1934), with forty pages of general text and two hundred full-page illustrations. It is not a specialist's book: the captions are short and uninformative and the oracles are not translated. White acknowledged his 'obligation to various members of the Museum' and noted that the line drawings drawn by Menzies were 'the method generally followed' in the museum. Only once is Menzies mentioned; on page 122 it is noted that 'Rev. J.M. Menzies, a missionary, who for many years had lived in the vicinity of the village [Xiaotun], in 1914 actually found fragments of inscribed bones on the surface of the soil, the site was definitely located, and the scientific public informed, by a publication of reproductions of 2,369 fragments issued by him in 1917.'[2]

Sidney Smith's letter was not a complete surprise to Menzies. During a visit to Toronto, his good friend W.R. Taylor, principal of University College, had already told him that White would be retiring soon. Menzies, who knew the ROM collections intimately and had the academic qualifications for a university professor, was the only logical choice. Moreover, the job could be his if he lobbied for it.[3] He gave Sidney Smith's enquiry 'a great deal of careful thought.' He asked for information about the university's plans to create a department rather than a School of East Asiatic Studies. The Board of Overseas Missions saw this as an ideal outcome, and Jesse Arnup wrote confidentially, 'You will be wondering about our plans for sending you back to Tsinan. There has been a hold-up for what is to us an outside reason. It is no breach of faith to say that your name has been before the University group for appointment as Director of the School of Chinese Studies at the University.'[4]

When severe fighting broke out near Jinan, the Canadian government refused to grant permission to its nationals to proceed to Shandong. On 13 March 1948 the Shandong governor urged the evacuation of Cheeloo University. That eliminated Menzies's preferred option of an early return to Jinan.

After consulting American academic friends Arthur Hummel, Mortimer Graves, and A.C. Wenley, Menzies wrote to Smith on 22 March, stating that he had decided to accept the offer of the headship. This was the most difficult decision he had made since 1905, when he had chosen to give up engineering and become a foreign missionary to China. 'Since then I have directed my life toward endeavouring to convince the peasants, students and scholars of North China that there is no contradiction involved in being a true Chinese, proud of his cultural tradition, a true scientist searching for truth wherever it may be found and a true Christian living a Christian life in his own Chinese society. This was but the expression of the three great passions of my life, my Sinophilia, my scientific bent, and my missionary purpose.'[5] Now he believed the call from his alma mater gave him another type of opportunity by serving China in Canada. 'The recent great misunderstandings that have arisen between the Western Europe cultural tradition and the Oriental ways of life have only accentuated the needs for such studies in Canada as elsewhere and it is the call of this need that has finally made me willing to change the place of my endeavour in Chinese studies from China to

Canada. These problems will not be solved or even fully understood in my lifetime but we can begin and as the Chinese say of a literary essay, "it is the beginning that is difficult."'[6]

James Menzies's acceptance of the University of Toronto's 'offer' was dated March 22nd, two months after Sidney Smith's initial enquiry. One week later, he learned that the position had been offered on 21 February to Lewis C. Walmsley, former principal of the Canadian School in West China. There seems to be contradictory evidence concerning the exact timing. On 10 March (supposedly eighteen days after Walmsley's appointment offer), W.R. Taylor, the chair of the official search committee, still wrote Menzies: 'After submitting the preliminary report ... I submitted another report to the President recommending that you be appointed as Keeper and Head of the Department and that after your arrival here further appointments on your advice could be made.'[7] Clearly other influences swayed the search committee and/or president of the university.

The search committee, headed by Principal Taylor, consisted of representatives from the museum and university as well as 'the heads of Theological Colleges and the Secretaries of Mission Boards, together with the Director of the School of Missions.'[8] White's retirement marked the end of an era. Despite a wartime boost in interest in Asia, the School of Chinese Studies never really got off the ground. It could not decide whether it was an academic department like Slavonic Studies or a school preparing 'missionaries-in-training, potential diplomats and businessmen for future work in China, on par with the Canadian School of Missions or Toronto Bible College. Symbolically, the committee recognized that China was no longer a theological but a political issue, as they started to dismantle the structures that had supported the missionary movement.[9]

At its first meeting, the search committee discussed the situation in general but no names were mentioned. At the second meeting, in early February, the same people were present, with the addition of Bishop White. Two candidates, Menzies and Walmsley, were discussed, but no decision was reached. Arnup informed Menzies confidentially, 'There are elements of delicacy in the whole matter,' and the decision was left in the hands of President Sidney Smith, with the counsel of Principal Taylor.[10]

Writing to Menzies a few weeks later, Taylor exposed the 'elements of delicacy' and his own despair over Bishop White's meddling: 'I found that White was campaigning, after his usual manner, on behalf of his favourites. I learned to my surprise, through an incidental remark of the President, that Miss [Helen] Fernald had been appointed Keeper by the Museum Board. I was somewhat aghast at this action of the Museum Board when the whole matter was still in review. Later I found that very strong pressure was being brought to bear by White for the appointment of Walmsley of West China to the language department. Both of these appointments, if ratified, would be in my opinion a backward step in the organization of the University. There would be no hope of any scientific production in the field of Chinese studies here under the direction of such persons as Walmsley and Miss Fernald since neither of them is an expert in Chinese studies.'[11] Clearly, the appointment of Walmsley was another triumph of Bishop White's influence over the established academic qualifications of James Menzies.

Menzies wrote Principal Taylor: 'President Smith's letter was direct and to the point. I was curtly dismissed and as a Canadian Highlander I was hurt, but what hurt most was that I saw that Toronto in Chinese studies was made a laughing stock in university circles in the U.S.A. and in the world at large for that matter.'[12] He was especially angry about the interference by Bishop White, 'my holy friend.' 'His actions at this time are exactly the same as in all his breaks with other people. He gets great crushes on people and then when things do not go entirely his way, he endeavours to destroy them. I am but one among many. He never forgave me because I willingly consented to having my Ph.D. thesis put under Professor Homer Thompson who gave me all the training I ever got in Toronto except what I learned from objects in the Museum and books in the Chinese library ... White wanted to give me a Ph.D., so I would be indebted to him for life. I wanted to do academic work worth a Ph.D. My whole struggle in Toronto was over the standards in academic work. White resented me even in the background when he knew I was critical of his lack of academic standards. Today he is more afraid of anyone with academic standards than anything else. He knows that good academic work by anyone will cast a shadow on the past.'[13] Nonetheless, Menzies told Taylor, 'I trust you will not worry about me. My heart is in China and we will probably, God willing, go back to China. I hope to North China and if possible to Cheeloo ... wherever it may be located.'[14] In April Menzies wrote Arnup: 'We ask that the Board of Overseas Missions will reaffirm our appointment to our work in China and that we be permitted to return whenever conditions make this possible.'[15]

Retirement

James and Annie Menzies waited impatiently as the geopolitical situation in China deteriorated. To keep their missionary status, they made 'super gifts' to the Board of Overseas Missions to pay their stipends. This required them to rearrange their finances and cash in funds set aside for retirement. Sympathetic with their situation, the board advised James to retire early on condition that he would be sent back to China if the situation changed. In May 1949 Arnup wrote to Menzies: 'It would be to your advantage to retire officially from the ministry and claim your credit in the Pension Fund ... I may add that this would not affect your chance of return to China if we find a place for you and you could physically qualify. We could appoint you without consideration of the fact that you had retired.'[16] In reply, Menzies sent the board another 'super gift' of $1000, stating he preferred to wait for a few more months until the situation in China might become clearer.

The People's Republic of China was founded on 1 October 1949. At first, the new government tolerated some Christian missions, especially those concerned with social welfare and education, while curtailing those primarily engaged in propagating religion. The 'bamboo curtain' fell a year later in the summer of 1950, when the Korean War broke out. Once again, most Western nationals were 'enemy aliens' and were ordered to leave the country. This was the fatal blow to the missionary enterprise in China. The 'reluctant exodus' of all missionaries and other foreigners began.

Before departure, many missionaries endured humiliating public trials and denunciation meetings. In Kaifeng Bishop White's protégé, now the bishop of Henan, Rev. Francis Tseng, launched a vitriolic attack on White as an agent of Western imperialism. Tseng 'had seen the treasures in Toronto and it had filled him with hatred to think that Dr. White, under the cloak of religion, had taken advantage of his position, stolen those treasures from China, and grown rich by so doing.'[17]

Menzies also came in for denunciation *in absentia*. The last missionary to leave Cheeloo, F.S. Drake, who had helped Menzies survey the ancient sites of Shandong in the 1930s, gave the authorities an old map that showed where he had buried the boxes of oracle bones in 1942, nine years earlier. All together, about 140 boxes of artefacts were eventually uncovered. In the highly politicized atmosphere of the new regime, this became a political event on the Cheeloo campus and in the city of Jinan, with a public exhibition and 'denunciation' meetings designed to 'expose the nature of the cultural imperialist, Menzies.'[18]

After all these years of waiting, James Menzies accepted 'honourable retirement' in April 1951. Co-signed by James and Annie, the letter to the board contained the following statement: 'We do not regret that we went as missionaries to Honan and North China nor do we consider that the life effort we put into the work there is lost. Unless a corn of wheat fall into the ground and be buried, it cannot bring forth fruit. We have faith that there will be a Christian harvest in China in God's good time. We loved and tried to understand the Chinese people in Honan and at Cheeloo University and we believe that the Christian Church will survive even though the persecution may be as severe as it has ever been in China's history. The United Church of Canada must not abandon the Christian Church in China but must continue to believe that it is our Christian duty to extend the Kingdom of God and the Gospel of Jesus Christ to China by whatever means is possible.' Still they had hope: 'If it is ever possible in the future for me to return to China for a short period to arrange about books and archaeological collection at Cheeloo University, that can be considered when the time comes.'[19]

When James and Annie had returned to Toronto in 1949, the financial help of the children enabled them to buy a small two-storey semi-detached house at 62 Tilson Road near Yonge Street and Eglinton Avenue. It cost $10,500, some $500 over their budget. As Marion recalled, James's cousin, a skilled carpenter, 'created a work place for my father in the center section of the attic under the eaves. A folding ladder in the clothes closet was the entrance to this place. He also built a dormer window to let in light and air. This primitive area became my father's study where he could work on his "Oracle Bones."'[20] Only after he gave up hope of going back to China did Menzies begin to retrieve the six crates of oracle bones from Tianjin that were still in storage. He started to bring a few artefacts to decorate the small house, and gradually transferred the rest of the collection to his attic study. Each fragile item had to be carried carefully up the ladder and through the trap door, where he laid them out on shelves, neatly arranged and catalogued.

Menzies's last years were very difficult. While on a 1955 visit to their daughter and son-in-law, now appointed to Trinidad, Annie Menzies discovered a lump on her neck. Back in Canada, she had to undergo painful radiation therapy five days a week. To complicate things, she broke her hip when she fell down stairs. The stress for James was great, and in turn his heart condition worsened. When Annie returned from hospital, he could not cope with making meals and moving her wheelchair. He went downhill physically and was confined to bed.[21]

There was one final indignity from Bishop White. In 1956 White published his last book, *Bronze Culture of Ancient China*. Even its title echoed the title of Menzies's rejected thesis, 'The Bronze Age Culture of China.' Here the effacement of Menzies was complete, as he is mentioned only in one footnote.[22]

When James Menzies received his copy, he commented to Sheila, Arthur's wife:

> Bishop White's book *Bronze Culture of Ancient China* is out and has provoked many thoughts. It is very ambitious and persevering of him to put it out at his age, but the material on which his groups of sets is based is founded entirely on my thesis written in 1942. I was sent a complimentary copy by the museum, sent 'at the request of Bishop White.' One appendix is a reprint of my findings on one halberd or '*Ko*' that fixes the date of one tomb from which a series of bronzes came. Naturally I have mixed feelings about it all. At least the photographs (90 of them) are valuable. He had them reserved for this publication for many years, at least 15 years. Perhaps I should be glad to have the information published since the depositing of 3 copies [of the thesis] in the Library of the University of Toronto is not considered publication. But, enough.[23]

Two months after making these comments, on 16 March 1957, James Menzies had a second heart attack and died, aged seventy-two. He was survived by his brother Robert and sister Margaret Judge, as well as his wife and children. The funeral, attended by hundreds of friends, was held at Bloor Street United Church, conducted by Dr George Pidgeon, the patriarch of the social gospel. James Menzies was buried in Mount Pleasant Cemetery. Annie sold the house on Tilson Road and moved to London to live with daughter Marion and her husband Jim Hummel, who was a United Church minister. She died on 18 October 1962, aged 80, and was buried beside her beloved husband – 'Old Bones.'

James Menzies was 'a man of many parts,' his old friend L. Carrington Goodrich, of Columbia University, wrote in an obituary in the *Journal of Asian Studies*. Goodrich described Menzies's achievements, such as his identification of the Waste of Yin and his book *Oracle Records from the Waste of Yin*, which contained only one inscription that 'proved to be a fake – a notable achievement for a pioneer work.' 'It was at the end of 1929 that I first met him and persuaded him to give a lecture on the Shang. My recollection of it is still a vivid one. Master of his subject he made it live, interspersing his talk with many valuable comments on comparable societies drawn from his first-hand knowledge of finds in the Near East,' which he had visited on his round-the-world trip. 'It is worth remembering, in conclusion,' Goodrich noted, 'that his is one of the few Western names, sometimes the only Western name, mentioned by Chinese scholars in connection with work on Shang inscriptions.'[24]

When Menzies came back to Canada on furlough in 1936, he was at the height of his missionary scholarship. For the next twenty years, believing his 'detainment' in North America would be temporary, he made an effort to prepare himself for better service when he would go 'home' to China. He wrote 'The Bronze Age Culture of China,' an academic masterpiece. His doctoral dissertation, *Shang Ko*, was a significant achievement, recognized when it was belatedly published by the ROM. Personal politics frustrated his work, however, which was a great loss to the scholarly community and Chinese studies in Canada. In this period, the only happy stretch was, ironically, the war years in the United States, when he worked as a propaganda expert.

Menzies never regretted his choice to be a China missionary, but his last years were ones of frustration. A wandering uprooted missionary until the end of his life, he found it difficult to reintegrate into Canadian society. His heart, his home, his soul were always among his students at Cheeloo and the poor illiterate peasants of North Henan.

Chapter 18

Conclusion

As a China missionary, James Mellon Menzies and his family joined a select company of Canadians, British, Americans, and others who chose to perform humanitarian and educational work overseas. He experienced the tides of twentieth-century history with his colleagues in North Henan and at Cheeloo University in neighbouring Shandong. Arriving during the high tide of Western imperialism after the Boxer rebellion of 1900, they watched as the Chinese Revolution seemingly swept away their work. Menzies's life highlights the complex context of Christian missions and the multiple forces that Protestant missionaries had to 'negotiate' for their work in China. In contrast to conventional views, this study argues that China's modern encounter with the West, particularly Christian missions, was not a linear process, but a dynamic and multi-dimensional discourse.

This book set out to study the life of one individual missionary in the context of his time and space. By avoiding the constraints of generic theoretical interpretations, it has attempted to capture what made James Menzies unique. It historicizes his life, work, and thought in the context in which he experienced it. With this contextualization, we are able to see the difficult 'negotiation' process that Menzies had at multiple levels and with multiple forces, including Chinese nationalism, Western imperialism, the evangelical mission, and his own personal interest in Chinese archaeology within that world. Without categorization, this approach shows the interaction between these issues/forces, and their impact on Menzies's life. If one simplistically put Menzies in a theoretical category, he might appear as an example of the *single-dimension* 'impact and influence' or 'cultural imperialist' theories, aiming to *destroy* Chinese tradition and culture. Such was definitely not the case, as our examination of his life and work has shown. At all times, he was an interactive medium at the very interface of two cultures, trying to embrace both.

The final evaluation of Menzies's life should focus on the three roles he played as a China missionary: as collector, archaeologist, and evangelical theorist. These roles shaped his experience from the moment he picked up his first fragment of oracle bone from the Waste of Yin. 'Do bones interest you?' the peasant boy asked. James Menzies's answer made him unique among China missionaries.

Missionary Collector

Menzies is known as an oracle-bone collector, but except for a few brief articles, no extensive study has been done about him in that capacity. Consequently, there have been different interpretations about his motivations. In addition, the exact nature of his collection, in both qualitative and quantitative terms, has remained a mystery. With the help of unpublished family papers, and archival and museum documents, we can provide a detailed discussion and evaluation of Menzies as a world-class collector. The Menzies Collections – some 35,000 oracles and thousands of other ancient objects – are detailed in the Epilogue, 'James Menzies's Legacy.' As this study shows, Menzies distinguished himself from other collectors in terms of collecting motivation, method, and achievement.

The Menzies collections had a high monetary value. However, family and archival documents and the disposition of these artefacts indicate clearly that the motivation behind his remarkable collecting efforts had never been monetary, but rather stemmed from a mixture of religious and academic interest. As his children recall, he always followed the principle of *bu zuo mai mai* (no business deals).

From the beginning to the end, Menzies kept the belief that his connection with the 'Waste of Yin' was 'providential,' that God had placed in his hands the oracle bones, the religious documents left by a people over three thousand years ago who were worshippers of *Shangdi*, the same name as the Protestants used to translate 'Jehovah God.' As he was a missionary, it is not hard to understand his claim that God appointed him custodian of his adobe city. Ever since the sixteenth century, both foreign and Chinese Christians had searched for a common ground or synthesis between Christianity and Chinese culture. The Jesuit Matteo Ricci had endeavoured to link Christianity to Confucius and Mencius by infusing Christian meaning into the loosely defined concept of *Tian*, or 'Heaven.' Some Protestant missionaries, such as Timothy

Richard, tried to prove a commonality between Christianity and Mahayana Buddhism. In his search for a link between Christianity and the Chinese, James Menzies went back to the beginning of Chinese civilization, before the time of Confucius and Gautama Buddha. He thought the inscribed oracles contained the key to a genuine synthesis between Christianity and ancient Chinese culture. This link became the driving force in his passion for oracle bones and other archaeological artefacts.

This religious motivation had been nurtured and strengthened by Menzies's growing interest in Chinese culture, his aesthetic appreciation of Chinese artefacts, and the frustration he felt with rural evangelism and Chinese nationalism. Starting with Chinese language classes in North Henan, he developed a lifelong bond with Chinese culture and arts. The lack of interest by educated Chinese in Christianity and particularly the anti-Christian movements in the 1920s galvanized him to seek a meaningful link between Christianity and Chinese culture. Collecting provided him with the necessary means to carry out this self-selected mission.

Menzies collected for his mission in China. This unique motivation led to unique collecting principles. By comparing him to other missionary collectors such as Bishop White, another Canadian missionary collector and scholar, we have been able to highlight Menzies's collecting principles. The first was his scientific approach to collecting. As he was not collecting for museums or the art market, what was essential was not the artefacts' artistic value but their scientific value, particularly the amount of information they revealed about China's past culture and beliefs. Therefore, for Menzies a broken shard of white pottery could be as important as an intact, beautiful vessel. As a direct result of this principle, he was able to build up a large collection with limited financial resources. This principle also determined that, except for a small number of fine items, his collection was not well suited for museum exhibition, as most items were broken. However, they were of high academic value because of the scientific ways in which they were collected and preserved, as well as for the knowledge accessed through the pieces themselves.

Second, Menzies always believed his collection should remain with him in China. Since his commitment to the mission cause was lifelong, he never made plans to send his collection out of China. The only institute to which he chose to donate the collection was Cheeloo University, in a private arrangement to protect it after the Japanese invasion. Unfortunately, this did not materialize as planned because of his absence from China and the swift political changes during the anti-Japanese war and the subsequent civil war. A small part of the Menzies collection did end up in Canada, six boxes stored in Tianjin that were sent out by his colleagues after the North Henan mission was disbanded in 1947. For years, these artefacts remained unpacked while Menzies and his wife were arranging for their return to China. Menzies gave some fine items from his collection to his family as presents on important occasions, but the bulk remained together, primarily with a view to academic study. In general, we think Menzies did stand by his self-imposed principle of keeping his collection in China. This was truly unusual for a collector at that time when foreign collectors missed no opportunity to export Chinese artefacts legally or illegally, paying no attention to Chinese sentiment and regulations.

What did Menzies accomplish as a collector? Many collectors have been remembered with museums or galleries named after them, but Menzies did not earn such an honour. We could say that he never thought of that kind of recognition. Otherwise, he would have cultivated relations with museums in the West, something he eschewed except for personal relations with individuals and his troubled relations with the ROM. His achievement as a collector is of a different kind.

The artefacts he collected are of great academic value for the study of early Chinese culture and religion. Even though most are broken fragments, often as small as a fingernail, their historic value was preserved by Menzies's attempt to preserve earth samples with each artefact whenever possible, and to attach a detailed registration note describing where and how each was discovered, along with his own evaluation. These artefacts, especially the oracles, fulfilled the mission that Menzies assigned for them. They provided him with rich information about the Shang people's life and beliefs, leading him to the conclusion that these early Chinese were truly worshippers of 'God' and therefore, in a religious sense, that the fundamental premise of Christianity was not totally foreign to the Chinese.

Since the Menzies collections have been divided among five Chinese and Canadian museums, their academic value has been shared by both Chinese and Western scholars. In quantitative terms, the Menzies collection is one of the important collections of early Chinese archaeological artefacts. This is particularly the case for his collection of oracles. Excluding those destroyed by warlord soldiers, the extant inscribed oracle bones collected by Menzies total 35,913 pieces. In the last hundred years, the Waste of Yin has yielded about 150,000 pieces of inscribed oracle bones. Menzies collected more than one-fifth, which made him the largest private collector of oracle bones. The other artefacts that he gathered number about 23,000 pieces. To better evaluate the Menzies collection, we also have to consider the fact that it was put together by an ordinary missionary with limited financial resources. It was mainly through his own economy that he helped collect and preserve these valuable Chinese artefacts.

By following the principles of 'no business deals' and keeping the artefacts in China, Menzies set an ethical and practical example for foreign scholars to participate in Chinese archaeology. With few exceptions, Western collectors of Menzies's time and earlier have been condemned as cultural imperialists and disliked by the Chinese. In the 1950s Menzies was also called a cultural imperialist, but as this study shows, he was perhaps one of the few exceptions among foreign collectors. He was indeed not beyond reproach: without the imperial intrusion into China, the Menzies collections would not exist. It was indeed the effects of imperialism that made it possible for him to collect and preserve such a large collection of Chinese archaeological artefacts. Still, we also have to recognize that the motivation behind Menzies's collecting efforts and the final disposition of his collection distinguished him from collectors who truly were cultural imperialists. He collected for his missionary cause in China and kept his collection in China too. If it had not been for the wars, Cheeloo University would have become the sole recipient of his entire collection and library.

It is not my intention to say that Menzies was a perfect collector and did nothing improperly. But the new evidence provided in this study indicates it is a great mistake to paint him simply as one more cultural imperialist. To do justice to him as a committed missionary scholar we have to acknowledge that he was an early pioneer of the principle 'collect for knowledge and keep in China,' now the universal standard for foreign archaeologists participating in field excavations there.

Missionary Archaeologist

The importance of the oracle inscriptions from the Waste of Yin for the study of Chinese history and archaeology cannot be overstated. Their discovery and identification as authentic ideographs written by the Shang people provided the first concrete evidence of a literate, urbanized Bronze Age in China. The excavation of Anyang by the Academia Sinica between 1928 and 1937 made the Waste of Yin the birthplace of modern Chinese archaeology.

The Waste of Yin was the central place in Menzies's intellectual life, wherever he was actually located. Wandering in his 'adobe city' in the cool of the evening on his daily walk, he found the meaning of his mission in China. There he built up his collection of bits and pieces he picked up from the surface, and started the transition from rural evangelism to scientific archaeology. If collecting helped build steps to reach China's past, archaeology provided Menzies with the key to the door for understanding China's ancient cultural and religious life.

Motivated by his self-proclaimed mission to indigenize Christianity in Chinese culture, Menzies became part of the drive for professionalism among Protestant missions in China. The difference was that his goal was not simply to introduce Western science and technology, but to prove through archaeological evidence the link between the Chinese and God, what he called 'Grace.' For this purpose, he was not satisfied with the status of an amateur archaeologist, but devoted himself with a strong spirit of professionalism. To serve his new mission, archaeology became his 'social gospel' and the *Cheeloo Quarterly* and university podiums because his pulpit. By the 1930s Menzies was one of the recognized archaeologists in China, a national and international authority on oracle-bone studies.

In addition to his own collection of oracles and other archaeological artefacts, Menzies made significant contributions to the early development of scientific oracle-bone studies. The foundation was the publication of oracle inscriptions that provided the basic materials for scholars. Already a major collector, Menzies published *Oracle Records from the Waste of Yin* in 1917. A decade later, he had substantially completed 'Oracle Records from the Waste of Yin, Part II,' not published at the time but consulted in draft copies by many Chinese scholars. All the inscriptions in Menzies's books were from his personal collection. While working at Cheeloo, he also published the collection of Paul D. Bergen. In total, Menzies drew or reproduced, translated, annotated, and published over five thousand oracle-bone inscriptions.

For a while after Wang Yirong's discovery of oracle bones in a Beijing drugstore in 1898, the value of these historical documents was doubtful because of the number of forgeries flooding the curio markets. With his years of experience in fieldwork, Menzies became one of the few experts at detecting forgeries. Of his five thousand inscriptions, only one forged oracle slipped past his eyes. His pioneering efforts helped establish criteria for distinguishing between real and forged oracles, thereby silencing the conservative historical school that challenged the authenticity of oracle bones.

Menzies also made significant achievements in matching broken oracle bones. After being buried underground for several thousand years, oracle bones broke into pieces during the process of excavation, shipping, and rubbing. As a result, pieces of one bone ended up in different collections. Even though Menzies was not the first to recognize the value in matching broken bone fragments, he and his assistant Zeng Yigong were responsible for the establishment of matching oracle-bone fragments as a field of oracle studies. Their publications restored the documentary value of many broken oracle bones.

As historical documents, inscribed oracles were dated according to the titles of Shang kings and queens. Wang Guowei first discovered this dating method and classified oracle inscriptions into historical periods. Wang made an important start, but Menzies was one of the scholars who further developed Wang's methodology of oracle periodization. In addition to correcting Wang's misinterpretation of the names of the Shang kings, Menzies discovered other particulars for determining the time period of oracle bones. One was the name of the diviners, another the pattern of chiselled hollows in oracle bones. Nowadays, these two particulars have become the basic criteria for dating oracle bones.

From the time he stumbled into the world of oracle bones, Menzies remained obsessed with Chinese archaeology, until the very end of his life. His years at Cheeloo University were his golden age as an archaeologist. Before he was appointed to Cheeloo in 1932, modern archaeology education did not exist there. He made Cheeloo the centre for oracle studies and taught the first courses in 'Oracle Bone Studies' and 'Archaeology.' He was probably the first foreign professor to teach these courses in Chinese. As a part of his archaeology education efforts, he established a study museum on the campus, exhibiting some of the best pieces from his collection. This museum became a unique feature of the Institute of Chinese Studies and helped enhance Cheeloo's international reputation.

Menzies was a far-sighted scholar with an inborn instinct for archaeology. This made it possible for him to play a pioneering role in several important areas of oracle-bone studies. At Cheeloo, while continuing his work on oracle publication, identification, and periodization, he also made efforts to apply the new information provided by oracle-bone inscriptions to the study of Shang culture and religion. Among his publications was *Jiagu Yanjiu* (Oracle Bone Studies). Printed as a text-book for his oracle course, this was the best work of its type published during his lifetime. It was the synthesis of his knowledge and experience with oracle-bone collection and study, accumulated over more than two decades.

Menzies carried on his interest in Shang culture and archaeology after his return to Canada in 1936. When working at the Royal Ontario Museum and doing his PhD program at the University of Toronto, he expanded his research scope from Shang bone culture to Shang stone and bronze culture, with more attention given to the latter. The results were 'The Bronze Age Culture of China' and *Shang Ko*.

'The Bronze Age Culture of China' was a general synthesis of Menzies's knowledge about ancient Shang culture. Although it has not been published, it remains a significant academic achievement. Unlike most publications, it was based upon primary archaeological and classical sources. The long bibliography of Chinese references and their application in the text are a testimony to Menzies's expertise in Chinese classics. 'The Bronze Age' also shed new light on important issues concerning early Chinese culture. Its hypothesis and analysis of the 'indigenous origin of Chinese bronze culture' directly challenged the accepted theory by Western scholars of the 'Western origin of Chinese civilization.' Menzies paid particular attention to the rivers of Siberia and northern route of ancient China's connection with the Middle East and Europe. His image of gloves with their central palms and extended fingers, used to explain China's cultural relations with other parts of the world, was brilliant and unforgettable. It showed his bold spirit in theoretical speculation and his ability to observe and visualize. He may not have been the first to articulate these ideas, but the contribution he made was to present them in a historical context constructed from both archaeological discoveries and Chinese classical records.

Shang Ko was originally the second part of 'The Bronze Age Culture of China,' separately revised and accepted as Menzies's doctoral dissertation. At that time, it was the most detailed typological study of the *ge* (which he spelled *Ko*), the unique and most common Chinese bronze weapon. The primary source for this study was 177 bronze *ge* in the ROM collections, which he classified into ten types and arranged in chronological sequence. Within this framework, he presented a grand picture of the Shang bronze industry, an enterprise controlled by the state and sustained with raw materials transported from as far away as Yunnan and Malaya. Menzies argued that *ge* was an indigenous Chinese weapon, similar to, but not a copy of, the European halberd. Its origin was the stone sickles used by farmers in north China. He was the first to introduce the concept of *ge* directly into English, instead of translating it into English. Menzies's hypothesis about the Shang bronze culture may not be correct in every aspect, but his views about its origin, scale of influence, and supplies of raw materials have been supported by recent archaeological discoveries in China.

For Menzies, the transition from rural evangelism to professional archaeology was not an easy one. Not only did he have to persuade his conservative colleagues in North Henan and Canada, but he had to re-educate himself in a very difficult subject. Sincerely believing in the possibility of discovering God in ancient China, he made himself an expert in Chinese archaeology. However, archaeology was never the end, but only the tool.

Evangelist: God in Ancient China

No matter how successful his efforts at archaeology and oracle-bone studies, Menzies always regarded himself as a missionary. In fact, his primary aim was to harness his scholarship to the good of his mission work. The central thesis of his life, 'God in Ancient China,' became the focus of his life and thought for half a century.

Menzies was initiated into mission policy and theory through his involvement with the YMCA and Student Volunteer Movement during his education at the University of Toronto's School of Practical Science. In 1910, en route to China, he attended the World Missionary Conference in Edinburgh, where he was exposed to the highest levels of mission-policy thinking. He exhibited a strong interest in Chinese culture almost as soon as he arrived at Zhangde and quickly developed his theory that the ancient Chinese were worshippers of 'God.' His evangelistic theory took shape in the late 1920s, influenced by two decades of rural evangelism in North Henan. Menzies had a rich knowledge of the common people and their culture, to which he allied a liberal outlook on the volatile Chinese situation, including a sympathy with Chinese nationalism and a progressive world view. He came to advocate a three-pronged mission theory – similar to the famous Three Self movement: indigenization, Christian higher education, and Chinese leadership.

Today, the concept of indigenization has become an indispensable idea of world Christianity. At Menzies's time, however, it was still a radical idea. His successful efforts in oracle studies and in dealing with the anti-Christian sentiment among Chinese intellectuals and students made Menzies a committed advocate of 'localizing' the gospel in Chinese culture. He believed that the Christian church in China depended largely on Christian leaders linking their message with Chinese culture. Only an indigenized faith would be able to face up to the agnosticism of the Confucian tradition and the new forces of anti-religious atheism and anti-foreign nationalism.

The theological foundation for Menzies's thought on accommodation was his interpretation of Shang religion, which he defined through three main concepts. The first was *Shangdi*, or 'God,' as a personal spiritual power, almighty but caring, just and omnipotent, in control of nature and human affairs. The second concept was ancestor reverence. The Shang royal family revered their ancestors and held extravagant ceremonies in their memory, but Menzies argued that the rationale behind this was different from that for ancestor worship as expounded by Confucianism. The Shang people revered their ancestors because they believed they were the medium between living humans and *Shangdi*. Since the ancestors had no independent power to answer petitions from their descendants, their role was limited to that of intermediaries.

A third concept Menzies expounded was *Tian* (Heaven), or *Tian Yi Shang* (the 'Heavenly City Shang'). Menzies maintained that the Shang people's concept, unlike the later Confucian concept of *Tian*, was not of a fearful spiritual Heaven but of a place where *Shangdi* dwelled with their ancestors. Because of this proximity, their ancestors were in a position to communicate directly with *Shangdi* on their behalf.

For Menzies, his theory of Shang religion was of great importance for the missionary enterprise. He believed he had found the response in archaeology to Chinese scholars' assertion that the Chinese were non-religious and had never believed in God. More importantly, he came to the conclusion that if the Chinese once had 'as good a primitive idea of God as the Hebrews before Moses,' Christianity as the Western revelation of God should not be seen as totally foreign. What Menzies attempted was no less than a redefinition of the missionary enterprise. The role of foreign missionaries was not to introduce a 'new' belief to the Chinese, but to help in the rediscovery and enhancement of the faith originally followed by the Chinese. Overcoming that faith's foreignness, Menzies maintained, made possible the integration of Christianity and China's unique past. In other words, the link between 'God' and Shang Chinese served to indigenize the Christian gospel in Chinese culture. As Menzies wrote to his Knox College classmates in the early 1950s, 'When one starts from the premise that God is the God of the Chinese and was so recognized by them, Christianity no longer becomes a foreign religion in the eyes of the Chinese and you have a firm foundation for your Christian preaching.'

The second component of Menzies's mission theory was Christian higher education. The Christian colleges in China should train leaders both for the church and for Chinese society. He insisted repeatedly that a living Chinese church needed well-educated leaders who were able to think and work independently and intelligently, and that Chinese society needed leaders with a strong sense of Christian morality. Although trained as a civil engineer, Menzies argued that science alone could not save China. Christian higher education should give students a broad and balanced education of 'faith plus science plus Chinese culture plus Western social science.' He particularly emphasized the importance of Chinese studies, but with both classical and modern focus, since a good basis would make it easier for graduates to integrate their faith into the Chinese society and make Christianity less foreign to the Chinese.

Menzies had a passion for Cheeloo University, which he felt represented the ideal of Christian higher education. Yenching and the elite Christian colleges had lost touch by turning out Westernized 'de-nationalized' graduates who mainly aspired to make money and serve the interests of political powers. He believed the graduates of Christian colleges should be ministers, teachers, doctors, and other educated young men and women with a 'Christian character.' In other words, they should be students committed to the Christian cause and willing to serve the common people.

Founding a living Christian church in China constituted the third component of Menzies's missionary policy. Challenged by Chinese nationalism, he became an advocate of native leadership of the Christian movement. He believed that the days of missionaries as leaders were over and that clinging to leadership roles could harm rather than help the Chinese church. Menzies was not a radical. He did not support unconditionally transferring power to Chinese leaders who were not well trained. As he wrote in 1934, 'We have far too many half trained and half baked people in the Church now. It is our curse. They are at the mercy of all emotional, political, racial, communistic winds and follow whatever wind blows the hardest ... Had they been better trained in history, culture, real knowledge of the world and its scientific advancement, they would never have allowed themselves to be so exploited.'[1] To prevent the church from being taken over by 'half-baked people,' Menzies argued for a gradual transition. As the first step, missionaries and their missions must trust their Chinese leaders. But more importantly, missionaries had to empower them as partners by providing the best possible education. Only an educated Christian leadership able to think and act intelligently and independently would be able to preserve what the missionaries had achieved, and take the gospel to the Chinese people.

Menzies was not a 'big' leader of the missionary movement but he was a big thinker with an active mind. By turning archaeology to the service of his mission in China, he pioneered a distinctive path for himself. Some of his ideas, such as the concept of *Shangdi* and its relation with the Christian concept of God, are still a matter of debate, but his theories on Christian higher education and indigenization of the gospel did reach and influence a large audience.

To conclude, Menzies was a unique China missionary. Quiet and non-provocative but still a man of commitment, he had the patience and flexibility to 'negotiate' the forces interacting within his life. This made it possible for him to make successful shifts in his life path from engineering to evangelism and then to archaeology. His change from rural evangelism to archaeology was not a change of heart or abandonment of the Chinese commoner. Archaeology was his way to serve the mission cause in China, since through archaeology he was able to link Christianity with the Chinese people. As he reflected late in life, 'While I have counted 1,000 persons baptized and many more prepared for the catechumens, yet perhaps my work on the bones permeated deeper into Chinese life than my work among the schools and churches of North Henan.'[2] His theory of *Shangdi* meant that the gospel was no longer a foreign religion, but also that the mission of the missionaries was not to 'convert' the Chinese. Rather, their role was to help the Chinese to rediscover the belief that their own ancestors followed. The concept of *Shangdi*, as believed by Menzies, provided a firm ground for the Chinese church to negotiate a legitimate space in Chinese society.

Menzies lived in two worlds, the secular and the religious. For him there was no wall between them. In 1907 he gave up engineering and chose to be a China missionary. From that time to the end of his life his heart was with the evangelistic cause in China. However, this religious commitment did not prevent him from using secular means to serve his missionary cause. Today, Menzies is remembered for what he achieved as a collector and archaeologist, but what has been ignored and forgotten was his attempt to place his scholarship within his missionary goals. For

Menzies, archaeology was just a tool for a higher purpose: to adapt the gospel to the Chinese context.

Menzies lived at the interface between two cultures. He made the journey to understand the Chinese; his goal was to indigenize Christianity within the Chinese context, to produce a living synthesis between Christianity and Chinese culture. This attitude indicates his open-mindedness and willingness to accept cultures different from his own. His accommodationist approach distinguished him from other missionaries who worked to 'give' the Chinese a belief and culture. However, his accommodation was limited to the culture and religion: it failed when confronted by Chinese nationalism. In other words, although Menzies went a long way towards understanding Chinese culture, in the end he never understood the real nature of twentieth-century Chinese nationalism and revolution.

Sadly, the Chinese Revolution meant that James Menzies did not receive due recognition during his lifetime. Shortly after his death in 1957, his wife Annie and his son Arthur met with the directors of the Royal Ontario Museum to discuss the Canadian portion of the Menzies collection. The international situation was unstable because of the Cold War, and the Canadian government did not have formal diplomatic relations with the People's Republic of China. As the best solution to a desperate situation, the Menzies family agreed to transfer a substantial portion of the collection to the museum. As part of this agreement finalized in 1960, the ROM and the University of Toronto established the Menzies Fund of $40,000, administered by the ROM, to publish his works and promote Chinese studies in Canada. It is appropriate, then, to end with a list of publications by and about James Menzies, which have 'rehabilitated' his memory in Canada and China:

- 1965, *Shang Ko*, published by the ROM.
- 1971, *The Menzies Collection of Shang Dynasty Oracle Bones*, volume 1, edited by James Chin-hsiung Hsü and published by the ROM.
- 1972, *Yin-hsü P'u-tz'u hou-pien* (Additional Collection of Oracle Records from the Waste of Yin), edited by James Hsü and published by Yee Wen Press (Taiwan).
- 1972, *Oracle Records from the Waste of Yin* (originally published by Kelly & Walsh in Shanghai in 1917), reprinted by Yee Wen Press.
- 1976, *The Menzies Collection of Shang Dynasty Oracle Bones*, volume 2, edited by James Hsü and published by the ROM.
- 1989, *Chinese Art from the Rev. Dr. James M. Menzies Family Collection*, by

Barry Till, catalogue for an exhibition at the Art Gallery of Greater Victoria, British Columbia.

- 1996, *Jiagu Yanjiu* (Oracle Bone Studies), reprinted by Qilu Press, Jinan.
- 1999, the Menzies family donated James Menzies's personal library, including his unpublished manuscripts and study notes, to Shandong University. The mayor of Qingdao, Wang Jiarui, the president of Shandong University, Zeng Fanren, and the Canadian ambassador, Howard Balloch, attended the ceremony.
- 2000, publication of *Ming I Shi ho ta di tsan ping* (Dr James Menzies and His Collections of Chinese Art). Jinan: Shandong University Press.

James Menzies's Legacy

James Mellon Menzies left two major legacies of international impact: his children and his archaeological collections.

Offspring

Three children were raised in unusual environments by kind and loving parents who guided their development of Christian characters that they were to express through their lives and careers. James gave them something more than conventional mishkids enjoyed, something they would never forget: a round-the-world tour that would last almost a whole year. As Marion remembered seventy years later, '[W]e were privileged, under the guidance of a father, interested in world archaeology, and Biblical historiography, to get a real feel for what we saw and to record and express ourselves about our experiences in our diaries ... But in residue, this world-wide experience and exposure gave each of us a strong personal memory of widely different historical cultures, yet a sense that all these regional, cultural, and religious differences could be pulled together in a modernized and caring world order.'[1]

When Marion reached Vancouver in the fall of 1932, immigration officials detained her because she had only $25.00 to her name. A telegram to Aunt Margaret Judge in Edmonton provided the assurance of adequate funds in Canada for her to attend university. Aunt Margaret was the stable rock that held the Menzies family together in Canada. She had cared for the aging parents until their death and now she and Uncle Jack opened their home to Marion while she attended the University of Alberta.

'The courses I took were largely decided by Dad with a view of eventual return to China as a missionary,' she remembered. 'Greek, Hebrew, and a grade 13 French, which I had failed at C[anadian] A[cademy, at Kobe]. In retrospect, I was not a good student at languages and would have enjoyed psychology and sociology more. I made a lot of friends and became involved with the Student Christian Movement and later the Oxford Group, just making its impression on university students.' The following year, 1933–4, she moved to Victoria College, the United Church college at the University of Toronto, living with a North Henan family, the Boyds. Besides numerous West China mishkids, Vic had an active association of Canadian Academy alumni who called themselves 'Chushinguru' (loyal retainers) after the Japanese story of the forty-seven samurai. Marion had a large circle of friends.[2]

In September 1934, when Frances was nineteen and ready to enter university, James and Annie decided that Annie should take her to Toronto and set up a home for the two girls. 'What a joy to be part of a family again!' Marion wrote. They rented a house on Cottingham Street within walking distance of the university and Annie managed to acquire furniture through a rather ingenious method: she put a classified ad in the newspaper offering, 'Will store furniture for use of same.' The family worshipped at Bloor Street United church, a former Presbyterian congregation that had a reputation as an intellectual 'university church.' Bloor Street had a long connection with North Henan including the Bloor Street hospital in Huaiqing built in memory of the murdered Dr James R. Menzies.[3] The minister was Rev. Dr George Pidgeon, one of the greatest preachers of his generation and first moderator of the United Church.

Arthur remained in the Canadian Academy for one more year, then joined the others in Toronto. Consequently, James lived as a bachelor for his last two years at Cheeloo, which allowed him to throw himself into his work without any distractions. He and Arthur spent the summer holidays of 1935 together, travelling through China visiting ancient sites, temples, and monasteries; they climbed Taishan, the sacred mountain in Shandong, and went home to Zhangde to inspect the excavation of Anyang. This experience cemented a special father/son relationship. In later years, James would confide in his son what he could not speak in public. Their letters form the backbone of this book.

That the world be both modernized and caring beyond regional and religious differences remained the Menzies' hope and faith. While the family was as poor as church mice, all three children went on to graduate education, Marion and Frances in social work and Arthur in Far Eastern history. After the Second World War, they all became involved in the reconstruction of China, their birthplace. Marion's service in UNRRA, Frances in the United Church, and Arthur at the Department of External Affairs continued the tradition of inculturation that James had exemplified. During the dark days of the anti-Japanese war and the civil war, as the forces combined to eventually destroy James's own career, their stories inevitably cheered him.

After his death in 1957, the Menzies children continued his legacy by distributing his collection of oracle bones and other ancient artefacts to the most appropriate institutions, considering the perilous state of world affairs. Although James Menzies has been recognized as an important collector and all major studies of oracle bones refer to him, no comprehensive study has been done of his collection. Few know what happened to the tens of thousands of artefacts, especially the 35,000 oracle bones, and so inevitably speculations and misunderstandings have arisen. To have a realistic evaluation of the James Mellon Menzies Collection, it is necessary to retrace the history of how he assembled his collections and how they were dispersed after he left China in 1936.

Assembling the Collection

When James Menzies discovered the Waste of Yin in 1914, he knew that he was looking at potsherds of a very early date and 'dragon bones' with characters on them, and he followed the trail until it disappeared at the edge of the Huan River. Shard by shard, tortoise shells and oracle bones, Menzies began assembling his collection that day.

The first evidence of his style of collecting was the thirty-eight artefacts, stone implements, and potsherds that he sent on loan to the Royal Ontario Museum in 1915. Menzies permanently donated these (without receiving a payment) to the ROM in 1942 with the request that they be kept together as representative artefacts from the surface of the Waste of Yin as he found it in February or March of 1914. These included the bronze axe, described in chapter 9, that he found beside the Zhang River. His 1917 book *Oracle Records from the Waste of Yin* contained line drawings of 2369 inscribed bones from his collection. That same year, when he joined the Chinese Labour Corps, he brought out a second box of artefacts, which he deposited in the ROM in 1921. These were also donated in 1942. He also collected a box of fragments from the battlefields of Flanders, which he sold to the ROM for a nominal fee.

By 1927 Menzies claimed to have about 50,000 ancient artefacts, mostly pieces of pottery, oracle bones, neolithic stone implements, bronze vessels and weapons, jade, and other objects. Not everything was destroyed during the Northern Expedition: he had taken his best pieces to Tianjin and Beidaihe. When he was assigned to teach at the North China Union Language School in 1927–8, he brought more than 20,000 pieces of oracle bones to Beijing in order to complete the second volume of his *Oracle Records from the Waste of Yin*. During this period he made rubbings of 2819 tortoise-shell and bone inscriptions. Since he expected to return to the language school after his furlough, he stored the bones and a few fine bronze vessels in the school's vault.[4] This collection remained there during the civil war.

In 1932, when Menzies was appointed to Cheeloo University as professor of archaeology, he took his collection from Zhangde, North Henan, to Jinan, Shandong. This became the basis for the university's archaeological museum that he created. He formed a strong bond with the university while handicrafting its archaeological education. Menzies hoped to work there for the rest of his life and expected eventually to donate his collection to that institution. Consequently, when he returned to Canada on furlough in 1936, he left everything at Cheeloo. He had no idea he would never be able to return. When full-scale war broke out between China and Japan, Jinan was a battlefield, eventually captured by the Japanese in 1938. Detained in North America, James Menzies worried about the safety of his collection, and indirectly arranged for its relocation. Hereby hangs a fascinating story with a happier ending than that attending the fossils of Peking Man, which disappeared in transit to 'safety' during the war.

Cheeloo University

The easiest part of the collection to deal with was the museum at Cheeloo, and in 1938 Menzies negotiated a purchase agreement with university president Liu Shuming. This agreement included only those artefacts that Menzies had loaned to the university museum; he remained the owner of the oracle bones and other archaeological specimens he had left at the campus. Several boxes were stored in the house of Dr William McClure, the respected elder missionary still teaching medicine after several decades at the university.

Four years later, in early 1942 after Pearl Harbor, the occupying Japanese military authorities closed the university. Menzies's colleagues helped hide his collections at different places on the campus. One crate of 'first class national treasures' was stored in the university's vault, while another was put into the loft above the foreign children's school. Others were buried on the campus.[5] These precautions were necessary since Cheeloo's archaeological collection was well known, and Japanese scholars and institutes were particularly interested in gathering ancient Chinese artefacts, leading to rapacious plundering of museums and private collections in the wake of the invading armies.

Chinese scholars knew of and were attracted by the Menzies collection even after Cheeloo had moved to wartime exile in Sichuan. One such was Hu Houxuan, a promising junior scholar at the History and Language Institute of the Academia Sinica, who was invited to work at Cheeloo in Sichuan in 1940. Decades later, he recalled: 'In 1939 Mr. Gu Jiegang accepted Cheeloo's invitation to head its Sinological Institute. He then invited Qian Mu and me to be the institute's researchers. He told me that Cheeloo had Menzies' large collection of oracle bones, which I could study.'[6] Since the collection remained behind Japanese lines, Hu had to wait until the war was over in 1945.

As soon as the Japanese surrendered, Hu requested that Cheeloo send him to Jinan to investigate the whereabouts of the collection. He wrote in his proposal: 'Our university is the pioneer in oracle bone study. In this field no other institute, Chinese or foreign, could compete with us ... Dr. Menzies is a worldwide-recognized scholar for his three-decade effort on oracle bones ... He started to collect oracle bones from the early years of the Republic. By 1936, his collection numbered from twenty to thirty thousands. It has all been sold to our university. So, Cheeloo's oracle bone collection is larger than that of Academia Sinica and in fact it is the centre of oracle bone study.'[7]

Hu was worried that the collection might be removed by the retreating Japanese. He continued: 'For our nation's culture, I do not mind the difficulties and hardship and want to go to Jinan to find and study the collection. This was my wish when I came to Qilu five and a half years ago ... This collection has about thirty thousand pieces of oracle bones. Of them, only two thousand were published. I plan to invite Dr. Menzies to come back to Qilu and study the bones together. We need only one year's time to accomplish this project.'[8] Unfortunately, Menzies never returned to China, and Hu was not given the opportunity to see the Menzies collection until the 1950s.

After the war, the Menzies collection also attracted the attention of the Chinese government. In early 1947 the Shandong provincial government asked Cheeloo to report on the collection. Aware that the bones were still on campus, it informed the university to take good care of them as the government was planning to nationalize the collection.[9] The following March, the military governor of Shandong, Wang Yaowu, informed the university that he could no longer guarantee the safety of Westerners and urged them to evacuate the city.

This crisis posed a problem for the collection. James Menzies was in Washington, DC, recovering from a heart attack. Both his daughters were in China: Marion with the United Nation's World Student Relief Organization, and Frances Newcombe as an evangelistic missionary in North Henan.[10] Arthur had joined the Canadian Department of External Affairs and was now head of the Far Eastern Division. If James had wanted to ship his artefacts out of China, he could have done so easily through his children's channels. 'How I would have liked to finish my work in Cheeloo,' he wrote to Arthur in April 1947, 'if it only meant handing things over to the university in a proper way, so that archaeology would have its settled place in the curriculum of studies.'[11]

When the foreigners started to evacuate Cheeloo in 1948, James Menzies asked his colleagues to send the collection to Nanjing or Shanghai for safekeeping. For this enterprise he involved Marion, Frances, and Arthur. The plan was to send the artefacts to either the Canadian consulate in Shanghai or the Canadian embassy in Nanjing. With the help of seven Henan students, a North Henan colleague, Dr Isabelle McTavish, packed the artefacts in more than one hundred wooden boxes. At this point, James Menzies changed his mind and gave up the idea of handing things over to the university in a proper way in favour of immediate transfer. He told Marion to inform Cheeloo to take over his collection and be responsible for its safety, except for one box of oracle bones.[12] The university decided to leave the collection on campus, while sending the single box to Shanghai in care of F.G. Ballachey, a Canadian diplomat.

In September 1948 Jinan was liberated by the CCP armies. For several years no one knew the whereabouts of Menzies's collection. By the middle of 1951, all the foreign staff except one British chemist had left Cheeloo. Before his departure, Francis Drake, who had accompanied Menzies on many archaeological surveys of Shandong, handed over to the university authorities an old map that showed where the bones had been buried in 1942. He also told them where other artefacts were hidden. Altogether, about 140 boxes of artefacts were uncovered. In the highly politicized atmosphere of that era, this discovery prompted a political event on the campus and in the city, with a public exhibition and 'denunciation' meetings to 'expose the nature of the cultural imperialist, Menzies.'[13]

At the time, the newspapers reported that the bones had all rotted to powder. This was not true: in fact, the bones were in good condition. In 1959 this collection was handed over to the Shandong Provincial Museum, where it has remained. The collection consists of 29,457 archaeological specimens, including 8080 oracle bones, 4000 pieces of pottery, 1000 porcelain articles, over 8000 bronze vessels and fragments, 700 jade items, 2000 stone implements, 2000 bone and horn implements, 500 bricks and tiles, and 200 other objects.[14]

Nanjing Museum

The single box of oracle bones sent from Jinan to Shanghai in July 1948 had an interesting journey. It consisted of 2390 tortoise shells and oracle bones collected by Menzies between 1914 and 1916, which he had reproduced in *Oracle Records from The Waste of Yin*. This was the box stored in the Cheeloo University vault during the Japanese occupation. It was a miracle that it survived.[15] Menzies hoped to republish these inscriptions in the form of ink rubbings, as he felt his early hand drawings were not accurate. This is why he insisted that the box be sent away from danger. He asked Arthur to get the Canadian embassy involved: 'I think it quite a suitable thing for the Embassy to do. It preserves cultural material that is internationally important. Please write to some one about it in case the box of bones is sent there by some one.'[16] He hoped that the bones should not remain at the Canadian embassy for a long time, expecting that they would eventually be returned to Cheeloo.[17]

Ballachey brought the box as arranged to the safely of Shanghai, whence it was sent on to the Canadian embassy at Nanjing. The embassy remained at Nanjing through the transition to the People's Republic in 1949. Although the Canadian ambassador was recalled after the outbreak of the Korean War in 1950, the chargé d'affaires Chester Ronning, born in China and the most fluent member of the international diplomatic corps, was the chief intermediary between China and the foreign powers during the tense negotiations concerning diplomatic recognition. In 1951, when the Canadian government declined to recognize the PRC, Ronning was recalled to Ottawa.

In the process of packing up the embassy, Ronning was surprised to find this box of 'first class national treasures' on the embassy premises. Aware of his precarious position as a diplomat in a hostile nation, he knew that the box could become a diplomatic bombshell if not dealt with carefully and confidentially. With the assistance of a 'Red' friend, Yang Xianyi, he donated the box to the Nanjing Museum, which was greatly pleased with this 'super gift.' The museum published an article in its journal, 'Good News: Our Newly Received Oracle Bones.' Nanjing Museum now had 2921 pieces of oracle bones, of which 2369 derived from the Menzies collection. In 1961 Hu Houxuan made a thorough study of these bones, comparing them with the drawings in *Oracle Records from the Waste of Yin*, and found only twenty-one original bones missing. It is useless to speculate what happened to them.[18] This box continued to trouble Ronning, however. When he crossed the border from China to Hong Kong, his luggage was searched several times and he was interrogated at length whether he was 'stealing' other national 'treasures.'[19]

National Palace Museum, Beijing

In 1928 Menzies left several boxes at the North China Union Language School in Beijing. When Menzies returned from his furlough in 1930 and was 'persuaded' to return to North Henan, he did not bother to recover this box, since he felt that as a foreign institute the language school was safe from the threat of continued civil turmoil. Principal W.H. Pettus was a trusted friend, who simply did not inform the authorities – Chinese and Japanese – of the boxes' existence. They remained in the vault throughout the 1930s and right until the end of the Japanese occupation in 1945.

In 1946, after the Japanese surrender, Pettus wrote to Menzies that the bones were safe and had been moved to another part of the building. James Menzies wrote back, 'asking him to send them by safe hand to Dr. E.B. Struthers [a North Henan colleague] to place with some of my other oracle bones in Cheeloo University vault. It would seem best to keep them together until such time as I can publish some of them. *Eventually I wish to give or donate them to Cheeloo University* [italics added]. It seems to me that the best use of them can be made in university work and I trust that Cheeloo will always maintain an interest in oracle bone studies.'[20] As Menzies explained to the Board of Overseas Missions: 'The things in Peking were left by Dr. Pettus in 1946 with the new Language School authorities until it was possible to have them sent to Tsinan Cheeloo University by safe hand. They should be left where they are until the situation becomes clearer.'[21] Pettus retired to the United States before he could carry out Menzies's request, and the bones remained at the North China Union Language School. The school was closed in 1949 and its buildings taken over by the Ministry of Culture.

The Menzies collection was sent to the Beijing Palace Museum, where it remained undisturbed in a warehouse until 1974. The transaction was not registered properly and even today no one is sure when and how these bones were acquired by the museum. Altogether, the Palace Museum collection contains 20,364 oracle bones, plus other neolithic and bronze artefacts from Anyang. When the Menzies boxes were brought from the school's vault, they were separated into two groups. The first consisted of three wooden cases containing 870 oracle bones and 164 other objects; the second of ten wooden cases and 167 parcels with an additional 19,494 oracle bones. This latter group was supposedly lost, and was rediscovered only in 1974 when the Palace Museum cleaned out its warehouse.

Unlike the box sent to Nanjing Museum, the rediscovery of this much larger collection was not publicized. Arthur Menzies arrived in Beijing that same year as Canada's ambassador to the People's Republic of China. To his deep regret, he learned nothing of this story during his three-year tenure.[22] The wars had thwarted James Menzies's wish to make Cheeloo the centre of oracle-bone studies. By accident the same circumstances favoured the Palace Museum, which now has the second largest collection of oracle bones, some 22,463 pieces. Of these 20,364 are from the Menzies collection.[23]

Toronto and Victoria

We have traced the history of Menzies's collections in China; in Canada, he left collections of artefacts to the Royal Ontario Museum in Toronto and the Art Gallery of Greater Victoria, British Columbia.

In June 1947 the North Henan mission was disbanded permanently. Hugh Mackenzie, the mission treasurer in Tianjin, warned the former missionaries to make arrangements to remove their personal effects stored in his house before the British Concession was closed and the house lost. Menzies, in Washington recovering from a heart attack, missed the notification. However, he subsequently requested that his personal items be sent to Canada and the archaeological objects remain in China.[24]

'We have a valuable collection of oracle bones and some archaeological objects in Mackenzie's attic,' he wrote to the Board of Missions. 'They are piled back of the chimney in the main attic. The bones are in two large wooden boxes and inside these outer wooden cases are tin or galvanized iron cases with galvanized iron drawers containing the bones. When we expected to be going out to China ourselves, we did not trouble anyone with information about them except Frances [Menzies] and Ervin [Newcombe, her husband] ... The bones and archaeological materials are to remain in China ... The bones in Tientsin are quite separate from another collection in the Language School Peiping.'[25]

Events were changing quickly in China. Mackenzie did not receive instructions in time and he shipped six boxes of artefacts stored in his attic directly to James Menzies, c/o the United Church of Canada, Board of Overseas Missions, in Toronto. As Menzies was still in Washington, the boxes were stored in Rawlinson's storage warehouse in Toronto for six years (1948–54).[26]

James Menzies's reaction to the arrival of the six crates was mixed. He was happy that they would be safer in Canada than in China during the civil war. At the same time, he was disturbed by the uncertain future, his own and that of his adopted homeland, China. He had been waiting to go back to Cheeloo, and even had his trunks packed and ready. 'Do not ask what I am going to do with the things. I do not know yet,' he wrote to Arthur in Ottawa.[27] 'I would store them just as is in Rawlinson's until I know what our future is to be. I still hope to go out to China when Cheeloo has a place for me to work whether in Hangchow or elsewhere.'[28] His intention was clearly to return these artefacts to Cheeloo when he returned.

For several years Menzies left the cases in storage. Only after he gave up hope of going back to China did he bring some home to continue his studies and to decorate his small house. He kept this collection until his death in 1957, even though he was approached several times by the Royal Ontario Museum to sell or donate the artefacts to complement the George Crofts and Bishop White collections. When he died, he left specific instructions for the disposition of his collection.

Two American friends, A.W. Hummel and L.C. Goodrich, who were both professors of Chinese, suggested that Annie Belle Menzies and the children sell the collection to an American institution, but they wanted to keep the collection in Canada for the moment.[29] This was the height of the Cold War and the revolutionary Maoist uncertainties in China, and Annie and Arthur felt that this personal collection could not be returned to China for the foreseeable future. They decided to transfer 80 per cent of the collection to the University of Toronto on behalf of the Royal Ontario Museum (which was then part of the university) in return for guaranteeing the publication of three books: James Menzies's PhD thesis on *ge*, the Shang ritual weapon; a set of reproductions featuring his collection of inscribed oracle bones and shells, about 4700 pieces; and another reproducing his collection of oracle bone rubbings.[30]

Two years later, in 1960, the Royal Ontario Museum formally aquired this collection. The Menzies Collection enhanced the museum's academic function and the ROM became *the* centre outside of China for scholars studing Shang bone culture. The ROM collection contains 7551 artefacts, including 5170 oracle bones and 2812 bone rubbings, 710 bronze vessels and fragments, and 639 pottery items. Frank Caro, a leading dealer in Chinese art who evaluated the collection, wrote to Arthur as the executor of his father's estate: 'The collection of your father was a great surprise to me. It was a very thrilling experience; of course the material is only study material and a great percentage of it is not marketable ... but for any serious student, they are most valuable.'[31] A decade later, Caro wrote: 'In my opinion, it is one of the best concerning archaeology. I have mentioned this to many scholars to go to Toronto and study the material as they will find more in the fragments than they would find elsewhere as your father had written on every wrapper where he found the bones and at what strata. In your collection are the only Shang tools that I have ever seen to clean and refinish the ritual bronzes after the mould was broken up.'[32]

The Menzies family retained a small part of the collections, several hundred artefacts including some of the best pieces. After Annie died in 1962, these were inherited by the children, Marion Hummel, Frances Newcombe, and Arthur Menzies, who already had the personal gifts James had given them over the years (such as Marion's roof tiles picked up from the Forbidden City in 1928).[33] In 1980 Barry Till, a curator from the Art Gallery of Greater Victoria, British Columbia, selected the best pieces for an exhibition at the gallery. Till's friendship went back to 1977, when Arthur was the Canadian ambassador to the PRC and Till was a 'colourful' exchange student whose intense interest in Chinese art and architecture led him into frequent transgressions of then-current restrictions on foreigners' access to 'out-of-bounds' historical sites.[34] Till wrote the exhibit catalogue, *Chinese Art from the Rev. Dr. James M. Menzies Family Collection*. Some of these artefacts have since been given to the Victoria gallery, while others remain there on loan.[35]

Oracle Bone Studies before 1914

The story of Wang Yirong's discovery of ancient Chinese writing on the so-called dragon bones in 1899 is well known. He was an eminent, classically trained scholar and palaeographer steeped in the old learning. His eyes and mind were already prepared to identify and decipher oracle-bone inscriptions. Even before his discovery there had been a long intellectual preparation among Chinese antiquarians that led him to his conclusion. In other words, it was only a matter of time before someone discovered the significance of oracle bones. More importantly, between 1899 and 1914, when James Menzies first visited the Waste of Yin, there was considerable scholarly discussion and publication of oracle bones in private collections.

This intellectual process was linked to two branches of classical learning. The first was *Kao Ju Xue* (Classical Textual Criticism), whose goal was to re-examine the Chinese classics and histories in order to (re)discover their original meanings. Along with this textual criticism, important developments were taking place in the study of palaeography or *Jin Shi Xue*. This branch of learning had started during the Song dynasty (960–1127 CE), been neglected during the following dynasties, and was revived in the early Qing (1644–1912). *Jin Shi* scholars tried to trace critically the evolution of Chinese ideographs by studying inscriptions on archaic bronzes and monuments. Their efforts cast doubts on the accuracy of Xu Shen's massive dictionary *Shuo Wen*, which for a century had been the authoritative reference for the origins and meanings of ideographs. With a shared spirit of doubt and modern criticism, these scholars freed themselves from the shackles of old authorities and were searching for new material and ideas.

The archaeologist Li Chi (pinyin Li Ji) summarized the situation: 'At this time, on the basis of the accumulated achievements of textual criticism and the study of stone and bronze inscriptions, cultivated in general among the intellectuals and the literati and encouraged by imperial sanctions of the Ch'ien Lung [Qian Long] and Chia Ch'ing [Jia Qing] eras (1736–1820), Chinese epigraphy had already advanced to a stage ready for new source materials and new ideas which were eagerly looked for and studied.'[1]

In 1982 *Lishi Jiaoxue* (Journal of History Education) published an article by the late Wang Xiang, one of the early collectors of oracle bones, which cast doubt on the story of Wang Yirong. Wang Xiang insisted that 'oracle bone inscriptions were first known in 1898,' and went on to claim that Wang Yirong's evidence was flawed. Wang could not have found inscribed characters as described because drugstores refused to buy dragon bones with characters, causing the peasants to scrape the characters off to get more money. Furthermore, Beijing did not have a drugstore named Daren Tang in 1899. The debate raged for a decade, until the challengers conceded their points, and in 1996 the 'Chronology of Early Chinese History in the Xia, Shang and Western Zhou' project confirmed the facts and the date of Wang Yirong's discovery.[2]

Wang Yirong became the first collector of oracle bones. He paid high prices for all the inscribed bones that a curio dealer named Fan Weiqing could supply, paying four *liang* (ounces) of silver per character.[3] He was secretive about his discovery, hoping to corner the market and collect all the bones himself. Unfortunately, his connection with oracle bones was short. During the Boxer Uprising of 1900 he was appointed by the Qing court to supervise the militia in Beijing, and when the allied forces sacked the city, Wang, together with his wife and daughter-in-law, committed suicide.[4]

As soon as Wang Yirong identified the oracle-bone script, a dedicated group of scholars began to collect and study inscribed bones. The most significant among them were Liu E, Sun Yirang, and Luo Zhenyu. Liu E, an eminent scholar-official and close friend of Wang Yirong, started to buy oracle bones in 1901. When he was exiled by the Qing court to the northwest in 1910, he already had a collection of about five thousand pieces of inscribed bones and tortoise shells. Unlike Wang, Liu E did not keep his discoveries secret. In 1903 he published ink-squeezes of his best pieces in a book entitled *Tieyun Canggui* (Tortoise Shell Collection by Tie Yun), the first published book of oracle-bone inscriptions. This spread the knowledge of oracle bones to a larger audience of scholars, who began to decipher the characters. In addition, Liu E was the first to date the inscriptions to the Shang dynasty, an important step in deciphering the inscriptions.[5]

The publication of Liu E's book caught the interest of a palaeographer named Sun Yirang, who published a book the following year, *Qiwen Juli* (Examples of Oracle Bone Inscriptions). This represented a pioneering inquiry into the structure and meaning of oracle-bone inscriptions. A year later, Sun Yirang published another book, *Ming Yuan* (Origin of Characters), which traced the development of archaic scripts at different periods of time.[6]

These pioneers approached the inscriptions from the narrow perspective of palaeography. It took another scholar, Luo Zhenyu (old spelling Lo Chen-yü) (1866–1940), to broaden the scope and make oracle bones a scientific subject. A friend of Liu E in Beijing, Luo Zhenyu made a significant contribution to the knowledge of the ancient Chinese language. He started to collect oracle bones in 1907 and by the 1930s had the largest collection among Chinese collectors. Unlike his predecessors, Luo was not satisfied with passively buying whatever the curio dealers offered while keeping the provenance a trade secret. After considerable research, in 1908 he identified that they came from Xiaotun, the Little Village built upon the lost *Yin Xu* (Waste of Yin) or *Da Yi Shang* (Great City of Shang), as recorded in the Classics. Luo publicized this source of the material in 1910 and sent people to Xiaotun to collect bones, instructing them not to neglect small, *inscribed* shell fragments.[7]

Luo's first book, *Yinshang Zhengbu Wenzi Kao* (A Treatise on Oracle Bone Inscriptions of the Yin-Shang, 1910), correlated the information from the oracle inscriptions with that found in the classical Chinese records such as the *Book of History*. He thus identified the names of the Shang kings, thereby pioneering a new way to study Shang history. Luo identified the geographic locations of the seven Shang capitals, reconstructed the genealogical tree of the royal family, and studied the methods of divination, though inevitably he made some errors.[8] He continued collecting and publishing the inscriptions until his death in 1940. His monumental *Yinxu Shuqi Qianbian* (Oracle Bone Inscriptions from the Waste of Yin, Part One, 1912) consisted of two thousand ink-squeezes of oracle-bone inscriptions selected from his collection of 20,000 to 30,000 bone and shell fragments. In 1915 he published *Yinxu Shuqi Houbian* (Oracle Inscriptions from the Waste of Yin, Part II), and in 1933, *Yinxu Shuqi Xubian* (Supplement to Oracle Inscriptions from the Waste of Yin).

Luo Zhenyu was the most important epigrapher and preserver of oracle-bone inscriptions during the early Republican period. He wrote and edited over one hundred books, of which ten concerned oracle-bone inscriptions. Sadly, his scholarly achievements were tarnished for a long time by his political conservatism and collaboration with the Japanese puppet state of Manchukuo under the last Qing emperor, Puyi. Luo was also criticized by Chinese scholars for academic dishonesty, specifically that he exploited his master–student relationship with Wang Guowei, the widely acknowledged master of Chinese learning.

Interest in oracle bones was not limited to Chinese scholars. The first foreign scholar was Rev. Frank H. Chalfant of the American Presbyterian Mission at Weixian, Shandong, who sold four hundred bones to the Museum of the Royal Asiatic Society in Shanghai in 1903. The following year, he and Rev. Samuel Couling of the English Baptist mission at Qingzhou sold a large number of bones, real and fake, to the Carnegie Museum, the Royal Scottish Museum, and the British Museum. In 1906 Chalfant sold a further 119 pieces to Princeton University, and in 1913 four large bones to the Field Museum, one of the aggressive collectors among museums.[9]

In 1906 Chalfant published *Early Chinese Writing*, the first account of oracle bones in English. This brought him to the attention of the British consul in Tianjin, L.C. Hopkins, who bought nine hundred inscribed bones. Hopkins afterwards published four articles on oracle-bones, making him the best-known foreign writer on oracle-bone inscriptions at the time.[10] Besides foreign scholars in China, sinologues and museums in Britain, France, Germany, the United States and particularly Japan collected oracle bones.

Thus, by the time Menzies 'visited' the Waste of Yin in 1914, there already existed a pool of knowledge about oracle-bone inscriptions, in both Chinese and English. It is not clear how much Menzies knew of this growing body of scholarship, since he never made a statement about what led him on, shard by shard. We can be certain, however, that he knew what he was looking at when the children showed him their cache of dragon bones with characters on them. It was, as he said, a providential act of God.

Notes

Abbreviations

ABM	Annie Belle Menzies (James's wife)
AEA	A.E. Armstrong, secretary of BOM
AM	Arthur Menzies (James's son)
BOM	Board of Overseas Missions (UCC)
DRM	David R. Menzies (James's father)
FMC	Foreign Mission Committee (PCC)
HYI	Harvard-Yenching Institute
JMM	James Mellon Menzies
JRM	Jane R. Menzies (James's mother)
MF Papers	Menzies Family Papers (private, with AM)
NHM	North Henan Mission
PCC	Presbyterian Church in Canada
ROM	Royal Ontario Museum
RPM	R.P. MacKay, secretary of FMC
SGS	School of Graduate Studies
SPA	Shandong Provincial Archives
UCA	United Church Archives
UCC	United Church of Canada
UTA	University of Toronto Archives
UT/WCW	Bishop White Papers, Thomas Fisher Rare Books Library, University of Toronto
WCW	William Charles White
WHG	W.H. Grant of NHM

Introduction

1 James Mellon Menzies [JMM], *Oracle Records from the Waste of Yin* (Shanghai: Kelly & Walsh Co. Ltd., 1917), Preface.

2 JMM to A.E. Armstrong [AEA], December 1929, United Church Archives, United Church of Canada, Board of Overseas Missions, North Henan Mission correspondence [hereafter UCC/NHM corr.], box 3/file 48 [3/48].

3 Lewis C. Walmsley, *Bishop in Honan: Mission and Museum in the Life of William C. White* (Toronto: University of Toronto Press, 1974), 141–2.

4 Lovat Dickson, *The Museum Makers: The Story of the Royal Ontario Museum* (Toronto: ROM, 1986), 76–7.

5 JMM to Currelly, 6 March 1940, Royal Ontario Museum [ROM], Currelly file.

6 The following chronological list is not complete, since it does not include the many missionary biographies and autobiographies that have also been published: Dora Hood, *Davidson Black: A Biography* (Toronto: University of Toronto Press, 1978); Munroe Scott, *McClure: The China Years* (Markham, ON: Penguin Books, 1979); Stephen Endicott, *James G. Endicott: Rebel Out of China* (Toronto: University of Toronto Press, 1980); Grant Maxwell, *China: Assignment in Chekiang: 71 Canadians in China, 1902–1954* (Toronto: Scarboro Foreign Mission Society, 1982); Alvyn Austin, *Saving China: Canadian Missionaries in the Middle Kingdom, 1888–1959* (Toronto: University of Toronto Press, 1986); Peter Stursberg, *The Golden Hope: Christians in China* (Toronto: United Church Publishing House, 1987); Rosemary Gagan, *A Sensitive Independence: Canadian Methodist Women Missionaries in Canada and the Orient, 1881–1925* (Montreal and Kingston: McGill-Queen's University Press, 1992).

7 Karen Minden, *Bamboo Stone: The Evolution of a Chinese Medical Elite* (Toronto: University of Toronto Press, 1994).

8 Jean-Paul Wiest, *Maryknoll in China: A History, 1918–1955* (Armonk, NY, and London: M.E. Sharpe, c. 1988), Introduction.

9 The Menzies Family Papers are held in trust by Arthur Menzies. The National Archives of Canada, which has made a preliminary sorting and indexing, will be the eventual depository for the papers.

10 Peter M. Mitchell, Margo S. Gewurtz, and Alvyn Austin, eds., *Guide to Archival Resources on Canadian Missionaries in East Asia, 1890–1960* (Toronto: University of Toronto – York University Joint Centre for Asia Pacific Studies, 1988).

11 W.A.P. Martin's mission theories are expressed in his two books, *A Cycle of Cathay* (New York: Fleming H. Revell, 1896, repub. Taipei: Ch'eng-Wen Publishing Co., 1966), and *Lore of Cathay* (New York: Fleming H. Revell, 1901). See also Ralph R. Covell, *W.A.P. Martin: Pioneer of Progress in China*

(Washington: Christian University Press, 1978). For Richard, see William E. Soothill, *Timothy Richard of China* (London: Seeley, Service & Co., 1924), and Paul Richard Bohr, *Famine in China and the Missionary* (Cambridge: Harvard University Press, 1972).

12 Soothill, *Timothy Richard*, 8.

13 James M. Menzies to Knox classmates, undated but probably early 1950, Menzies Family Papers (hereafter MF Papers).

14 Wang Yuxin and Yang Shengnan, eds., *A Century of Oracle Bone Studies* (Beijing: Social Science Press, 1999), 135–6.

15 Claire Huot, Cultural Counsellor, Canadian embassy at Beijing, 'J. Menzies Conference Report,' sent to Bruce Jutzi as an e-mail on 11 September 2000.

Chapter 1: Rural Ontario, 1885–1903

1 JMM to David R. Menzies [DRM], 21 February 1919 and completed 30 April, MF Papers.

2 The Menzies Clan Society, *The Clan Menzies* (1974), MF Papers.

3 George Leslie Mackay, founder of the first Canadian foreign mission, to Taiwan in 1871, and Jonathan Goforth, founder of the North Henan mission, both came from this 'porridge and catechism' Presbyterian piety.

4 JMM to Annie Belle Sedgwick Menzies [ABM], 21 February 1951, MF Papers; Marion F. Menzies Hummel, *Memoirs of a Mishkid* (Beamsville, ON: privately published, 2000), 3.

5 For Doherty Organ Factory, see Clinton Centennial Committee, *History of Clinton 1875–1975* (Clinton, ON: Centennial Committee, 1975), 72–3, 126–7.

6 Interview with AM, 19 July 1997.

7 JMM to R.P. Mackay [RPM], secretary of Foreign Missionary Committee of the Presbyterian Church in Canada, January 1910, MF Papers.

8 AM interview.

9 DRM to JMM, 2 December 1894, MF Papers.

10 Jane R. Menzies [JRM] to JMM, June 1900, MF Papers; and AM interview.

11 Hummel, *Memoirs of a Mishkid*, 4.

12 DRM to JMM, 1 March 1901, MF Papers. The information about Leamington High School is from a brief history of the school from 1896 to 1906, also in MF Papers.

Chapter 2: Toronto, 1903–1905

1 JMM to JRM, 17 November 1903, MF Papers.

2 JMM to AM, 28 August 1949, MF Papers.

3 John Webster Grant, *A Profusion of Spires: Religion in Nineteenth-Century Ontario* (Toronto: University of Toronto Press, 1988), 175.

4 Richard White, *The Skule Story: The University of Toronto Faculty of Applied Science and Engineering, 1873–2000* (Toronto: University of Toronto Press, 2000), 13.

5 Ibid., 86.

6 W. Stewart Wallace, *A History of the University of Toronto, 1827–1927* (Toronto: University of Toronto Press, 1927), 215.

7 White, *Skule Story*, 53, 64.

8 Ibid., 27–8.

9 Ibid., 70, 76.

10 Robin S. Harris and Ian Montagnes, *Cold Iron and Lady Godiva: Engineering Education at Toronto 1920–1972* (Toronto: University of Toronto Press, 1973), 27.

11 JMM to JRM, 17 November 1903, MF Papers.

12 DRM to JMM, 26 March 1906, MF Papers.

13 DRM to JMM, 22 January 1906, MF Papers.

14 JMM to R.P. MacKay [RPM], secretary of Foreign Mission Committee [FMC], letter of application, January 1910, MF Papers.

15 JMM to AM, 19 November 1933, MF Papers.

16 DRM to JMM, 3 February 1910, MF Papers.

17 Ruth C. Brouwer, *New Women for God: Canadian Presbyterian Women and India Missions, 1876–1914* (Toronto: University of Toronto Press, 1990), 82.

18 Ibid., 83.

19 Mary MacGregor to JMM, 25 January 1904, MF Papers.

20 Grant, *Profusion of Spires*, 171.

21 'University of Toronto YMCA,' 1907, University of Toronto Archives [UTA], A73-005-240.

22 JMM to RPM, January 1910, MF Papers.

23 Austin, *Saving China*, 85.

24 'University of Toronto YMCA Annual Report, 1907–08,' UTA, B79-0052-008. See also Ernest R. Sandeen, *The Roots of Fundamentalism: British and American Millenarianism 1800–1930* (Chicago: University of Chicago Press, 1970), 132–4.

25 There has been considerable scholarly attention to the SVM: see Valentin H. Rabe, *The Home Base of American China Missions, 1880–1920* (Cambridge: Harvard University, Council on East Asian Studies, 1978); and Nathan D. Showalter, *The End of a Crusade: The Student Volunteer Movement for Foreign Missions and the Great War* (Lanham, MD: Scarecrow Press, 1997).

26 Grant, *Profusion of Spires*, 187.

27 Brouwer, *New Women for God*, 23.
28 Austin, *Saving China*, 96–7.
29 JMM to RPM, January 1910, MF Papers.
30 JMM to JRM, 14 February 1908, MF Papers.
31 JMM diary, 1905, MF Papers.
32 Brian J. Fraser, 'James A. Macdonald and the Theology of the Regenerators, 1890–1914,' in Michael D. Behiels and Marcel Martel, eds., *Nation, Ideas, Identities: Essays in Honour of Ramsay Cook* (Toronto: Oxford University Press, 2000), 3–15.
33 'University of Toronto YMCA Annual Report, 1907–08,' 9–10, UTA, B79-0052-008.
34 Ibid., 3.
35 Murray G. Ross, *The Y.M.C.A. in Canada: The Chronicle of a Century* (Toronto: Ryerson Press, 1951), 216–17.
36 JMM to RPM, January 1910, MF Papers.

Chapter 3: From Commitment to Departure, 1905–1910

 1 JMM diary, 4 September 1905, MF Papers.
 2 Ibid., 7 September 1905.
 3 JMM to RPM, January 1910, MF Papers.
 4 Ross, *Y.M.C.A. in Canada*, 128.
 5 Shirley S. Garrett, *Social Reformers in Urban China: The Chinese Y.M.C.A., 1895–1926* (Cambridge: Harvard University Press, 1970), 44. Among notable Canadians in the Chinese YMCA was Harry Hussey, who went out as a YMCA architect and ended up as a personal adviser to Chiang Kai-shek. His autobiography is enjoyable: *My Pleasures and Palaces: An Informal Memoir of Forty Years in Modern China* (Garden City, NY: Doubleday, 1968).
 6 JMM to RPM, January 1910, MF Papers.
 7 JMM diary, MF Papers.
 8 JMM to RPM, January 1910, MF Papers.
 9 RPM to ABM, 20 February 1911, and AEA to JMM, 26 July 1915, United Church of Canada Archives, Presbyterian Church in Canada, Board of Foreign Missions [after 1910; hereafter PCC/NHM corr.].
10 JMM to parents, letters dated July and August, 1907, MF Papers.
11 Brian J. Fraser, *Church, College, and Clergy: A History of Theological Education at Knox College, Toronto, 1844–1994* (Montreal and Kingston: McGill-Queen's University Press, 1995), 93–4, 116.
12 Ibid., 97.
13 Ibid., chaps. 4 and 5.

14 Austin, Saving China, 116–17.

15 Fraser, *Church, College, and Clergy*, 106.

16 JMM to ABM, 1947, MF Papers.

17 JMM to RPM, January 1910, MF Papers.

18 JRM to JMM, 29 March 1908, MF Papers.

19 JMM diary, 1908, MF Papers.

20 Showalter, *End of a Crusade.*

21 'University of Toronto YMCA Annual Report, 1908–09' and 'University of Toronto YMCA Annual Report, 1909–10,' UTA, B79-0052-008.

22 JMM diary, 1908, MF Papers.

23 Hummel, *Memoirs of a Mishkid*, 5–7.

24 Ibid., 6, 36.

25 JMM to JRM, 5 March 1910, MF Papers.

26 AEA to JMM, 20 January 1910, PCC/NHM corr., 3/31.

27 DRM to JMM, 19 January 1910, MF Papers.

28 DRM to JMM, 3 February 1910, MF Papers.

29 JMM to DRM, 21 February 1910, MF Papers.

30 Friends to JMM, May 1910, MF Papers.

31 JMM to ABM, 1947, MF Papers.

Chapter 4: North Henan, 1910

1 JMM to parents, September 1910, MF Papers.

2 Hummel, *Memoirs of a Mishkid*, 9.

3 JMM to parents, 18 November 1910, MF Papers.

4 Walmsley, *Bishop in Honan*, 20–5; Austin, *Saving China*, 128.

5 William C. White, *Without the Gate: A Brief Record of Work among Lepers in Fuhkian* (Toronto: Missionary Society of the Church of England in Canada, 1904).

6 Walmsley, *Bishop in Honan*, 90.

7 Ibid., 92.

8 Ibid., 100; Austin, Saving China, 131–2.

9 Walmsley, *Bishop in Honan*, 101–2.

10 Walmsley alludes to White's troubles (101–4). Austin, *Saving China*, 133–6, notes that personality conflicts within the mission became so acrimonious that White was recalled to Canada to face an enquiry. Most of the complaints were similar to Maude's.

11 Immanuel C.Y. Hsü, *The Rise of Modern China* (New York: Oxford University Press, 1975), chap. 17.

12 Jonathan D. Spence, *To Change China: Western Advisors in China, 1620–1960* (Boston: Little, Brown, 1969).

13 Kenneth Scott Latourette, *A History of Christian Missions in China* (New York: Russell & Russell, 1967), 539, 606, 724, and 773.

14 Gagan, *A Sensitive Intelligence*, 4–5.

15 Austin, *Saving China*, chap. 2, 'The Old Homestead of China.'

16 Margo S. Gewurtz, '"Their Names May Not Shine": Narrating Chinese Christian Converts,' in Alvyn Austin and Jamie Scott, eds., *Canadian Missionaries, Indigenous Peoples: Representing Religion at Home and Abroad* (Toronto: University of Toronto Press, 2005), 135–6.

17 W. Harvey Grant, *North of the Yellow River: Six Decades in Honan 1888–1948* (Toronto: United Church of Canada, 1948); and Murdoch Mackenzie, *Twenty-five Years in Honan* (Toronto: Presbyterian Church in Canada, Board of Foreign Missions, 1913), chap. 3.

18 Shi Shangang, *Heluo Wenhua Lungang* (An Outline of Heluo Culture) (Zhengzhou: Henan People's Press, 1994), chap. 1.

19 Grant, *North of the Yellow River*, 7.

20 Ibid., 8, and Mackenzie, Twenty-Five Years in Honan, 104–5.

21 Grant, *North of the Yellow River*, 8.

22 Margo S. Gewurtz, '"The Cinderella of Mission Work": Canadian Missionaries and Educational Modernization in North Henan, 1890–1925,' in Lin Zhiping, ed., *Christianity and China's Modernization* (Taipei: Yuzhouguang Press, 1993), 664–7.

23 Song Jiaheng and Li Wei, *Jianada Chuanjiaoshi Zai Zhongguo* (Canadian Missionaries in China) (Beijing: Dongfang Press, 1995), part 2.

24 Austin, *Saving China*, 115–17.

25 Margaret H. Brown, *History of the Honan (North China) Mission of the United Church of Canada, Originally a Mission of the Presbyterian Church in Canada, 1887–1951* (typescript in UCA), chap. XLVI-11.

26 Ibid., XLVI-2.

Chapter 5: The Early Years

1 Peter Stursberg, *The Golden Hope,* 136–7.

2 JMM to parents, 27 October 1910, MF Papers.

3 Ibid.

4 Ibid.

5 W.H. Grant [WHG] to RPM, 30 January 1914, PCC/NHM correspondence, 4/5.

6 Brown, History of Honan Mission, chap. XLV, 'Wuan's Problems 1910–15,' XLV-1.

7 Ibid., XLV-2–3. Yuile also supported his niece Margaret King in the China Inland Mission, because she found the Presbyterian mission too liberal: see

'Not the Marrying Sort – Margaret King,' in Phyllis Thompson, *Each to Her Post: Six Women of the China Inland Mission* (London: Hodder and Stoughton, 1982) 63–82.

8 Brown, *History of Honan Mission*, XLV-3 and XLV-15.

9 Ibid., XLV-11.

10 Ibid., XLV-13 and 16.

11 JMM to AM, 27 November 1942, MF Papers.

12 Austin, *Saving China*, 118–20.

13 WHG to RPM, 2 December 1910, PCC/NHM corr., 3/38.

14 JMM to AM, 9 December 1951, MF Papers.

15 Rosalind Goforth, *Goforth of China* (Grand Rapids, MI: Zondervan Publishing House, 1937), 87

16 Hugh Mackenzie to RPM, 22 July 1913, PCC/NHM corr., 4/48.

17 JMM to parents, 19 May 1913, MF Papers.

18 W.C. White to American Council of Learned Societies, 19 February 1932, copy in MF Papers.

19 JMM to parents, 18 November 1910, MF Papers.

20 Si Deao, ed., *Zhonghua Guizhu* (All China to God) (Beijing: China Social Sciences Press, 1985), 188–99.

21 Robert A. Mitchell to AEA, 8 April 1911, PCC/NHM corr., 3/34.

22 JMM to parents, 18 November 1910; and JMM to Classmates of Knox College, 22 October 1951, MF Papers.

23 JMM to parents, 18 November 1910, MF Papers.

24 JMM to Knox classmates, 22 October 1951, MF Papers.

25 AM to Linfu Dong, 19 April 1999.

26 Hummel, *Memoirs of a Mishkid*, 10–11.

27 Austin, *Saving China*, 118.

28 Margo S. Gewurtz, '"Their Names May Not Shine": Narrating Chinese Christian Converts,' in Alvyn Austin and James S. Scott, eds., *Canadian Missionaries, Indigenous Peoples* (Toronto: University of Toronto Press, 2005). Mackenzie wrote the anniversary history, *Twenty-five Years in Honan*.

29 WHG to RPM, 23 July 1912, PCC/NHM corr., 4/42.

30 WHG to RPM, 23 July 1912, ibid., 4/42 and 9/137.

31 See Gewurtz, '"The Cinderella of Mission Work."'

32 Ibid.

33 Song and Li, *Jianada Chuanjiaoshi* (Canadian Missionaries), 112.

34 Wang Huiguang, 'History of Binying Middle School,' *Wenfeng Wenshi Ziliao* (Wenfeng Historical Material Collection), no. 2, September 1989.

35 ABM to David R. Menzies, 24 April 1915, MF Papers.

36 Ibid.

37 Presbytery Minutes, February 1915, PCC/NHM corr., 12/17.
38 R.A. Mitchell to RPM, 10 October 1914, PCC/NHM corr., 4/55.
39 This and the following paragraphs: PCC/NHM corr., 5/61, Arthur W. Lochead to RPM, 18 October 1915.
40 Ibid.
41 Ibid.
42 Ibid.
43 Ibid.
44 'Honan Presbytery Minutes,' 1926, UCC/ NHM corr., 6/56.
45 JMM to parents, 13 June 1916, MF Papers.
46 JMM to ABM, 4 August 1916, MF Papers.

Chapter 6: Somewhere in France, 1917–1920

1 Tsing Yuan, 'The Japanese Intervention in Shantung during World War I,' in Alvin D. Cox and Hilary Conroy, ed., *China and Japan: Search for Balance since World War I* (Santa Barbara: ABC-Clio, 1978), 19–34.
2 Austin, *Saving China*, 188–91.
3 Nicholas J. Griffin, 'Britain's Chinese Labour Corps in World War I,' *Military Affairs* 40:3 (October 1976), 102.
4 Peter M. Mitchell, 'Canada and the Chinese Labour Corps 1917–1920: The Official Connection,' in Min-sun Chen and Lawrence N. Shyu, eds., *China Insight: Selected Papers from the Canadian Asian Studies Association Annual Conference Proceedings, 1982–1984* (Ottawa: Canadian Asian Studies Association, 1985), 7–30.
5 Margo S. Gewurtz, 'For God or for King: Canadian Missionaries and the Chinese Labour Corps in World War I,' in Chen and Shyu, eds., *China Insight*, 32.
6 R.A. Mitchell to RPM, 10 October 1914, PCC/NHM corr., 4/55.
7 Ibid., 5/73, 'The War and China,' 10 September 1917. It is not clear whether this report was from the North Henan mission.
8 Murdoch Mackenzie to RPM, 25 January 1917, PCC/NHM corr., 5/73.
9 List of 'Honan Missionaries Who Served with the Chinese Labour Corps in World War I, 1917–1920,' UCA, Chinese Labour Corps, 1/1 [hereafter PCC/CLC corr.]
10 Gewurtz, 'For God or for King,' 31–5.
11 JMM to British Legation, December 1916, MF Papers.
12 JMM to ABM, 23 April 1917, MF Papers.
13 Hummel, *Memoirs of a Mishkid*, 19.
14 JMM to AM, 25 November 1945, MF Papers.

15 Hummel, *Memoirs of a Mishkid*, 18–19.
16 Gewurtz, 'For God or for King.'
17 Interview with AM, July 1996, York University.
18 JMM to grandchildren, 1 December 1956, MF Papers.
19 JMM to ABM, 8 May 1917, MF Papers.
20 JMM to ABM, 21 May 1917, MF Papers.
21 Ibid.
22 For Canadian censorship, see Mitchell, 'Canada and the Chinese Labour Corps.'
23 RPM to John Griffith, 2 June 1917, PCC/NHM corr., 5/70.
24 JMM to ABM, 1 June 1917, MF Papers.
25 JMM to ABM, 27 May 1917, MF Papers.
26 JMM to ABM, 1 June 1917, MF Papers.
27 JMM to ABM, 13 June 1917, MF Papers.
28 For the deployment of the CLC, see Griffin, 'Britain's Chinese Labour Corps.'
29 JMM to ABM, 18 November 1917, MF Papers.
30 JMM to ABM, 10 December 1917, MF Papers.
31 Ibid.
32 Griffin, 'Britain's Chinese Labour Corps,' 105.
33 JMM to parents, 3 February 1918, MF Papers.
34 JMM to ABM, 19 December 1917, MF Papers.
35 Gewurtz, 'For God or for King,' 41. See also G. Ross to St John's Presbyterian Church, 17 March 1918, PCC/CLC corr., 1/2.
36 JMM to RPM, 1918, PCC/NHM corr., 6/75; and RPM to JMM, 18 February 1918, PCC/CLC corr., 1/ 2.
37 JMM to RPM, 1918, PCC/NHM corr., 6/75.
38 JMM to parents, 27 June 1918, MF Papers.
39 JMM to ABM, 20 May 1918, MF Papers.
40 JMM to parents, 27 June 1918, MF Papers.
41 JMM to parents, 3 February 1918, MF Papers.
42 JMM to mother, December 1918, MF Papers.
43 JMM to ABM, 12 November 1918, MF Papers. Note that despite his unusual empathy with the Chinese labourers, Menzies could occasionally, in exasperation, indulge in the derogatory terminology often applied to them at that time.
44 W.H. Grant to British Legation, Beijing, 7 May 1919, PCC/NHM corr., 6/84.
45 S.C. Newburn to F.H. Keefer, 13 June 1919, ibid., 6/83.
46 Gewurtz, 'For God or for King,' 49. Although Menzies's rank was that of captain, one typed document listed him as a major: PCC/CLC corr., 1/1.
47 JMM to ABM, 29 September 1919, MF Papers.

48 J.E.B. Martin, 1 September 1919, MF Papers.
49 JMM to father, 21 February 1919, MF Papers.
50 Hummel, *Memoirs of a Mishkid*, 20.

Chapter 7: Rest and Return, 1921–1927

1 Hummel, *Memoirs of a Mishkid*, 20–9.
2 Austin, *Saving China*, 191.
3 Because of his work in Shandong and Shanxi during the great famine of 1877–9, Timothy Richard was called 'the Founder of Famine Relief in China': Bohr, *Famine in China*.
4 Gewurtz, 'Famine Relief in China,' 8.
5 Brown, *History of the Honan Mission*, 11–17.
6 See Andrew J. Nathan, *A History of the China International Famine Relief Commission* (Cambridge: Harvard University Press, 1965).
7 Interview with AM, July 1996, York University.
8 O.J. Todd to S.H. Littell, 3 March 1925, MF Papers.
9 JMM to parents, 6 April 1925, MF Papers.
10 JMM to ABM, 11 and 13 September 1916; and JMM to AM, 26 August 1951 and 2 March 1952, MF Papers.
11 Scott, *McClure: The China Years*, 197–207.
12 Hummel, *Memoirs of a Mishkid*, 27–8.
13 JMM to AM, 27 November 1949, MF Papers.
14 JMM to mother, 26 November 1922, MF Papers.
15 ABM diary, 9 April 1915, MF Papers.
16 JMM to father, 18 March 1926, MF Papers.
17 ABM, 'Itinerating in Honan,' pamphlet published by North Henan Mission, 1932, MF Papers.
18 JMM to children, undated. See the NHM's request for the FMB to send more evangelists: 'Shall We Retreat?' *Honan Messenger*, no. 3, 1925, MF Papers.
19 JMM to mother, 26 November 1922, MF Papers.
20 Ibid., and JMM to parents, 2 August 1925.
21 JMM to parents, 29 August 1913, MF Papers.
22 JMM to AEA, 9 December 1923, PCC/NHM corr., 8/121.
23 Scott, McClure, 209.
24 Liu Shiwu, 'Junxian Fuqiushan Miaohui' (Junxian Fuqiushan Temple Fair), *Hebi Wenshi Ziliao* (Hebi Historical Material Collection), no. 6, 1992; Margo S. Gewurtz, 'Issues in the History of Canadian Missionaries in China: Examples from North Henan,' in Song and Li, *Jianada Chuanjiaoshi* (Canadian Missionaries), 24–6.

25 Hummel, *Memoirs of a Mish Kid,* 12. See also 'Peitaiho,' draft article by John Fraser, former *Globe and Mail* correspondent in Beijing, MF Papers.
26 JMM to parents, 4 September 1928, MF Papers.
27 'Rocky Point Association Membership Agreement,' revised in 1939, MF Papers.
28 AM to sisters Marion and Frances, 27 March 1983, MF Papers.
29 Hummel, *Memoirs of a Mishkid,* 33.
30 AM to Marion and Frances, 27 March 1983, MF Papers.
31 Margaret E. Webb, 'The Education of Ruth Jenkins: A Canadian Missionary in China, 1920–27' (PhD dissertation, Syracuse University, 1996), 93.

Chapter 8: Converts, Education, and Nationalism

1 For the effect of popular theatricals on the Boxers, see Joseph W. Esherick, *The Origins of the Boxer Uprising* (Berkeley: University of California Press, 1987).
2 For detailed studies of Chinese peasant culture, see David Johnson, Andrew J. Nathan, and Evelyn S. Rawski, eds., *Popular Culture in Late Imperial China* (Berkeley: University of California Press, 1985).
3 Ralph R. Covell, *Confucius, the Buddha, and Christ: A History of the Gospel in Chinese* (Maryknoll, NY: Orbis Books, 1986), Introduction.
4 The final reports were published in Song and Li, *Jianada Chuanjiaoshi* (Canadian Missionaries). See also Margo S. Gewurtz, 'Do Numbers Count? A Report on a Preliminary Study of the Christian Converts of the North Henan Mission, 1890–1925,' *Republican China* 10:3 (June 1985), 18–26.
5 Song and Li, *Jianada Chuanjiaoshi* (Canadian Missionaries), 85.
6 Ibid.; PCC/NHM corr., box 14.
7 Interview with AM, July, 1996.
8 For 'feminist' movements in the Methodist Women's Missionary Societies, see Gagan, *A Sensitive Intelligence.* For the Anglican mission in Henan, see Webb, 'Education of Ruth Jenkins.'
9 Margo S. Gewurtz, 'Issues in the History of Canadian Missionaries in China: Examples from North Henan,' in Song and Li, *Jianada Chuanjiaoshi* (Canadian Missionaries), 29–31.
10 Song and Li, *Jianada Chuanjiaoshi* (Canadian Missionaries), 81.
11 JMM to AEA, 9 December 1923, PCC/NHM corr., 8/121.
12 JMM to parents, 20 January 1924, MF Papers.
13 This and the following are found ibid., and in JMM to AEA, 9 December 1923, MF Papers.
14 The most comprehensive examination of single women and missionary wives is Dana Lee Robert, *American Women in Mission: A Social History of Their Thought and Practice* (Macon, GA: Mercer University Press, 1996).

15 AM, 'Toast to Frances on Her 80th Birthday,' 1995, MF Papers.
16 Interview with Marion Menzies Hummel, September 1996.
17 This idea of missionaries as 'new gentry' was developed by Gewurtz in 'Famine Relief in China.'
18 Min-Chin Chou, *Hu Shih and Intellectual Choice* (Ann Arbor: University of Michigan Press, 1984); and Chow Tse-tsung, *The May Fourth Movement* (Cambridge: Harvard University Press, 1964).
19 Chou, *Hu Shih*, chap. 4.
20 Jessie G. Lutz, *China and the Christian Colleges, 1850–1950.* (Ithaca: Cornell University Press, 1971), chap. 7.
21 Ibid., 234. See also Alvyn Austin, 'Wallace of West China: Edward Wilson Wallace and the Canadian Educational Systems of West China,' in Austin and Scott, eds., *Canadian Missionaries, Indigenous Peoples.*
22 Lutz, *China and the Christian Colleges*, chap. 7.
23 Hsü, *Rise of Modern China*, chap. 22.
24 Ibid.
25 John Foster, 'The Imperialism of Righteousness: Canadian Protestant Missions and the Chinese Revolution, 1925–1928' (PhD dissertation, University of Toronto, 1977) compared the differing reactions of the Canadian missions to the Chinese nationalist movement: the Presbyterians in North Henan, Shanghai, and Canton, Methodists in Sichuan, and Anglicans in Kaifeng. He concluded the NHM was the most conservative and intransigent Canadian mission.
26 Interview with Wang Huiguang, Anyang, August 1996.
27 J.G. Bompas to AEA, 5 August 1925, PCC/NHM corr., 9/141.
28 JMM to parents, 4 September 1928, MF Papers.
29 JMM to parents, 2 August 1925, MF Papers.
30 Song and Li, *Jianada Chuanjiaoshi* (Canadian Missionaries), 154.
31 'The Official Proclamation of the Christian Church at Chihsien [Weihuei],' UCC/NHM corr., 8/141.
32 Bompas to AEA, 5 August 1925, UCC/NHM corr., 9/141.
33 'Demands of Chinese Workers at Hwaiking Station, Honan,' UCC/NHM corr., 8/143.
34 Odoric Y.K. Wou, Mobilizing the Masses: Building Revolution in Henan (Stanford: Stanford University Press, 1994), chap. 1.
35 'Inventory of Mission Property in Honan,' PCC/NHM corr., 1/14.
36 Quoted in Philip West, *Yenching University and Sino-Western Relations 1916–1952* (Cambridge: Harvard University Press, 1976), 7.
37 'Resolution Adopted by Conference of Canadian Foreign Mission Boards and Societies,' Toronto, 18 February 1926, PCC/NHM corr., 1/14.
38 W.H. Grant to AEA, 10 November 1925, ibid., 1/16.

39 'Honan Mission General Report for 1928,' UCC/NHM corr., 3/40; and correspondence between the mission and the Chinese Synod in 1928, ibid., 3/36. See also Song and Li, *Jianada Chuanjiaoshi* (Canadian Missionaries), 115.

Chapter 9: The Waste of Yin, 1917–1927

1 Brown, *History of the Honan Mission*, LXXVII-14
2 JMM to parents, 4 September 1928, MF Papers.
3 Ibid.
4 JMM, *Oracle Records from the Waste of Yin* (Shanghai: Kelly & Walsh Co. Ltd., 1917).
5 Stursberg, *The Golden Hope* and Barry Till, *Chinese Art from the Rev. Dr. James M. Menzies Family Collection* (Victoria: Art Gallery of Greater Victoria, 1989).
6 JMM to AEA, 9 December 1929, UCC/NHM corr., 3/48.
7 See website, 'Yin Ruin's Museum of Anyang Henan Province,' at http://www.ayyx.com/en/left6.htm ('ayyx' refers to Anyang-Yin Xu).
8 JMM, *Yinxu Buci* (Oracle Records), Preface.
9 Li Chi, *Anyang*, 51–2.
10 For Luo Zhenyu, see ibid., 23–30.
11 Zhang Kunhe, 'Ming Yishi yu Qilu Daxue Jiagu Yanjiu' (James Menzies and Oracle Bone Study at Qilu University), in *Jinan Wenshi Zilao Xuanji* (Jinan Historical Documents Collection), vol. 11, October 1995. In September 1996 I interviewed Zhang Kunhe at his home in Jinan.
12 Hu Houxuan, *Yinxu Fajue* (The Excavation of the Waste of Yin) (Shanghai: Xuexi and Shenghuo Press, 1955), 9; J. Gunnar Andersson, *Children of the Yellow Earth: Studies in Prehistoric China* (London: Kegan Paul, Trench, Trubner, 1934), chap. 5.
13 JMM, *Jiagu Yianjiu* (Oracle Bone Studies) (Jinan: Cheeloo University Press, 1933), chap. 2.
14 This point is confirmed by many letters in both the Menzies Family Papers and the Bishop White Papers in the Thomas Fisher Rare Books Library, University of Toronto (cited as UT/WCW Papers).
15 Shandong Provincial Museum, 'List of Menzies Collection.'
16 Interview with AM, September 1996.
17 'List of Stone Axes and Other Objects Sent by James M. Menzies to Royal Ontario Museum of Archaeology in 1915, Together with Present ROM Acquisition Numbers and Notes on Objects by James M. Menzies.' MF Papers.
18 Ibid. In 1942 Menzies donated them to the museum.
19 Toronto *Globe*, 20 July 1917; *Presbyterian Record*, 17 August 1917.

20 ABM to JMM, July 1918, MF Papers.
21 Ibid. These artefacts were also donated to the museum in 1942.
22 JMM to C.T. Currelly, 6 March 1940, ROM, Registrar's Office, JMM file.
23 Dong Zuobin, *Jiagu Nianbiao* (Oracle Bone Chronicles) (Nanjing: Academia Sinica, 1937), 8.
24 Menzies, *Yinxu Buci* (Oracle Records), Preface.
25 JMM to C.T. Currelly, 6 March 1940, ROM, Registrar's Office, C.T. Currelly file.
26 JMM to AM, 12 September 1954, MF Papers.
27 Interview with Marion Menzies Hummel, September 1996.
28 Dong, *Jiagu Nianbiao*, 20.
29 Menzies, *Yinxu Buci* (Oracle Records), Preface.
30 JMM to AM, 19 November 1933, MF Papers.
31 ABM to JMM, 1935, MF Papers.

Chapter 10: Museums and Collectors

1 Alvyn Austin, 'Missionaries, Scholars, and Diplomats: China Missions and Canadian Public Life,' in Marguerite Van Die, ed., *Religion and Public Life in Canada: Historical and Comparative Perspectives* (Toronto: University of Toronto Press, 2001), 131. Austin refers to the ROM as 'a vast storehouse of missionary collections,' a view disputed by many others.
2 The volume edited by Alvyn Austin and Jamie Scott, *Canadian Missionaries, Indigenous Peoples*, has four chapters on missionary collections in Canadian museums, including one by Linfu Dong.
3 Charles Trick Currelly, *I Brought the Ages Home* (Toronto: Ryerson Press, 1956), vii.
4 Ibid., 241–4.
5 Ibid., 247–8. Currelly devoted twelve pages to Crofts, and only three to White and two to the temple frescoes he acquired. Dickson, Museum Makers, rectified this, with two pages on Crofts – noting that Currelly pressured the University of Toronto to confer an honorary doctorate on him – and a whole chapter on White.
6 Dickson, *Museum Makers*, 76.
7 Ibid., 85–6. At page 78, Dickson stated: 'In his passion for collection he [White] appeared as clever and as ruthless as any gifted dealer. He knew about people who had fallen on hard times and might be persuaded to part with their treasures for a small price. He kept his eye on people who were ailing and might die soon, at which time certain pieces he desired might be easy to obtain.'

8 Ibid., 77.
9 Warren I. Cohen, *East Asian Art and American Culture* (New York: Columbia University Press, 1992), 95.
10 Cohen, *East Asian Art*, 118–21.
11 Currelly, *I Brought the Ages Home*, 249. Until the 1950s most books on the history of Chinese art had photographs of objects from the ROM: see, for example, Laurence C.S. Sickman and Alexander Soper, *The Art and Architecture of China* (Harmondsworth, UK: Penguin, 1956).
12 Walmsley, *Bishop in Honan*, 144–5.
13 Foster, 'Imperialism of Righteousness,' 257.
14 Walmsley, *Bishop In Honan*, 141–2.
15 Charles Taylor, 'Bishop William White,' in *Six Journeys: A Canadian Pattern* (Toronto: Anansi, 1977), 52–3.
16 White became an expert on Chinese Jews, as his 700-page compendium attests: *Chinese Jews: A Compilation of Matters Relating to the Jews of K'aifeng Fu*, 3 vols. (Toronto: University of Toronto Press, 1942; repr. in 1 vol., 1966). See also Walmsley, *Bishop in Honan*, 137–8.
17 Walmsley, *Bishop in Honan*, 143–4.
18 Ibid., 139.
19 Ibid., 147.
20 JMM to WCW, 25 May 1932, UT/WCW Papers.
21 JMM to WCW, 19 January 1931, ibid.
22 JMM to WCW, 1 July 1933, ibid.
23 JMM to WCW, 25 May 1932, ibid.
24 JMM to WCW, 22 September 1933, ibid.
25 Dickson, *Museum Makers*, 77; Chi, *Anyang*, 63.
26 JMM to WCW, 18 May 1932, UT/WCW Papers.
27 Dickson, *Museum Makers*, 77.
28 Walmsley, *Bishop in Honan*, 147.
29 Austin, *Saving China*, 225.
30 Song and Li, *Jianada Chuanjiaoshi*, 283.
31 ABM to JMM, 8 November 1934, MF Papers.
32 William Charles White, *Tombs of Old Lo-yang: A Record of the Construction and Contents of a Group of Royal Tombs at Chin-ts'un, Honan, Probably Dating 550 B.C.* (Shanghai: Kelly and Walsh, 1934), ix.
33 Ibid., 1, 3.
34 I.H. Wei to WCW, 7 September 1934, ROM, Far Eastern Department, Bishop White Papers.
35 Wei to WCW, 28 December 1935, ibid.
36 Wei to WCW, 11 March 1937, ibid.

37 These bronzes seem to have been White's only coup after he returned to Henan in 1947. It is not known how he got them out of China. He was proud of his adventure and displayed the items in the ROM. After seeing the display, Menzies wrote to his son, 'Bishop White has brought back some Shang bronzes from China. I saw them in the museum on display. I wonder how he managed it.' See JMM to AM, 16 August 1947, MF Papers.

38 Currelly to JMM, 12 January 1927, ROM, Currelly file.

39 Walmsley, Bishop in Honan, 158.

40 Cohen, *East Asian Art*, 115.

41 Walmsley, *Bishop in Honan*, 145.

42 Austin, *Saving China*, 298.

43 Walmsley, *Bishop in Honan*, 192.

44 WCW to Miss Greenway, 26 April 1932. East Asian Dept., ROM. As China traditionally lacked a form of minted coin or currency above the basic-level copper 'cash,' the Mexican dollar became the most common standard in all trade and commerce during the nineteenth and early twentieth centuries.

45 ROM, Registrar's Office, C.T. Currelly file.

46 JMM to ABM, 15 March 1935, MF Papers.

47 JMM to ABM, 23 February 1936, MF Papers.

48 'Catalogue of Cheeloo Museum,' 16 June 1936, MF Papers. Menzies compiled this catalogue before he left Cheeloo in 1937.

49 'Minutes of Cheeloo Emergency Administrative Committee,' 23 November 1937, Shandong Provincial Archives, File J109-01-379.

50 'Shantung Christian University Sinological Research Institute: Eighth Yearly Report,' ibid., File J109-03-11.

51 Tian Mu, 'Chedi Suqing Diguo Zhuyi Wenhua Qinlue de Yingxiang' (Eliminate Completely the Influence of Imperialist Cultural Invasion), *Da Zhong Daily*, 28 April 1952.

52 'Memorandum of an Agreement between Annie Belle Menzies and Arthur R. Menzies and the Governors of the University of Toronto,' 1960, MF Papers.

53 JMM to AM, 21 July 1949, MF Papers.

54 JMM to AM, 5 July 1951, MF Papers.

55 JMM to White, 18 March 1932, UT/WCW Papers.

Chapter 11: Interlude, 1927–1928

1 Hummel, *Memoirs of a Mishkid*, 37.

2 'The North China Union Language School,' bulletin for the school year of 1919–20. PCC/NHM corr., 6/87.

3 WHG to RPM, 6 February 1922, ibid., 7/105.

4 W.B. Pettus to Honan Mission, 8 December 1927, UCC/NHM corr., 2/27.

5 AEA to JMM, 26 December 1924, PCC/NHM corr., 8/133.

6 WHG to AEA, 22 December 1927, UCC/NHM corr., 2/27.

7 WHG to AEA, 19 December 1927, ibid. Bishop White also refused to send his missionaries to NCULS because of the Beijing accent.

8 WHG to AEA, 22 December 1927, ibid.

9 JMM to H.S. Forbes, 11 December 1927, ibid.

10 WHG to AEA, 19 December 1927, ibid.

11 AEA to WHG, 30 January 1928, UCC/NHM corr., 3/36.

12 AEA to WHG, 23 January 1928, ibid.

13 AEA to WHG, 6 March 1928, ibid.

14 AEA to WHG, 3 April 1928, ibid.

15 Hummel, Memoirs of a Mishkid, 39–41.

16 JMM to parents, 4 September 1928, MF Papers.

17 ABM to parents, December 1928, MF Papers.

18 Hummel, *Memoirs of a Mishkid*, 42–3.

19 ABM to AEA, 18 March 1929, UCC/NHM corr., 3/45.

20 Hummel, *Memoirs of a Mishkid*, 59.

21 Ibid., 74.

22 Ibid., 78.

23 Ibid., 90.

24 Ibid., 90–3.

25 AEA to WHG, 11 October 1929, UCC/NHM corr. In his reply to Badi, AEA noted his appreciation of Menzies's skills, but 'Menzies' work is in China.'

26 Hugh Mackenzie [HM], Tianjin, to AEA, 6 March 1929, ibid., 3/45.

27 AEA to HM, 15 April 1929, ibid.

28 AEA to WHG, 23 November 1929, UCC/NHM corr., 3/48.

29 AEA to JMM, 25 November 1929, ibid.

30 JMM to AEA, 9 December 1929, ibid.

31 JMM to AEA, 25 April 1930, MF Papers.

32 JMM to AEA, 9 December 1929, UCC/NHM corr., 3/48.

33 Ibid.

34 Ibid.

35 JMM to George H. Chase, Dean of Harvard Graduate School, 30 December 1929, MF Papers.

36 JMM to John Leighton Stuart, 20 February 1930, Yale Divinity Library, R611, 343/5264.

37 JMM to AEA, 1 January 1930, MF Papers.

38 Ibid.

39 'Menzies' speech to the Foreign Mission Board,' April 1930, MF Papers.

40 Feng Youlan (old spelling) published *A History of Chinese Philosophy* in Chinese in 1931 with the Shen Chou Publishing Co., Shanghai. It was translated into English in 1952 by Princeton University Press, and became the standard Western survey during the 1960s.

41 David E. Mungello, *Curious Land: Jesuit Accommodation and the Origins of Sinology* (Wiesbaden: Franz Steiner, 1985); George Dunne, *Generation of Giants: The Story of the Jesuits in China in the Last Decades of the Ming Dynasty* (South Bend, IN: Notre Dame University Press, 1962).

42 'Menzies' speech,' April 1930, MF Papers.

43 JMM to AEA, 9 December 1929, UCC/NHM corr., 3/48.

44 AEA to WHG, 10 May 1930, ibid., 3/45.

Chapter 12: Marking Time, 1930–1931

1 Hummel, *Memoirs of a Mishkid*, 94.

2 Ibid., 95–9.

3 Fang Hui, 'Cong Chuanjiaoshi dao Kaoguxuejia' (From Missionary to Archaeologist), in Song and Li, *Jianada Chuanjiaoshi* (Canadian Missionaries), 198.

4 Meng Shikai, 'Jiaguxue de Fazhan yu Shangdaishi Yanjiu' (The Development of Oracle Bone Study and the Study of Shang History), in Yindu Xüekan, ed., *Quanguo Shangshi Xueshu Taolunhui Lunwenji* (Seattle: University of Washington Press, 1977), 38–42.

5 JMM, *Oracle Records from the Waste of the Yin*, Preface.

6 JMM to AM, 28 November 1945, MF Papers.

7 Ibid.

8 Andersson, *Children of the Yellow Earth*, 163–87. See also Li Chi, *Anyang*, 38–42.

9 Li Guangmo, 'Li Ji yu Yinxu Kaogu' (Li Ji and Archaeological Study of the Waste of Yin), in Yindu Xüekan, ed., *Jiaguwen yu Yinshang Wenhua Yanjiu* (Oracle Bone Inscriptions and Yinshang Culture Studies) (Anyang, 1992).

10 JMM to AM, 11 July 1941, MF Papers.

11 JMM to parents, 6 April 1925, MF Papers.

12 AM to Frank Caro, 18 May 1958, MF Papers.

13 ABM to children, 25 October 1932, MF Papers.

14 Interviews with Zhang Kunhe in Jinan, and AM in Ottawa, 1996.

15 JMM to G.H. Chase, 30 December 1929, UCC/NHM corr., 3/48.

16 The W.B. Pettus papers and the records of NCULS (which moved to Berkeley, California, in 1942) are at the Claremont Colleges, California. See *Connections: A Newsletter from the Libraries to the Faculty at The Claremont Colleges*, Fall 2000; website at www.cgu.edu/faculty/reganj/spcoll.html.

17 For a memoir by W. Perceval Yetts, see Hopkin's translation of a Song
    dynasty study by Dai Tong, *The Six Scripts: or, The Principles of Chinese Writings*
    (Amoy: A.A. Marcal, 1881; repub. Cambridge: Cambridge University Press,
    1954). See also Li Chi, *Anyang*, 21.

18 George D. Wilder and J.H. Ingram, *Analysis of Chinese Characters* (Beijing:
    College of Chinese Studies, 1934; repr. New York: Dover Publications,
    1974).

19 R.R. Sowerby, *Sowerby of China: Arthur de Carle Sowerby* (Kendal: Titus Wilson
    & Son, 1956). The records of the Shaanxi–Gansu Expedition are in the
    Smithsonian Institution Archives, RU 7263, 'Arthur de Carle Sowerby
    Papers, 1904–1954.' Robert Sterling Clark and Arthur de C. Sowerby,
    Through Shen-kan: The Account of the Clark Expedition in North China,
    1908–1909 (London: Unwin, 1912). Jonathan Edwards Sinton, 'Arthur de
    Carle Sowerby: A Naturalist in Republican China' (Bachelor's thesis,
    Harvard University, 1986).

20 Shandong Province Archives, 'Harvard-Yenching Institute,' File J100-01-100,
    'Memorandum on the Policy and Procedure of the Harvard-Yenching
    Institute Concerning Educational Activities in China.'

21 Dwight Edwards, *Yenching University* (New York: United Board for Christian
    Higher Education in Asia, 1959), 88.

22 West, *Yenching University*, 23–7. See also J.L. Stuart, *Fifty Years in China: The
    Memoirs of John Leighton Stuart, Missionary and Ambassador* (New York: Ran-
    dom House, 1954); and Yu-ming Shaw, *An American Missionary in China: John
    Leighton Stuart and Chinese-American Relations* (Cambridge: Harvard Univer-
    sity, 1992).

23 West, *Yenching University*, 90–1. In 1926 Yenching moved to the handsomest
    university campus in China, 200 acres of gardens of former Manchu officials
    five miles west of Beijing near Tsinghua and the Summer Palace.

24 *Beloit Daily News*, 9 September 1958. Biographical entry in Gerald H. Ander-
    son, ed., *Biographical Dictionary of Christian Missions* (New York: Macmillan
    Reference USA, 1998), 544. See also West, *Yenching University*, 27–9.

25 Egan, *A Latter-day Confucian*, 89, 102, 109.

26 Philip Yuen-sang Leung, 'From Periphery to Core: Chinese Studies at
    Christian Colleges in Republican China,' paper prepared for the research
    project Thirteen Points of Light: Christian Colleges/Universities and
    Modern China's Transformation (1996–8), Chinese University of Hong
    Kong; see www.cuhk.edu.hk/his/2002/chi/staff/leung/confu_christ/
    christ02.htm. See also West, *Yenching University*, 74–6.

27 JMM to White, 5 May 1932. University of Toronto Archives, Bishop W.C.
    White Papers (cited as UT/WCW papers).

28 Chen Weizhan, 'Rong Geng Xiansheng Yu Jiaguwen Yanjiu' (Rong Geng and Oracle Bone Inscription Study), *Yindu Xüekan*, no. 3 (1994).

29 *China Journal of Science and Arts*, December 1934. Some of J.C. Ferguson's papers are at the ROM.

30 Hood, *Davidson Black*. See also Li Chi, *Anyang*, 42–6. Black was so beloved that every year, on the anniversary of his death, the entire department of anatomy would visit the European cemetery in Beijing to place flowers on his grave.

31 Susan N. Erickson, 'Forging New Directions in Art Collecting and Research: Berthold Laufer's Expeditions to China,' in *Association of Asian Studies Abstracts 1996*, session 143: 'The Cultivation and Reception of Chinese and Japanese Art Collecting in Early Twentieth-Century America.'

32 Quoted in K.S. Latourette, Review of Arthur Hummel, ed., *Eminent Chinese of the Ch'ing Period, American Historical Review* 50, no. 4 (July 1945), 803–5.

33 Biographical information from the Arlington National Cemetery website, at www.arlingtoncemetery.com/cwbishop.htm.

Chapter 13: Next Stage, the 1930s

1 JMM to J.L. Stuart, 20 February 1930, Yale Divinity Library, R611, 343/5264.

2 JMM, *Oracle Records from the Waste of the Yin*, Preface.

3 James Chin-hsiung Hsü, preface to *Yin-hsü P'u-tz'u Hou-pien* (Additional Collection of Oracle Records from the Waste of Yin) (Toronto: Royal Ontario Museum, 1977).

4 JMM to parents, 4 September 1928, MF Papers.

5 JMM to G.H. Chase, 30 December 1929, UCC/NHM corr., 3/48. This proposal was written in Boston, and a copy sent to AEA.

6 JMM to J.L. Stuart, 20 February 1930, Yale Divinity Library.

7 Ibid.

8 Li Chi, *Anyang*, 56–8.

9 Li Chi is mentioned in every reference history of archaeology. For a bibliography, see *Qing zhu Li Ji xian sheng qi shi sui lun wen ji* (Symposium in Honor of Dr Li Chi on His Seventieth Birthday) (Taipei: Qing hua xue bao she, 1965). Guolong Lai, 'Digging Up China: Nationalism, Politics and the Yinxu Excavation, 1928–1937,' in *Abstracts of the 1999 Association of Asian Studies Annual Meeting* (11–14 March 1999, Boston), argues that 'Yinxu was in fact selected by cultural conservatives as the first site for national archaeology in order to refute the "Doubting Antiquity" scholars and to sustain tradition.'

10 Li Chi, *Anyang*, 51–2.

11 Ibid., 60.

12 Interview with Li Guangmo in Beijing, 1996.

13 Li Chi, *Anyang*, 20, 267 n. 6.

14 Ibid., 68–71.

15 JMM to Knox classmates, early 1950s, MF Papers.

16 L.J. Davis to NHM Council, 9 January 1932, UCC/NHM corr., 4/78.

17 AEA to NHM Synod, 16 May 1932, ibid., 4/79.

18 'Second Annual Report of the Research Institute of Chinese Studies,'
    Shandong Province Archives (SPA), Qilu University, File J109-03-11 (cited as
    SPA/Qilu).

19 L.J. Davis to NHM Council, 9 January 1932, UCC/NHM corr., 4/78

20 Ibid. See also Philip West, 'Christianity and Nationalism: The Career of Wu
    Lei-ch'uan at Yenching University,' in John King Fairbank, ed., *The Mission-
    ary Enterprise in China and America* (Cambridge: Harvard University Press,
    1974), 227–8.

21 W.B. Chang, 'Religious Life in Cheeloo,' UCC/NHM corr., 8/118.

22 JMM to AEA, 6 January 1934, ibid., 6/96.

23 Charles Hodge Corbett, *Shantung Christian University (Cheeloo)* (New York:
    United Board for Christian Colleges in China, 1955), 184.

24 Lutz, *China and the Christian Colleges*, 161.

25 'Shantung Christian University,' UCC/NHM corr., 5/61.

26 Quoted in Peter M. Mitchell, 'The Missionary Connection,' in Paul B. Evans
    and B. Michael Frolic, eds., *Reluctant Adversaries: Canada and the People's
    Republic of China, 1949–1970* (Toronto: University of Toronto Press, 1991),
    22.

27 WHG to RPM, 30 January 1914, PCC/NHM corr., 4/51.

28 RPM to R.A. Mitchell, 30 June 1915, ibid., 5/59.

29 John Griffith to RPM, 21 July 1916, ibid., 5/67; AEA to R.F. Moorsheed, 16
    November 1916, ibid., 5/64.

30 Corbett, Shantung Christian University, 103.

31 SPA/Qilu, File J109-01-693.

32 Corbett, *Shantung Christian University*, 103; AEA to WHG, 7 January 1928,
    UCC/NHM corr., 3/36.

33 RPM to W.L.M. King, 26 May 1924, PCC/NHM corr., 8/126.

34 Corbett, *Shantung Christian University*, 163–5.

35 Ibid., 142–3.

36 Ibid., 171.

37 Ibid., 112–13.

38 Jonathan D. Spence, *The Search for Modern China* (London: Huchinson,
    1990), 418–19.

39 ABM to children, 12 January 1933, MF Papers.

40 Interview with Zhang Kunhe, at Jinan, 1996.

41 Zhang Kunhe, 'Ming Yishi yu Qilu Daxue Jiagu Yanjiu' (Menzies and Oracle Bone Study at Qilu University), in *Jinan Wenshi Ziliao Xuanji* (Jinan Historical Material Collection), vol. 11 (October 1995).

42 'Memorandum on the Policy and Procedure of the Harvard-Yenching Institute Concerning Educational Activities in China,' SPA, 'Harvard-Yenching Institute,' File J100-01-100.

43 'Program of the Harvard-Yenching Institute in its Relation to the Correlated Program for Christian Higher Education in China,' ibid., File J109-01-98.

44 Leung, 'From Periphery to Core.'

45 Minutes of HYI, Meeting of Educational Committee, 8 February 1933, SPA/Qilu, File J109-01098.

46 Serge Elisseeff to JMM, 27 November 1934, ibid., File J109-01098. Serge Elisseeff (1889–1975) was born at St Petersburg and educated in Berlin. He had 'determined to make himself the first fully qualified European Japanologist' and enrolled at Tokyo Imperial University at 19. After escaping from the Russian Revolution, he taught Japanese literature at the Sorbonne in Paris, and in 1934 was appointed professor at Harvard University and director of the HYI. During his long, groundbreaking career at Harvard, which lasted until 1957, he supervised the growth of East Asian studies and the Yenching library. See '75th Anniversary of the Harvard-Yenching Library to Be Celebrated in October 2003,' in the Edwin O. Reischauer Institute of Japanese Studies newsletter *Tsushin*, vol. 9, no. 1 (Spring 2003).

47 JMM to AEA, 23 March 1936, UCC/NHM corr., 7/115.

48 'Observations by Professor Elisseeff on the Work of the Six Affiliated Universities Based on His Visit to China during 1936–37.' SPA/Qilu, File J109-01099.

49 JMM to AEA, 14 March 1936, UCC/NHM corr., 7/115.

50 B.A. Garside to Jesse H. Arnup, 7 March 1935, ibid., 7/106.

51 Corbett, *Shantung Christian University*, 216.

52 Lutz, *China and the Christian Colleges*, 292.

53 JMM to AEA, 14 March 1936, ibid., 7/115.

54 Ibid.

55 Ibid.

56 Ibid.

57 Ibid.

58 Ibid.

59 JMM to ABM, 14 October 1935, MF Papers.

60 JMM to AEA, 6 January 1934, UCC/NHM corr., 6/96.

61 JMM to AEA, 23 March 1936, ibid., 7/115.
62 JMM to ABM, 29 August 1934, MF Papers.
63 B.A. Garside to AEA, 30 December 1940, UCC/NHM corr., 10/165.
64 JMM to AEA, 26 February 1944, ibid., 11/187.

Chapter 14: Mature Archaeologist, the 1930s

1 Dunne, *Generation of Giants*, Prologue.
2 Meng, 'Jiaguxue de Fazhan' (Development of Oracle Bone Studies).
3 JMM, 'A Critical Study of the Divinatory Inscriptions from the Collection of
   Paul D. Bergen,' *Cheeloo Quarterly* (Jinan), nos. 6 and 7 (1935). Bergen was
   an American who went to China in 1883 and became principal of Kuang
   Wen (pinyin Guangwen) College, a predecessor of the arts college at
   Cheeloo. Cheeloo's science building was named in his honour. He donated
   his collection of 74 oracle bones and tortoise shells to the Guangzhi Yuan,
   the university museum. To protect the fragile fragments, he had pasted
   them onto pieces of thick black paperboard that were displayed in glass
   cases. When Menzies noticed tiny red spiders had slipped into the cases
   and were eating the paste, he disassembled the whole collection, catalogued
   and transcribed it, and published the ink rubbings and hand drawings with
   translations into modern Chinese.
4 Bernhard Karlgren, 'Some Fecundity Symbols in Ancient China,' *Bulletin of
   the Museum of Far Eastern Antiquities* (Stockholm), no. 2 (1930). This article
   was translated and published in *Cheeloo Quarterly*, no. 2 (1933).
5 JMM, 'Critical Study.'
6 Ibid.
7 Yan Yiping, *Bogenshi Jiucang Jiagu Wenzi Kaoshi* (A Critical Study of the
   Divinatory Inscriptions from the Collection of Paul D. Bergen) (Taiwan: Yee
   Wen Publishing House, 1978), 8.
8 Although JMM was recognized as an expert at matching bone fragments, he
   never wrote anything concerning his methodology.
9 *Cheeloo Quarterly*, no. 2 (1933).
10 Ibid. Menzies developed the idea of *Tian Yi Shang* (Heavenly City of Shang)
   in his 'The Bronze Age Culture of the Shang Dynasty,' the draft of his
   doctoral thesis.
11 According to Li Xueqing, these skull inscriptions are now in Taiwan, although there is no clue when and how they arrived there. Perhaps it was
   with the flight of the Academia Sinica.
12 JMM, 'A Comparative Study of Luo Chen-yu's *Earlier Compilation,*' *Cheeloo
   Quarterly*, no. 2 (1933). This article, one of the first studies of Shang military
   strategy, is still a valuable reference.

13 Wang Yuxin, 'The Publication of *Jiagu Yanjiu*,' in *Wen Wu*, 20 April 1997.
14 Ibid.
15 Luo Zhenyu, *A Critical Study of Inscriptions from the Waste of Yin*, 1915; and Wang Guowei, 'Former Lords and Former Kings of the Yin [Whose Names] Appear in Divinatory Inscriptions,' 1917.
16 JMM, *Jiagu Yanjiu*, 87; see also 'The Bronze Age Culture of China' (draft), 123–4.
17 JMM, 'Bronze Age Culture,' 123–4.
18 'Shantung Christian University, Sinological Research Institute Seventh Yearly Report.' Yale Divinity Library, File RG 11.255-4145.
19 Zeng Yigong, '*Yinxu Shuqi Houbian* Jiaoji,' in *Sinological Annual*, Cheeloo University, 1939.
20 Hu Houxuan, *Jiaguxue Shangshi Luncong* (Oracle Bone Studies and Shang History), part II (Chengdu: Cheeloo University Press, 1944).
21 Zeng Yigong, *Jiagu Zhuicun* (Jinan: Cheeloo University Press, 1938). Zeng left Cheeloo in late 1941, when the Japanese closed the university, and returned to Beijing. He kept contact with Menzies for some time. According to Li Xueqin, Zeng was persecuted during the Cultural Revolution and his correspondence with Menzies was burned.
22 JMM to WCW, 22 April 1933, and JMM to WCW, 24 June 1933. UT/WCW papers.
23 Chen Mengjia, *Yinxu Buci Zongshu* (A Comprehensive Study of the Oracle Bone Inscriptions from the Waste of Yin) (Beijing: Science Press, 1956), 135–6.
24 Li Xüeqin, 'Yinxu Wang Buci de Fenlei yu Duandai-Xü' (Introduction to Classification and Periodization of Royal Inscriptions from the Waste of Yin), *Wen Wu* (Archaeological Artefacts), no. 6 (1992).
25 Wang Yuxin and Yang Kainan, eds., *Jiaguxue Yibai Nian* (A Century of Oracle Bone Studies) (Beijing: Shehui Kexue Wenxian Chubanshe, 1999), 136.
26 Rong Geng, 'Jiaguxue Gaikuang,' *Lingnan Xuebao* 7, no. 2 (1947).
27 Chen, 'Rong Geng.'
28 Hu Houxuan, *Zhanhou Nanbei Suojian Jiagu Lu* (Collection of Oracle Bones Seen in North and South China after the War), 1951, Preface. Hu reiterated this in view *Yinxu Fajue* (Excavation of the Waste of Yin), 1955.
29 James Hsü, preface to JMM, *Yin-hsü P'u-tz'u Hou-pien.*
30 JMM to WCW, 27 December 1933, UT/WCW papers.
31 Zeng Yigong to JMM, 20 February 1940, MF Papers.
32 Chen, 'Rong Geng.'
33 Annual reports of the Institute of Chinese Studies from 1933 to 1937, SPA/ Qilu, File 109-03-11. It is impossible to know how much research Menzies had carried out on each of these topics. He brought a few manuscripts and

two boxes of card indexes when he returned to Canada in 1936. He left much material in Jinan, some of which was lost in the great confusions caused by the wars. The manuscripts and index cards in Toronto were recently sent back to Shandong by Arthur Menzies.

34 L.C. Porter to JMM, 6 June 1936, ibid., File J109-01-98.

35 Ibid.

36 'Shantung Christian University Sinological Research Institute, Sixth Yearly Report,' Yale Divinity Library, File RG 11.255-4145.

37 Serge Elisseeff to Liu Shuming, 30 December 1936, SPA, File J109-01-98.

38 L.C. Porter to JMM, 1 December 1932, SPA, File J109-01-101.

39 Zhang, 'Ming Yishi yu Qilu.'

40 Interview with Zhang Kunhe, Jinan, 1996.

41 JMM to G.H. Chase, Dean of School of Graduate Studies, Harvard University, 18 November 1933, SPA, File J109-03-11.

42 Interview with Fang Hui, archaeologist from Shandong University, 1998. F.S. Drake became a professor of Chinese studies at Hong Kong University in the 1950s.

43 Li Chi, *Anyang*, 20.

Chapter 15: Frustrating Exile, 1936–1941

1 Hummel, *Memoirs of a Mishkid*, 106–7.

2 Lutz, *China and the Christian Colleges*, 337–51

3 Corbett, *Shantung Christian University*, 238.

4 Ibid., 363.

5 Li Chi, *Anyang*, 95–119.

6 Ibid., 121.

7 Ibid., 128.

8 Egan, *Latterday Confucian*, 150. This work is the best description of the war years at Yenching.

9 Lutz, *China and the Christian Colleges*, 366.

10 West, *Yenching University*, 174–5.

11 Corbett, *Shantung Christian University*, 237–45. See also Lutz, *China and the Christian Colleges*, 368–70.

12 See Gu Jiegang, *The Autobiography of a Chinese Historian*, trans. by A.W. Hummer (Leyden: E.J. Brill, 1931).

13 Xiaoqing C. Lin, 'The Meaning of State, Society, and Profession to Twentieth-Century Chinese Scholars,' *Association of Asian Studies Abstracts* 1997, session 73, 'Between Professionalism and Politics: The Role(s) of Chinese Professionals in the Republican Era.'

14 Li Chi, *Anyang*, 123.

15 Hu Houxuan, 'Wangshi Suoyi.' (Reflection on Past Events). *Zhungguo Wenwu Bazo*, 20 July 1977. See also SPA/Qilu, File J109-03-2.

16 E.H. Cressy to A.E. Armstrong [AEA], 22 May 1936, MF Papers.

17 University of Toronto Archives, School of Graduate Studies [UTA/SGS], File A84-0011-068.

18 L. C. Porter to JMM, 6 June 1936, SPA, 'Ming Yishi,' File J109-01-101.

19 Walmsley, *Bishop in Honan*, 165–7; Dickson, *Museum Makers*, 79–81. White would later write Cody's biography.

20 *Museum Makers*, 79, 86.

21 Walmsley, *Bishop in Honan*, 168.

22 Dickson, *Museum Makers*, 82–3, describes White's relationship with F.S. Spendlove, later curator of the Canadian department. Currelly's successor, Gerard Brett, demanded that 'Bishop White would be retired before he took up his office' (104).

23 Walmsley, *Bishop in Honan*, 169–70.

24 Obituary at University of British Columbia, Department of Classical, Near Eastern and Religious Studies, website: http://www.cnrs.ubc.ca/homer/homer.htm.

25 'A Brief History of Anthropology at University of Toronto,' University of Toronto, Department of Anthropology.

26 UTA/SGS, File A84-0011-068.

27 JMM to Currelly, 6 March 1940, ROM, Registrar's Office, C.T. Currelly files.

28 AEA to JMM, 10 January 1938, ibid., JMM file.

29 JMM to AEA, 3 January 1940, UCC/NHM corr., 10/166.

30 James M. Menzies, 'Introduction' to An Exhibition of Ancient Chinese Ritual Bronzes, Detroit Institute of Arts, 1940.

31 JMM to Currelly, 6 March 1940, ROM, Currelly file.

32 William C. White, *Bone Culture of Ancient China: An Archaeological Study of Bone Material from Northern Honan, Dating about the Twelfth Century, B.C.*, published by the University of Toronto Press for the ROM, Museum Studies no. 4 (1945). The issues White discusses were much better presented by H.G. Creel in *The Birth of China* (1937).

33 JMM to Currelly, 6 March 1940, ROM, Currelly files.

34 Ibid.

35 Lewis C. Walmsley to AM, 2 December 1970, MF Papers.

36 Walmsley, *Bishop in Honan*, 171.

37 Dickson, *Museum Makers*, 75.

38 JMM to Currelly, 6 March 1940, ROM, Currelly file.

39 Ibid.

40 Ibid.
41 JMM to AM, 22 September 1941, MF Papers.
42 JMM to AEA, 3 January 1941, UCC/ NHM corr., 10/166.
43 Ibid.
44 Walmsley, *Bishop in Honan*, 171.
45 WCW to AEA, 24 January 1941, UCC/NHM corr., 10/166.
46 AEA to JMM, 12 February 1941, ibid.
47 JMM to AM, 23 September 1941, MF Papers.
48 JMM to Homer A. Thompson, 17 August 1942, MF Papers.
49 Thompson to WCW, 30 August 1942, MF Papers.
50 Ibid.
51 'Decision of the Directors of the Royal Ontario Museum of Archaeology re
    the Rev. J.M. Menzies, and the material assembled by him in his research
    work at the Museum,' signed by WCW and JMM, on 15 October 1942,
    MF Papers.
52 Gerard S. Brett, director of the ROM's Museum of Archaeology, to JMM,
    29 October 1942, MF Papers.
53 As was the custom, the abstract of the thesis was printed for the oral exami-
    nation; a copy is in UCA, JMM bio file, 'Programme of the Final Oral Exami-
    nation for the Degree of Doctor of Philosophy of James Mellon Menzies.'
54 H.A. Thompson to JMM, 20 November 1942, MF Papers.
55 C.T. Currelly, 'Foreword' to White's *Tomb Tile Pictures of Ancient China*
    (Toronto: University of Toronto Press, 1939).

Chapter 16: American Interlude and Postwar Hiatus, 1942–1947

1 Egan, *Latterday Confucian*, 171–2, 177.
2 Ibid., 70.
3 Corbett, *Shantung Christian University*, 244–5. Repatriation occurred under a
   diplomatic exchange agreement negotiated by the American and Canadian
   governments and the Japanese government through the intermediary of the
   International Red Cross and the Swiss government. The Japanese ship
   Asama Maru picked up US and Canadian diplomats and some other of their
   citizens from China, Korea, and Japan, and carried them to Lorenzo
   Marques in East Africa. There they were exchanged for Japanese diplomats
   and citizens arriving on the neutral Swedish vessel S.S. *Gripsholm*. The latter
   then took the American and Canadian repatriates around the Cape of Good
   Hope and across the South Atlantic to New York.
4 Austin, *Saving China*, 275–83.
5 Andrew Thomson to JMM, 5 October 1942, MF Papers.

6 JMM to AM, 11 August 1943, MF Papers.
7 Ibid., 18 March 1943.
8 Hummel, *Memoirs of a Mishkid*, 104–5, 112–13. See also her letter to Linfu Dong, June 1999.
9 John King Fairbank, *Chinabound: A Fifty-Year Memoir* (New York: Harper & Row Publishers, 1982), 182.
10 Peter M. Mitchell, 'The Missionary Connection,' in P.M. Evans and B.M. Frolic, eds., *Reluctant Adversaries: Canada and the People's Republic of China 1949–1970* (Toronto: University of Toronto Press, 1991), 33. Arthur Menzies appears frequently throughout this book.
11 George E. Taylor to AM, 3 April 1943, MF Papers.
12 JMM to AM, 2 April 1943, MF Papers.
13 JMM to AEA, 26 February 1944, UCC/NHM corr., 11/187.
14 Arthur Menzies, 'Foreword' to *Yin-hsü P'u-tz'u Hou-pien* (Additional Collection of Oracle Records from the Waste of Yin, 1972), UCA, JMM bio file.
15 'Connections: A Newsletter from the Library to the Faculty of the Claremont Colleges,' Fall 2000, http://www.cgu.edu/faculty/reganj/spcoll.html.
16 JMM to AM, 25 November 1945, MF Papers.
17 JMM to ABM, December 1944, MF Papers.
18 Hummel, *Memoirs of a Mishkid*, 126.
19 Feng Yu-lan, *A History of Chinese Philosophy*, pub. in Chinese (Shanghai: Shen Chou Publishing Co., 1931), trans. D. Bodde (Princeton: Princeton University Press, 1952). See also Feng Yu-lan, *The Hall of Three Pines: An Account of My Life*, trans. D.C. Mair (Honolulu: University of Hawaii Press, 2000).
20 JMM to AM, 26 April 1946, MF Papers.
21 JMM to AM, 25 November 1945, MF Papers.
22 JMM to AEA, 2 September 1945, UCC/NHM corr., 11/192.
23 AEA to JMM, 17 September 1945, ibid.
24 JMM to AM, 22 November 1946, MF Papers.
25 JMM to AM, 4 August 1947, MF Papers
26 JMM to J.H. Arnup [JHA], 12 November 1947, UCC/NHM corr., 12/209.
27 Dr G. Burton Queen to JHA, 7 November 1947, ibid.
28 JMM to JHA, 27 September 1948, ibid., 12/220.
29 JMM to AM, 11 December 1947, MF Papers.
30 Hummel, *Memoirs of a Mishkid*, 20.
31 Ibid., 121. Marion's report (co-authored by William Paget) on 'Communist Educational Policies in Certain North China Rural Areas in 1947–48' appeared as a supplement to Sir Michael Lindsay's *Notes on Educational Problems in Communist China*, published by the Institute of Pacific Relations (March 1950), 146–73.

32 Austin, *Saving China*, 202–3.
33 Hummel, *Memoirs of a Mishkid*, 195–7. See also Arthur Menzies, 'Toast to Frances and Ervin Newcombe at Dinner Celebrating Their 50th Wedding Anniversary,' 15 May 1995, MF Papers.
34 Arthur R. Menzies, 'On Assignment: The Distinguished Diplomat Reflects on Forty-one Years in the Foreign Service,' *Vic Report* (Toronto, Alumni of Victoria College), Summer 1983, 5–8.
35 See Terry A. Crowley, *Marriage of Minds: Isabel and Oscar Skelton Reinventing Canada* (Toronto: University of Toronto Press, 2003).
36 Mitchell, 'The Missionary Connection,' 33.
37 JMM to AM, 28 April 1947, MF Papers.
38 JMM to AM, 1 September 1948, MF Papers
39 JMM to AM, 2 October 1948, MF Papers
40 AM to Linfu Dong, 5 May 2001.
41 JMM to AM, 15 March 1947, MF Papers
42 JMM to AM, 3 March 1947, MF Papers
43 JMM to AM, 15 March 1947, MF Papers
44 AEA to JMM, 24 June 1947, UCC/NHM corr., 12/209.
45 See Stephen Endicott, *James G. Endicott: Rebel Out of China* (Toronto: University of Toronto Press, 1980).
46 Hummel to JMM, 28 April 1947, MF Papers.
47 JMM to AEA, 27 July 1946, UCC/NHM corr., 12/198.
48 JMM to AEA, 20 December 1946, ibid.
49 JMM to AM, 1947 [specific date], MF Papers.
50 JHA to Wu Keming, 31 January 1947, UCC/NHM corr., 12/209.
51 AEA to JMM, 27 March 1947, ibid.
52 JMM to AEA, 1 April 1947, ibid.
53 JMM to AM, 31 March 1947, MF Papers.

Chapter 17: The Last Stage, 1948–1957

1 Sidney Smith to JMM, 21 January 1948, MF Papers.
2 William Charles White, *Bone Culture in Ancient China*, viii, 122.
3 JMM to AM, 1947, with no specific date, MF Papers.
4 JHA to JMM, 13 February 1948, MF Papers.
5 JMM to Sidney Smith, 22 March 1948, MF Papers.
6 Ibid.
7 W.R. Taylor to JMM, 10 March 1948, MF Papers.
8 JHA to JMM, 13 February 1948, MF Papers.
9 Austin, 'Missionaries, Scholars, and Diplomats,' in Van Die, ed., *Religion and Public Life in Canada*, 130–52.

10 JHA to JMM, 13 February 1948, MF Papers.

11 W.R. Taylor to JMM, 10 March 1948, MF Papers.

12 JMM to Taylor, 7 April 1948, MF Papers.

13 Ibid.

14 JMM to Taylor, 9 April 1948, MF Papers.

15 JMM to JHA, 21 April 1948, UCC/NHM, 12/209.

16 JHA to JMM, 11 May 1949, ibid.

17 Walmsley, *Bishop in Honan*, 191–3.

18 Tian Mu, *Da Zhong Daily*, 28 April 1952.

19 JMM to JHA, 4 April 1951, UCC/NHM corr., 12/209.

20 Hummel, *Memoirs of a Mishkid*, 133.

21 Ibid., 144–5.

22 White, *Bronze Culture of Ancient China*, 196–9.

23 JMM to Sheila Skelton Menzies, 4 January 1957, MF Papers.

24 L. Carrington Goodrich, *Journal of Asian Studies*, August 1957, 672–3.

Chapter 18: Conclusion

1 JMM to ABM, 29 August 1934, MF Papers.

2 JMM to Knox Classmates, early 1950s, MF Papers.

Epilogue: James Menzies's Legacy

1 Hummel, *Memoirs of a Mishkid*, 90.

2 Ibid., 100–1. *Chushingura*, or the 'Tale of Forty-seven Ronin,' denotes a
    famous Japanese incident in 1702 that, from those feudal times until the
    present, represents absolute dedication and unshakeable loyalty. See
    http://www.samurai-archives.com/ronin.html for a brief outline of the
    actual incident.

3 Austin, *Saving China*, 192.

4 'Mr. Menzies' Things in the Vault,' MF Papers. The language school was
    located at No. 5, Dongsi Toutiao, Beijing.

5 Andrew Thomson to JMM, 5 October 1942, MF Papers.

6 Hu Houxuan, 'Wangshi Suoyi.' Hu's decision to join Cheeloo caused some
    tension between Cheeloo and Academia Sinica. When Cheeloo was accused
    of stealing unpublished studies on oracle bones, it threatened to take
    Academia Sinica to court if it did not retract its accusations: see Shandong
    Provincial Archives, 'Qilu University,' file J109-03-2.

7 Ibid., file J109-03-8.

8 Ibid.

9 'Qilu University,' file J109-01-693.

10 Interview with Marion Menzies Hummel, September 1996, Ottawa.

11 JMM to Arthur Menzies [AM], 28 April 1947, MF Papers.

12 Ibid. Also G.K. King to Friends, 1 July 1948, MF Papers. King's letter was published in Chinese, in *Yindu Xuekan* (Journal of Yin Capital), no. 3 (1996). In his comments, the archaeologist Fang Hui misinterpreted Menzies's intention in sending the single box to Shanghai, stating that he intended to ship the bones to Canada: Fang Hui, 'Guanyu Ming Yishi Shoucang de Yi Feng Xin' (A Letter about the Menzies Collection), ibid. See also his chapter 'Ming Yishi Shoucang Jiqi dui Zhongguo Kaogu de Gongxian' (Menzies and His Collection of Chinese Cultural Relics and His Contribution to Chinese Archaeology) in Song and Li, *Jianada Chuanjiaoshi* (Canadian Missionaries), 186–213.

13 Tian Mu, *Da Zhong Daily*, 28 April 1952.

14 Fang Hui, 'Ming Yishi Shoucang Jiqi dui Zhongguo Kaogu de Gongxian.'

15 JMM to AM, 28 July 1948, MF Papers.

16 JMM to AM, 24 July 1948, MF Papers.

17 JMM to AM, 3 August 1948, MF Papers.

18 Yin Huanzhang, 'Ben Yuan Xinhuo Buci Xixun' (Good News: Our Newly Received Oracle Bones), in *Nanbuo Xunkan* (Journal of Nanjing Museum), no. 37 (May 1951).

19 Chester Ronning, *A Memoir of China in Revolution: From the Boxer Rebellion to the People's Republic* (New York: Pantheon Books, 1974).

20 JMM to AM, 11 June 1946, MF Papers.

21 JMM to Miss Granston, 11 June 1947, UCC/NHM corr., 12/208.

22 Interview with AM, July 1996, York University.

23 Hu Houxuan, 'Bashiwu Nian Lai Jiaguwen Cailiao zhi Zai Tongji' (Recalculation of Oracle Bones Discovered in the Past 85 Years), in *Shixüe Yuekan* (Monthly Journal of Historical Studies), no. 5, 1984.

24 JMM to Miss Granston, 11 June 1947, UCC/NHM corr.

25 Ibid.

26 AM to Linfu Dong, 5 May 2001.

27 JMM to AM, 1 September 1948, MF Papers.

28 JMM to AM, 2 October 1948, MF Papers.

29 AM to Annie Belle Menzies, 12 January 1958, MF Papers.

30 AM to Linfu Dong, 5 May 2001.

31 Frank Caro to AM, 19 March 1958, MF Papers.

32 Frank Caro to AM, 28 February 1969, MF Papers.

33 Arthur Menzies, 'Dr. James M. Menzies: His Interest in Chinese Archaeology and Art,' in Barry Till, *Chinese Art from the Rev. Dr. James M. Menzies Family Collection* (Victoria: Art Gallery of Greater Victoria, 1989).

34 Interview with Peter Mitchell. As the cultural officer in Beijing under Arthur Menzies at that time, Mitchell was the Ministry of Education's contact person for such problems with Canadian exchange students.
35 AM to Linfu Dong, 5 May 2001.

Appendix: Oracle Bone Studies

1 Li Ji, *Anyang*, 6.
2 Ma Rusen, 'Guanyu Yanjiu Yinxu Jiaguweng de Shuping' (Review of Studies of Yin-Shang Oracle Bone Inscriptions), in Yindu Xuekan, ed., *Jiaguwen yu Yinshang Wenhua Yanjiu* (Oracle Bone Inscriptions and Yin-Shang Culture Studies) (Zhengzhou: Zhengzhou Guji Press, 1992).
3 According to Wang Guowei, Wang Yirong instructed his family and the dealer to keep silent about the discovery in order to collect all the available bones. See Chen Mengjia, *Yinxu Buci Zongshu* (A Comprehensive Study of the Oracle Bone Inscriptions from the Waste of Yin) (Beijing: Science Press, 1956), 647.
4 Ibid., chapter 20.
5 Ibid., 647.
6 Dong, *Jiagu Nianbiao*, 23.
7 Chen, *Yinxu Buci Zongshu*, 650.
8 Dong, *Jiagu Nianbiao*, 28.
9 Ibid. See also Hu Houxuan, Yinxu Fajue. Frank Herring Chalfant died in 1914. In 1935 *The Couling-Chalfant Collection of Inscribed Oracle Bones/K'u Fang-erh shih ts'ang chia ku pu tz'u* was published, with 'sketch plates' drawn by Chalfant and edited by Rowell S. Britton (Shanghai: Commercial Press, 1935). The 'General Note' states: 'Distribution of the collection: Royal Scottish museum, Edinburgh, Scotland ... 760 pieces ... Acquired from Couling in 1909. Carnegie museum, Pittsburgh, Pennsylvania, U.S.A. ... 438 pieces ... Acquired from Chalfant in 1909. British museum, London ... 485 pieces ... Acquired from Couling in 1911. Field Museum of Natural History, Chicago, Illinois, U.S.A. ... 4 pieces ... Acquired from Chalfant in 1913.'
10 L.C. Hopkins, 'Chinese Writing in the Chou Dynasty in the Light of Recent Discoveries,' *Journal of the Royal Asiatic Society of Great Britain and Ireland* (1911); 'Royal Relic of Ancient China,' *Man* (1912); 'A Funeral Elegy and a Family Tree Inscribed on Bone' (1912); 'Dragon and Alligator being Noted on Some Ancient Inscribed Bone Carvings' (1913). See Dong, *Jiagu Nianbiao*.

Bibliography

Primary Sources

Archives in China

Beijing Library, Beijing
Beijing Palace Museum, Beijing
Shandong Provincial Archives, Jinan
Shandong Provincial Museum, Jinan

Archives in Canada and the United States

Anglican Church of Canada General Synod Archives, Toronto
Presbyterian Church in Canada Archives, Toronto
Royal Ontario Museum, Toronto
United Church of Canada Archives, Toronto
   Presbyterian Church in Canada, Foreign Missions Board (to 1925)
    United Church of Canada, Board of Overseas Missions (after 1925)
University of Toronto Archives, Toronto
University of Toronto Library, Thomas Fisher Rare Books Library: Bishop
   William C. White Papers
Yale Divinity Library, New Haven, Connecticut

Menzies Family Papers (MFP) and Collections

The MFP contains correspondence of four generations of the Menzies family. It currently is in the hands of Arthur Menzies, but is to be transferred to the National Archives of Canada, Ottawa. The family still owns a few ancient artefacts.

Other family papers and collections have been deposited in museums and institutions in China and Canada, as outlined in the Epilogue.

Books, Pamphlets, Articles, and Drafts by James Mellon Menzies

Prehistoric China, Part One: Oracle Records from the Waste of Yin. Shanghai: Kelly &
    Walsh Co. Ltd., 1917.
'The Culture of the Shang Dynasty.' In *The Smithsonian Report for 1931.* Washing-
    ton: Smithsonian Institution, 1931.
'Christianity in China in Marco Polo's Time.' *Honan Quarterly*, 1932.
Jiagu Yanjiu (Oracle Bone Studies). Jinan: Cheeloo University Press, 1933.
'A Comparative Study of the New and Old Editions of Luo Zhenyu's *Earlier
    Compilation of Written Inscriptions from the Waste of Yin* and the Resultant Newly
    Discovered Historical Materials.' *Cheeloo Quarterly*, no. 2 (1933).
'Nixon Xiansheng Suocang Qintong Shizi Yanjiu' (A Study of the Bronze
    Crosses from the Nixon Collection). *Qida Jikan* (Qilu Quarterly), no. 3
    (1934).
'Bergen Jiucang Jiagu Wenzi' (A Critical Study of the Divinatory Inscriptions
    from the Collection of Paul D. Bergen). *Cheeloo Quarterly*, nos. 6 and 7 (1935).
'Early Chinese Ideas of God.' *Honan Quarterly*, April 1935.
God in Ancient China. Jinan: Cheeloo University Press, 1936.
'God in Honan.' *New Outlook* (Toronto, United Church of Canada journal),
    1939.
'The Bronze Age Culture of China.' Draft of dissertation, 1941, unpublished.
Shang Ko. Doctoral dissertation, University of Toronto, 1942, published Toronto:
    Royal Ontario Museum, 1964.
Yin-hsü P'u-tz'u Hou-pien (Additional Collection of Oracle Records from the
    Waste of Yin). Ed. James Chin-hsiung Hsü. Taiwan: Yee Wen Publishing Co.,
    1972.
Yan Yiping. *Bogenshi Jiucang Jiagu Wenzi Kaoshi* (translation of 'A Critical Study of
    the Divinatory Inscriptions from the Collection of Paul D. Bergen'). Taiwan:
    Yee Wen Publishing House, 1978.

Other Primary Sources

Brown, Margaret H. *History of the Honan (North China) Mission of the United Church
    of Canada, Originally a Mission of the Presbyterian Church in Canada, 1887–1951.*
    4-volume typescript in United Church Archives, 1970.
– *MacGillivray of Shanghai: The Life of Donald MacGillivray.* Toronto: Ryerson
    Press, 1968.

Corbett, Charles H. *Shantung Christian University (Cheeloo).* New York: United Board for Christian Colleges in China, 1955.

Currelly, Charles Trick. *I Brought the Ages Home.* Toronto: Ryerson Press, 1956.

Goforth, Rosalind. *Goforth of China.* Grand Rapids, MI: Zondervan Publishing House, 1937.

Goodrich, L. Carrington. Obituary of JMM. *Journal of Asian Studies,* August 1957: 672–73.

Grant, W. Harvey. *North of the Yellow River: Six Decades in Honan, 1888–1948.* Toronto: United Church of Canada, 1948.

Hsü, James Chin-hsiung. *The Menzies Collection of Shang Dynasty Oracle Bones.* Toronto: Royal Ontario Museum, 1977.

Hummel, Marion F. Menzies. *Memoirs of a Mishkid.* Beamsville, ON: privately published, 2000.

Karlgren, Bernhard. 'Some Fecundity Symbols in Ancient China.' *Bulletin of the Museum of Far Eastern Antiquities* (Stockholm), no. 2 (1930).

de Lacouperie, Albert Terrien. *Western Origin of the Early Chinese Civilization.* (Translated. Osnabrück: O. Zeller, 1965).

Li Chi. *Anyang.* Seattle: University of Washington Press, 1977.

Mackenzie, Murdoch. *Twenty-five Years in Henan.* Toronto: Presbyterian Church in Canada, Board of Foreign Missions, 1913.

Martin, William Alexander Parsons. *A Cycle of Cathay; Or China South and China North with Personal Reminiscences.* New York: Fleming H. Revell, 1896, Repub. Taipei: Cheng-Wen Publishing Co., 1966.

– *Lore of Cathay.* New York: Fleming H. Revell Co., 1901.

Menzies, Arthur. 'Dr. James M. Menzies: His Interest in Chinese Archaeology and Art,' letter to Song Jiaheng, 6 July 1992, MF Papers.

– 'Foreword' to *Yin-hsü P'u-tz'u Hou-pien* (Additional Collection of Oracle Records from the Waste of Yin, 1972).

– 'On Assignment: The Distinguished Diplomat Reflects on Forty-one Years in the Foreign Service.' *Vic Report* (Toronto, Alumni of Victoria College), Summer 1983.

Reichelt, Karl L. *Religion in Chinese Garment.* Trans. J. Tetlie. London: Luterworth Press, 1951.

– *Truth and Tradition in Chinese Buddhism.* Trans. K. Van Vagenen Bugge. New York: Paragon Book Reprint, 1968.

Till, Barry. *Chinese Art from the Rev. Dr. James M. Menzies Family Collection.* Victoria: Art Gallery of Greater Victoria, 1989.

White, William Charles. *Bone Culture of Ancient China: An Archaeological Study of Bone Material from Northern Honan, Dating about the Twelfth Century, B.C.* Royal Ontario Museum Studies no. 4. Toronto: University of Toronto Press, 1945.

- *Bronze Culture of Ancient China.* Toronto: University of Toronto Press, 1957.
- *Canon Cody of St. Paul's Church.* Toronto: Ryerson Press, 1953.
- *Chinese Jews: A Compilation of Matters Relating to the Jews of K'aifeng Fu.* 3 vols. Toronto: University of Toronto Press, 1942; repr. in 1 vol. 1966.
- *Tombs of Old Lo-yang: A Record of the Construction and Contents of a Group of Royal Tombs at Chin-ts'un, Honan, Probably Dating 550 B.C.* Shanghai: Kelly and Walsh, 1934.
- *Tomb Tile Pictures of Ancient China.* Toronto: University of Toronto Press, 1939.
- *Without the Gate: A Brief Record of Work among Lepers in Fuhkian.* Toronto: Missionary Society of the Church of England in Canada, 1904.

Secondary Sources in English

Allen, Richard, ed. *The Social Gospel in Canada.* Ottawa: National Museums of Canada, 1975.
Andersson, J. Gunnar. *Children of the Yellow Earth: Studies in Prehistoric China.* London: Kegan Paul, Trench, Trubner, 1934.
Austin, Alvyn J. *Saving China: Canadian Missionaries in the Middle Kingdom.* Toronto: University of Toronto Press, 1986.
- 'Missionaries, Scholars, and Diplomats: China Missions and Canadian Public Life.' In Marguerite Van Die, ed., *Religion and Public Life in Canada: Historical and Comparative Perspectives.* Toronto: University of Toronto Press, 2001.
- 'Wallace of West China: Edward Wilson Wallace and the Canadian Educational Systems of West China.' In Jamie Scott and Alvyn Austin, eds., *Canadian Missionaries, Indigenous Peoples: Representing People at Home and Abroad.* Toronto: University of Toronto Press, 2005.
Baker, D. *Religious Motivation: Biographical and Sociological Problems for the Church Historian.* Oxford: Oxford University Press, 1978.
Barnett, Suzanne Wilson, and John King Fairbank, eds. *Christianity in China: Early Protestant Missionary Writings.* Cambridge, MA: Harvard University Press, 1985.
Barr, Pat. *To China with Love: The Lives and Times of Protestant Missionaries in China, 1860–1900.* London: Secker & Warburg, 1972.
Bishop, Carl Whiting. *Man from the Farthest Past.* New York: Smithsonian Institution, 1930.
- *Origin of the Far Eastern Civilizations: A Brief Handbook.* Washington: Smithsonian Institution, War Background Studies, 1942.
Bohr, Paul Richard. *Famine in China and the Missionary: Timothy Richard as Relief Administrator and Advocate of National Reform, 1876–1884.* Cambridge, MA: Harvard University Press, 1972.

Brouwer, Ruth Compton. *Modern Women Modernizing Men: The Changing Missions of Three Professional Women in Asia and Africa, 1902–69.* Vancouver: UBC Press, 2002.

– *New Women for God: Canadian Presbyterian Women and India Missions, 1876–1914.* Toronto: University of Toronto Press, 1990.

Carpenter, Joel A., and Wilbert R. Shenk, eds. *Earthen Vessels: American Evangelicals and Foreign Missions, 1800–1980.* Grand Rapids, MI: William B. Eerdmans, 1990.

Chou, Min-Chin. *Hu Shih and Intellectual Choice.* Ann Arbor: University of Michigan Press, 1984.

Chow, Tse-tsung. *The May Fourth Movement.* Cambridge, MA: Harvard University Press, 1964.

Clinton Centennial Committee. *History of Clinton 1875–1975.* Clinton, ON: Centennial Committee, 1975.

Clyde, Paul H., and Burton F. Beers. *The Far East: A History of the Western Impact and the Eastern Response, 1830–1965.* 4th ed. New York: Prentice-Hall, 1966.

Cohen, Paul A. *China and Christianity: The Missionary Movement and the Growth of Chinese Antiforeignism, 1860–1870.* Cambridge, MA: Harvard University Press, 1963.

– *Discovering History in China: American Historical Writing on the Recent Chinese Past.* New York: Columbia University Press, 1984.

Cohen, Warren I. *East Asian Art and American Culture.* New York: Columbia University Press, 1992.

Cook, Ramsey. *The Regenerators: Social Criticism in Late Victorian English Canada.* Toronto: University of Toronto Press, 1985.

Covell, Ralph R. *Confucius, the Buddha, and Christ: A History of the Gospel in Chinese.* Maryknoll, NY: Orbis Books, 1986.

– *W.A.P. Martin: Pioneer of Progress in China.* Washington: Christian University Press, 1978.

Cracknell, Kenneth. *Justice, Courtesy and Love: Theologians and Missionaries Encountering World Religions, 1846–1914.* London: Epworth Press, 1995.

Creel, Herrlee Glessner. *The Birth of China: A Study of the Formative Period of Chinese Civilization.* New York: Reynal & Hitchcock, 1937.

Dickson, Lovat. *The Museum Makers: The Story of the Royal Ontario Museum.* Toronto: Royal Ontario Museum, 1986.

Dunne, George. *Generation of Giants: The Story of the Jesuits in China in the Last Decades of the Ming Dynasty.* South Bend, IN: Notre Dame University Press, 1962, 1985.

Edwards, Dwight. *Yenching University.* New York: United Board for Christian Higher Education in Asia, 1959.

Egan, Susan Chan. *A Latterday Confucian: Reminiscences of William Hung (1893–1980)*. East Asian Monographs. Cambridge, MA: Harvard University Press, 1987.

Elman, Benjamin A. *A Cultural History of Civil Examinations in Late Imperial China*. Berkeley: University of California Press, 2000.

Endicott, Stephen. *James G. Endicott: Rebel Out of China*. Toronto: University of Toronto Press, 1980.

Fairbank, John King. *Chinabound: A Fifty-Year Memoir*. New York: Harper & Row, 1982.

– 'The Many Faces of Protestant Missions in China and the United States.' In J. Fairbank, ed., *The Missionary Enterprise in China and America*.

Fairbank, John King, ed. *The Missionary Enterprise in China and America*. Cambridge, MA: Harvard University Press, 1974.

Fairbank, John King, Edwin O. Reischauer, and Albert M. Craig. *East Asia: The Modern Transformation*. Boston: Houghton Mifflin, 1965.

Findlay, James F. Jr. *Dwight L. Moody: American Evangelist, 1837–1899*. Chicago: University of Chicago Press, 1969.

Finkel, Alvin, Margaret Conrad, and Veronica Strong-Boag. *History of the Canadian Peoples*. Vol. 2. *1867 to the Present*. Toronto: Copp Clark Pitman, 1993.

Foster, John. 'The Imperialism of Righteousness: Canadian Protestant Missions and the Chinese Revolution, 1925–1928.' PhD dissertation, University of Toronto, 1977.

Fraser, Brian J. *Church, College, and Clergy: A History of Theological Education at Knox College, Toronto, 1844–1994*. Montreal and Kingston: McGill-Queen's University Press, 1995.

– 'James A. Macdonald and the Theology of the Regenerators, 1890–1914.' In Michael D. Behiels and Marcel Martel, eds. *Nation, Ideas, Identities: Essays in Honour of Ramsay Cook*. Toronto: Oxford University Press, 2000.

– *The Social Uplifters: Presbyterian Progressives and the Social Gospel in Canada, 1875–1915*. Waterloo: Wilfrid Laurier University Press, 1988.

Frolic, B. Michael, and Paul M. Evans, eds. *Reluctant Adversaries: Canada and the People's Republic of China, 1949–1970*. Toronto: University of Toronto Press, 1991.

Gagan, Rosemary. *A Sensitive Independance: Canadian Methodist Women Missionaries in Canada and the Orient, 1881–1925*. Monteal and Kingston: McGill-Queen's University Press, 1992.

Gewurtz, Margo S. '"The Cinderella of Mission Work": Canadian Missionaries and Educational Modernization in North Henan, 1890–1925.' In Lin Zhiping, ed., *Christianity and China's Modernization*. Taipei: Yuzhouguang Press, 1993.

- 'Do Numbers Count? A Report on a Preliminary Study of the Christian Converts of the North Henan Mission, 1890–1925.' *Republican China* 10:3 (June 1985).
- 'Famine Relief in China: North Henan in the 1920s.' University of Toronto–York University Joint Centre for Asia Pacific Studies, Working Paper Series no. 50 (1987).
- 'For God or for King: Canadian Missionaries and the Chinese Labour Corps in World War I.' In Min-Sun Chen and Lawrence N. Shyu, eds., *China Insight: Selected Papers from the Canadian Asian Studies Association Annual Conference Proceedings, 1982–1984*. Ottawa: Canadian Asian Studies Association, 1985.
- 'Issues in the History of Canadian Missionaries in China: Examples from North Henan.' In Jiaheng Song and Li Wei, *Jianada Chuanjiaoshi Zai Zhongguo*. Beijing: Dongfang Press, 1995.
- 'Women and the Building of the Christian Church in Rural North Henan, 1888–1912.' In *Proceedings of ICANAS*, vol. 4, *Eastern Asia: History and Social Science*. Lewiston, NY: Edwin Mellen Press, 1993.
- Garrett, Shirley S. *Social Reformers in Urban China: The Chinese YMCA, 1895–1926*. Cambridge, MA: Harvard University Press, 1970.
- Gauvreau, Michael. *The Evangelical Century: College and Creed in English Canada from the Great Revival to the Great Depression*. Montreal and Kingston: McGill-Queen's University Press, 1991.
- Gernet, Jacques. *China and the Christian Impact: A Conflict of Cultures*. Cambridge: Cambridge University Press, 1985.
- Grant, John Webster. *A Profusion of Spires: Religion in Nineteenth-Century Ontario*. Toronto: University of Toronto Press, 1988.
- Griffin, Nicholas J. 'Britain's Chinese Labour Corps in World War I.' *Military Affairs* 40:3 (October 1976).
- Harris, Robin S., and Ian Montagnes. *Cold Iron and Lady Godiva: Engineering Education at Toronto 1920–1972*. Toronto: University of Toronto Press, 1973.
- Hood, Dora. *Davidson Black: A Biography*. Toronto: University of Toronto Press, 1978.
- Hopkins, Lionel C. 'Chinese Writing in the Chou Dynasty in the Light of Recent Discoveries.' *Journal of the Royal Asiatic Society of Great Britain and Ireland*, 1911.
- Hopkins, Lionel C., trans. Dai Tong, *The Six Scripts: or, The Principles of Chinese Writings*. Amoy: A.A. Marcal, 1881; repub. Cambridge: Cambridge University Press, 1954.
- Hsü, Immanuel C.Y. *The Rise of Modern China*. New York: Oxford University Press, 1975.
- Hunter, Alan, and Kim-Kwong Chan. *Protestantism in Contemporary China*. Cambridge: Cambridge University Press, 1993.

Hussey, Harry. *My Pleasures and Palaces: An Informal Memoir of Forty Years in Modern China.* Garden City, NY: Doubleday, 1968.

Joukowsky, Martha. *A Complete Manual of Field Archaeology.* New York: Prentice-Hall, 1980.

Latourette, Kenneth Scott. *A History of Christian Missions in China.* New York: Russell & Russell, 1967.

Lemon, James T. *City of Toronto Annexation Map.* Toronto: University of Toronto, Department of Geography, 1977.

– *Toronto since 1918: An Illustrated History.* Toronto: James Lorimer, 1985.

Leung, Philip Yuen-sang. 'From Periphery to Core: Chinese Studies at Christian Colleges in Republican China.' Paper prepared for the research project 'Thirteen Points of Light: Christian Colleges/Universities and Modern China's Transformation' (1996–8), Chinese University of Hong Kong. http://www.cuhk.edu.hk/his/2002/chi/staff/leung/confu_christ/christ02.htm.

Lian, Xi. *The Conversion of Missionaries: Liberalism in American Protestant Missions in China, 1907–1932.* University Park: Pennsylvania State University Press, 1996.

Ling, Qi Ki. *The Changing Role of the British Protestant Missionaries in China, 1945–1952.* London: Associated University Presses, 1999.

Lutz, Jessie G. *China and the Christian Colleges, 1850–1950.* Ithaca, NY: Cornell University Press, 1971.

Maxwell, Grant. *China: Assignment in Chekiang: 71 Canadians in China, 1902–1954.* Toronto: Scarboro Foreign Mission Society, 1982.

Michael, Franz, and George Taylor. *The Far East in the Modern World.* 3rd ed. Hinsdale: Dryden Press, 1975.

Miller, Stuart Creighton. 'Ends and Means: Missionary Justification of Force in Nineteenth-Century China.' In J. Fairbank, ed., *The Missionary Enterprise in China and America.*

Minden, Karen. *Bamboo Stone: The Evolution of a Chinese Medical Elite.* Toronto: University of Toronto Press, 1994.

Mitchell, Peter M. 'Canada and the Chinese Labour Corps 1917–1920: The Official Connection.' In Min-Sun Chen and Lawrence N. Shyu, eds., *China Insight: Selected Papers from the Canadian Asian Studies Association Annual Conference Proceeding, 1982–1984.* Ottawa: Canadian Asian Studies Association, 1985.

– 'The Missionary Connection.' In P.M. Frolic and B.M. Evans, eds., *Reluctant Adversaries.*

Mitchell, Peter M., Margo S. Gewurtz, and Alvyn Austin, eds. *Guide to Archival Resources on Canadian Missionaries in East Asia, 1890–1960.'* Toronto: University of Toronto–York University Joint Centre for Asia Pacific Studies, 1988.

Moulder, Frances. *Japan, China and the Modern World Economy: Toward a Reinterpre-*

tation of East Asian Development, ca. 1600 to ca. 1918. Cambridge, MA: Cambridge University Press, 1979.

Mungello, David E. *The Chinese Rites Controversy: Its History and Meaning.* Nettetal: Steyler Verlag, 1994.

– *Curious Land: Jesuit Accommodation and the Origins of Sinology.* Wiesbaden: Franz Steiner, 1985.

Nathan, Andrew J. *A History of the China International Famine Relief Commission.* Cambridge, MA: Harvard University Press, 1965.

Peck, James. 'The Roots of Rhetoric: The Professional Ideology of America's China Watchers.' *Bulletin of Concerned Asian Scholars* (October 1969).

Piggin, Stuart. 'Assessing Missionary Motivation.' In D. Baker, ed., *Religious Motivation: Biographical and Sociological Problems for the Church Historians.* Oxford: Oxford University Press, 1978.

Rabe, Valentin H. *The Home Base of American China Missions, 1880–1920.* Cambridge, MA: Harvard University, Council on East Asian Studies, 1978.

Rawski, Evelyn S., David Johnson, and Andrew J. Nathan, eds. *Popular Culture in Late Imperial China.* Berkeley: University of California Press, 1985.

Ronning, Chester. *A Memoir of China in Revolution: From the Boxer Rebellion to the People's Republic.* New York: Pantheon Books, 1974.

Ross, Murray G. *The Y.M.C.A. in Canada: The Chronicle of a Century.* Toronto: Ryerson Press, 1951.

Sandeen, Ernest R. *The Roots of Fundamentalism: British and American Millenarianism 1800–1930.* Chicago: University of Chicago Press, 1970.

Schlesinger, Arthur Jr. 'The Missionary Enterprise and Theories of Imperialism.' In J. Fairbank, ed., *The Missionary Enterprise in China and America.*

Schrecher, John E. *Imperialism and Chinese Nationalism: Germany in Shantung.* Cambridge, MA: Harvard University Press, 1971.

Scott, Munroe. *McClure: The China Years.* Markham, ON: Penguin Books, 1979.

Sharpe, Eric J. *Karl Ludvig Reichelt, A Biography.* Hong Kong: Dao Feng Shan, 1984.

Shih, Vincent Y.C. *The Taiping Ideology: Its Resources, Interpretations, and Influences.* Seattle: University of Washington Press, 1967.

Showalter, Nathan D. 'Evangelizing the World in This Generation: The Impact of the Ideology of the Student Volunteer Movement for Foreign Missions, 1886–1914.' Consultation Paper for North Atlantic Missiology Project, Cambridge University, March 1998.

Sickman, Laurence C.S., and Alexander Soper. *The Art and Architecture of China.* Harmondsworth, UK: Penguin, 1956.

Sinton, Jonathan Edwards. 'Arthur de Carle Sowerby: A Naturalist in Republican China.' Bachelor's thesis, Harvard University, 1986.

Soothill, William E. *Timothy Richard of China.* London: Seeley, Service & Co., 1924.

Sowerby, Arthur de Carle, and Robert Sterling Clark. *Through Shen-kan: The Account of the Clark Expedition in North China, 1908–1909.* London: Unwin, 1912.

Sowerby, R.R. *Sowerby of China: Arthur de Carle Sowerby.* Kendal: Titus Wilson & Son, 1956.

Spence, Jonathan D. *God's Chinese Son: The Taiping Heavenly Kingdom of Hong Xiuquan.* New York: W.W. Norton, 1996.

– *The Memory Palace of Matteo Ricci.* New York: Viking Penguin, 1984.

– *To Change China: Western Advisors in China, 1620–1960.* Boston: Little, Brown, 1969.

Stursberg, Peter. *The Golden Hope: Christians in China.* Toronto: United Church Publishing House, 1987.

Taylor, Charles. 'Bishop William White.' In *Six Journeys: A Canadian Pattern.* Toronto: Anansi, 1982.

Teng, Ssü-yu, and John King Fairbank, eds. *China's Response to the West: A Documentary Survey, 1839–1923.* Cambridge, MA: Harvard University Press, 1954.

Varg, Paul A. *Missionaries, Chinese and Diplomats: The American Protestant Movement in China, 1890–1952.* Princeton, NJ: Princeton University Press, 1958.

Wallace, W. Stewart. *A History of the University of Toronto, 1827–1927.* Toronto: University of Toronto Press, 1927.

Walmsley, Lewis C. *Bishop in Honan: Mission and Museum in the Life of William C. White.* Toronto: University of Toronto Press, 1974.

Watson, William. *China Before the Han Dynasty.* London: Thames & Hudson, 1963.

Webb, Margaret E. 'The Education of Ruth Jenkins: A Canadian Missionary in China, 1920–27.' PhD dissertation, Syracuse University, 1996.

West, Philip. *Yenching University and Sino-Western Relations, 1916–1952.* Cambridge, MA: Harvard University Press, 1976.

Westfall, William. *Two Worlds: The Protestant Culture of Nineteenth-Century Ontario.* Kingston and Montreal: McGill-Queen's University Press, 1989.

White, Richard. *The Skule Story: The University of Toronto Faculty of Applied Science and Engineering, 1873–2000.* Toronto: University of Toronto Press, 2000.

Whyte, Bob. *Unfinished Encounter: China and Christianity.* London: Fount Paperbacks, 1988.

Wiest, Jean-Paul. *Maryknoll in China: A History, 1918–1955.* Armonk, NY: M.E. Sharpe, 1988.

Wilder, George D., and J.H. Ingram. *Analysis of Chinese Characters.* Beijing: College of Chinese Studies, 1934, repr. New York: Dover Publications, 1974.

Wood, J. David. *Making Ontario: Agricultural Colonization and Landscape Re-creation before the Railway.* Montreal: McGill-Queen's University Press, 2000.

Wou, Odoric Y.K. *Mobilizing the Masses: Building Revolution in Henan.* Stanford: Stanford University Press, 1994.

Yuan, Tsing. 'The Japanese Intervention in Shantung during World War I.' In Alvin D. Cox and Hilary Conroy, eds., *China and Japan: Search for Balance Since World War I.* Santa Barbara, CA: ABC-Clio, 1978.

Secondary Sources in Chinese

Chen Mengjia. *Yinxu Buci Zongshu* (A Comprehensive Study of the Oracle Bone Inscriptions from the Waste of Yin). Beijing: Science Press, 1956.

Chen Weizhan. 'Rong Geng Xiansheng Yu Jiaguwen Yanjiu' (Rong Geng and Oracle Bone Inscription Study). *Yindu Xuekan*, no. 3 (1994).

Dong Zuobin (Tung Tzo-pin). *Jiagu Nianbiao* (Oracle Bone Chronicles). Nanjing: Academia Sinica, 1937.

Fang Hao. *Fang Hao Liushi Ziding Gao* (Anthology of Fang Hao). Taipei: Taiwan Xüesheng Shuju, 1969.

– 'Mingmo Qingchu Tianzhujiao Shiying Rujia Xueshuo zhi Yanjiu' (Accommodation of the Catholic Church in China with Confucianism in Late Ming and Early Qing). In *Fang Hao Liushi Ziding Gao.* Taipei: Taiwan Xuesheng Shujü, 1969.

Fang Hui. 'Guangyu Ming Yishi Shoucang de Yi Feng Xin' (A Letter Concerning the Menzies Collection). *Yindu Xuekan*, no. 3 (1996).

– 'Ming Yishi Shoucang Jiqi dui Zhongguo Kaogu de Gongxian' (The Menzies Collection and His Contributions to Chinese Archaeology). In Song and Li, *Jianada Chuanjiaoshi Zai Zhongguo.*

He Tianxing. 'Jiaguwen Yi Xian yu Gudai Shuo' (Oracle Bone Inscriptions Discovered in Earlier Times). *Xue Shu* (Academics) 1 (February 1930).

Hu Houxuan (Hu Hou-hsüan). 'Bashiwu Nian Lai Jiaguwen Cailiao Zhi Zai Tongji' (Recalculation of Oracle Bones Discovered in the Past 85 Years). *Shixüe Yuekan* (Monthly Journal of Historical Studies), no. 5 (1984).

– *Jiagu Tanshi Lun* (The History of Oracle Bone Studies). Beijing: San Lian Press, 1982.

– *Jiaguxue Shangshi Luncong* (Oracle Bone Studies and Shang History), Part II. Chengdu: Cheeloo University Press, 1944.

– 'Wuangshi Suoyi' (Reflection on Past Events). *Zhongguo Wenwu Bao*, 20 July 1997.

– *Wushi Nian Jiaguwen Faxian de Zongjie* (A Summary of the Studies of Oracle Bone Inscriptions in the Past Fifty Years). Shanghai: Commercial Press, 1950.

– *Yinxu Fajue* (The Excavation of the Waste of Yin). Shanghai: Xuexi and Shenghuo Press, 1955.

Li Guangmo. 'Li Ji Xiansheng Xue Xing Jilüe' (Biographical Sketch of Li Ji). Beijing: 1995.

– 'Li Ji yu Yinxu Kaogu' (Li Ji and Archaeological Study of the Waste of Yin). In Yindu Xüekan, ed., *Jiaguwen yu Yinshang Wenhua Yanjiu* (Oracle Bone Inscriptions and Yinshang Culture Studies). Anyang, 1992.

Li Xüeqin. 'Yinxu Wang Buci de Fenlei yu Duandai-Xü' (Introduction to Classification and Periodization of Royal Inscriptions from the Waste of Yin). *Wen Wu*, no. 6 (1992).

Liu Shiwu. 'Junxian Fuqiushan Miaohui' (Junxian Fuqiushan Temple Fair). *Hebi Wenshi Ziliao* (Hebi Historical Material Collection), no. 6, 1992.

Ma Rusen. 'Guanyu Yanjiu Yinxu Jiaguwen de Shuping' (Review of Studies of Yin-Shang Oracle Bone Inscriptions). In *Jiaguwen yu Yinshang Wenhua Yanjiu* (Oracle Bone Inscriptions and Yinshang Culture Studies). Zhengzhou: Zhengzhou Guji Press, 1992.

Ma Yusen. *Yinxu Jiaguwen Yinlun* (A Study of Oracle Bone Inscriptions from the Waste of Yin). Changchun: Dongbei Normal University Press, 1988.

Meng Shikai. 'Jiaguxue de Fazhan yu Shangdaishi Yanjiu' (The Development of Oracle Bone Studies and the Study of Shang History). In Yindu Xüekan, ed., *Qüanguo Shangshi Xueshu Taolunhui Lunwenji*, 38–42. Seattle: University of Washington Press, 1977.

– *Yinxu Jiaguwen Jianlun* (A Study of Oracle Bone Inscriptions from the Waste of Yin). Beijing: Wen Wu Press, 1980.

Shi Shangang. *Heluo Wenhua Lungang* (An Outline of Heluo Culture). Zhengzhou: Henan People's Press, 1994.

Si Deao, ed. *Zhonghua Guizhu* (China to God). Beijing: Chinese Social Sciences Press, 1985).

Song Jiaheng and Li Wei. *Jinada Chuanjiaoshi Zai Zhongguo* (Canadian Missionaries in China). Beijing: Dongfang Press, 1995.

Song Xinchao. *Yinshang Wenhua Quyu Yanjiu* (A Study of Yinshang Cultural Areas). Xi'an: Shannxi People's Press, 1991.

Tao Feiya and Liu Tianlu. *Jidu Jiaohui yu Jindai Shandong Shehui* (Protestantism and Modern Shandong Society). Jinan: Shandong University Press, 1994.

Tetsuro Saiki. '"Fangdi Kao" Bu' (Supplement to the Study of Fangdi). In *Jiaguwen yu Shang Wenhua Yanjiu* (Oracle Bone Inscriptions and Shang Culture Study). Zhengzhou: Zhengzhou Guji Press, 1992.

Wang Huiguang. 'Binying Zhongxüe de Lishi' (History of Binying Middle School). *Wenfeng Wenshi Ziliao* (Wenfeng Historical Material Collection), no. 2 (September 1989).

Wang Yuxin. *Jiaguxue Tonglun* (A Comprehensive Study of Oracle Bone Inscriptions). Beijing: Chinese Social Science Academy, 1987.

– 'The Publication of *Jiagu Yanjiu*.' *Wen Wu*, 20 April 1997.

Wei Jüxian. 'Qinhan Shi Faxian Jiaguwen' (Oracle Bone Inscriptions Discovered in the Qin-Han Period). *Shuo Wen Yuekan* (Monthly Journal of Shuo Wen) 1:9 (1939).

– *Zhongguo Kaoguxue Shi* (History of Chinese Archaeology). Shanghai: Commercial Press, 1937.

Yin Huanzhang. 'Ben Yuan Xinghuo Buci Xixun' (Good News: Our Newly Received Oracle Bones). *Nanbo Xunkan* (Journal of Nanjing Museum), no. 37 (May 1951).

Zeng Yigong. *Jiagu Zhuicun* (Matched Oracle Bones). Jinan: Cheeloo University Press, 1938.

– '*Yinxu Shuqi Houbian* Jiaoji' (Notes on the Later Supplement of Oracle Bone Inscriptions from the Waste of Yin). *Qilu Guoxue Huibian* (Cheeloo Sinological Annual). Qilu: Qilu University Press, 1939.

[Zhang Guangzhi] Kwang-chih Chang. *Zhongguo Qingtong Shidai* (The Bronze Age of China). Hong Kong: Hong Kong Zhongwen Daxue Zhongguo Wenhua Yanjiu So, 1982.

Zhang Guangzhi and Li Guangmo, eds. *Li Ji Kaoguxue Lunwen Xuanji* (Selected Articles by Li Ji on Archaeology). Beijing: Wen Wu Press, 1990.

Zhang Kunhe. 'Ming Yishi yu Qilu Daxue Jiagu Yanjiu' (Menzies and Oracle Bone Study at Qilu University). In *Jinan Wenshi Ziliao Xuanji* (Jinan Historical Material Collection), vol. 11 (October 1995).

Illustration Credits

Board of Foreign Missions, Presbyterian Church in Canada: Canadian Presbyterian mission in North Honan (from Rev. Murdoch Mackenzie, D.D., *Twenty-five Years in Honan* [Toronto: Board of Foreign Missions, Presbyterian Church in Canada, 1912], 30).

Arthur Menzies: family reunion, 1921; Student Volunteer Movement conference, 1908; Ireland, 1910; Menzies in his study in Wuan; James and Annie's wedding; Menzies in the Chinese Labour Corps; Shen Dasao, 1919; donkey riding, 1923; Beidaihe cottage; Capernaum, 1929; Arthur on the Huan River; corn field over Anyang excavations; dolmen, 1935; Mount Tai, 1935; James and Annie with grandchildren; James and Annie, 1952; Marion Menzies in China, 1948; Arthur Menzies.

James Menzies: halbert drawing (from James Menzies, 'A Study of the Characteristic Weapon of the Bronze Age in China in the Period 1311–1039 B.C.' [PhD dissertation, University of Toronto, 1942], ill. 74).

Royal Ontario Museum: oracle bone fragments (from James Hsü, *The Menzies Collection of Shang Dynasty Oracle Bones*, vol. 1 [Toronto: Royal Ontario Museum, 1970], plate 277).

Thomas Fisher Rare Books Library, Bishop W.C. White papers: map of Changte/Anyang, box 34/2; White and company at the Anglican mission, box 38/21.

United Board for Christian Colleges in China: archaeological museum at Cheeloo University (from Charles Hodge Corbett, *Shantung Christian University (Cheeloo)* [New York: United Board for Christian Colleges in China, 1955], n.p.).

United Church Archives: excavating the Wastes of Yin, ca. 1931, 1999.001P1592.

Index